BEYOND DOLBY (STEREO)

BEYOND DOLBY (STEREO)

CINEMA IN THE DIGITAL SOUND AGE

MARK KERINS

INDIANA UNIVERSITY PRESS

Bloomington & Indianapolis

This book is a publication of

Indiana University Press
601 North Morton Street
Bloomington, Indiana 47404-3797 USA

www.iupress.indiana.edu

Telephone orders   800-842-6796
Fax orders   812-855-7931
Orders by e-mail   iuporder@indiana.edu

Library of Congress Cataloging-
in-Publication Data

Kerins, Mark.
  Beyond Dolby (stereo) : cinema in
the digital sound age / Mark Kerins.
    p. cm.
  Includes bibliographical
references and index.
  Includes filmography.
  ISBN 978-0-253-35546-1 (cloth : alk.
paper) -- ISBN 978-0-253-22252-7
(pbk. : alk. paper) 1. Sound motion
pictures. 2. Sound--Recording and
reproduction--Digital technique. 3.
Computer sound processing. I. Title.
  PN1995.7.K47 2010
  791.43024--dc22

                           2010015343

1 2 3 4 5   16 15 14 13 12 11

CONTENTS

ACKNOWLEDGMENTS

It has been nearly a decade since I first considered surround sound as a possible research project. During those years, numerous friends, colleagues, and family members have been an invaluable support in my personal and professional life. I cannot possibly name all those who deserve my gratitude, lest this list of thank-yous take up the entire book. I must, however, specifically mention a few people and organizations without whom this book would not exist.

Without Angelo Restivo, Dave Koenig, Beth Lange, and the Kimberly-Clark Corporation, the very idea for this project might never have occurred to me. Dave and Beth gave me the K-C job that funded my first 5.1 system; Angelo's seminar on "Image/Sound Aesthetics" introduced me to film sound theory and encouraged me to examine why movies seemed so different on my new system than on my old one. And as parts of this book build directly on my graduate work, I also must express my gratitude to my dissertation committee of Chuck Kleinhans, Scott Lipscomb, and David Tolchinsky for their advice, guidance, and insights throughout my years at Northwestern.

SMU's Meadows School of the Arts generously provided summer writing support in 2008 and a sabbatical in 2009, both of which were instrumental in finishing this book on time. Meadows, SMU's University Research Council, and Northwestern University's Graduate School also provided grant support for research trips and conference travel critical to developing this project. A Sam Taylor Fellowship from the United Methodist Church's General Board of Higher Education and

Ministry allowed me to have most of my interviews professionally transcribed; thanks to Dan Betsill for his assistance in transcribing several others. Obviously Indiana University Press's support for this book was essential; Jane Behnken and Katie Baber guided me smoothly through the publishing process and were always ready to answer even the most basic of questions.

In terms of the content, this project owes a huge debt to Jay Beck, Michel Chion, Gianluca Sergi, and William Whittington: their groundbreaking work provides a crucial foundation without which my own would not be possible. I have also been fortunate enough to be on conference panels with thoughtful sound scholars like Randolph Jordan, Elisabeth Weis, and Benjamin Wright—their ideas have inspired and pushed me. Portions of this work were presented at the 2003 through 2008 Society for Cinema and Media Studies (SCMS) conferences and at the 2008 *Screen* Studies Conference; feedback from fellow panelists and attendees at these conferences was immensely helpful in shaping the final product.

Several people were invaluable during the writing process itself. Adam Marshall offered crucial insights at two key points—in particular, he proposed a way to organize the first section that gave it a logic and flow it had been sorely lacking. The aforementioned Whittington and an anonymous reviewer likewise offered suggestions about my original proposal that have strengthened the final work. My thanks to both of them, and doubly to Whittington for serving as a reviewer of the complete manuscript—his thoughtful comments and suggestions at that point guided me through one final rewrite. My wife, Jessica, had perhaps the most difficult task of all: serving as the day-in-and-day-out sounding board for my ideas and generally listening to me ramble about surround sound incessantly—her patience in this was much appreciated. Finally, John and Eva Kerins deserve tremendous gratitude for taking on the arduous task of critiquing the entire first draft of the manuscript—and doing an amazing job at it. On behalf of those who will read this book (the true beneficiaries of their work), a *huge* thank you to them for helping me make the argumentation cleaner and the writing clearer. I count myself blessed to have such great parents.

I have saved the most important thank you for last: that to the film sound professionals who so graciously gave of their own time to help me with this project. Several of them not only discussed their own work and thoughts but also gave me valuable feedback on my early ideas about the "digital surround style"; all were instrumental in helping me develop the concepts set forth in this book and ensure that those abstract ideas meshed with real-world practices. So a massive thank you to (in alphabetical order): Erik Aadahl, David Bondelevitch, Midge Costin, Thom "Coach" Ehle, Stephen Flick, Tomlinson Holman, Marti Humphrey, Gary Johns, Suhail Kafity, Richard King, Mike Knobloch, Albert Lord, Paul Massey, F. Hudson Miller, Glenn Morgan, R. J. Palmer, Christopher Reeves, and Mike Thomson. David Bondelevitch, Midge Costin, Mike Knobloch, and David Tolchinsky deserve special praise for using their own contacts to put me in touch with additional potential interviewees.

This book is humbly dedicated to these artists and their colleagues in the world of film sound, where the best work paradoxically tends to be that which draws the least attention to itself. To these amazing filmmakers: your work has not gone unheard, and I only hope you feel this book does it justice.

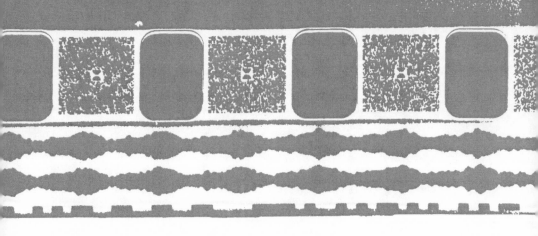

BEYOND DOLBY (STEREO)

INTRODUCTION

Audiences around the world listen to, as well as look at, a movie; sound technology impacts on the way films are made and received as much as image technology; the soundtrack is an area of creativity as fertile and exciting as any in filmmaking, yet the majority of scholars and critics have by and large remained impervious to all things sound for nearly a century.

GIANLUCA SERGI IN *THE DOLBY ERA*

The title of this book can be read as either *Beyond Dolby* or *Beyond Dolby Stereo*.

This first might seem misleading. The film industry has certainly *not* moved "beyond" Dolby; the company remains a major player in cinema sound, and today any feature film print, DVD, or high-definition television broadcast includes a Dolby-encoded soundtrack. Indeed, Dolby's legacy would be difficult to overstate. The company pioneered a host of noise reduction techniques adopted across all areas of sound recording and playback; created Dolby Stereo, the dominant sound system in the 1980s; launched Dolby Digital, the first successful digital surround sound format to hit the market; and since then has remained at the forefront of film sound by developing more advanced formats like Dolby Surround EX and Dolby TrueHD.

With all these successes to its credit, and a conscious effort by Dolby Laboratories to market not just its technologies but the "Dolby" brand itself,[1] today "Dolby" is often seen as synonymous with "high-quality cinema sound." But this association grossly oversimplifies the current state of sound technology in the film industry. Dolby Stereo was introduced in the 1970s and was adopted as the exhibition standard after its highly touted use in blockbuster films like *Star Wars* (1977) and *Superman* (1978). Throughout the 1980s and into the 1990s, Dolby Stereo and Dolby SR (an enhanced version of Dolby's original system) enjoyed massive success; like the monophonic systems they had replaced, though, these formats too were eventually supplanted. In the early 1990s, the first digital surround sound (DSS) systems appeared, offering a full "5.1 channels" of sound in comparison to the 4 of Dolby Stereo (the ".1" referring to a low-frequencies-only channel). The systems were a hit, and by 1995 most studios had adopted an all-digital release policy.[2]

Today Dolby Stereo is rarely heard in American theaters, making *Beyond Dolby (Stereo)* seem an appropriate title for a work on digital sound-era cinema. The simpler title *Beyond Dolby* has its merits as well, though. In what limited academic work exists on contemporary cinema sound or on film sound technologies, scholars often even describe modern film sound as "Dolby sound" and assume—apparently not recognizing that sound technology has shifted under their feet—that today's soundtracks rely on the same rules as their Dolby Stereo–based forerunners. In particular, "Dolby sound" is often used interchangeably with "surround sound," suggesting that Dolby Stereo is a suitable stand-in for *all* surround sound systems. The truth is that in key ways Dolby Stereo actually has more in common with the *monophonic* systems it replaced than it does with the digital surround systems that replaced it.

Unfortunately, the conflation of "Dolby" with "surround" has kept film scholarship from addressing this latter shift from one multi-channel technology to another. The goal of the present work is to remedy that oversight, demonstrating that digital surround sound has had crucial implications for production practices, cinematic aesthetics, and film theory—read as *Beyond Dolby*, this work's title is intended not to minimize the significance of Dolby or its technologies but to acknowledge that digital surround has made the cinema of today something quite different from its Dolby Stereo–era counterpart. In short, *Beyond Dolby* is a conceptual call to arms: for the field of cinema studies to accurately investigate and comprehend contemporary cinema, it must move its understanding of film sound beyond Dolby and into the digital surround age.

SURROUND SOUND IN CINEMA SCHOLARSHIP

For years now, any new works dealing with film sound have been obligated to begin, like the quotation that opens this work, by lamenting film studies' history of marginalizing the topic. Thankfully this no longer seems necessary, not only because this complaint has been repeated so often but also because current scholarship is increasingly working to address it. Indeed, the editors of the 2008 collection of sound-oriented essays *Lowering the Boom* write of sound studies that "the subject has most certainly arrived, and this notable shift over the past decade places sound studies at the vanguard of academic discourse."[3] Recent works such as *Lowering the Boom*, the essay collection *Sound and Music in Film and Visual Media,* and William Whittington's *Sound Design & Science Fiction* forcefully demonstrate just how much visuals-only scholarship has been missing.

Yet even as interest in film sound in general has exploded, scholars have thus far failed to tackle the unique features of today's digital surround–equipped films. In part this is because most work on film sound has focused on the period surrounding the introduction of sync sound; relatively little has addressed more modern practices. To be sure, the transition to sound is an attractive scholarly topic of inquiry, as it held the potential for "cinema" to develop in a variety of different ways. Leading Soviet filmmakers of the time, for example, famously set forth a vision for the use of sync sound based on the principles of montage and collision, even as they (correctly) predicted that the industry would end up using the new technology primarily to make "talking films." Even within the American industry, whose filmmakers did not have this sort of philosophical opposition to "talkies," early film sound technicians developed two different (and incompatible) models for how the soundtrack "should" sound: some argued for fidelity to the profilmic event, while others promoted a more "designed" representation.[4] Clearly the question of how movies "should" sound was an important one in the years immediately after the transition to sync sound.

Much work on film sound suggests that such debates were resolved long ago, and that any later changes in sound usage represent only minor alterations to an established set of aesthetic and industrial practices. To some extent this is true—the completely collision-based use of sync sound described by Sergei Eisenstein and his colleagues, for instance, is certainly a rarity in mainstream feature film. Yet sound technology has continued to progress, and these advances have altered the cinema more than those believing the question of film sound settled in the 1930s acknowledge.

A few recent works challenge this mindset; Gianluca Sergi's *The Dolby Era* and Jay Beck's "A Quiet Revolution" show that the development and widespread success of Dolby Stereo had significant implications for cinematic aesthetics and the film industry itself. Sergi even goes so far as to argue that the introduction of Dolby Stereo led to changes "so pervasive as to make it possible to suggest that they ushered in a new 'era' of cinema."[5] In contradicting the view of film sound aesthetics as a "settled," unchanging entity, Sergi and Beck perform a valuable service. At the same time, their works' emphasis on the importance of Dolby Stereo reinforces the accepted link between "Dolby" and contemporary film sound, and it suggests the later introduction of digital surround sound was of minimal importance.

Yet this is patently untrue, particularly in the case of surround usage—one of the factors affecting the design of digital surround sound (i.e., "DSS") systems was filmmakers' desire to move *beyond* the limited surround capabilities of Dolby Stereo. Tellingly, neither Sergi nor Beck devote much attention to surround itself, instead focusing on the development, deployment, and industrial implications of the Dolby Stereo format. Whittington's *Sound Design & Science Fiction* does include a thoughtful chapter on Dolby Stereo–based surround sound; its observations, though, are specifically tied to surround's relation to science fiction and not generally applicable across genres. And all these works dwell exclusively on Dolby Stereo's impact on the *soundtrack*, with little discussion of the way sound and image interact or the ramifications of surround sound for the filmic image.

While work on Dolby Stereo–based surround is limited, work on DSS is essentially non-existent. Richard Maltby's *Hollywood Cinema*, for instance, has an entire chapter on "Technology," including a section specifically on digital technologies, but devotes only a scant half paragraph to digital surround. Vivian Sobchack's "When the Ear Dreams: Dolby Digital and the Imagination of Sound," discussed in depth in chapter 4, directly tackles digital surround sound but takes as its objects of analysis several Dolby trailers she specifically notes do *not* use DSS in the same way as mainstream feature films.[6] Indeed, perhaps the most frank recognition of DSS's importance to mainstream film comes in its brief mention in *The Dolby Era*. Writing that digital sound's "consequences for audiences are unquestionable," Sergi suggests that "we might be about to enter a new stage of the Dolby era" and hints that the greater options it offers for use of the surround channels will likely require "a reassessment of the relationship between screen sound and surround sound."[7] This intriguing proposal is sidestepped, though, by Sergi's assertion—without further discussion—that digital sound systems probably rely on the same screen-centric notion of cinema sound as their mono and Dolby Stereo predecessors did.

This overall lack of attention to the possibilities of digital surround is unfortunate given that multi-channel sound is such an integral part of contemporary cinema. Re-recording mixer Marti Humphrey (*The Grudge, The Exorcism of Emily Rose, Drag Me to Hell*) says that questions about multi-channel usage rarely arise in his work today—not because multi-channel is not important, but rather because digital surround has been the established norm for over a decade and the major issues of how to deploy it were discussed years ago.[8] Clearly, film scholarship lags well behind film production in its consideration of surround—as if all films were being made in color but all analysis of them ignored that and treated them as if they were in black and white. This analogy hardly overstates the case—as this book will show, the adoption of digital surround sound not only had the predictable effect of opening up new creative possibilities for sound design but also affected cinematography, editing, and even more abstract ideas about how cinema works. In short, digital surround sound has affected all areas of filmmaking and film scholarship.

The wording of this claim holds two potential pitfalls. One is the implication that the key change in the move from Dolby Stereo to digital surround sound is the replacement of an *analog* soundtrack with a *digital* one. The term "digital surround sound" conveniently highlights the fact that the transition from Dolby Stereo to modern surround systems occurred in the context of the transition from analog to digital soundtracks, but from an aesthetic standpoint these digital soundtracks did not introduce creative capabilities beyond those of the best analog formats that preceded them. As chapter 1 will show, the primary significance of the move to "digital" surround sound was that the high compression ratios and low monetary costs of digital encoding schemes allowed high-quality, discrete multi-channel soundtracks to emerge as a true *standard*, rather than being limited to a few high-end theaters as they had been in the past. Thus this book is not as much about *digital* surround sound as it is about a particular *form* of surround sound that came to prominence when it was adopted as the standard for digital soundtracks.

The other possible concern is that of technological determinism. Certainly any study that takes as its principal question the effects of a new technology runs the risk of veering into this territory. The aim here is not to argue that digital surround appeared and suddenly all of cinema was irrevocably changed. Quite the opposite is true—as discussed in chapter 5, even today some filmmakers are reluctant to exploit the capabilities of this technology and instead continue with the same stylistic practices they were using before DSS's introduction. But the advent of DSS technology *did* have significant consequences for filmmaking and for cinema as an institution. This work will seek to provide a balanced assessment of digital surround sound's impact, identifying and analyzing DSS's effects on the cinema while acknowledging the limits of those changes and the factors that have hindered or promoted them.

STRUCTURAL PLAN OF ATTACK

This project's fundamental question—how has digital surround sound affected the cinema?—is broken down into three smaller ones, which parallel the book's division into three sections. The first and longest of these sections deals with film production and style. After a brief recounting of the history behind digital surround's development and its adoption by the film industry, it explores the array of visual and aural aesthetic traits linked to DSS. Some of these, such as more precise placement of sounds around the soundscape, derive directly from digital surround sound's technological capabilities. Others, such as an increased use of close-up shots, reflect more complex interactions between the soundtrack and image. All of these traits, as demonstrated in chapter 4, ultimately serve a common goal tied to the spatial re-lationship between the audience and the diegetic space portrayed onscreen. The section concludes by considering the industrial and stylistic concerns affecting the deployment of this DSS-based aesthetic in Hollywood films.

After this examination of digital surround's influence on filmmak-ing practices, the book moves from the realm of production into that of critical studies; its second section takes on textual analysis. Years of visu-ally oriented film scholarship have left a legacy of methods ill equipped to deconstruct complex multi-channel soundtracks or to combine sonic analyses with image-based ones. Yet studying contemporary films de-mands precisely such techniques. This section begins by developing an approach to conducting close readings of DSS soundtracks that incorporates both the elements of the soundtrack themselves and their placement in the multi-channel soundscape. Building off this work, it then analyzes the advantages and shortcomings of existing models for image/sound interaction. Finally, it combines and expands the stron-gest components of these models, as well as a few new ones, to create a comprehensive methodology for audio-visual analysis.

The book's third and final section addresses the ramifications of DSS for film theory. In doing so, it integrates the results of the previ-ous two sections: the stylistic issues raised in the first and the analysis tools developed in the second are both brought to bear on key theo-retical concepts. In keeping with this conceptual move away from the specifics of film aesthetics and analysis into more abstract realms, this section adopts a marked change in strategy from its predecessors. Where the first section offered a general understanding of DSS's ef-fects on cinematic aesthetics, and the second developed a model for textual analysis useful in studying *any* type of film, the third makes no such claims to completeness. Instead, each chapter in this section interrogates a *single* concept from film scholarship in the light of digital surround sound. Though not as far reaching as that of the previous sec-tions, this approach effectively demonstrates the significance of DSS to film theory. The specific issues explored—the rift between body and voice, apparatus theory, and psychoanalysis—have been chosen because multi-channel sound has obvious and significant implica-tions for them. A variety of other areas could equally well have been included if space had allowed; the conclusion suggests a few of these as possibilities for future inquiries.

METHODS AND SCOPE: HOLLYWOOD,
INTERVIEWS, AND SOUND DESIGN

As a complete work, then, this book shows the ramifications of digital surround for film aesthetics, analysis, and theory. It relies on two primary sets of evidence to do so. One is actual film practice. For the book's first section on film style, multiple examples support virtually every claim made, showing how each argument is evidenced in a variety of scenes, sequences, and/or entire films. The more conceptual questions raised by later chapters are often difficult to fully explore through this excerpt-based approach. Thus each chapter in the latter two sections concludes with an in-depth investigation of a single film, which serves to tie the often abstract issues raised in these chapters back to real-world filmmaking. For example, chapter 8 ("Body and Voice") demonstrates DSS's implications for synchronization through *Fight Club* (1999), which splits one character into two voices and two bodies. Chapter 10 similarly uses the 2007 musical *Hairspray* to illustrate its psychoanalysis-based discussion, showing how that film's shifting use of surround signifies the degree to which the "real" is spreading into "reality." Overall, this mixture of numerous but brief examples and infrequent but in-depth case studies illustrates that the issues being discussed are widely important—rather than unique to any particular film—without sacrificing the more profound insights available through close analysis.

The vast majority of this book's cinematic examples are mainstream Hollywood fare, as are all five detailed case studies (including *Disturbia* [2007], *The Matrix* [1999], and *Joy Ride* [2001] in addition to the aforementioned *Fight Club* and *Hairspray*). The question this book asks is straightforward—how has digital surround sound affected the cinema?—but the boundaries of that question are not. How any given cinematic tool (such as DSS) is deployed in actual movies depends not just on the tool itself but on the time period and country in which the film was made, on the personnel and budget involved, on the genre and story of the film, and so on. Investigating digital surround sound's effect across *all* of cinema would hence be an unmanageably massive undertaking. Focusing on Hollywood feature filmmaking sacrifices a degree of breadth in the interests of a deeper look at DSS's implications.

Additionally, Hollywood features have historically been the movies with the time, money, and expertise to make the most use of digital surround. Hollywood therefore provides the largest body of DSS-equipped work to examine, allowing for broad generalizations to be developed in the context of, then tested on, as wide a filmic sample as possible. And the book's mix of high-profile films from the entire spectrum of Hollywood filmmaking makes it likely that any reader can find examples with which he or she is familiar. That said, as discussed in chapter 5, the resources required to fully exploit the possibilities of DSS are still substantial; just because a film is *released* with a digital soundtrack does not mean that soundtrack was carefully crafted to take full advantage of DSS's extensive multi-channel capabilities. This project's citations thus skew toward bigger-budget films (including action films, animated features, and prestige pictures) simply because those are the films where, as a practical matter, DSS *can* have the greatest impact.

As a final note about the films explored, they are necessarily fairly recent; digital surround was not introduced until the 1990s. This seeming limitation has a significant upside in the context of film scholarship. Too often, work on modern cinema sound has focused on a small number of films. *Apocalypse Now* (1979), *Citizen Kane* (1941), and *The Conversation* (1974), for example, have been analyzed repeatedly, while the vast majority of other films have been ignored entirely. This sense of a "canon" creates the unintended but nonetheless salient impression that sound is only important in a select few cases and can be ignored in others. By relying on a wide variety of newer examples, this project confirms that digital surround's impact can be felt across the cinematic spectrum, not just in those films where the soundtrack draws the most attention.

The second set of evidence on which this book relies is two rounds of interviews I conducted with film sound professionals. My list of interviewees included sound editors, sound designers, re-recording mixers, executives, and engineers—in short, people from all areas of the post-production audio spectrum. Their collective credits include many of the biggest movies from the past twenty years, dozens of Emmy and Oscar nominations, and awards from professional organizations including the Cinema Audio Society (CAS) and the Motion Picture Sound Editors (MPSE). The first group of interviews covered their working methods, their approaches to film sound in general and to multi-channel sound in particular, and their personal perspectives on how the move to digital surround sound has affected filmmaking. These interviews were crucial in understanding how DSS was viewed by those in the film industry, including the ways it was used and—just as importantly—the reasons it was sometimes *not* used.

Interviewing filmmakers for background information is hardly un-common in film scholarship; *The Dolby Era* devotes fully four of its eight chapters to printing in their entirety interviews with key figures in the development and use of Dolby Stereo. My second round of interviews, however, added a valuable and unusual component to this project. Two years after the first round, I met again with many of the same people, as well as with some new ones. This time I brought a list of my ideas about the effects of digital surround on visual and aural aesthetics, and I let the filmmakers consider whether those claims reflected their own experiences and explain where they disagreed. The conclusions in this book, particularly its first section on style and production practices, thus reflect not just my own research and opin-ions but also those of the people responsible for *making* some of the very soundtracks the work explores. This back-and-forth approach is a distinctive feature of this project and ensures that even its more abstract notions about filmmaking and cinema remain grounded in real-world practices.

By virtue of its interviews with practicing filmmakers, this book necessarily describes the effects of DSS in the context of the contem-porary feature film industry. Here again it is crucial to define limits to this particular investigation. This work *will* consider the ways in which the culture and industrial organization of modern Hollywood affect digital surround's use. It will *not*, however, analyze the origins of those factors themselves, which would veer far from its central concerns into another project altogether. As an example of this distinction, industry practices traditionally separate sound *mixing* from sound *editing*: dif-ferent people, working in different spaces, take the lead in each area.

This separation has implications for the way DSS's multi-channel capabilities are used, and chapter 5 will investigate these in detail. That exploration, though, will focus on *how* the mixing/editing split impacts the use of surround sound, rather than analyzing the historical roots *of* this organizational scheme. Other social and industrial factors influencing DSS's application are handled similarly.

PRODUCTION TERMINOLOGY

Portions of this book inevitably include technical discussion of sound technology and details of the audio post-production process. Since people without backgrounds in sound production may find its arguments of interest, this book is intended to be readable to an audience not already familiar with the nuances of film sound. In deference to this goal, it briefly defines possibly unfamiliar concepts when they are first used and minimizes the use of specialized language wherever possible. Despite these efforts, this work is not a production handbook, and it is not meant as a primer on audio post-production. Readers desiring such an introduction can consult Elisabeth Weis's "Sync Tanks: The Art and Technique of Postproduction Sound" for a concise but thorough summary of the process, or Vincent LoBrutto's *Sound-on-Film*, a collection of interviews with personnel from every area of film sound, for a more detailed explanation of film sound production and post-production.

To facilitate accessibility to a wide audience, a few audio-related terms that will be used extensively deserve some explanation from the start. The ubiquitous phrase "sound design" is convenient, yet ambiguous—it has no agreed-upon definition even within the industry. Fortunately, Whittington's *Sound Design & Science Fiction* does an excellent job explaining how sound design has developed, both as a process and as a term. Rather than repeat that work, this book will simply follow its lead by employing "sound design" as a loose but overarching label for the artistic components of the audio post-production process, including (among other tasks) developing the soundtrack's arc across an entire film, creating unique sounds and effects, and deciding which sounds will go where in the multi-channel soundscape. Although this working definition does not always correspond to the term's use within the industry, it fits well with what most non-specialists imagine "sound design" to entail.

"Sound designer," the job title from which "sound design" derives, is equally tricky. This designation was originally created to describe a single person who would oversee the creative aspects of a film's sound from start to finish. Today, though, the "sound designer" credit may mean a number of things, which is why some within the film industry dislike it. Sometimes it labels the person with ultimate creative control over the soundtrack, but it may instead be used for the person who created a film's signature sound effects, or for something else entirely. This book ignores that particular quandary by using "sound designer" as several of its interviewees do: not to designate a single particular job, but as a handy credit for work encompassing one or more portions of the sound design process described in the preceding paragraph.

Other personnel credits in film sound denote more specific types of work. "Sound editors" are found in every area of the soundtrack (a "dialogue editor" or a "music editor" is a specific type of sound editor); all piece together portions of numerous sound recordings and place them at the appropriate points of the film. As discussed in chapter 5, sound editors today often make the initial decision about which sounds go to which audio channel, though these panning choices may be changed later. "Re-recording mixers," often referred to simply as "mixers" in this work, are responsible for taking the multiple tracks of audio assembled by the sound editors and ensuring that they play together smoothly in the final soundtrack. This involves tweaking the levels of each sound; adding any necessary reverb, equalization, or other processing; and orchestrating the final panning of sounds to the proper locations in the multi-channel soundscape.

Finally, this book occasionally employs the word "filmmakers." Entertainment press and the general public tend to equate "filmmaker" with "director." This usage, however, devalues the creative role played by many others in the production and post-production fields, implying that their work is not "making films." This book will therefore employ "filmmakers" as a convenient catchall, including not just directors but also producers, sound editors, mixers, and everyone else involved in the process. A note of caution, though—my interviewees are not consistent in their use of "filmmakers," sometimes meaning it to include sound personnel such as themselves and sometimes not. In these cases context should indicate the intended connotation.

DIGITAL SOUNDTRACKS AND THE
CHALLENGE OF TECHNOLOGY

This book's subtitle, *Cinema in the* Digital *Sound Age*, and its central question of the effect of *digital* surround, warrant a brief word about "the digital." Digital technology is the foundation of this entire project in two different ways. First, prior to the introduction of DVD—a digital format—it would not have been possible to write this book; the only way for anyone to hear a film's full 5.1-channel soundtrack would have been in a theater, making close analysis of its multi-channel use impossible. Second, the importance of 5.1-channel sound itself is (as chapter 1 will show) inextricably linked to the advent of the digital technologies that allowed it to become the standard for both theatrical and home exhibition.

Nevertheless, this book is not *about* the difference between analog and digital sound per se. 5.1-channel soundtracks existed long before the advent of DSS, though it was digital techniques that made them commonplace. And digital technology was integrated into the audio post-production process years before the introduction of digital surround sound systems for exhibition. It is the ramifications of cinema adopting a new technology—which *happened* to be digital—that are at stake here. Audiophiles may debate whether digital sound can ever be as good as pristine, high-quality analog sound, but as digital surround sound is the current standard for cinema sound, any question of what would be the "best possible" system is beside the point.

One challenge particular to the digital era, though, *has* affected this project: the proliferation of different versions of the same movie. A single DVD may include two or three different cuts of a film, as well as multiple soundtracks to each. The *Terminator 2: Judgment Day* (1991) Ultimate Edition DVD, for example, includes three different versions of the film. For each of these the disc offers Dolby Digital and DTS digital soundtracks, both in 5.1 with additional encoded content playable on a 6.1-channel system, as well as a Dolby Stereo track and a commentary track. In total, *twelve* different feature/soundtrack combinations could be selected from this one DVD.

Compounding the issue of proliferation, none of the soundtracks on the DVD is necessarily the original theatrical soundtrack. Many films are remixed for home release, leading to the possibility of significant differences between the theatrical and home versions of a soundtrack. This is a significant concern for a project like this one, which relies heavily on close examinations of film soundtracks. It is difficult to conduct a close reading of a film or sequence thereof in the theatrical environment, and hence most of the analyses presented here are based on DVD and/or Blu-Ray copies of the films in question. In most cases differences between the theatrical mix and the home mix are minor, designed mainly to compensate for the spatial differences between theaters and home viewing environments.[9] It is, therefore, *unlikely* that different versions of a movie's soundtrack will exhibit *major* differences; nevertheless, given the variety of soundtracks available, this book's filmography specifies the particular release and soundtrack studied for each film.[10]

That studios and filmmakers expend the time, money, and energy to remix film soundtracks to match the spatial characteristics of the home market is evidence enough of their belief in surround's importance to the modern motion picture experience. This book aims to convince cinema scholars of the same by showing that film analysis and film theory can both benefit from close attention to the cinema's multi-channel soundtracks. For too long even sound-oriented work in our field has tended to operate with sonic blinders on that keep it from hearing anything other than what comes from the screen; it is now time to crank up *all* the cinema's speakers and find out what they have to say.

1

PRODUCTION AND STYLE

CINEMA'S HIDDEN MULTI-CHANNEL HISTORY AND THE ORIGINS OF DIGITAL SURROUND

It was at the 1987 October SMPTE meeting. People were saying, "How many channels should there be [in the digital sound standard for cinema]?" And people said two . . . people said four . . . one said eight. And I put my hand up and said, "five point one." Everybody went, "What is he talking about?"

TOMLINSON HOLMAN, AUDIO ENGINEER AND INVENTOR OF THX

Today, digital "5.1" sound—the "5" referring to the configuration's five full-range channels and the ".1" to its bass-frequencies-only low-frequency effects (LFE) channel—is commonplace is homes and nearly ubiquitous in theaters. But in the late 1980s, when Holman made his proposal to the Society of Motion Picture and Television Engineers (SMPTE), no one was sure what form cinematic digital sound would take or how successful it would be. The movie industry, after all, had a long history of introducing new sound technologies only to quickly discard them.

This book is ultimately less interested in the factors leading *to* the adoption of 5.1-channel digital surround sound as the exhibition standard than in the ramifications—both for filmmaking and for film studies—*of* that decision. That said, digital surround sound (DSS) did not spontaneously spring, fully matured, out of a vacuum; its design and effects are rooted in earlier systems' successes and failures. Understanding DSS and its effects thus requires knowing a bit about the long history of multi-channel sound in the cinema. A detailed exploration of the entire history of multi-channel cinema sound in all its forms, however, would take the space of an entire book. This chapter thus offers an intentionally incomplete history, focusing only on events and technologies directly relevant to the eventual creation and standardization of 5.1 digital surround sound.[1]

This condensed history can be conceptually split into four parts. First, an overview of the history of multi-channel sound in cinema demonstrates where DSS draws inspiration from previous systems. Understanding why some of these systems succeeded while others did not—in particular why technologies representing technical or aesthetic "improvements" over the prevailing standards of the time often failed—will provide crucial context about the factors necessary for DSS (or any other new sound system) to be widely accepted. The second phase of this historical exploration is a close look at Dolby Stereo, digital surround sound's immediate predecessor as the exhibition standard. Many of the specific technical specifications of DSS are direct responses to the strengths and weaknesses of Dolby Stereo; understanding Dolby Stereo helps explain the design of DSS systems and why the film industry was willing to embrace DSS. Third, an examination of the companies, technologies, and outside factors involved in the launch of DSS and its subsequent expansion from the cinema to the home and other venues explains how DSS became common enough to affect the way filmmakers make movies. Finally, a brief exploration of the limitations of 5.1-channel digital surround sound offers ideas about where sound technology might be headed in the future, a question that will come into play in chapter 5 when considering the likely longevity of filmmaking practices based in 5.1-channel sound.

THE ORIGINS OF MULTI-CHANNEL

Though multi-channel sound (i.e., soundtrack formats with two or more distinct channels of audio) may be considered by many theatergoers a relatively recent innovation, its roots reach back decades. Like other technologies, it has an intricate history of success and failure, progress and regression, that precludes a simple "technological developmental" history. Its development has been influenced not just by advancements in technology but also by aesthetic practices, the economics of the film industry, audience/consumer expectations, and the growth of the home market. While the *introduction* of digital surround sound in the 1990s was a clear technological change, DSS's widespread *success* reflected lessons learned over the previous sixty years about the importance of these other factors to the viability of a new system.

The idea of multi-channel sound predates cinema itself by at least sixteen years, to Alexander Graham Bell's experiments on two-channel sound transmitted by two telephones in 1879.[2] Other sound pioneers continued to play with the effects of two-channel audio *transmission*, but cinema would first be invented and then "find its voice" with 1927's *The Jazz Singer* before the first multi-track *recordings* were made. In 1928, Bell Labs recorded an orchestra onto a disk using two separate tracks—instead of using the two tracks to record sounds from two different microphones, though, this design split the signal from one microphone, putting the high-frequency component of the sound on one track and the low frequencies on another to improve the sound quality.[3] Four years later, Bell Labs made another two-track recording, this time using two distinct audio channels; this 1932 record is the first known example of a true "stereo" recording.[4]

A year later, Bell Labs transmitted a *three*-channel orchestral mix from Philadelphia to front right, front center, and front left speakers in Washington, D.C.[5] The choice of three unique audio channels here was dictated by aesthetic concerns: while Bell engineers agreed that "an infinite number of front loudspeaker channels was desirable,"[6] the use of left, center, and right channels seemed to adequately produce the effect of a "full" stereophonic field without the "hole in the middle" effect common to reproductions using only two (front left and front right) channels.[7] The experiment was a success—"various orchestral sounds seemed to come from the appropriate places, and a moving source such as a man walking across the stage and talking seemed at the receiving end to move about"[8]—but left unresolved a question of major interest to those concerned with the deployment of multi-channel sound into film theaters: what was the best way to utilize a multi-channel configuration as part of a motion picture? Several years later, in 1937, the first documented presentation of multi-channel audio synched to film would highlight that this issue was anything but settled: a demonstration by Bell Labs paired a three-channel frontal sound mix with visuals for three scenes, each of which employed the multi-channel soundtrack in a different way. Jay Beck characterizes the three approaches as deriving from different implicit goals:

> This demonstration film showed that three basic factors were considered in the development of multi-track sound. First, a musical "binaural model" where the fidelity was related to the fixed position of the auditor and a stationary sound source. Second, a spectacular "stereophonic model" where the intent was to imitate motion even if it exaggerated the scale of the sound event. And third, a more complex "constructed model" where stationary and moving objects were depicted in spatial accord with the image.[9]

These three models correspond, respectively, to multi-channel being used (a) to match a sound to its source's (horizontal) position in the visual field, (b) to heighten the "spectacle" of the film by calling attention to a moving sound, and (c) to create a narrative space. This first test of cinematic multi-channel thus presciently included the three most common uses to which multi-channel would be put over the years.

The film industry had not been idling while Bell Labs and others were experimenting with multi-channel sound systems. As early as 1927, exhibitors were trying out systems that allowed them to send different sounds to different loudspeakers. Their motivations were initially quite different from those of Bell Labs. Rather than trying to correlate the reproduction of sounds with their sources' locations onscreen, movie theater owners were trying to maintain the conventions of the silent era, where (live) music typically originated from a pit in front of the screen, while at the same time recognizing that synchronized dialogue suggested speakers be located behind the screen to "match" the onscreen images. In other words, they were trying to recreate the spatial organization of the legitimate theater. Since films at this time were released with only one audio track, the task of switching the soundtrack back and forth between two sets of speakers—one behind the screen, one in the orchestra pit—fell to the projectionist, who "needed to know the soundtrack like an orchestra conductor."[10] Not surprisingly, this convoluted arrangement did not last long, as sound technicians quickly recognized that having music coming from behind the screen with the dialogue was perfectly acceptable to audiences.[11]

These switching systems, though only briefly used, demonstrate that even from its earliest days the sound cinema has flirted with the possibilities of multiple-speaker configurations, with a few forward thinkers suggesting as early as 1928 that switching mechanisms could move sounds among several speakers behind the screen, thereby placing sounds as horizontally and vertically close to their sources as possible. In 1940, after over a decade of "pure" monophonic cinema, Warner Brothers' Vitasound became the first standardized multi-speaker system. Like the music/dialogue switching system described above, Vitasound was not a true multi-*channel* system but rather a multi-*speaker* one. It had, however, two major differences from its forerunner. First, it employed speakers surrounding the audience. Second, instead of relying on a projectionist to switch the sound between the two tracks, Vitasound used a control track between the sprocket holes of the filmstrip to turn these surround speakers on and off; a similar method would be used by multi-channel systems of the 1950s. Vitasound reflects Beck's "stereophonic model," in that the surround speakers were used to heighten the *spectacle* of film—all dialogue was kept tied to the screen, and the surround speakers were only engaged for loud portions of the film where the music and effects could spread out into the theater.[12]

The first true multi-*channel* sound film, with *unique* audio channels feeding different speakers, came not long after Vitasound's debut with Walt Disney's *Fantasia* (1940). *Fantasia*'s sound system, developed by RCA and Walt Disney Studios and dubbed "Fantasound," involved two technical advances over Vitasound.[13] For one, not only did it spread three speakers horizontally behind the screen to allow sound to come from multiple places across the width of the image, it fed those three speakers from three *different* recorded channels.[14] Second, the Los Angeles premiere of the film saw the use of a "surround channel," with ninety-six smaller speakers around and behind the audience coming to life for specific sound effects and for the sound of a large chorus singing at the end of the film.[15] The film's multi-channel mix itself was a hybrid between "correct" spatial reproduction of the orchestral recordings that dominated the musically driven film (Beck's "binaural model") and a more "spectacular" approach (Beck's "stereophonic model") that moved sounds out of their orchestral configuration when doing so might be more engaging for the audience: "Duplication of an original distribution of sound sources was a *secondary* consideration, and the choice of directions from which sounds were to come was to be entirely at the discretion of the directors, musicians, and technicians."[16] Intriguingly, one of the configurations tried but ultimately abandoned during the three-year process of developing Fantasound was a 3-channel front and 2-channel surround setup similar to the 5.1-channel arrangement DSS systems would adopt half a century later.[17]

Despite the efforts of *Fantasia*'s makers to create a unique sound experience, only six theaters nationwide were equipped for Fantasound; everyone who saw the film in other theaters heard the then-standard monophonic sound rather than the complete "sound environment" intended by the filmmakers.[18] While a number of factors played into its failure, the expense and technical complexity of Fantasound exhibition must bear the most blame. Fantasound required not just additional speakers both behind the screen and out in the auditorium but also an additional projector. Since *Fantasia*'s multi-channel soundtrack could not fit in the small space reserved for the soundtrack on a standard 35mm print, Disney had opted for a more complicated system. The finished movie featured three channels of optical sound and one control track (which, like that of Vitasound, turned the surround speakers on and off) on one strip of 35mm film and the image on another—theaters using Fantasound thus needed to have two linked projectors kept in exact synchronization.[19] Ultimately, though this dual system provided both a multi-channel experience and higher-quality sound reproduction than standard 35mm projection,[20] the costs and difficulties of equipping theaters with Fantasound proved overwhelmingly prohibitive, and the first true multi-channel sound system disappeared after being deployed in only a few theaters and a single film.

WIDESCREEN REJUVENATES SURROUND

After *Fantasia*'s failed multi-channel release, little happened in the world of multi-channel sound for about ten years. By the end of World War II, though, two new technologies had appeared in the United States that would further the cause of multi-channel sound: better loudspeakers utilizing permanent magnets (developed as part of the war effort) and magnetic audio recording tape (a German invention obtained by the Allies during their offensive into Germany).[21] These new tools were put into use in film exhibition and production, respectively, almost immediately after the war. Magnetic tape held particular promise, as it was both easier to use and produced higher-quality recordings (with less distortion, less noise, and a wider range of frequencies) than the 35mm optical recordings the industry had been using.[22] But any potential gains in sound quality from these new technologies went unheard by audiences due to the limited capabilities of the monophonic optical soundtracks used in exhibition. Thus in the early 1950s, experiments began with using magnetic soundtracks on release prints. Magnetic "stereophonic sound" soon appeared in a variety of formats, each usually utilizing one rear channel (then called the "effects channel") and three or more channels arranged in a horizontal spread behind the screen.[23]

These various systems achieved multi-channel sound through two different technical approaches. Cinerama, Warnerphonic sound, and early Todd-AO films all relied on a dual-projection system like that used for *Fantasia*, with the soundtrack on a separate piece of 35mm magnetic stock run in sync with one or more film projectors.[24] In contrast, Super Panavision 70, later Todd-AO releases, and Twentieth-Century Fox's CinemaScope system put image and sound on the same piece of film via "striping," or gluing magnetic tape along the edges of a film print.[25] Fox's system had a major advantage over all the other formats, as its single-strip system offered widescreen aspect-ratio images and multi-channel sound using the standard 35mm projectors that exhibitors already owned (Todd-AO's single-strip system used 70mm prints), with only a new lens required for the image and a new magnetic head for the sound. Yet the success of Fox's system stemmed as much from the studio's business practices as from any technical advantages: Fox simply *required* theaters wanting to show any of its CinemaScope films, including many of the studio's high-profile releases, to install both the aural and visual components of the CinemaScope system.[26] By the end of the 1950s, more than ten thousand theaters had installed a stereophonic sound system.[27]

The "effects channel" out in the auditorium quickly became a problem for the 1950s multi-channel systems. One issue was its technical limitations—it was of lower sound quality than the other channels and hence necessitated the use of a control signal that could turn the surround speakers on and off to avoid hiss when no surround effects were present.[28] A bigger difficulty, though, was the fundamental aesthetic question of what should be done with the channel when it *was* on. Mixers initially took differing approaches to this problem. Some films, such as *Around the World in 80 Days* (1956), used the surround channel for effects such as placing the viewer "inside" a train;[29] Cinerama movies placed all sorts of offscreen sounds in the surround channel; and a few early multi-channel releases even placed dialogue in the surrounds.[30] But perhaps because audiences were reportedly "overwhelmed" by these initial experiments with surround effects, filmmakers quickly reined in their uses of the "effects channel" for narrative films.[31] Many studios using the CinemaScope system left it completely empty,[32] and Fox Studios had to exhort its own filmmakers to take advantage of the channel's possibilities.[33]

When Fox relented on its "stereo-equipped theaters only" policy and began shipping CinemaScope prints in both four-channel magnetic and monophonic optical versions, it marked the beginning of the end for the effects channel. The only studio that had been seriously pushing use of the effects channel forced itself into the position of making four-channel stereo films that could be mixed down to a monophonic soundtrack and still make sense. As filmmakers could no longer count on their stereo or surround effects being heard as such, it made no sense to even try to employ them; by the late 1950s, the few four-channel CinemaScope films released almost never used the effects channel, and (aside from music, which was still recorded in stereo) the front channels essentially contained monophonic sounds panned to the various speakers.[34] As use of the format's multi-channel capabilities slowly dwindled, Fox predictably moved away from its dual print system of providing either magnetic-striped or monophonic optical prints in favor of a mono-only system.[35]

Given that magnetic sound provided a clear technical and aesthetic improvement over the monophonic optical tracks that preceded and followed it, its failure deserves some explanation. Economics played a major role: aside from their high installation costs for theater owners, both the dual-projector and "striping" processes of exhibiting magnetic stereo sound were expensive for the distributor—the striped prints used for CinemaScope cost *seven times* as much as those with standard optical soundtracks.[36] In a decade where domestic film attendance sank over 50 percent, studios were willing to try these expensive experiments, and initially it seemed the expense of magnetic stereo might be justified. *This is Cinerama* (1952), the first Cinerama film, made up for the extraordinary expense of its three-projector image and six-track magnetic sound by playing in one theater for over two years, grossing $4.5 million—at a time when tickets cost only about $2 each. By the end of its run it was the third highest grossing film in history despite only ever playing in seventeen theaters.[37] The less-exorbitant costs of CinemaScope likewise produced results. Even toward the end of the 1950s, when Fox was shipping both monophonic and magnetic-striped prints, about three-fourths of Fox's income on a film came from the less than one-fourth of theaters playing the magnetic stereophonic version.[38] But as it became clear that theatrical audiences were declining despite Hollywood's best technical efforts, the high costs of magnetic striping became prohibitively expensive relative to their return. Compounding this problem was that the revenue streams with which the motion picture industry was replacing its falling U.S. theatrical revenues—overseas markets and domestic television—required monophonic sound mixing: foreign theaters were unlikely to have multi-channel capabilities, and television at the time was purely monophonic. Creating multi-channel mixes was therefore largely counterproductive, as any films mixed in stereo would later have to be remixed into mono.

Economics alone, though, cannot explain the failure of CinemaScope. John Belton has argued persuasively for an audience perception–centered explanation. He contends that stereo became associated with "spectacle," while the old monophonic systems to which audiences were accustomed were still viewed as more "realistic." Noting both that the films released in stereophonic CinemaScope tended to be of genres known for "spectacle," such as musicals (*Oklahoma!* and *West Side Story*) and biblical or historical epics (*Ben-Hur, Lawrence of*

Arabia, The Alamo), and that magnetic sound survived in the six-track stereo sound of large-format systems such as M-G-M Camera 65, Super Panavision, and 70mm Todd-AO, he writes:

> Stereo thus continued to be connected not with the average movie-going experience of the 1950s audience but rather with special pre-sentation large-screen processes and with blockbuster spectacles. . . . Through its usage as an element of spectacle and through its identifica-tion with the genres of spectacle, stereo sound became associated for audiences not so much with greater realism as with greater artifice.[39]

In other words, audiences had been taught by their long experience with monophonic cinema sound (and radio and records) that sounds were supposed to remain centered behind the screen. While they were willing to accept stereo sound for films that foregrounded the "spec-tacular experience," such as those they went to see played in Cinerama or 70mm, they refused to make the same allowance for the movies they saw in their everyday theaters. Combined with the partly economics-driven relegation of stereo to special venues, this conception of mono sound as the "norm" formed a vicious circle; stereo was pushed out of the mainstream because it was viewed as too spectacular, and it was viewed as spectacular because it was used in large-screen presentations of "blockbuster spectacles" but not for mainstream exhibition.

Scattered experiments in multi-channel sound continued in the large-format market through the 1950s and 1960s.[40] One of these, a 70mm six-track magnetic system, is noteworthy as the first multi-channel system with a constant signal-to-noise ratio on all channels, allowing "panning" between any channels with no perceptible loss of sound quality; this advance was hailed for its "greater sonic realism," as it at last allowed continuous use of the rear channels without the hiss inherent in their earlier incarnations.[41] Sound could now constantly surround the audience—leading to the present moniker for the rear speakers, the "surrounds." Yet while these rear channels *could* handle any sounds the front channels could, filmmakers still employed them only for ambience and occasional effects; the guiding principles of surround mixing, rooted in 1950s audiences' distraction by the effects channel, were that "in ambience the watchword is subtlety"[42] and that the listener should not even be consciously aware of the surround channel unless it failed.[43]

DOLBY STANDARDIZES SURROUND

After the demise of multi-channel in mainstream 35mm presentation, monophonic optical sound once again dominated, and theatrical sound systems would remain unchanged through the 1960s and most of the 1970s. Audio quality in many theaters actually decreased over this time period as exhibitors, faced with declining audiences, chose to economize on equipment and hence often did not repair or replace old and broken speakers and projection heads.[44] Ironically, this negligence encouraged further audience decreases due to the concurrent introduction of home formats with high-fidelity audio, notably LPs with two-channel and even four-channel (quadraphonic) sound. When audiences—particularly the young adults on whom the film industry so heavily relies—could hear quality multi-channel sound at home, many of them chose not to attend movie theaters where they were confronted with crackling, monophonic sound. To meet the newly heightened sonic expectations of their audiences, film industry engineers once more set out to improve cinema sound technology.[45]

Their first attempt came in 1974, when Universal Studios premiered its Sensurround system with the disaster film *Earthquake*. Like the widescreen and multi-channel processes of the 1950s, Sensurround attempted to draw patrons to movie theaters with promises of "technology impossible to duplicate at home."[46] Sensurround was used to create powerful ultra-low-frequency rumbles (some below the limits of human hearing) that shook audiences and theaters in concert with explosions and other appropriate onscreen stimuli (like *Earthquake*'s titular event). It also used a control track to "steer" other sounds to the Sensurround speakers to create a more "enveloping" sense of destruction.[47] Released in monophonic and multi-channel magnetic (four-track 35mm and six-track 70mm) versions that could function either with or without the Sensurround equipment, *Earthquake* screenings employed anywhere from one to seven separate audio and Sensurround channels, depending on the theater.

While Sensurround's rumbles and shakes created a novel audience experience, the system was never able to overcome certain limitations inherent in its design. For one, Sensurround was itself a monophonic system; though it could be used with the CinemaScope and 70mm multi-channel magnetic formats, the expanded dynamic and frequency ranges it offered only applied to the single Sensurround channel, not the other sound channels. Additionally, Sensurround required exhibitors to rent Universal's proprietary equipment. This arrangement allowed high-end exhibitors to draw crowds but limited the system's reach, as the earlier failure of magnetic multi-channel had left many theater owners unwilling to pay for a new and unproven system. Facing these problems and—by the late 1970s—competition from Dolby Stereo, Sensurround disappeared as a release format in 1981 after use on only five films. The system remains noteworthy, however, for its use of a discrete low-frequency-only channel, an idea that would resurface a decade later as part of the digital surround sound specifications.

While Sensurround had been developed from scratch for the cinema, many 1970s film sound engineers saw adapting quadraphonic sound as a more promising avenue. "Quad" sound had enjoyed minor success as a home music format, using a "matrixing" process to encode four channels of audio into two for recording on a stereo LP; the proper decoder would then convert these two channels back into (approximations of) the original four. Matrixing held obvious appeal for the film industry, which had long struggled to fit multiple channels of audio into the limited space available on 35mm film prints. Quintaphonics, the first quadraphonics-based system, debuted with *Tommy* (1975), based on an album by The Who that had been recorded and released in quad. Quintaphonics expanded quad's four channels to five—three across the screen (L, C, R) and stereo surrounds (LS, RS)—with three-channel magnetic striping providing a quad matrix and a non-matrixed center front channel.[48] The matrix allowed placement of sounds in any corner of the theater; the non-matrixed center channel served to stabilize the onscreen audio. To facilitate the smooth movement of sounds around the theater, the system also took the bold step of using matched front and rear speakers.[49]

Despite its potential, Quintaphonics quickly disappeared, in large part due to the arrival of what would quickly become the 800-pound gorilla of theatrical sound, Dolby Stereo. Like Quintaphonics, Dolby Stereo used matrixing to encode four channels (three front, one surround) into two. It also incorporated noise reduction technology into the encoding process to give its optical soundtracks wider frequency and dynamic ranges than their monophonic counterparts.[50] But the key to its success was that Dolby took to heart one of the lessons of magnetic sound's failure and gave studios and exhibitors a better-sounding *and no more expensive* alternative to mono sound. Instead of requiring costly magnetic striping or a cumbersome dual-projector arrangement, Dolby used a traditional optical soundtrack, taking advantage of matrixing and noise reduction to fit the (encoded) data for four tracks into the same area of the print that the monophonic soundtrack had traditionally occupied. Thus film prints with Dolby Stereo could be made for the same price as those with mono sound and would even play back on mono projectors.

The new system did have its disadvantages. Dolby's matrixing setup offered limited mixing possibilities compared with a fully discrete four-channel system or even the matrixed Quintaphonics system. In response to the negative audience reactions encountered by multichannel dialogue and effects in the 1950s, Dolby's matrix emphasized the front center channel as the source of most sounds—indeed, the original Dolby Stereo system did not even provide for a surround channel, and when one was finally added it had only about half the frequency range of the front channels.[51] Compounding matters further, to ensure backward compatibility with monophonic theaters, no sounds crucial to a film could be encoded in the surround channel, as Dolby's matrixing process ensured they would vanish upon playback in a mono theater. Compared to its competitor Quintaphonics, "Dolby Stereo was a giant step *backwards* in the history of film sound evolution."[52]

The system's limitations made some sense at the time. Given its creators' concern with anchoring most sounds to the center of the screen, the fact that its matrix prohibited certain types of mixes—such as playing something in the left and right channels but not in the center—could be interpreted as a method of keeping mixers from doing anything "wrong."[53] Similarly, Dolby Stereo's surround capabilities were *intentionally* limited so filmmakers would not be tempted to put crucial information in the surrounds.[54] Indeed, the consultants Dolby provided to productions using Dolby Stereo acted as much to limit experimentation as to help filmmakers work with the Dolby system.[55]

Recording and mixing films for the new (pseudo-) four-channel system was more expensive than making monophonic films, and "probably would not have been sustained—after all, it cost more,"[56] if not for the bevy of sound-intensive films that quickly followed Dolby Stereo's introduction. Indeed, one can hardly talk about Dolby Stereo without at least mentioning 1977's *Star Wars*. The opening scene, where a giant spaceship audibly travels from the back of the theater to the front, showcased the powerful capabilities of the new audio format and catapulted Dolby Stereo into the public consciousness.[57] The wild success of Dolby Stereo films such as *Star Wars* showed exhibitors that audiences noticed quality sound, and they rushed to install Dolby's system in their theaters. Less than three years after *Star Wars* premiered, the Dolby Stereo format had already been used on 85 feature films, and decoding equipment had been installed in over 1,200 theaters.[58]

Ironically, much of Dolby Stereo's success can be attributed to its association in the public consciousness with spectacular effects that were not supported by its standard 35mm incarnation. The vast bass-driven audio of the opening scene in *Star Wars* mentioned earlier, for instance, was only achieved through a "work-around" of the standard Dolby Stereo setup. For the film's 70mm showcase prints, engineers utilized the "left center" and "right center" speakers still present in most larger theaters from the Todd-AO era to add a "Baby Boom" channel, which provided the Dolby Stereo setup with the additional low-frequency power they desired.[59] Those seeing the film on 35mm with a true four-channel Dolby Stereo soundtrack missed much of this experience, yet public perception (encouraged by Dolby) was that the amazing 70mm presentation *was* Dolby Stereo:

> As a company, Dolby Laboratories has actively maintained the illusion that Dolby Stereo was a singular design entity providing a singular cinematic aesthetic effect. Despite the extreme heterogeneity of its origins, and the dual technological platforms of 35mm and 70mm, Dolby Stereo functioned as a singular entity in the marketplace.[60]

Like *Star Wars*, many later films associated with Dolby Stereo in the public consciousness used special audio setups not part of the Dolby Stereo specifications, such as a dedicated subwoofer track (1977's *Close Encounters of the Third Kind*) or stereo surrounds (1978's *Superman*).[61] *Apocalypse Now* (1979), which birthed the term "sound designer," even used an entirely different multi-channel configuration that more closely resembled Quintaphonics but was marketed simply as Dolby Stereo.

1.1. Even early in the Dolby Stereo era, some filmmakers found that system's multi-channel capabilities too limiting and modified its configuration to fit their own needs. *Superman* (1978) split the single surround channel of Dolby Stereo into "left surround" and "right surround" so its hero could sonically fly around the auditorium space.

THE PROBLEM OF DOLBY STEREO

Dolby Stereo deserves credit for being the first format to supplant monophonic optical sound as a viable *standard* for theatrical exhibition. And to be sure, it represented a significant improvement over the status quo: it offered cinema improved dynamic and frequency ranges and "cleaner" sound—capabilities further enhanced in the 1980s by Dolby SR, which applied improved noise reduction techniques to the Dolby Stereo matrix.[62] Not surprisingly given these strengths, the format enjoyed a success unrivaled by any previous multi-channel system, with tens of thousands of theaters around the world eventually installing Dolby Stereo systems. And although Dolby Stereo's multi-channel capabilities were far from perfect, having *any* multi-channel format as a standard was crucial to accustoming audiences to experiencing all types of movies in some form of stereo. Indeed, Dolby Stereo remains important even today—all 35mm film releases include a Dolby Stereo track for backward compatibility with the few remaining theaters without digital sound systems and to serve as a backup to the digital soundtracks for those theaters with digital systems installed.

Yet from the very start of the Dolby Stereo era, filmmakers found it necessary to circumvent Dolby's standard system to achieve the aural effects they desired, as shown by 1977's *Close Encounters of the Third Kind*, 1978's *Superman*, and 1979's *Apocalypse Now*. As Tomlinson Holman notes in his book *5.1 Surround Sound: Up and Running*, Dolby Stereo's "dynamic range and difficulties with recording for the matrix make this format seem rather prematurely grey."[63] Holman lists numerous problems with the matrix, including that level imbalances anywhere in the signal path would significantly skew the whole soundfield; that the matrix decoders often steered sounds to the wrong speakers when multiple sound sources were present at once; and that the width of the perceived soundfield behind the screen varied depending on whether dialogue was present or not.[64] The encoding process also made the surround channel highly dependent on the rest of the soundtrack, as sound editor David Bondelevitch (former president of the Motion Picture Sound Editors or MPSE) noted: "Oftentimes the surrounds tend to disappear because if there's a lot of loud stuff coming up the center, like dialogue, the stuff that would be in the surrounds gets sucked back to the screen."[65] Stanley Kubrick ultimately found playback of matrixed sounds so unpredictable that he chose to continue making his films in mono throughout the era of Dolby Stereo's dominance.[66]

In the end, the legacy of Dolby Stereo would be one of missed opportunities, particularly with respect to surround sound. *Apocalypse Now* editor and sound designer Walter Murch, for instance, felt that the quad sound used in that film offered much more powerful surround possibilities than Dolby Stereo:

> [Quad can] create the illusion of a sound moving in all four quadrants of the room. Mono surround, 35mm Dolby optical, pretty much ties you to the idea of some mixture of front and back. Since quadraphonics gives you a left back and a right back, you can steer that sound through 360 degrees.[67]

Dolby Labs, meanwhile, viewed use of surround channels to pan sounds around the soundscape or provide spot effects as a "gimmick" to be avoided. When Dolby highlighted the possibilities of "ambience effects" in its system as an improvement over both mono and magnetic

sound, it left unspoken its system's inability to use the surround channel in any way *other* than for these sorts of effects. As Jay Beck points
out, Dolby's claim

> of the "emergence" of a new sound aesthetic in the use of [Dolby Ste-
> reo] ambience hides the fact that no other aesthetic could possibly have
> emerged simply because of the system's design. The screen centrality
> and the lack of divergence inherent in Dolby Stereo ensured that all
> dialogue and main sound effects would be channeled to the screen
> speakers and not the surrounds.[68]

As Dolby Stereo spread as the standard for film sound, the company's
initial design choices came to form the "rules" of acceptable sound—
and surround—mixing practices. Despite its promises of a "new aesthetic," the system actually reinforced and codified the norms of monophonic, screen-centric cinema rather than opening up the possibilities
of what full-fledged surround could do. Dolby's monophonic-based
conception of how multi-channel "should" be used and the technical
limitations of the Dolby Stereo matrix, rather than filmmakers' wishes,
would continue to dictate sound design practices through the 1980s
and early 1990s.

DIGITAL SURROUND'S PRE-HISTORY

Cognizant of Dolby Stereo's limitations, many filmmakers saw in
digital sound—technology using ones and zeroes rather than literal
analogues of soundwaves to represent sounds—the potential for advancement beyond the capabilities of Dolby Stereo. At the time the
Dolby Stereo system was developed, digital sound was in its infancy
and hardly ready for widespread deployment; a series of tests in the
early 1970s had demonstrated that the digital techniques of the time
were inadequate for a practical cinema sound system.[69] By 1987,
though, digital technology had advanced enough that SMPTE began
work on a digital sound standard for film based on two specific objectives. First, that any digital multi-channel system should use fully
discrete channels rather than matrix encoding to avoid encountering
Dolby Stereo's problems with sounds not playing back in the correct
channels. Second, that the new digital system should have at least

CD-quality sound so that cinematic systems could catch up with home audio.[70]

What remained to be determined was the number of channels the new standard would require. As Tom Holman recalled in this chapter's epigraph, a range of suggestions was proposed: the four-channel (left/center/right/surround) configuration used by Dolby Stereo, a five-channel system mimicking Quintaphonics and the "split surround" 70mm version of Dolby Stereo, a six-channel system (five front channels plus one surround) like that used by Todd-AO, and others. Ultimately, after Holman explained to everyone what a "tenth" of a channel was, his "5.1"-channel configuration was agreed upon as the minimum standard for digital surround sound systems.[71]

5.1 mimics the Quintaphonics setup, though with discrete rather than matrixed channels, and adds a separate LFE channel that covers a frequency range only about one-tenth that of the others—hence the ".1."[72] While it may seem curious to dedicate an entire channel to low frequencies, two physical laws make this a useful design. First, it takes considerably more raw sound energy for a low-frequency sound to reach a given loudness level than it does for a higher frequency one[73]—a good example of this is Jabba the Hutt's deep bass voice in *Return of the Jedi* (1983), which carries much more acoustic energy (and uses almost all the available amplitude of the optical soundtrack) than the other characters' "normal" frequency voices, yet does not sound much louder.[74] The LFE channel allows soundtracks to provide the same range of volumes to low-frequency sounds as they do to higher-frequency ones. Second, the human ability to localize sound is much weaker at low frequencies; below roughly 80 Hz, sounds simply cannot be located with any accuracy at all.[75] A single LFE channel thus serves the dual function of creating "enveloping" bass sound and giving added emphasis to localized sounds coming from any of the full-range channels, as the human brain uses higher-frequency sounds and onscreen visual cues to "localize" sounds coming from the LFE channel.[76]

With a technical standard in place, development on digital sound systems continued in earnest. But SMPTE's specifications were only one of the design elements faced by engineers working on these technologies. The failure of sound exhibition technologies like Fantasound in the 1940s and magnetic multi-channel in the 1950s had demonstrated that even systems offering a substantial, noticeable improvement over the standard of the day were susceptible to failure if they failed to meet the practical and economic needs of the industry. Thus for a new system like DSS to replace a thoroughly tested one like optical analog sound (whether monophonic or Dolby Stereo), it would have to meet three additional criteria. First, it would have to be as robust and manageable as the system it replaced. Second, it would have to be backward compatible with existing analog sound systems. And third, it would have to be cost effective—studios wanted neither to pay more for prints nor to maintain dual inventories as they had during the magnetic era. This last criterion was particularly critical: a major reason Dolby Stereo was so successful despite its matrix encoding scheme was that it had no economically viable competition, as no one had been able to devise a non-matrixed method for fitting more than two channels onto 35mm film without using (expensive) magnetic striping.

The importance of meeting these three practical requirements was aptly demonstrated by the failure of the first digital sound system to make it to market—which met none of them. Cinema Digital Sound, or CDS, was a joint venture between Eastman Kodak and Optical Radiation Corporation and hoped to win market share by beating its competitors (including Dolby) to the playing field. In this respect its plan worked: CDS was the first digital sound system to be used on a major release, with a number of 70mm prints of 1990's *Dick Tracy* employing a 5.1-channel CDS soundtrack.[77] The *Dick Tracy* screenings went smoothly,[78] but CDS's second appearance two weeks later, with the big-budget Tom Cruise vehicle *Days of Thunder* (1990), was an unmitigated disaster. At the film's Hollywood premiere, featuring a 70mm print with a CDS digital soundtrack, the processor used to decode the soundtrack overheated and started a fire in the projection room.[79] Obviously the industry bigwigs present were not impressed— "this town is not too forgiving of that,"[80] as Dolby consultant Thom Ehle noted—and the system was used on less than ten films after *Days of Thunder*.[81]

CDS made its last public appearance in July 1992, a month after Dolby had premiered its own digital sound system, Dolby SR-D (today known as Dolby Digital), with *Batman Returns*.[82] This coincidence of timing suggests CDS's failure can be attributed to the power of the

Dolby name—despite a two-year head start, CDS disappeared immediately upon head-to-head competition with the company behind Dolby Stereo, Dolby noise reduction, and a host of other audio advancements. In truth, the bigger issue was that CDS simply did not fulfill the criteria for a successful sound system. Most importantly, its digital soundtrack occupied the space normally reserved for the analog soundtrack, meaning that CDS prints could not play in any theater without a CDS system installed and hence were not backward compatible. Requiring different prints for analog systems and digital ones was problematic not only for the studios, who would have had to maintain dual print inventories, but also for exhibitors: multiplex owners who had upgraded some, but not all, of their theaters to the CDS system would be unable to move their prints between theaters over the course of a film's run. A CDS print was thus only useful as long as it could fill the theaters that had been upgraded to the new system, in most multiplexes the largest of their auditoriums. The elimination of the analog soundtrack concerned exhibitors for another reason as well—should the relatively untested CDS system fail during a screening, the rest of the movie would play with no sound at all.

DIGITAL SOUND ARRIVES IN TRIPLICATE

Dolby SR-D and the other two digital sound systems that soon followed were successful in large part because unlike CDS, they had been developed with an eye to the practical concerns of robustness, backward compatibility, and economic viability. Demonstrating robustness was a relatively straightforward engineering and testing problem. Digital sound technology was already successfully employed throughout the film post-production pipeline, as well as in consumer formats (i.e., the compact disc)—engineers merely needed to build upon these existing technologies.[83] To further ease exhibitors' concerns about robustness, all post-CDS digital systems kept the analog Dolby Stereo track in its traditional place and designed their systems such that in the case of any problem with the digital soundtrack during projection, playback would simply revert to the Dolby Stereo system. Thus the worst-case scenario would be not the "no sound at all" of a failing CDS system, but the four-channel-matrixed Dolby Stereo sound to which audiences were already accustomed. Keeping the Dolby Stereo track in place also ensured backward compatibility and eliminated concerns about maintaining dual print inventories.

When Dolby's SR-D format premiered in 1992, the *San Francisco Chronicle* called the system "a significant breakthrough in sound,"[84] and audiophile magazine *Stereo Review* described it as "a precursor of and foundation for future home media" that would affect "*all* of audio, or very close to that."[85] Despite these rave reviews, SR-D's debut went largely unnoticed by the general public. Even the ads for *Batman Returns* mentioned nothing about the new sound system. That such a big change garnered so little notice likely stemmed from its extremely limited initial deployment: only ten theaters in the United States and Canada were set to show *Batman Returns* in digital surround when it was released,[86] and the situation in Britain was even worse, with only one theater equipped with SR-D when the film premiered there a few weeks later.[87] Price was the key issue—retrofitting an existing theater with SR-D cost around $20,000 at the time, and with SR-D-encoded prints backward compatible with analog systems, most theaters chose to use *Batman Returns*'s Dolby Stereo soundtrack rather than pay for the new system.[88]

This high cost of adoption kept Dolby's system from spreading quickly enough to keep competitors out of the market. A year after SR-D's introduction, the DTS system developed by Digital Theater Systems debuted in *Jurassic Park* (1993). But where only a handful of the theaters showing *Batman Returns* had installed Dolby's digital system, *Jurassic Park* opened in over a thousand DTS-equipped theaters, so that about 80 percent of the movie's American audience heard it in DTS.[89] This disparity stemmed from two elements. First, exhibitors could purchase DTS's system for about $4,000, a mere fifth the cost of adopting Dolby's SR-D. Second, and perhaps more importantly, Dolby needed to convince studios and filmmakers to embrace its system, while DTS already had the weight of an entire studio and one of the most successful directors of all time behind it. After hearing an early demonstration of their system, Steven Spielberg not only bought a stake in Digital Theater Systems and agreed to use the new technology for *Jurassic Park* (a pre-ordained summer blockbuster) but also convinced Universal Pictures to help finance the fledgling company and commit to releasing *all* its future pictures in DTS.[90] To support its investment, Universal went to the trouble of noting in newspaper advertisements for *Jurassic Park* which theaters featured DTS so audiences knew where they "should" go.[91] Dolby had been the first to demonstrate the feasibility of digital surround sound, but it was DTS that brought it to the masses.

A mere week after DTS premiered, a third system entered the increasingly crowded marketplace: Sony's Sony Dynamic Digital Sound (SDDS), which debuted in *Last Action Hero* (1993).[92] Sony's system added two more full-range channels behind the screen to the 5.1 minimum specified by the SMPTE standard and adopted by SR-D and DTS, resulting in a 7.1-channel setup with five front channels and two surrounds. On the surface this seems an odd decision—by the 1990s the rise of the multiplex and the corresponding decline of "picture palaces" had dramatically decreased average theater screen sizes, so that three front channels seemed more than enough to fill most screens. But in choosing to base its SDDS system on the Todd-AO sound systems, which placed five front channels across the ultra-wide screens of the 1950s,[93] Sony was making a calculated decision intended to help its new format survive competition with the year-older Dolby system and the Spielberg-backed DTS. A 7.1 setup was of little use to the multiplex market, but it *did* offer owners of high-end, large-screen theaters something Dolby and DTS systems could not. Sony's gamble paid off, and while the SDDS system never achieved the same level of penetration as Dolby or DTS, its 7.1-channel configuration allowed it to become a viable competitor for the next decade.

THE SECRETS OF DSS'S SUCCESS

Digital surround sound arrived at an opportune moment to capitalize on growing public perceptions of "digital" as a synonym for "better." As one *Stereo Review* writer commented in late 1992,

> The word "digital" is to this decade as "transistor" was to the Fifties and Sixties, with implications and resonances that reach beyond the specific technology it names. It gleams with the promise of a cleansed, transformed future, of something new under the sun and better on the horizon.[94]

This trend was not lost on the creators and marketers of DSS systems. Shortly after the debut of Dolby's new system, its name was changed from "Dolby SR-D," a label intended to exploit the industry's familiarity with Dolby SR, to "Dolby Digital." Upon its introduction a year later, DTS showed it had learned from Dolby's initial marketing error by adopting for its own logo a shiny disc with "the *digital* experience" (emphasis in original) emblazoned across it—a marketing image allying DTS not just with the buzzword "digital" but also with the compact disc, the hot consumer technology of the day.

In addition to this fortuitous timing, digital surround sound offered clear advantages over Dolby Stereo, the exhibition standard it sought to replace: more audio channels, greater frequency and dynamic ranges, and fully discrete encoding with none of the Dolby matrix's limitations. Yet for all these elements favoring its success, several economic obstacles threatened to derail digital surround early on. One of these was standardization. Only a couple years after DSS's introduction, virtually every major release featured a digital soundtrack—but not all prints used the same digital system, as each studio had allied with a specific format. Sony's Columbia Pictures naturally used Sony's SDDS system; Universal continued its support of DTS; and Disney and Paramount employed Dolby Digital.[95] Thus equipping a theater to show films from every studio required the installation of all three competing systems. While a few of the biggest venues did exactly that, for most theaters this was a financially impossible proposition. It made sense for the industry to agree on a standard, but with two of the three systems having direct studio backing, no company was willing to cede defeat, and some concern arose over a "format war" before a compromise was reached.[96]

Through a combination of luck and strategic planning, no technical conflicts prevented printing multiple digital sound formats on the same film—each DSS system had opted for a different placement of its soundtrack. Dolby Digital used small blocks of data placed in between the sprocket holes on one side of the film, as the company's research had determined that this was an area of the print unlikely to be badly scratched or dirtied. SDDS used the outer edges of the filmstrip outside the sprocket holes, an area less protected than that between the sprocket holes but offering additional space for the extra data required by SDDS's 7.1 configuration. And DTS took the most radical approach, placing its soundtrack on a separate CD-ROM and printing only a simple timecode track—for maintaining synchronization between disc and film—on the film print itself. This dual-media system allowed DTS to use a higher bitrate, and hence less compression of the original audio data, than its sound-on-film competitors, but it was at first met with skepticism—as one person familiar with DTS's marketing plans noted, "An industry unaccustomed (since Vitaphone) to sound on disc worried that the CD-ROMs would not show up with the prints."[97] In the end DTS alleviated exhibitor concerns by emphasizing that the soundtrack and print would ship together in the same containers, making the possibility of the soundtrack not arriving no greater than that of an entire reel doing the same.

The three formats' differing placements meant that the Dolby Digital and SDDS soundtracks, as well as the DTS timecode track, could all be printed on the same piece of film without interfering with each other, the image, or the Dolby Stereo soundtrack. Within a short time reason prevailed, and each studio agreed to include multiple digital soundtracks on its releases—provided the specific DSS system it had backed was among them. This plan worked, and finally allowed 5.1 surround to supplant Dolby Stereo as the dominant soundtrack configuration: "at the point we got the quad negative and were able to put all three digital formats on one piece of sound negative was about the time that the studios said, 'Every movie we do is going to be digital. We'll have a 5.1 mix.'"[98] Today, high-profile releases from major studios feature all three digital soundtracks on each print, enabling 5.1 playback in theaters with *any* variety of digital surround system.

The standardization issue was only part of the economic problem faced by digital surround. In the first few years of DSS's history, the question for exhibitors was often not *which* sound system to install but *whether* to install one at all. As noted above, digital sound systems were not cheap—even the relatively inexpensive DTS system cost a minimum of about $3,500 per theater, and that price could go much higher if the theater did not already have a decent speaker system. Few theater owners were willing to bear these costs without a clear reason to do so. Just such a good reason soon appeared, in the form of audience preferences. Studios and exhibitors had proved with magnetic sound and Dolby Stereo that they were willing to pay for new technologies *if* those enhancements proved successful in enticing audiences to the

1.2. A frame from *Twilight* (2008) shows the multiple soundtracks included on modern 35mm prints. Immediately to the right of the image is the DTS timecode track (the dots and dashes), which keeps the film synched to the DTS soundtrack on a CD-ROM. Just right of the timecode track is the two-channel analog Dolby Stereo track. The Dolby Digital soundtrack is encoded in the blocks of digital data between the right set of sprocket holes; each data block has a tiny Dolby logo at its center. The data for the SDDS track runs along both outside edges of the print and looks similar to the Dolby Digital data but takes up significantly more room.

theater. In the case of digital surround, audiences did seem to appreciate its potential and were willing to seek out theaters offering the new sound technology. Those theater owners who had installed DSS systems found it worth the costs of additional advertising space to note in their newspaper ads that their theaters used digital sound systems—for some time even denoting (for those theatergoers who had a preference) whether each theater's system was Dolby Digital, DTS, or SDDS.

Had only a small minority of theaters offered digital sound, this distinction may not have had much impact since the number of digital screenings would be small relative to the number of filmgoers wishing to see a particular film. The period of digital surround sound's adoption, however, overlapped with two other developments in the film industry. One was a theater-building boom, which saw a 50-percent increase in the total number of screens over just a few years.[99] While exhibitors had been reluctant to upgrade the sound systems in their older theaters, these new theaters were built with DSS technology already installed, vastly increasing digital surround's penetration despite the relatively small number of "conversions." The other important development was a move away from "platform" releases to "saturation booking" (releasing a movie in 2,000+ theaters simultaneously). With greater competition for opening weekend audiences, and the numerous recently constructed theaters all having digital systems, those theater owners who had been on the fence about digital sound found it necessary to upgrade merely to keep from falling behind their competition.[100]

SURROUND SOUND MOVES TO THE HOME

By the early 2000s, digital surround sound was the clearly established norm for theatrical exhibition. At the end of 2003, for instance, there were 35,361 indoor screens in the United States.[101] At the same point, SDDS was installed on about 7,000 screens, DTS about 23,000, and Dolby Digital about 35,000.[102] Although these numbers include venues outside the United States and double-count those few theaters that are equipped with more than one of the three systems, they indicate that a decade after DSS's introduction, the vast majority of U.S. screens were equipped with a digital sound system.

But theatrical exhibition is only one portion of the movie industry. More people today watch movies at home than in theaters, and home video sales net the film industry more revenue than theatrical exhibition.[103] Because the home market is so crucial, filmmakers have to be careful about how they use new technologies like digital surround sound. As an example, the makers of *Jurassic Park* knew they *could* use the 5.1 DTS soundtrack to place sounds very specifically—for instance, a particular sound could be mixed to the right surround speaker only. What they could *not* do, though, was make it *crucial* to know that particular sound came from the right surround speaker, as viewers watching *Jurassic Park* later on video or television would not receive this piece of information. For filmmakers to freely exploit *all* the capabilities of digital surround, 5.1 sound systems would have to spread from theaters into the home.

Multi-channel home sound systems already existed, of course. Since the earliest days of stereo videotapes, ambitious consumers had been connecting their VCRs to their existing music systems, creating a basic stereo effect. In 1982 Dolby introduced Dolby Surround decoding, which allowed audiences to watch their video cassettes in a simplified version (L/R/S) of Dolby Stereo. Dolby Surround cleverly took advantage of a fact of which consumers had been largely igno-rant—that to save the costs of remixing soundtracks, film studios simply dumped their films' existing Dolby Stereo soundtracks into the two audio tracks available on hi-fi VHS and laserdisc.[104] This cost-cutting method had inadvertently created large libraries of "stereo" VHS tapes that were already Dolby Stereo–encoded, and Dolby Surround offered the technology to decode them. Thanks in part to this ready supply of surround-encoded soundtracks, Dolby Surround was a rousing success.

Five years later, Dolby Pro Logic debuted, adding to the Dolby Surround format the center channel and steering effects of theatri-cal Dolby Stereo.[105] Those willing to invest in a Pro Logic processor and two or three more speakers (in addition to the two most people already had for their home stereos) could, in theory, experience sound equal to that of their local theater.[106] By 1998 over thirty-one million homes—about a third of all U.S. households—had Dolby Surround or Pro Logic decoders, and almost all prime-time television was broadcast with some form of Dolby Surround encoding.[107]

As digital surround sound became common in theatrical venues, demand for 5.1-channel home systems grew. DTS broke into the home first, simultaneously introducing a home version of DTS for laserdisc and compact disc;[108] Dolby quickly followed suit with a consumer version of Dolby Digital.[109] Despite technical differences from their theatrical counterparts, the DTS and Dolby home DSS systems kept the same name and logos to encourage the perception that consumers could *literally* bring the theatrical experience home. After some debate, Sony decided that the SDDS brand would retain more of its prestige as a high-end format if it remained a theatrical-only format;[110] this marketing decision made sense given that their system was installed primarily in the largest and best-equipped theaters but was probably also influenced by the fact that the 7.1-channel SDDS configuration did not lend itself to home installations, where three front channels were more than adequate.

The laserdisc format never achieved mainstream success, and until the late 1990s most people had little experience with 5.1-channel sound in their homes. In 1997, however, the consumer market was transformed by the introduction and rapid spread of DVD, which quickly became the most quickly adopted home electronics product ever.[111] For comparison, at the *height* of its popularity about 1 percent of U.S. households had laserdisc players, while only five years after its U.S. debut DVD already had household penetration of over 25 percent.[112]

As DVD took off, it increased consumer awareness about digital soundtracks, since the DVD specifications required each DVD to carry Dolby Digital and/or DTS soundtracks. Sales of DVD players drove a massive increase in sales of home theater products such as receivers and speakers, as home cinephiles endeavored to take full advantage of the 5.1 soundtracks on their DVDs.[113] Those who already had Dolby Surround or Pro Logic home multi-channel systems upgraded to digital 5.1 systems;[114] others purchased home-theater-in-a-box units bundling a DVD player with a 5.1 sound system. Between 2000 and the end of 2005 the number of American homes with home theater systems went up by over 70 percent,[115] and this rate of increase shows no signs of slowing down. Home-theater-in-a-box sales alone almost doubled between 2006 and 2007, and in 2008 the Consumer Electronics Association felt comfortable writing that "home theater went mainstream long ago."[116]

DVD also helped digital surround expand into television. Not long after DVD debuted, media companies realized that they had a backlog of extant TV programming that some consumers might be willing to purchase on the new format. TV on DVD proved a huge success, and filmmakers working on current programming soon realized that mixing their television programming in 5.1 would help their DVD sales on the back end. As sound editor Bondelevitch explains,

> The real place you see surround on television is on shows that are looking into the DVD market as a primary source of income . . . so far pretty much everything that's been released on DVD has been a hit, or at least made its money back. So I think we'll continue to see DVD as a major driving factor in TV.[117]

Another sound editor, Glenn Morgan (*Open Water, Star Trek, Monster's Ball*) recalled convincing the producers of a made-for-TV movie to mix in 5.1 rather than stereo with just that argument: "I said, 'You know this is all going to go to video, to DVD.' Let's cut to the chase and do it right."[118] Eventually 5.1 was specified as the required audio format for high-definition television, which cemented this shift in broadcast sound mixing.[119]

VARIATIONS IN 5.1 CONFIGURATIONS

The adoption of 5.1 as the HDTV standard would appear to mark the final phase of technological convergence: with home, theatrical, and broadcast systems all employing 5.1 digital surround sound, a single sound mix would seemingly work in all contexts. In practice, the situation is more complex. One issue is the differences between speaker configurations in homes and those in cinemas. Movie theaters, for instance, spread the three front channels of a 5.1-channel configuration *behind* the screen, while in home setups the left and right speakers are generally placed some distance *outside* the width of the screen. Using the same mix in both cases can quickly become troublesome—a sound originating from an onscreen source near the left edge of the frame may be mixed to the left front channel for theatrical release, but if the same mix is used in a home setup most viewers would perceive the difference between the onscreen source and its offscreen sonic source.[120]

Home and theatrical systems also differ in their surround speaker configurations. Most theatrical setups use an "array" of surround speakers, meaning that multiple speakers are placed along the side walls and back of the theater, with those to the left of the theater's centerline receiving the soundtrack's left surround signal and those to the right receiving its right surround signal. Most 5.1-channel home systems, for logistical and economic reasons, instead employ only two "point source" surround speakers, one for each rear channel. In many cases the home and theatrical setups behave similarly, especially when the surround effects in question are of a subtle nature, such as reverb effects or ambiences—in the case of quiet ambience effects a surround array becomes almost necessary in a large theater, while two point sources are more than adequate in a home environment.

For more aggressive surround effects, though, the systems can sound quite different. The sequences inside John Malkovich's head in *Being John Malkovich* (1999), for instance, place sounds that would be heard specifically through Malkovich's left or right ear (i.e., a phone conversation) in the surround channel on the proper side. In the array system, these sounds seem to come from one whole side of the theater, a considerably better "hearing through Malkovich's ears" effect than that created by home systems, which place the same sounds noticeably behind, rather than next to, the viewer. On the other hand, many "spot" sounds—those one would expect to come from a specific, identifiable location—fare better in home systems. Depending on a person's location in the theater, an array can make a sound that is intended to originate from the rear of the theater seem to come from the side or even the front—a telephone ring in *Spider-Man 2* (2004), for instance, seems to be spread along an entire wall of the theater rather than originating from an actual phone somewhere.

This highlights a final difference between theatrical and home multi-channel sound systems: cinematic installations need to have a wider range of "acceptable" seating than home theaters. Home systems generally need to sound good only from a few listening positions, while for a large theater it may be necessary to have acceptable sound from several hundred positions that vary in horizontal placement, distance from the screen, and even vertical relationship to the screen. Engineers and architects try to design theaters to provide a good listening experience from anywhere in the theater, and the best theaters may even tweak the amplification and delay of each speaker in the surround array to "standardize" the sound experience throughout the auditorium.[121] Still, it is simply impossible to make a theater that will sound equally good (and have the same front-to-surround balance) heard from a seat on the left edge of the front row, from the middle of the auditorium, or from the back right corner.

Thus for theatrical exhibition, mixers tend to be very careful about how they use (possibly troublesome) spot effects. Many consumers, though, prefer just the opposite. Having shelled out significant amounts of money for their surround sound systems, they want to hear those systems used to their full capacity. Barbara Klinger notes that home theater owners tend to consider mainly the technical quality of their images and how actively they use the surround channels when rating DVDs, largely ignoring the content of the film itself: "the clarity of the transfer and the film's delivery of the kind of audio-visual spectacle that best exhibits the prowess of the playback equipment are pervasive and potent aspects of the hardware aesthetic shared and propagated by collectors."[122] A glance at fan-written DVD reviews confirms this: films are praised for aggressive use of the surround speakers and criticized for "tamer" mixes.[123]

Given the above differences between home and theatrical digital surround systems, it is not surprising that most studios remix some or all of their films for DVD release. As yet, however, no clear guidelines for what constitutes the "proper" mixing for home systems have emerged. Some movies are not changed at all, others are remixed for the home on a traditional theatrical sound stage, and still others are mixed using a consumer home theater setup for monitoring—a practice allowing even further variation between techniques, as different studios and/or mixers use different definitions of "normal" consumer speakers and room arrangements. At the moment no strong impetus exists to standardize these practices, and for the time being it appears DVD sound mixes will continue to be created using a variety of aesthetic and technical strategies.

THE FUTURE OF DIGITAL SURROUND TECHNOLOGIES

Despite these issues, the deployment of the 5.1 format across homes *and* theaters has, for the first time, made it possible for filmmakers to take full advantage of digital surround sound's capabilities and make aesthetic decisions based on what is *best* for a given project rather than limiting themselves to what will play back well in non-5.1 venues.[124] This raises a couple of important questions. First, now that filmmakers can safely assume their work will be heard in 5.1, precisely how are they choosing to deploy digital surround's capabilities? Second, how do those choices about the soundtrack affect other aspects of filmmaking?

But before concluding this discussion of digital surround sound's history and moving on to those issues, it is worth briefly speculating on the future of cinema sound. One near certainty is that the three digital surround systems in today's marketplace will eventually become two. Dolby Digital and DTS both remain strong presences in both the home and theatrical markets, but SDDS has long lagged behind its competitors in number of theatrical installations and in the early 2000s stopped selling new theatrical sound systems entirely. Though it continues to support existing theatrical installations by pushing studios to include SDDS soundtracks on new releases, the last full 7.1-channel SDDS release was in June 2007 (the animated feature *Surf's Up*); since then all SDDS releases have used the same 5.1-channel configuration as Dolby Digital and DTS, negating the SDDS format's one advantage over its competitors.[125] With no current engineering or development staff, the next major shift in sound technology will likely push SDDS out of the digital surround business entirely.[126]

Dolby and DTS, meanwhile, face a different challenge: remaining relevant as data storage becomes less of an issue in both the home and theatrical markets. The initial demand for Dolby Digital and DTS stemmed from their success in compressing DSS's 5.1 channels of audio enough that a feature-length 5.1 soundtrack could be included on the film print (Dolby) or on one or two CD-ROMs (DTS). But these compression schemes are not as valuable in formats where storage is less of an issue. Indeed, some Blu-Ray discs have taken advantage of that medium's massive storage capabilities to bypass Dolby and DTS encoding by offering uncompressed 5.1 audio. If theatrical exhibition moves away from film prints to a completely digital format, as many expect, DTS and Dolby may similarly see their compression schemes deemed unnecessary—an uncompressed 5.1-channel soundtrack requires only a fraction of the bandwidth necessary for (even compressed) theatrical-quality video. In response to this shift in the industry's needs, both companies have introduced new lossless codecs (coding schemes allowing the original master audio to be *exactly* reconstructed from the compressed data) that offer significant reductions in storage relative to uncompressed audio, leaving more bandwidth available for video or other information with no loss in sound quality. That these codecs, Dolby TrueHD and DTS-HD Master Audio, have already proven popular on Blu-Ray suggests Dolby and DTS will remain viable for the foreseeable future, especially as the original Dolby Digital and DTS codecs are still widely used.[127]

The most obvious way in which digital surround systems have continued to advance since their debut is not through improved codecs but through their expansion to support greater numbers of audio channels. Experimental data shows that increasing the number of distinct audio channels in a sound system continues to provide noticeable

improvement until the system has between twenty and thirty channels.[128] The original 5.1 configuration specified by SMPTE in the late
1980s, though a marked advance over Dolby Stereo, thus left significant
room for future improvement. SMPTE's standard was a compromise
between filmmakers' desire for better multi-channel capabilities, what
would be financially feasible, and the reality of what the industry would
accept. After the first viable digital 5.1 systems were introduced, it was
not long before sound engineers began developing ways to expand it;
as Tom Holman explains, "the platform [5.1] was there for art to be
made. As an engineer, I moved on to the next platform to work on *it*."[129]

The first addition to 5.1 was a back surround (BS) channel, which
allowed for panning directly over the audience from back to front or
vice versa. George Lucas specifically requested a system that could
do this for the podrace sequence in 1999's *Star Wars Episode I: The
Phantom Menace*, and Dolby Laboratories obliged. Their system, titled
Dolby Digital Surround EX, used a matrixing process similar to that of
Dolby Stereo to encode the BS channel into the LS and RS channels
provided in the Dolby Digital standard.[130] DTS debuted its 6.1 DTS-ES
configuration shortly thereafter; DTS-ES added a discrete (non-matrixed) back surround channel to the 5.1-channel DTS specification.[131]

At the moment, there seems to be little push to go beyond the 6.1
and 7.1 systems in use today. In part this represents a practical limit to
the existing frameworks; as Dolby consultant Thom Ehle notes, "to
put more channels in the [Dolby Digital] system is rewriting the whole
thing. . . . It's safe to say that we're fully utilizing the data we have
on the film at this point [with Surround EX]."[132] Dolby TrueHD and
DTS-HD Master Audio offer support for up to 7.1 channels in home
systems, though in a different configuration (three front and four rear
channels) than the 7.1 SDDS system. A few Blu-Ray releases have used
this format, but as it differs from theatrical setups and most consumers
are not yet willing to fill up their living rooms with more speakers, it
is unlikely 7.1 will have much impact in the immediate future. And
while a few electronics manufacturers have begun including circuitry
to handle configurations with even more channels—fall 2009 saw at
least two brands of 9.2-channel receivers introduced—no media yet
exists to take advantage of these expanded setups, nor does any appear
to be immediately forthcoming.[133] "5.1 will be the standard for awhile

for home viewing," as sound editor Christopher Reeves (*Alias, Fringe, The Practice*) succinctly puts it.[134]

Any major expansion of the 5.1 configuration in theatrical exhibition will likely not occur until the film industry shifts entirely to digital projection. Both SMPTE and the industry consortium "Digital Cinema Initiative" (DCI) have issued technical specifications for digital projection, which include support for up to sixteen audio channels. With two of these channels reserved for hearing- and visually impaired information, an expanded multi-channel configuration could include up to fourteen channels.[135] These channels could be deployed in any number of ways—no standard arrangement has yet been adopted—but one likely possibility is the so-called "10.2" configuration developed by Tomlinson Holman, who was part of the committee that created the DCI specs. A 14-channel design most accurately described as "12.2" but dubbed "10.2" for marketing purposes ("Twice as good as 5.1"),[136] this system offers significantly improved spatialization and envelopment capabilities compared to 5.1.

As demonstrated throughout this chapter, however, technical capabilities are but one factor affecting changes in sound technology; considerations such as backward compatibility, robustness, economics, and audience expectations often play a more important role in determining the success or failure of a given system. Given the expense required to outfit a theater with a 10.2 system[137] and current audience satisfaction with 5.1, 10.2 is unlikely to see widespread use in the immediate future. The home market may also impede its adoption—even the stripped-down home version of 10.2 requires twelve speakers, and it is hard to see many consumers willing—or even *able*—to double the number of speakers in their living rooms. With a majority of a contemporary film's revenue coming from the home market, even if theaters *did* install 10.2 systems, filmmakers would be hesitant to fully exploit those capabilities lest their movies not make sense when heard on a home system. Ultimately, economics, logistics, and audience preferences will play a major role in deciding when and if the film industry moves beyond the current 5.1-channel standard; whether 10.2 will eventually become an exhibition standard like Dolby Digital or an impressive but impractical system like Fantasound remains to be seen.

2

THE SOUND OF 5.1:
AURAL AESTHETICS

The design, technical considerations, and specifications that
went into the digital sound track are to provide a medium
that theoretically has no limitation. The digital medium
is not the restrictive part of the process anymore.

ROBERT WARREN, DOLBY ENGINEER

When 5.1-channel digital surround sound (DSS) first appeared in the
early 1990s, it offered filmmakers better dynamic range, more channels, and greater flexibility for placement of sounds within the multi-
channel environment. Few of these capabilities, however, could be
exploited to their fullest at this early stage in the digital era. Relatively
few exhibitors had installed DSS systems, so filmmakers had to ensure
that their soundtracks would still play back acceptably when down-
mixed to Dolby Stereo, which far and away dominated the theatrical
sound market.

Today the landscape is quite different. The theater-building boom
of the 1990s and audience preferences for digital sound systems made
5.1 the de facto standard for theatrical exhibition; the growth of DVD
and accompanying explosion in home theater accomplished the same
purpose in homes. With 5.1 digital surround sound the norm for both
theatrical and home exhibition, contemporary filmmakers can feel
reasonably confident in employing digital surround's full capabilities

without worrying about how their work will sound in Dolby Stereo or another less versatile format.

The advent of digital surround certainly did not *force* filmmakers to change their stylistic or technical approaches—anything that could be done in the Dolby Stereo or monophonic eras could still be done with DSS. But just as football players and coaches alter their strategies to adapt to rule changes, changing a cinema technology (a "rule" of how movies operate) affects the stylistic choices filmmakers make (how they "play the game"). Film history is rich with examples of technology influencing aesthetics: sync sound, color, 3-D, and CGI all caused substantial changes to film style. This chapter will explore the new aesthetic possibilities offered by digital surround sound and consider how these possibilities can be—and already have been—exploited.

SOME MOVIES GET LOUDER . . .

Digital surround sound provides a significantly larger dynamic range than Dolby Stereo and Dolby SR (the dynamic-range-enhanced version of Dolby Stereo). In lay terms, dynamic range is the difference between the loudest and softest sounds a system can reproduce. From a technical standpoint, it is measured in decibels (dB) and can be found by adding a format's *headroom* (how much louder than a designated reference level a signal can be before it distorts or clips) to its *signal-to-noise ratio* (the distance between that reference level and the inherent noise of the system). The dynamic range of any format is dictated by a number of criteria that influence these two technical measures. For analog systems, one crucial factor is the amount of *space* available to record the audio data. In the case of a 35mm filmstrip, the Dolby-encoded soundtrack must fit into the narrow gap between image and sprocket holes, which is only about 2mm wide. Because of this limitation, Dolby SR film soundtracks only achieve a dynamic range of about 78 dB—far less than Dolby SR encoding offers in other formats with more space for the soundtrack.[1]

In contrast, all three digital surround formats have a dynamic range of over 100 dB. To put this into a practical context, listeners perceive a "doubling" in volume for each 10 dB a sound's loudness increases; hence a dynamic range of 100 dB provides more than a *fourfold* improvement over one of 78 dB in the difference between the loudest and softest sounds that can be produced. Sound engineer Robert Warren offers a useful analogy: "this digital bucket of water quantitatively could hold roughly five to ten times as much as the analog bucket of water."[2] Digital surround's wide dynamic range means that within any given movie, it can include both very loud sounds *and* very soft ones, in theory surpassing the capabilities of Dolby Stereo and Dolby SR on both ends.

On the high end of the volume spectrum, differences in headroom are particularly important, since the amount of headroom determines how much louder than its "average" volume level a soundtrack's loudest parts can be. In the late sixties, monophonic sound had headroom of about 6 dB, meaning "the loudest sounds in the film could be six decibels over the level of average dialogue." This restriction was so limiting that Walter Murch (*Apocalypse Now, The English Patient, Cold Mountain*) recalls intentionally violating accepted mixing standards in such a way as "to 'trick' the projectionists to give my sound tracks an extra two or three decibels [of headroom]." This strategy backfired in the case of *The Godfather Part II* (1974), resulting in Murch having to remix (and the studio having to reprint) the entire film.[3]

Dolby SR offered a moderate improvement upon monophonic sound, with between 6 and 12 dB of headroom depending on the frequency of the sound. Digital sound represents a much more significant change: DSS systems have 20 dB of headroom across the entire frequency spectrum.[4] Since a 10 dB difference represents a doubling of perceived loudness, these numbers mean that relative to the "average" volume level of a soundtrack—for instance, the level of most dialogue—a digital soundtrack can make loud sounds that are more than *twice as loud* as the loudest sounds possible with Dolby SR. Much of Leos Carax's 1999 film *Pola X*, for example, employs a relatively "normal" average volume level, but one scene is given added aural emphasis by virtue of being much, much louder not only than the rest of the film, but than would have even been *possible* in the Dolby Stereo or monophonic eras.

In a properly calibrated theatrical setup, DSS soundtracks can get loud enough to approach the human threshold of pain. Filmmakers understandably needed some time and practice to determine how best to use this capacity for extremely high volume levels. Early in the DSS era, some films were predictably mixed *very* loud, often at the request of their directors. As one sound editor recalls,

> When the digital format came out. . . . there were, in my opinion, a series of not very good and just painful mixes. Directors thought it was good: "My movie is going to be the best movie ever" . . . it was the big action pictures, they used to *have* to be loud.[5]

The problem with this approach, of course, was that while sitting in mixing studios for hours and days on end accustomed filmmakers to these extremely high volume levels, what they saw as *normal* was well beyond what most audiences considered *comfortable*—notes Dolby consultant Thom Ehle, "You may think it's great and exciting and normal, but it's not. . . . about 90 percent of America just doesn't want to listen to stuff that loud at any time."[6] After audiences began to complain about movies being too loud,[7] the overall volume level of film mixes came back down somewhat.[8]

Still, overly loud mixes remain a concern among film sound professionals, many of whom find that only the high end of DSS's dynamic range is being used:

> A lot of movies are just loud all the time. . . . *Underworld* was probably the loudest movie I've seen in a long time. Every single kick, punch, whatever it was—everything had to be as loud as possible. Whereas a movie like that could have been a lot more effective had it been quieter in scenes instead of just loud all the time.[9]

Echoing this sentiment, one sound designer simply says, "I find movies are becoming sonically inappropriately loud. Unnecessary."[10] And a recent online discussion among film sound professionals centered around a posting titled "The Future for Hollywood Sound. . . ," which asked, "As Hollywood movies are getting bigger and more technologically advanced . . . is the sound just getting louder?"[11]

DSS actually expands *both* ends of the dynamic spectrum—so while soundtracks "can physically be louder than [they] used to be,"[12] they *can* also be quieter. The problem is one of usage. Many movies are "shifting the whole thing upwards and louder and not necessarily using the other side, quiet and silence, in interesting ways";[13] as one sound editor acknowledges, "Dynamic range, yes, we definitely have it and *can* use it. I would just argue that we *don't*."[14] And famed sound designer Walter Murch jestingly complains, "We've actually got too *much* dynamic range. We have to control it in the mixing or else we will blast people out of the theaters."[15]

Film sound professionals, who seem as frustrated as anyone with the push toward ever-increasing volume levels, suggest that the directors demanding their films be "louder and louder"[16] may simply be responding to exhibition conditions. Sound designer Randy Thom (*Ratatouille, Harry Potter and the Goblet of Fire, Cast Away*) explains:

> The well-known fact that nearly all theaters play films at a lower level
> than they were mixed ironically causes many directors to insist that
> their films be mixed even louder in a desperate effort to compensate for
> the anticipated reduction, which of course causes the theaters to turn
> the sound down even more, etc., etc. ad infinitum.[17]

Re-recording mixer Andy Daddario (the *Rush Hour* series, *Wedding Crashers*) confirms this assertion, writing that even though the SMPTE specifies that the volume level on a Dolby Digital processor should be set to 7, "For one chain in particular it is dictated that all films play at 6 . . . [and] I've found them as low as 4½."[18]

In their defense, theater owners play films at lower volumes than official standards dictate in an effort to provide the best possible moviegoing experience. The screens in some multiplex theaters are packed so close together, with so little soundproofing between them, that soundtracks played at their full intended volume bleed into neighboring theaters. Turning down the volume prohibits this bleed, though a better solution would be sonically isolating each theater in the first place.[19] Additionally, while *features* are mixed to play properly using a particular volume setting, the *trailers* that show beforehand are often mixed much louder. This too contributes to exhibitors' tendency to play movies too quietly: "Theatre playback levels are set by the complaints generated by the loudest element of the show. If the playback level is set to accommodate the loudest trailer, the feature will play at the same reduced level."[20]

Efforts are underway to address this problem by standardizing loudness levels across theater chains,[21] but another factor may also contribute to the problem of obscenely loud sound: the belief among some directors, producers, and executives that contemporary moviegoers have short attention spans and expect massive and constant stimuli from their entertainment. From this perspective, the trend toward constantly loud movies "is driven mostly by studio executives and producers who are paranoid that the audience will stop paying attention if they aren't constantly assaulted, both visually and audibly."[22] Or as one sound designer more succinctly puts it, "they think that as long as you make it louder, the audience is going to like it."[23] This offers one explanation for the exceptionally loud trailers that force exhibitors to lower the volume levels in their theaters: those overseeing these trailers believe that audiences associate "loud" with "good entertainment."

. . . OTHER MOVIES GET SOFTER . . .

Digital surround sound's wide dynamic range derives not just from its ability to produce very loud sounds but also from its exceptionally low inherent noise. All sound reproduction systems inherently produce unwanted background noise, but the specific amount of this depends on the medium. Consumer audio cassettes, for instance, have a *lot* of noise, while—as listening to the same album on both formats confirms—compact discs have relatively little. In the film world, analog optical sound-on-film systems like Dolby SR and Dolby Stereo are noisy enough that their intrinsic noise is audible, as a background hiss, in a soundtrack's quiet moments. The high signal-to-noise ratio of DSS, on the other hand, means that what little background noise exists in these systems is quieter than the ambient room noise of a theater, and hence imperceptible.

Digital surround can thus offer more profound silences than earlier systems. A scene from *Terminator 2: Judgment Day* (1991) highlights the creative possibilities made possible by this capability:

> When the Terminator shoots the T1000, which has been frozen by liquid nitrogen, the balance of sound changes radically. The ambient noises of the steel mill drop away completely, thus emphasizing the silence—a feature that the digital format is uniquely qualified to handle because it does not carry the noise artifacts that analog sound formats do.[24]

The opening sequence of *Contact* (1997) similarly uses silence to great effect. The movie begins with a tracking shot that starts at the earth and moves out until it encompasses the entire galaxy. While this scene begins with sound, it ends in the total silence of empty space. Here even the quiet speaker hiss of a Dolby Stereo "silence" would be reassuring, but director Robert Zemeckis refuses to temper the scene with any such aural object. Instead, he uses the total silence made available by DSS to emphasize the feeling of emptiness this scene engenders. Director Mike Figgis—who used total silence for the heart attack scene in *Leaving Las Vegas* (1995)—confirms this effect: "It's very disconcerting for an audience. . . . suddenly, it's so quiet in the cinema that you can literally hear everything, and you don't have the protection of this sound blanket of mush, or just ambient noise, or whatever, which we come to expect of a soundtrack."[25]

Partially for this reason, "complete" silences are rare. "Relative" silence, though, is an increasingly important element of contemporary filmmaking. Paul Théberge has argued compellingly that many films and television programs rely on an interplay between sound and relative silence as a structuring device.[26] His version of "relative" silence is admittedly broad and builds on Michel Chion's definition of silence as "the negative of sound we've heard beforehand or imagined";[27] in Théberge's words, "'silence' is always relative, and relational to sounds heard in the context of the film itself."[28] Thus in a movie where some segments feature music, sound effects, and dialogue, any section (however loud) where one or more of these elements drops out could be considered "relatively silent" due to the perception of the missing element.

Digital surround's increased dynamic range allows increased flexibility in the use of "relative" silence, since even sounds played at a "normal" volume can be *relatively* silent in the context of a noticeably louder or busier soundtrack. The climax of the 2008 film *Frost/Nixon*, for instance, uses relational silence to focus the audience's ears and emotional attentions on the moment when Frost finally draws an admission of wrongdoing out of the ex-president. In earlier segments of their conversations, the soundtrack included not only Frost and Nixon's dialogue but also the sounds of the television crew around them, the room tone of the location, and Foley. But for this key moment, everything *but* Nixon's voice drops out of the soundtrack. The effect fits

2.1. "Relative silence": everything but Nixon's voice drops out
of the soundtrack at the climax of *Frost/Nixon* (2008).

the story—everyone in the room is hanging on his every word at this
point—even as it breaks from the "realistic" soundtrack of prior scenes.
And this moment is made all the more gripping by the low background
noise of the digital surround format; it really seems that Nixon's voice is
the *only* sound in the theater. *Superman Returns* (2006) takes a similar
approach when a surgeon is picking shards of kryptonite from the hero's
body: all sounds other than the clank of the shards dropping onto a
table disappear. In both cases, while the emphasized sounds (Nixon's
voice and the clinks of shards hitting metal) are actually fairly loud,
the soundtrack *seems* silent due to its relative emptiness.

. . . AND SOME DO BOTH

The concept of silence as being relative to other parts of the soundtrack,
rather than a *total lack* of sound, hints at a key effect of digital surround
sound's increased dynamic range: the ability to create better dynamic
contrasts between loud and soft. As Tomlinson Holman puts it, "In
1977 a Dolby A stereo sound track playing Dolby Stereo sounded dramatic, but by [early 1990s] standards it sounds rather limited . . . it
takes at least Dolby SR to light up the pilot light. The digital systems
go a step beyond that."[29] One common approach filmmakers use to
heighten the perception of dynamic contrast is to exploit both the

loud and soft extremes of a soundtrack's capabilities in close succession. "Sometimes a moment of silence before a loud event can make it seem louder and punchier," sound editor Steve Bissinger (*3:10 to Yuma*, *Marie Antoinette*) explains. "So it's possible for an audience to experience parts of a movie as being 'loud' without the track actually reaching ridiculous decibels."[30]

This sound design tactic can be employed with any sound system; preceding a loud sound with silence always makes the loud sound seem louder than it really is. Sound designer Erik Aadahl (*Transformers*, *Kung Fu Panda*, *The New World*) recalls that *The Mosquito Coast*, released in 1986 in Dolby Stereo, had "the biggest explosion anyone had ever heard." The sound crew accomplished this by removing *all* sound—dialogue, ADR (Automated Dialog Replacement), Foley, sound effects, and so forth—for several moments before the explosion occurred.[31] Other filmmakers affirm that this strategy has been a part of their creative arsenal since well before digital sound. George Watters II, supervising sound editor on such films as *The Rock* and *Pearl Harbor*, notes that lowering loudness levels before and after a particularly loud sound helps "give the audience some breathing room,"[32] and sound designer Gary Rydstrom (*Finding Nemo*, *A.I.*, *Jurassic Park*) explains his strategy for creating drama in the firefighting scenes of the 1991 (Dolby Stereo) film *Backdraft* as an exercise in contrasts: "Just before an explosion, I like to have a moment of silence or expectation, have an explosion preceded by a sucking in of air, a light high sound, then a rest, and then the explosion coming in as a surprise."[33]

Though this strategy of pairing loud and soft sounds is itself not new, the huge dynamic range of DSS soundtracks makes them particularly well suited to such an approach. The louder or softer the soundtrack can be, the more striking it is for it to jump to the other end of the dynamic spectrum, since "to a certain degree loudness is determined by one's perception of the event as being loud (relative to the events surrounding it)."[34] DSS allows for the creation of sounds that seem louder than *any* sound created in a monophonic or Dolby Stereo system ever could on the one hand, and silences that can seem proportionately quieter on the other.

The two mixes of *The Exorcist* (1973, 2000) offer a compelling demonstration of this difference. For a moment where the film cuts from the possessed girl screaming and shrieking to her mother sitting in a deserted hallway, director William Friedkin wanted to heighten the contrast between the two shots through dynamics. So when mixing the original version he made the screaming as loud as possible, and then for the silent shot cut *blank film* into the magnetic soundtrack to ensure that *nothing* was on the soundtrack at that point—given the limited dynamic range of the monophonic soundtracks in use at the time, "he pushed the envelope of the technology that he had then as far as he possibly could."[35] For the 2000 "director's cut" re-release, Friedkin had the film remixed from scratch. According to Richard King, supervising sound editor for the re-release, the added dynamic range of digital surround, as well as its multi-channel configuration, allowed them to finally achieve what Friedkin had wanted in the first place:

> We were able to do everything he wanted done and actually accentuate that moment by having the screaming almost come from all around you, and then the silence was that much greater . . . the noise was much more deafening, so the silence was more effective.[36]

The scene from *Terminator 2* described earlier, where the background sounds fade away to nothingness, similarly draws an immediate contrast "with a crash of sound" as a gun fires and the T1000 shatters.[37]

Examples of filmmakers pairing true silences with loud transient sounds like explosions to exploit digital surround sound's full dynamic range can be found in a wide variety of films. *Fahrenheit 9/11* (2004), a seemingly non-sound-driven documentary, prefaces the sound of a plane crashing into the World Trade Center with a brief instant of silence (and a simple black screen), heightening our horror as we wait for what we know is about to happen. The climactic duel between Dumbledore and Voldemort in *Harry Potter and the Order of the Phoenix* (2007) employs a similar device, draining away all sound for a moment just before one of Voldemort's attacks, then letting his magic explode through the 5.1 soundscape and the diegetic world. On an absolute level the sound of this spell is no louder than those before it, but the instance of silence beforehand makes it seem much more powerful. An earlier film in the same series, *Harry Potter and the Prisoner of Azkaban* (2004), similarly drops out all sounds just before Harry shouts the crucial spell that prevents his godfather's death.

Perhaps the example that speaks most directly to the impact of digital surround sound is a chase scene from George Lucas's *Star Wars*

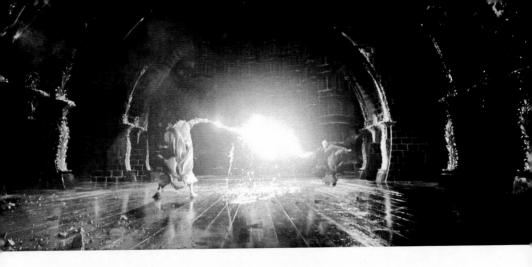

2.2. An instant of silence in the middle of this battle between Dumbledore and Voldemort heightens the perceived power of the spell launched immediately afterward. *Harry Potter and the Order of the Phoenix* (2007).

Episode II: Attack of the Clones (2002), where Obi-Wan Kenobi is chasing Jango Fett through an asteroid field. To distract his pursuer, Fett launches a series of bombs that, in keeping with the *Star Wars* franchise's tradition of ignoring the laws of physics, cause huge, theater-rattling explosions. The explosions are reasonably loud on their own, but Lucas makes them sound even louder than they actually are by dropping out *all* other sounds from the soundtrack about a half second before each one. Heightening the contrast in volume between the explosions and the sound immediately preceding them, he literally gets "more bang for his buck." Tellingly, this loud/soft pairing is a strategy Lucas did *not* use in his pre-DSS-era space battles; the opening space battle of the first *Star Wars* film, for example, instead *filled* the soundtrack with music, laser shots, and virtually non-stop explosions.

Creating dynamic contrast does not require playing loud and soft sounds in close succession; filmmakers can also explore dynamic range over the course of an entire movie. Walter Murch explains this strategy in terms of classical music:

> You could listen to a symphony played at full blast with all the instruments at the same level for about ten minutes, and then it would begin to pall on you. What the musicians of the nineteenth century began to discover . . . was the idea of dynamics within each movement, of shrinking the orchestration down to a single instrument and then expanding it outward again at the right moment. It's an approach that generally characterizes nineteenth-century music and is well suited to film.[38]

Finding ways to orchestrate this alternation of loud and soft sounds, Murch suggests, is particularly important today, when digital surround soundtracks carry the real danger of being so overwhelming (through DSS's multi-channel capabilities and enormous dynamic range) that "the real subject matter of the film can be crushed by the film's ability to represent it."[39]

An alternate way for filmmakers to exploit dynamic contrast over an entire film is to push the volume levels toward one end of DSS's dynamic range for most of the film's length, then use the other end to make a single moment seem exceptionally loud or exceptionally quiet. This approach can be very powerful, as filmmaker Robert Arnott attests:

> I went to see *The Fall* in the Sunshine cinema on Houston in NYC. I'm used to that cinema, its speakers, the space, so I was taken aback with how quiet the movie was! The whole soundscape was about 4 dB quieter than similar films I'd seen in the same auditorium. It paid off in the climax of the film though: there's a dream sequence and a single gunshot breaks the quietness. Bang!—no decay, no precedents in the film for anything near that loudness. Extremely effective! Whenever I'm talking to a director about the importance of dynamic range I always bring up *The Fall*.[40]

Unfortunately, this type of high-concept use of dynamic contrast is relatively rare, as Arnott acknowledges: "It [*The Fall*] absolutely blew me away because I've never seen that approach taken to such extremes before."[41]

In part, the rarity of such an effect can be attributed to industrial and economic constraints (detailed in chapter 5) hindering the ability of filmmakers to conceive and execute comprehensive sound design plans. But just as importantly, designing an entire soundtrack with dynamic contrast in mind requires a level of thoughtfulness about sound that many directors and producers do not possess. As Steve Bissinger explains,

> The problem is, this involves restraint when mixing other effects, some of which might sound really cool a bit louder, but . . . might not leave room for that loud explosion downstream to feel loud (relative to the rest of the track). The temptation . . . is to go for the "cool" effect in the mo-

ment to add energy to the scene, rather than feel the flow of the longer form with an eye towards giving the dynamics room to grow when they need to.[42]

The capacity for dynamic contrast is thus one aesthetic possibility offered by DSS but only rarely fully exploited.

DISCRETE CHANNELS AND COMPLEXITY

When most people think about digital sound, "improved dynamic range" is not the first issue that comes to mind. That honor would go to DSS's multi-channel capabilities. "5.1" is now a part of everyday language, a fact that speaks not only to digital surround's ubiquity in contemporary media but to DSS's fundamental association with multi-channel sound. As sound designer Richard King (*The Dark Knight, War of the Worlds, Magnolia*) recalls, when remixing *The Exorcist*, Friedkin instructed him to use more surrounds so it would "sound like a modern movie."[43]

Considered purely in terms of channel configuration, digital surround sound may not at first seem to offer much of an improvement over its immediate predecessor. Dolby Stereo ostensibly includes four channels—left, center, and right front plus mono surround—and, ignoring for the moment the LFE channel, digital surround systems employ the same basic setup other than splitting the mono surround channel into stereo. But as detailed in the last chapter, the technical limitations of matrix encoding and Dolby's views on proper mixing strategies placed significant constraints on how the pseudo-four-channel Dolby Stereo setup could be used. Digital surround sound, in contrast, offers completely *discrete* audio channels, meaning that the content in each one of its six channels is completely independent of what is in the others.

An important ramification of this more flexible mixing environment is the ability for literally *more sounds* to play at the same time. While any number of sounds *can* always be mixed together, mashing more than a few into the same channel makes it difficult to hear *any* of them clearly. Sound designer Steve Flick (*Spider-Man, Starship Troopers, Leatherheads*), for instance, notes that "Monaural's a much more difficult format to work with. . . . You are pared down to less [while still trying] to tell an effective story."[44] Sound editor Midge Costin (*Armageddon, Crimson Tide, Hocus Pocus*) shares the same sentiment, dryly noting, "How much can you really squeeze into a mono single track?"[45] As Dolby Stereo still required most important sounds to be mixed to the center channel, its adoption as a replacement for mono sound did little to alleviate this problem.

Digital sound, on the other hand, provided *five* separate channels across which sounds could spread. Filmmakers eagerly took advantage of this option, as Flick attests: "If you get too many elements piled on top of one another, it becomes less dynamic. So sometimes I have a tendency to move stuff into the surrounds and have more all at once."[46] Indeed, psychoacoustics confirms that increasing the number of channels actually increases the number of individual sounds the audience can hear. One factor is competition between sounds:

> When collapsed to one speaker or headphones, one sound of greater amplitude can cover another sound, creating a condition known as masking. . . . Variations of sound location, density, and volume in the surround channels can punctuate events on screen without the loss of intelligibility that might occur if the entire sound track was limited to the center speakers.[47]

Additionally, the human brain "sorts" sounds in part by comparing the sounds coming from one ear to those coming from the other; if two sounds originate in different places—such as different speakers in a movie theater—it is easier for the brain to separate them and hear each individually.

The net result of these psychoacoustic phenomena is that digital surround sound allows filmmakers to put more *separately perceptible* sounds in the soundtrack at any given moment. "Greater complexity, there's no doubt about that, more perceptible sounds, absolutely," says Tomlinson Holman about the effect of digital surround on aural aesthetics.[48] Mike Knobloch, an executive at Universal Pictures, confirms that sound designs that would have been too busy in earlier eras can now be made to work thanks to the discrete multi-channel configuration of DSS systems: "Sometimes there is room for very kinetic and dense music and sound effects and dialogue to all coexist in a 5.1 world where they couldn't necessarily coexist in a stereo or mono world."[49]

Digital systems with 6.1- or 7.1-channel configurations can at times push this capability even further. Dolby's website claims its 6.1 system "improves lifelike atmospheres and quiet effects . . . Surround EX is not just louder or bigger, but more like real life."[50] And SDDS executive Gary Johns notes that with SDDS's 7.1 setup, "you'll hear things that you wouldn't normally hear [in 5.1]"—he cites a quiet scene from *The Patriot* (2000) as an example, pointing out that in SDDS, "you can hear the leaves rustle, and you can hear the little sounds that you wouldn't hear otherwise, because they are isolated."[51]

More *perceptible* sounds is the key change here. In making the first sync sound films, re-recording was essentially impossible, and a section of dialogue (for instance) in the completed film would contain only those other sounds actually present when the dialogue was recorded.[52] Over the years, changes in post-production technologies—notably the shift from sound-on-film or sound-on-disk recording in the early days of sync sound, to magnetic tape in the 1950s, to digital systems in the 1980s and 1990s—have made it possible to mix together ever-increasing numbers of sounds. Today, a virtually infinite number of different sounds can be combined, as digital techniques have eliminated the "generation loss" problems of analog systems where each stage of re-recording or transfer adds noise to the signal. William Whittington has argued that the shift from analog to digital in the post-production realm has made soundtrack construction more complex, pointing out that at places in *Terminator 2: Judgment Day* one hundred original sounds are playing at once.[53] Walter Murch concurs, arguing that

> the general level of complexity . . . has been steadily increasing over the eight decades since film sound was invented. . . . Seventy years ago, for instance, it would not be unusual *for an entire film* to need only fifteen to twenty sound effects. Today that number could be hundreds to thousands of times greater.[54]

To be clear, this represents a different *type* of complexity from that spurred by digital surround systems. That one hundred sounds play at the same moment in *Terminator 2* implies that extensive sound design was involved in the creation of that film, not necessarily that one hundred sounds will be *perceived* at any single moment. Any given sound effect in a contemporary film likely incorporates several different original recordings that *sound* like a single effect when combined—as a sound designer acknowledges, "it is not always obvious what it took to get the final result: it can be simple to be complex, and complicated to be simple."[55] The tyrannosaur roar in *Jurassic Park*, for instance, was composed of a variety of animal noises, carefully combined by the sound crew to create a "single" sound the audience would believe as the bellows of a large dinosaur.[56]

While a theoretically limitless number of sounds can be used in the *creation* of a soundtrack, perception has much stricter limits. Psychoacoustic research shows that humans can only pay attention to a limited number of sounds at once; re-recording mixers know this and hence shape their soundtracks to focus audience attention on only two (or at most three) perceived aural objects at a time.[57] Murch suggests a "Law of Two-and-a-half" to achieve a balance between clarity and density—that is, between awareness of individual elements and of their combination. This approach, which limits the number of "similar" sounds that are played at the same time, allows the listener to hear both the forest *and* the trees.[58] He allows that this law can be extended, perhaps even doubled, when "dissimilar" sounds are combined, to allow at most perhaps five layers of *useful* sound.[59]

DSS's discrete channels make it possible for audiences to *hear* more sounds at once; the limitations described above beg the question of how useful that capability is if those audiences can only *process* a small fraction of the sounds they are hearing. Occasionally, filmmakers may *want* a mix to include more sounds than an audience can process, since this strategy creates particular emotions. "There may be instances in the thick of a battle where you just want to overwhelm the audience and just throw things at them," remarks sound designer Richard King. But this approach can only be used sparingly, since it can alienate an audience; as King cautions, "You want them to feel like they're being overwhelmed or in the midst of chaos, but you want to be real careful about where you do that and for how long you subject them to that."[60] In most cases, less is more. Sound designer Erik Aadahl, for example, argues that sound design fundamentally requires guiding the audience's attentions to key sounds, not trying to overwhelm them: "I don't like just every speaker blaring, it's just overwhelming and unlistenable and not very fun to me. I really like to hear this, then this, and then this, not everything all at once."[61] By and large, most sound designers and mixers follow the same approach, not simply assuming that they can fill up each of DSS's different audio channels to "get away with" overly busy soundtracks.

Nevertheless, filmmakers have found digital surround sound's potential for highly complex soundscapes useful in particular situations—specifically, those where they want to include a lot of different sounds but it is not necessary that the audience be able to *process* them all. Action films are the most obvious beneficiary of this strategy. The soundtrack to *Terminator 2*, for instance, not only incorporates thousands of original sounds but also features sections with dozens of *perceptibly different* sounds playing simultaneously. Its biggest action sequence, an extended freeway chase, moves a huge number of sounds around the multi-channel soundscape. Whether or not the audience actually notices all the individual sounds is irrelevant—in either case the feeling created is one of intense movement, speed, and action.

This "wall of sound" approach to sound design is not, however, used only for action scenes. A montage sequence in *Kinsey* (2004) employs an even more complex mix than that of *T2*'s freeway chase. While the title character crisscrosses the country interviewing people for his sex study, the faces of his various interviewees appear onscreen over a U.S. map. Their voices also begin to mingle together and spread throughout the theater as they recount their stories. By the montage's end, all five main sound channels are playing different sets of voices. These voices remain individually discernable, and audience members can choose if they want to focus on any particular voice to hear its story; alternately, they can simply listen to the mix as a whole, which continuously shifts focus among different voices. The result either way is a feeling of being overwhelmed by the number of different points of view present, an emotion made more powerful by the clear sense that this is not just "walla" sound but a vast collection of *individual voices*, all of whom have something worth saying.

ANY SOUND, ANYWHERE

Digital surround sound's discrete channel system is not, of course, used only to increase soundtrack complexity. It also allows filmmakers to place each element of the soundtrack precisely in any of the five channels around the theater. This ability is probably DSS's single most important technical improvement over Dolby Stereo, whose matrixing system's limitations resulted in screen-centric mixes not very different from those of the monophonic era. Of particular note is that DSS allows *any* sound to be placed in one or both surround channels—channels that in the Dolby Stereo era could contain only sounds that were not of narrative importance and fell within a narrow frequency range.

This capability has encouraged a vastly different use of multi-channel than the one most scholarship on surround sound, treating *technical limitations* specific to Dolby Stereo as carved-in-stone *rules* for multi-channel, describes. A 1995 essay by Rick Altman, for instance, asserts that audiences expect spatial fidelity from the front channels in a multi-channel setup but have markedly different expectations for the surround channel, which "is released from the standards we apply to the front channels" and in which "any effect, however farfetched, will be deemed acceptable."[62]

Soundtracks today, contrary to Altman's description, use all five of DSS's main channels *together* to build multi-channel environments, and they assume that audiences will understand sounds originating in the surround channels to be part of the same diegetic space as those originating onscreen. As an example, a scene in *Gladiator* (2000) where Maximus (the film's hero, played by Russell Crowe) walks from a small enclosed space out into a giant arena uses a gradual movement of sounds through all five channels. At the start of the scene, we hear the sounds of the small "waiting area" where Maximus is preparing to do battle; muffled sounds from outside also play in the background. As Maximus moves out to the arena, the camera moves with him and the soundtrack begins to shift. It gradually introduces the sounds of the arena (now heard without the "muffling" effect) to the front center, then the entire front, then gradually the entire theater (as the sounds of the original waiting area fade out in the rears). This design effectively conveys the overwhelming sensation of moving from a tiny underground tunnel to a gigantic stadium filled with cheering spectators, and it is made more effective by the way all the main channels are used together to precisely shape the move between these two spaces.

A more complex multi-channel-driven movement through space can be heard in the opening scene of *Contact* described earlier. The film opens on earth, then the camera begins tracking backward away from our planet through the outer reaches of the solar system all the way into deep space. As the camera pulls back, the soundtrack conveys that earth's radio and television signals are traveling out into space by moving recognizable music and news clips from the back of the theater to the front. In other words, as the camera moves away from the earth, the sounds of history whiz by the audience—the effect is that of traveling backward both spatially and temporally. A similar sound effect (that of moving back into history) could possibly be created in a monophonic or Dolby Stereo environment—but this would not have the same psychological and narrative power as actually hearing history fly by. And as with the *Gladiator* example above, this effect requires treating all the channels as equals rather than sticking to antiquated concepts about what each channel should or should not do.

To be sure, Dolby Stereo–era mixing practices have not disappeared entirely. Most dialogue continues to reside in the front center channel, and many filmmakers still have some reservations about using the surround channels *too* aggressively. The difference is that the way a given movie uses surround can now be dictated by what is appropriate for the *story* rather than by technology. The sound design to the 2000 musical *Dancer in the Dark* provides an implicit commentary on this difference. Paul Théberge notes that most of that film's diegetic sound is played in mono, while its musical numbers are in full stereo.[63] In the context of the movie, this binary approach creates a sharp contrast between the monotonous real life of its heroine Selma (played by pop singer Björk)—a poor factory worker going blind—and her exciting, life-affirming fantasy world, in which the musical sequences occur. But it also suggests the inability of monophonic-based sound and its "rules" to accommodate Selma's creativity and imagination, which can only be rendered in multi-channel.

Ultimately filmmakers using surround today strive to strike a balance between the traditions of the past and the freedom of the present—any sound *can* go anywhere in the theater, but not every sound *should* go anywhere. If an object is supposed to be moving, for instance, using the full 5.1 soundscape for panning its sound is effective and gives a better sense of motion.[64] But it is not necessarily a good idea to fill the surround channels with sound all of the time—good multi-channel design requires picking the right sounds to pan and the right moments to use the surrounds aggressively. As Gary Rydstrom remarks,

> People love surrounds in movies, but they're not effective if you always
> have sounds playing in the surrounds. You have to pick your moments
> when you want something to pass overhead or really fill out the theater.
> . . . If there's a grenade launch and you haven't had too much going on
> in the surrounds and it shoots out of the surrounds, it's more effective.[65]

Offscreen sounds in the surrounds can also be used effectively, notes
another sound designer, to draw the attentions of an onscreen character
or build suspense—but these effects can be distracting unless "the story
lends itself to that."[66]

A key consideration in multi-channel mixing is that surround effects should not distract the audience through the "exit door effect"
(alternately called the "exit sign effect"), where the audience believes
a sound in the surrounds actually originates within the theater and
looks away from the screen to find out the sound's source. Re-recording
mixer Paul Massey (*Walk the Line*, the *Pirates of the Caribbean* and
Night at the Museum series), for instance, points out that the mix in
Master and Commander: The Far Side of the World places sounds all
throughout the soundscape but carefully avoids putting effects in the
surrounds that would draw attention away from the screen:

> For a lot of the background sounds and the walking on deck and such
> from a below-deck perspective, it worked very well to be all around us
> in the surrounds and in the front . . . there is nothing percussive only
> in the back that would draw you away from the front. It all worked
> together. . . . if you are looking at a ship scene from a deck perspective
> and you suddenly hear a rope crinkle, or some specific mast crack, or
> something behind you, it is distracting to the point where you are pull-
> ing people away from the story[67]

One way to avoid the exit door effect is to eliminate the image
track entirely, making it irrelevant whether the audience's attentions are
distracted from the screen. The trailer for 2003's *The Texas Chainsaw
Massacre* remake employs this strategy with great success. While the
screen remains blank, a man's heavy footsteps methodically pursue a
woman—represented by her screams and running footsteps—around
the multi-channel space of the theater, beginning in the back right
channel and continuing around the front of the theater to the chase's
end in the front left channel. After the chainsaw roars into action, a
simple title card reveals the name of the movie. In a mono environment, this trailer would be simply a lot of footsteps, a couple screams,

2.3. The short *Lifted* (2006) uses careful placement of sounds around the multi-channel soundscape to indicate diegetic action beyond the edges of the frame. Here the abductor-in-training reacts to the offscreen sounds of an examiner making notes about his poor performance.

and a saw powering up; in the multi-channel realm it becomes a clear and engrossing chase with no visuals required.

Few films, of course, leave the screen blank for long stretches of time. More often, the exit door effect is prevented by ensuring that sounds either originate onscreen before panning into the surrounds or have clearly established diegetic sources. Pixar's 2006 short *Lifted* provides an excellent demonstration of how a film can exploit DSS's full panning and placement capabilities without triggering the exit door effect. Directed by sound designer and re-recording mixer Gary Rydstrom (*Saving Private Ryan*, *Minority Report*), this film tells—without any dialogue—the story of an alien attempting, under the watchful eye of his trainer, his first human abduction. As he futilely attempts to control the tractor beam that will pull the human out of a window and into their spaceship, he bangs the sleeping human body all around the bedroom, causing a giant mess.

Throughout the piece, Rydstrom uses carefully panned sound effects to suggest both this (often offscreen) havoc and other diegetic sounds outside the borders of the frame, such as the trainee's whining during a shot of his teacher making notes about his performance. One of the film's funniest moments even relies on a surround effect: the abductor-in-training at last succeeds in directing the human out of the bedroom window—a success quickly marred by the fact that immediately after the body flies offscreen, a crash in the right surround channel reveals that it has hit a tree. This sound effect cues a cut to a wider shot revealing the body wedged in the tree's branches. In this and other situations, Rydstrom carefully places sounds around the theater to heighten his film's drama and/or comedy. But since all these sound effects have clearly indicated sources within the diegesis (even if those sources are not onscreen at the moment), the sound design never becomes distracting or "too big" for the story.

PANNING AND DIALOGUE

Lifted shows that filmmakers can use DSS to aggressively place and pan sound effects—without distracting the audience—to a degree impossible in Dolby Stereo. An even better indication of how much digital surround's discrete channel design has affected mixing practices is that dialogue is slowly being liberated to move around the theater like other elements of the soundtrack. One of the cardinal principles of multi-channel panning has been to keep dialogue front and center; filmmakers using magnetic stereo in the 1950s quickly learned this lesson, and the Dolby Stereo system appearing twenty years later technologically codified this aesthetic guideline. But now that the discrete channels of digital surround have made it technically possible to place dialogue elsewhere in the theater, some filmmakers are breaking with decades-long conventions to take advantage of this capability.

This strategy is not without its dangers, if for no other reason than that audiences are unaccustomed to it. As sound editor David Bondelevitch remarks, "I can think of some examples where . . . you hear somebody talking or somebody suddenly yell in the surrounds—they just end up distracting the audience."[68] Sound editor Christopher Reeves offers a slight clarification on this perspective, suggesting that background dialogue (i.e. "walla") can be moved out of the center channel since it normally does not draw too much attention to itself.[69]

When filmmakers *do* move non-background dialogue around the 5.1 environment, they tend to do so in a conservative way, challenging the assumption that all dialogue must remain in the front center channel without fully abandoning it. Dialogue might be panned, for example, at points of a film where a tight correspondence between image and sound is not expected and hence audiences are more open to unusual techniques. The *Kinsey* montage discussed earlier, for instance, gradually spreads the voices of its researchers' interviewees around the whole soundscape, but it is clear in this case that no literal correspondence between image and sound is intended. In fact, while some of the voices in the montage are first heard in sync with onscreen faces, others are never associated with onscreen elements, and ultimately both types of voices spread into the surrounds even as some of the speakers' faces remain onscreen. The same fundamental principle is at play in the scene near the end of *Terminator 2* where the T1000 (played by Robert Patrick) is melting in a pit of molten steel. Despite the T1000 remaining onscreen in a close shot, its screams whip around the surround channels.[70] While this violates conventions of spatial matching between image and sound, it fits with the "spectacle" of the scene overall, recognizing that audiences are not expecting unadulterated realism out of this scene. Moreover, the T1000's screams are, like the voices in the *Kinsey* montage, primarily *effects* rather than dialogue whose semantic meaning the audience is expected to decode.

Transitory panning is another way for filmmakers to "bend" the rule that dialogue belongs in the front center channel without breaking it—in these cases voices are briefly placed offscreen but "rehabilitated" once they have served their purpose. As one sound editor explains, panned dialogue is often most palatable when it is used only briefly, such as when someone yells something from offscreen before the camera cuts to show that person.[71] An example of this type of transitory dialogue panning is a sound transition between two scenes in *Ratatouille* (2007). At the end of a scene in Gusteau's restaurant, the soundtrack introduces the beginning of a speech by Django (father of the film's rat hero Remy). Django (voiced by Brian Dennehy) is speaking in the rat's nest where Remy's family lives, but his line begins a few seconds before the image track cuts away from the restaurant. Overlapping image and sound from different scenes is a common transitional device used to smooth over the edit between two locales; what is unusual here is that during the time the dialogue of one space overlaps with the image of the other, *Ratatouille* mixes Django's voice to all five main channels. The rationale for this mixing strategy seems to be to keep the audience from assuming a particular spatial relationship between the two places and is therefore short lived—once the camera cuts to the rat's nest and Django appears onscreen, it is no longer necessary, and the dialogue quickly collapses back to the front center.

The 2007 teen comedy *Superbad*—hardly considered a surround-intensive movie—similarly pans dialogue out of the center where it is useful to the narrative purposes of the story. A good example is a scene where the film's three friends Seth (Jonah Hill), Evan (Michael Cera), and Fogell (Christopher Mintz-Plasse) are discussing their after-school plans during home economics class. They are interrupted by a comment from their teacher, whose voice originates offscreen in the front right audio channel. Most obviously, this choice to initially place her dialogue outside the center channel provides a spatial match between the soundtrack and the diegetic world, letting us know where the teacher is relative to Seth and company; her voice returns to the center when the image track cuts to show her. But this mixing strategy also sonically literalizes her role as an "outsider." With the students' voices in the center channel where movie dialogue is "supposed" to be, her voice (exhorting her pupils to focus on their class assignment) represents a jarring and unwelcome intrusion of the "real world" of work and school into the fantasy world of the movie, where the only thing that matters is the evening's party plans. She is not only in a different audio channel from her students and their lives, she is in a different *world*.

Not all filmmakers have restrained their panning of dialogue out of the center to brief moments or places where the specific words said are not crucial. Indeed, some have abandoned any pretense of keeping dialogue rooted to the front center, instead panning it uncompromisingly wherever they feel it should go and trusting the audience to keep

2.4. Fogell is distracted from his conversation with Seth and Evan by the offscreen voice of their teacher yelling at him. *Superbad* (2007).

up. *Strange Days* (1995), for example, pans voices all around the audience to simulate the experience of real life, where dialogue *can* come from all sides. Rydstrom, the film's sound designer, acknowledges that this was an unusual tactic to take, but points out that "It's dangerous to have rules" and asserts that accurately spatializing the dialogue was the right decision for a story partly about a technology that captures real experiences.[72]

Where *Strange Days* employs panned voices to create a better match between soundtrack and diegetic world, the same device can be used to *prohibit* a match from being made between the two. Gore Verbinski's *The Ring* (2003) at one point mixes a child's voice into all five channels simultaneously so that it *cannot* be associated with a single location. In this scene, the lead character is recalling something her son had said to her, and it is his voice that plays all around the auditorium. The effect is to add an ethereal, voice-in-the-head effect that not only fits the eerie tone of the horror film but also helps code this bit of dialogue as "not-really-there," especially in contrast to the tightly localized, front center channel-mixed voice of the mother that immediately follows.

As a third possibility, a film can play with both approaches, using the multi-channel environment to *suggest* a spatial match between sound and image but then thwart those expectations. *Girl, Interrupted* (1999) provides a prime example of this strategy. Susanna (Winona Ryder), the main character, is getting ready to leave her mental institution when another patient, Lisa (Angelina Jolie), steals her diary. As Susanna desperately searches a set of underground tunnels for Lisa, Lisa's voice jumps from one speaker to another, suggesting both the literal difficulty Susanna is having locating Lisa in any one place and the underlying sense that Lisa has some sort of strange power over Susanna. *Spider-Man* (2002) utilizes a similar tactic in the scene that reveals that Norman Osborn (Willem Dafoe) has a split personality—the voice of his Green Goblin personality moves from speaker to speaker while his Osborn personality futilely tries to locate the Goblin.

Though it does not employ the type of surround-driven "tricks" of *The Ring*, *Spider-Man*, or *Girl, Interrupted*, the 2006 Pixar film *Cars* is more consistently aggressive about panning dialogue than any of these films. Throughout the film, voices are panned within the 5.1 soundscape to match the position of their sources relative to the camera position implied by the image track. Sometimes this is as simple as panning a voice from right to center to left as a character moves across the width of the screen. In other places entire conversations take place in one or both of the rear channels while the image track shows someone watching (and listening to) the offscreen characters who are speaking, such as when Mater (voiced by Larry the Cable Guy) and Lightning (Owen Wilson) return from tractor tipping and Sally (Bonnie Hunt) watches them approach her motel. In both cases, the makers of *Cars* carefully avoid panning voices into the surrounds unless those voices are recognizably those of established characters, are tied to the world of the film with visual cues, or both—a strategy that prevents even the movie's lengthier segments of offscreen dialogue from eliciting the exit door effect. Given that neither critics nor audiences registered any complaints about—or even notice of—*Cars'* extensive dialogue panning, it seems clear that the filmgoing public is not distracted by dialogue being anywhere in the soundscape, at least if that panning is done intelligently. To be sure, *most* movies still place *most* dialogue front and center *most* of the time, a convention unlikely to change. But now that DSS has given filmmakers the *option* of breaking from this practice where appropriate, they are increasingly choosing to do so.

FULL-FREQUENCY CHANNELS

Digital surround sound's discrete channel configuration means that any sound can in *theory* be mixed to anywhere in the theater; this is only possible in *practice*, though, because all five main channels in a DSS configuration are required to be "full range"—that is, able to contain and reproduce sounds in the full range of human hearing, from 20 Hz to 20,000 Hz.[73] No widely adopted film sound system prior to DSS offered this capability. When SMPTE was developing the specifications for digital motion picture soundtracks, however, it recognized that the advantages of discrete channels would be partially lost if frequency limitations meant that the surround channels could only handle certain types of sounds. Hence SMPTE stipulated that *every* main channel be able to reproduce *all* audible frequencies.

The combination of full-range channels with a discrete channel configuration means not only that any sound can be *placed* in any channel, but that sounds can smoothly be panned *from* one channel to another. While brief stereo "fly-bys" across the front speakers have long been a staple of multi-channel soundtracks, digital surround sound represents the first commonplace system where sounds can move not just across the screen but all throughout the theater. *Apocalypse Now* famously panned helicopter sounds throughout the auditorium—but the full splendor of this multi-channel mix was only heard by viewers in a few showcase houses, as the standard 35mm Dolby Stereo prints of *Apocalypse Now* did not even include a surround channel.[74]

Filmmakers quickly found exciting uses for this newfound capability after DSS's debut—1990's *Days of Thunder*, one of the very first films with a digital 5.1 soundtrack, panned car engine sounds in a circle around the audience during some racing scenes to create the feeling of being "inside the track."[75] Several of the examples mentioned earlier in this chapter—including *Kinsey, Contact, Lifted,* and *Girl, Interrupted*—likewise depend not just on DSS's discrete configuration, the context in which they were introduced, but also on its full-range channels.

Indeed, virtually every contemporary surround mix relies on DSS's ability to seamlessly pan sounds of *any* frequency between the front and rear channels. The lengthy podrace sequence of 1999's *Star Wars Episode I: The Phantom Menace,* for example, pans the sounds of the podracers between every pair of channels imaginable: ships fly from front to back, left to right, corner to corner, and so on. Crucially, the "podracer" sound effect includes both high-frequency and low-frequency components, meaning that this extensive panning is only possible because all of DSS's channels support the full range of audible frequencies. More subtly but no less effectively, *The Matrix* (1999) employs slow audio pans through the entire theatrical soundspace during some of its "bullet-time" effects, where the visual and aural positions of moving bullets change drastically over the course of a single shot.

DSS's full-frequency channels can also be exploited in ways not dependent on a discrete configuration. A good example of this type of use is the soundtrack to 1995's *Crimson Tide.* During the film's numerous scenes set inside a submarine, the soundtrack incorporates a constant low rumbling in all five channels, emphasizing the claustrophobic nature of life in a sub by literally *surrounding* the audience with a continual engine noise that cannot be escaped.[76] Significantly, portions of this rumble sound fall below the lower frequency limit of the Dolby Stereo surround channel, meaning this claustrophobic effect is only possible because *all* DSS's channels are full range. But as the rumbling does not differ significantly from channel to channel, it does *not* depend on the fact that DSS uses a discrete format.

LOW-FREQUENCY EFFECTS

One channel in the 5.1 digital surround configuration does not have full-range capabilities: the ".1" low-frequency effects (LFE) channel. As explained in the last chapter, this channel was included in the DSS

2.5. The podrace sequence in *Star Wars Episode I: The Phantom Menace* (1999) demonstrates digital surround sound's unique technical capabilities: the LFE channel makes the podracers seem "powerful," and the discrete, full-range channel configuration enables the sounds of the racers to smoothly move around the auditorium to match the visuals.

specifications for psychoacoustic reasons; since much more powerful audio signals are required to make low-frequency sounds seem equal in volume to those of higher frequencies, a dedicated LFE channel was necessary to give filmmakers flexibility in their use of low-end sounds. That is, the LFE ultimately functions as a way around previous systems' technical limits on how loud sounds at the low end of the audible spectrum could get. As this rationale would suggest, the LFE channel is perhaps most commonly used simply to get low-frequency sounds up to desired levels; as sound editor Reeves explains, editors do cut some sounds specifically for the LFE channel, but more often "what they send to the boom track [i.e., the LFE channel] are the real low end frequencies that are in your regular track."[77]

The Phantom Menace adopts this approach, harnessing the LFE channel to give needed volume and power to a key sound effect. Perhaps because *The Phantom Menace* was George Lucas's first chance to explore the possibilities of digital surround, he made the sound of the film's "podracers" a primarily low-frequency rumble. This rumble, residing mostly in the LFE channel, was paired with a bit of high-end sound that could be panned to the other five channels to perceptually move the pods around the theater. Since podracers are essentially jet engines tied to a seat, the logically "correct" sound for them *would* be a low-end rumble like a jet engine. Yet DSS's capabilities were as much a factor in this sound design decision as any question about what a podracer would "really" sound like—without the LFE channel, the podracer effect could not have been made loud enough. Tellingly, both Lucas and sound designer Ben Burtt were intimately involved with 1983's *Return of the Jedi*, where the low-frequency voice of Jabba the Hutt had been difficult to adequately reproduce in Dolby Stereo—and the podracers required significantly more volume than Jabba's voice. Their decision to convey the raw power of the podracers through loud low-end sounds thus demonstrates Lucas and Burtt's awareness of, and willingness to rely on, the improved low-frequency capabilities DSS and its dedicated LFE channel offered.

Often the LFE channel is used not as part of a particular recurring sound effect like a podracer engine but rather in short bursts to give an added "weight" to explosions or other effects that need to seem bigger than they really are. Examples of using the LFE for this sort of "quick hit" can be found in just about any action film from the last ten years, but a particularly revealing one comes from a scene late in *The Matrix*: when a glass building is about to shatter after being hit by a helicopter, a low rumble in the LFE adds a sense of power and size to what would otherwise be the weak-sounding, primarily high-frequency sound of glass breaking. The same low/high approach is taken in the asteroid chase scene of *Attack of the Clones* mentioned earlier. The audience-felt power of Jango Fett's bombs—their "earth-shaking" force obliquely referenced by Obi-Wan's description of them as "seismic charges"—comes almost solely from their high-energy, low-frequency components in the LFE. By pairing these bass sounds with higher frequencies that move through the five (discrete) main channels, the filmmakers create a perceptual effect of the entire sound (low and high) moving through the theater.

Though low-frequency effects are most frequently associated with explosions, they can of course be used on other sounds as well. Sound editor Hudson Miller (*National Treasure, Hitch, Man on Fire*) recalls that the 70mm six-track magnetic release of 1986's *The Color of Money* used the boom channel (as the low-frequency track 70mm six-track included was known) to add weight and character to the primarily high-frequency sound of a cue hitting balls.[78] *Lifted* similarly uses the gradual growth of a low-frequency rumble to suggest the approach of the UFO outside the human's bedroom before we see any visual evidence of it. And films with scenes in dance clubs or other bass-heavy environments often employ the LFE channel to emphasize a rhythm that is felt as much as heard. As these examples show, filmmakers deploy the LFE channel in a variety of ways, even if most of the time its effects are designed to go consciously unnoticed.

FROM THE AURAL TO THE VISUAL

From a technical standpoint, digital surround sound represented a major improvement over Dolby Stereo. More importantly for film style, each of its technical advances—a wider dynamic range, discrete and full-range main channels, an LFE channel—opened up new aesthetic possibilities for what filmmakers could do with their soundtracks. Motion picture soundtracks, however, do not operate in isolation. Film is an audiovisual medium encompassing both *sound* and *image*—and to this point the discussion has largely ignored the latter. Sound design decisions are rarely made without consideration for the images with which the soundtrack will be paired, and thus it is important to consider what changes in visual style accompanied the new sound design possibilities introduced by DSS. The next chapter will do just this, examining how the adoption of digital surround affected cinematography and editing practices.

3
THE LOOK OF 5.1:
VISUAL AESTHETICS

If people are thinking about [sound] early on, when they're shooting
and when they're editing, you approach the film differently. You
think about how you're going to use sound, what you put in the
background of scenes—the length of your cuts might change.

GARY RYDSTROM, SOUND DESIGNER

A film's soundtrack does not operate in isolation, but rather as part of
a larger whole; changes in film sound technology thus have an impact
beyond the soundtrack. The advent of the "talkie," for instance, led to
significant shifts in the ways films were shot and edited. Silent films
of the late 1920s had an average shot length of five seconds overall,
with about three-fourths having an average shot length between four
and seven seconds.[1] With the introduction of sync sound, average shot
lengths nearly doubled to around 10.8 seconds; films also showed more
variation in the tempo of their cutting than they did in the silent era,
with average shot lengths ranging from six to fourteen seconds depending on the specific film.[2] And this was not a temporary aberration while
filmmakers and engineers worked to overcome the initial technical difficulties of sound shooting; over every six-year period from 1934 to 1987,
average shot lengths were never again as low as nor as homogenized
as those of the late silent era.[3] This measurably clear shift to longer
shots was but one effect of the transition to sound on visual style; that

technological change also sparked a decrease in camera movement and an increase in scene length.

Later innovations in sound technology similarly affected cinematic visuals, and digital surround sound (DSS) is no exception to this pattern. Determining exactly *what* shifts in visual aesthetics its use has provoked, however, is no easy task. In the last chapter, the technical differences between Dolby Stereo and digital surround sound served as a guide to considering how DSS might have affected filmmakers' aesthetic choices in the aural realm. This approach does not work when exploring the visual realm, however, since no technological differences differentiate the *image* tracks of DSS-equipped films from those of their predecessors. Moreover, many factors—production technologies, cultural norms, trends in non-film media, economic concerns, and so on—affect shifts in cinematic style. Given this breadth of influences and the lack of a specific change in imaging technology tied to DSS, it is nearly impossible to point to specific changes in visual style and claim them unequivocally as results of the move to 5.1 digital surround.

This chapter will thus take a more heuristic approach than the last, exploring ways in which digital surround is *linked* to shifts in cinematographic and editing practices rather than asserting a specific cause-and-effect relationship. Additionally, this analysis will necessarily be audio-visual rather than purely image-driven, since it deals with the ramifications of an *audio* technology on the *visual* field.

THE "SUPERFIELD" AND THE "POOR LITTLE SCREEN"

The effects on the filmic image of digital surround's immediate predecessor provide a useful starting point for this exploration. Michel Chion, one of the few film theorists to have written about the implications of multi-channel sound (which he calls multitrack) for cinematic visuals, argues that from the time Dolby Stereo was first introduced, its multi-channel capabilities were used to expand the world of the film beyond the screen:

> We also must not forget that the definitive adoption of multitrack sound occurred in the context of musical films like Michael Wadleigh's *Wood-stock* or Ken Russell's *Tommy*. These rock movies were made with the

intent to revitalize filmgoing by instituting a sort of participation, a communication between the audience shown in the film and the audience in the movie theater. The space of the film, no longer confined to the screen, in a way became the entire auditorium, via the loudspeakers that broadcast crowd noises as well as everything else.[4]

Chion dubs this "space of the film" that spreads from the screen into the entire theater the "superfield." Specifically, he defines the superfield as "the space created, in multitrack films, by ambient natural sounds, city noises, music, and all sorts of rustlings that surround the visual space and that can issue from loudspeakers outside the physical boundaries of the screen."[5]

In other words, the superfield is the sensation of a complete space, produced by a multi-channel ambience. This suggests a reversal of cinematic hierarchy: where historically it has been the responsibility of the *image* to explain the soundtrack by visually confirming the sources of sounds, it is now the *soundtrack* that provides the context of the image. "There is always 'more' of the diegesis than the camera can cover at any one time," writes Mary Ann Doane, and thus the effect of surround sound is "precisely to diminish the epistemological power of the image, to reveal its limitations."[6] Expanding beyond the edges of the frame, the sonic world literally becomes *bigger* than the image, which reveals only a small fraction of the world created by the superfield:

> Sound and sounds in the surrounds offer access into areas the image is not willing or is unable to go. In these instances, the sound design has not just achieved an equal status with the image. It has in fact surpassed it.[7]

As scholar Claude Bailblé poetically lamented at the dawn of the Dolby Stereo era, the "poor little screen," long the sole focus of cinema, would quickly find its role diminished once sounds could originate elsewhere in the theater.[8]

With the advent of surround sound, narrative and structural responsibilities that have traditionally been the purview of the image have been taken over by the soundtrack. Specifically, the soundtrack now assumes the task of guiding the audience and creating a coherent narrative space. "The superfield," Chion writes, "provides a continuous and constant consciousness of all the space surrounding the narrative action";[9] Slavoj Žižek concurs, noting that with Dolby Stereo "it is now the soundtrack that functions as the elementary 'frame of reference' enabling us to orient ourselves in the diegetic space."[10] And taking this argument one step further, William Whittington argues that surround sound renders the image superfluous to the creation of diegetic space: "cognitive geography is offered through echoes, reflections, and reverberations, which create spatial anchors or cues. Spaces, then, can exist without image-based referents. No image is necessary."[11]

Of course, the advent of multi-channel sound has not caused cinema to discard the image in favor of audio-only movies. But multi-channel *has* had an effect on visual style due to its ability to provide *stability*. In *Audio-Vision*, Chion sets up a dichotomy within the broad category of offscreen sound, dividing it into "active" and "passive"; the former is sound that "raises questions" while the latter is essentially ambient noise. Chion finds that "Dolby multitrack has naturally favored the development of passive offscreen space over active," arguing that the superfield "provides the ear a stable place" through reliance on passive offscreen sound.[12] The result is that multi-channel, while challenging the long-standing hierarchy subordinating the soundtrack to the image, simultaneously offers the image a heretofore unparalleled degree of freedom. Relying on the soundtrack to function both as a frame of reference for the diegetic space *and* as a source of the stability and coherence that classical continuity practices (180-degree rule, eyeline matches, etc.) must traditionally provide, the image track is free to explore new patterns and constructions: "Instead of establishing space (sound now does this), the image selects viewpoints into it."[13]

The most notable effect of this shift has been to alter the "dramaturgy of the establishing shot."[14] Specifically, "the Dolby Stereo soundtrack effectively guides the spectator in the same way as the establishing shot . . . creating a new regime of acoustic attraction that destabilizes the narrative centrality of the *frame*."[15] With the constant, enveloping ambient sound of the superfield creating the narrative space, the establishing shot is no longer necessary—its function is fulfilled by the soundtrack. Žižek explains:

> Bombarding us with details from different directions (dolby stereo [*sic*] techniques, etc.), the soundtrack takes over the function of the estab-

lishing shot. The soundtrack gives us the basic perspective, the "map" of the situation, and guarantees its continuity, while the images are reduced to isolated fragments that float freely in the universal medium of the sound aquarium.[16]

New visual elements must fill the void left by the missing establishing shot. Žižek's phrase "isolated fragments" suggests that in multi-channel cinema, *multiple* images have supplanted the wide, all-encompassing establishing shot of previous eras, with each individual shot offering only a fraction of the information the absent master shot would have. Chion, writing that "we have seen the establishing shot give way to the multiplication of close-up shots of parts and fragments,"[17] offers the same assessment.

SHORTCOMINGS OF THE SUPERFIELD

These comments by Žižek and Chion referred specifically to the effects of Dolby Stereo on shooting and editing practices. Thus while they provide a useful starting point for examining the ramifications of digital surround sound, they should be carefully tested rather than unquestioningly accepted as accurate analyses of the way cinema and surround sound function today. To examine the validity of these Dolby Stereo–based claims in the digital surround era, they will be considered in the context of a test case—the first battle sequence of Steven Spielberg's World War II drama *Saving Private Ryan* (1998), which depicts the D-Day Allied landing on Omaha Beach. This is an ideal sequence to analyze for two reasons. First, Hollywood recognized the film as a whole as an exemplar of *all* aspects of contemporary filmmaking, awarding it Oscars for Sound, Sound Effects Editing, Cinematography, Editing, and Direction. The D-Day sequence in particular is frequently cited by film sound professionals as one of the best and most forward-thinking uses of 5.1 surround. These praises may make it seem like a poor choice for a "test case," as they acknowledge that *Saving Private Ryan* is not an "average" movie. Yet this is precisely the second reason it is an excellent film through which to consider the effects of DSS—it demonstrates the *potential* of digital surround to affect cinematographic and editing practices when considered from the start as an integral part of the filmmaking process; that some contemporary films continue to employ a monophonic or Dolby Stereo–era style shows only that not all filmmakers *choose* to embrace DSS's full range of capabilities.

Saving Private Ryan's beach landing sequence seems in many ways to fit with the concept of the superfield. The soundtrack creates a complete and consistent world that keeps us oriented in the filmic space; in Žižek's words, it provides a "map" of the film's environment that allows the sequence to make sense without an establishing shot. In fact, not only does the image track not include a master shot, it offers *no* clear logical progression from one shot to the next. That is, while all the shots serve to move the film *narrative* forward, the editing does not have a clear *spatial* style—the direction the camera faces in one shot has no apparent bearing on where it faces in the next. The visuals are fragmented, with a large number of shots—primarily close-ups— jammed together, leaving it to the soundscape to maintain our spatial orientation. All this appears to align with the Dolby Stereo–based claims made by Chion and Žižek about the superfield and its effects on film visuals.

A closer inspection of *Saving Private Ryan*, however, reveals several ways in which it contradicts those claims. For one, Chion insists that the superfield relies on *passive* sound that "provides the ear a stable place." Yet the highly volatile multi-channel soundscape of this sequence hardly provides the ear a "stable place," as Chion suggests it should. Sounds zip around the space, with flying bullets and echoing explosions drawing our attentions—precisely Chion's definition of *active* offscreen sounds. One might argue that the superfield, by definition, consists only of ambience and noises, and that "active" sounds like the bullets, shouts, and explosions in this sequence should hence be considered as "effects" somehow separate from the superfield constructed by the rest of the soundtrack. Yet any such separation is impossible. The entire soundtrack (and the entire environment) is filled with these effects; the "ambience" of the space literally *is* active, drawing the audience's attentions as well as those of the soldiers storming the beach, for whom *not* paying attention to the questions raised by the soundscape could be fatal.

Additionally, both Chion and Žižek describe the multi-channel aural environment as continuous. The soundtrack to the *Saving Private*

Ryan sequence, though, is quite aggressively *not* continuous. Not only does it shift as the camera moves to different spaces (underwater, on the beach, inside a German bunker), it changes with almost *every* cut in the image track. Specifically, the aural perspective it presents shifts with each visual cut to reflect the orientation of the particular shot onscreen at that moment. So, for example, when the camera is facing toward the German bunkers, the sounds of machine gun bullets whiz from the front of the theater to the back, while when the camera is facing the other direction the same sounds move from back to front.

Narratively, this sequence's frenetic, highly active approach to sound design—as well as to the visuals—makes sense as a way of dramatizing the chaos of battle.[18] And in terms of literal realism, it makes sense to ensure that the spatialized sonic environment matches the physical orientation of the implied viewer suggested by the onscreen visuals. Yet even if these factors provide a clear rationale for the surround mixing style used by *Saving Private Ryan*, it is crucial to recognize that adopting such a style flies in the face of conventional wisdom and long-standing audio editing and mixing practices, which maintain that the soundtrack should be as free as possible of noticeable cuts. Indeed, writing in the early 1990s just before the introduction of the first DSS systems shifted the sound/image relationship, Rick Altman went so far as to suggest that audiences *require* a continuous soundtrack to help them cope with the frequent jumps that pervade the image track:

> The spectator might fight to integrate the multiple positions allotted by the film into a single unified home. While this wanderlust is partially cured by a learned, and thus historically grounded, ability to insert shots of various scales into a coherent *Gestalt* of filmic space, it is only with the aid of a continuous-level sound track that the spectator finds a comfortable home. By holding the auditor at a fixed and thus stable distance from all sound sources . . . Hollywood uses the sound track to anchor the body to a single continuous experience.[19]

In particular, traditional practices designed "to hide the work of production" require that the soundtrack not cut *at the same time as the image*, lest it draw attention to the cut in the image track: "Only in exceptional cases are sound and image cut at exactly the same point. The continuation of the same sound over a cut on the image track diverts attention from that cut."[20] *Saving Private Ryan*'s multi-channel soundtrack, whose jumps are timed to *match* cuts in the image track, adheres to precisely the opposite principle.

This difference hints at the fundamental disparity between the sound/image relationship of *Saving Private Ryan* and that of the superfield. Chion claims that the sonic superfield retains a semi-independence from the visuals with which it is paired and "does not depend moment by moment on what we see onscreen."[21] *Saving Private Ryan's* opening stands in direct opposition to this assertion, with sound and image tightly woven together, each affecting the other. Every cut in the image track changes the soundtrack, while on several occasions aural elements guide the visuals, as when the sound of an offscreen explosion cues the image track to show the explosion's source. Clearly, this tight relationship represents something quite different from the relative sound/image independence—where the image track cuts between various shots while the soundtrack offers "a single continuous experience"—presumed by much cinema sound scholarship and illustrated by Chion's Dolby Stereo–driven superfield.

THE ULTRAFIELD

Where the superfield is passive, continuous, and stable, the soundtrack to *Saving Private Ryan* is active, jumpy, and constantly shifting. Not coincidentally, these distinctions correspond precisely to the technological differences between the quasi-four-channel-matrixed Dolby Stereo system and the discrete, five-full-range-channel DSS systems. That the superfield is, in the digital surround era, no longer an accurate way of conceptualizing the use of multi-channel sound reflects the practical reality that at the time of the superfield's conception Dolby Stereo was the only multi-channel system in common use. Even if they had wanted to do so, filmmakers of the time simply *could not* have created a soundtrack like that of *Saving Private Ryan*—its constantly shifting soundscape relies too heavily on the unique capabilities of digital surround systems.

Yet the concept of the superfield should not be discarded too quickly in the wake of DSS. Some of Chion and Žižek's specific ideas about *how* the superfield functions are Dolby Stereo–specific and now outdated. But the fundamental concept that multi-channel ambiences are at the core of surround sound aesthetics remains a provocative principle for understanding how *any* multi-channel soundtrack might function. Indeed, in the DSS era multi-channel ambiences remain central to surround usage—they are just used in a somewhat different way. Rather than rendering the superfield *extinct*, DSS has allowed it to *evolve* beyond the limits of Dolby Stereo.

To distinguish between the superfield's Dolby Stereo–limited and DSS-based versions, I dub this updated superfield the *ultrafield*. It differs from the Dolby Stereo–based superfield in two key conceptual ways. First, it sacrifices the "invisibility" of sound editing and mixing to embrace digital surround's aforementioned capabilities to exploit active and changing sounds. Where the superfield maintains a sonic continuity, the ultrafield constantly shifts sounds around the multi-channel environment. Second, it encompasses a much broader array of sonic elements than its predecessor. Where Chion limited the superfield to ambient sounds and noises, the ultrafield encompasses not just these background sounds but the *entire* aural world of the film, including sound effects, dialogue, and diegetic music.

In a more practical sense, the difference between the superfield and the ultrafield centers on the relationship between image and sound. The superfield relies on a *constant* sonic space to ground freely moving and cutting images; the ultrafield allows for a *shifting* aural environment that functions in *dialogue* with the visual one. As an example, *Saving Private Ryan*'s aural elements often drive cuts in the image track—yet one might just as easily say that the visual elements of the sequence drive changes in the soundtrack. As the multi-channel sound space shifts with each cut to keep itself oriented to the image track, the *sonic* space changes to match the *visual* one onscreen. This represents a break from earlier Hollywood practices, which aimed to maintain a stable multi-channel environment—the ultrafield seeks not to provide a *continuous* aural environment, but rather to *continuously* provide an *accurate* spatial environment where aural and visual space match. In short, the ultrafield is the three-dimensional sonic environment of the diegetic world, continuously reoriented to match the camera's visual perspective.

Through use of the ultrafield, the soundtrack continues to function as a frame of reference as it did with the superfield, but it now

3.1. In the middle of a battle sequence in *Transformers* (2007), the ultrafield provides information about what is happening all around, including *where* the various combatants and firefights are, while Captain Lennox phones headquarters for help. The action scenes in this film rely on the soundtrack to provide spatial information, since the visuals often do not.

does so through a *shifting* soundscape that varies with what is seen onscreen. Sound designer Glenn Morgan notes, for instance, that matching the spatial orientation of the image was a key consideration in the location recordings collected at Yankee Stadium for 1999's *For Love of the Game*. For the large portion of the movie that takes place within the stadium, Morgan got recordings from different perspectives all around the stadium. All of these recordings were then timed to the onscreen action so that "no matter where the camera angle moved to, the sound could move with the camera angle."[22] Another sound editor, Suhail Kafity (*Pearl Harbor, Apocalypto, Harold & Kumar Go to White Castle*), cites the example of *Spy Game* (2001), where the image track cut between so many things so quickly—"the picture moves around and you had things happening here, and here, and here"—that it fell to the surround environment to clarify the audience's spatial orientation at any given moment: "the sound running around you, that sold your story, that became part of your story."[23]

Speed (1994) employs the same ultrafield-based approach, most obviously during the elevator sequence in the film's first act. As police officers Jack Traven (Keanu Reeves) and Harry Temple (Jeff Daniels) try to secure an elevator whose brakes and cable have been rigged to explode unless a ransom is paid, the sounds of their movements travel down the elevator shaft to another elevator. There those sounds are heard by the scheme's mastermind (Dennis Hopper), who by recognizing *where* those sounds originated figures out that Traven and Temple are trying to thwart his plan. The film consistently maintains a spatial match between image and sound; for instance, for several shots showing the bomber looking up toward the camera above him and listening carefully to the noises coming down the elevator shaft, the sounds made by the officers atop the rigged elevator are precisely mixed to the surround channels to signify their position relative to the bomber and the camera. The opening heist scene of *The Dark Knight* (2008) likewise provides a continuous orientation to the space of a bank lobby by panning sounds—including the bank robbers' voices—to the appropriate on- or offscreen locations suggested by the visuals.

Not all contemporary films rely on an ultrafield-based soundtrack. As Tomlinson Holman ambivalently remarks, the idea of the sonic environment shifting in response to the picture edit "is true and it's not true. There are times when the ambience is used as continuity, to take a picture cut but keep it constant so you're saying you are still in the same space. But there are other times where [sound continuity] is definitely broken so that you know you're shifting spaces."[24] The major factor limiting use of the ultrafield is a concern that breaking the soundtrack's flow can be disconcerting; as sound editor Midge Costin notes, "it brings too much attention to itself."[25] Re-recording mixer Marti Humphrey agrees, and notes that this is particularly true when dealing with dialogue: "if you start swinging dialogue to match every single perspective you're seeing, you're going to run people out of the audience. It was tried in the fifties; it didn't work."[26]

Ultimately, digital surround sound does not dictate that the ultrafield be deployed at all times, and few movies use it through their entire length. Yet even those with reservations about ultrafield-driven sound design agree that, for better or worse, this approach is growing ever more common. Explains sound editor David Bondelevitch:

> Normally I would tell people that you don't change sound perspective on every shot. . . . You wouldn't want to point out the picture edits by jumping back and forth. But I do find now more than ever that people

are breaking that rule. For a sound effect, for instance, if you go from a wide shot where it's on the left to a close-up where it's in the middle, back to the wide shot where it's on the left, that you will actually shift position of that sound effect back and forth, which not that long ago would have been considered an intrusion in the flow of the soundtrack. But today, you do it more.[27]

One key effect of this rise in ultrafield usage is that the impact of digital surround and the ultrafield on film visuals—specifically, on editing and shooting strategies—has become increasingly apparent.

STABILITY AND SPACE IN THE ULTRAFIELD

Since the ultrafield is based on the superfield, the effect on film visuals of that Dolby Stereo–based sonic strategy is worth reexamining in the context of the DSS-based ultrafield. With the rise of the superfield, the soundtrack took over some responsibilities normally associated with the image, including setting up the diegetic environment and providing audiences a sense of continuity. The superfield accomplished the first of these by offering "a continuous and constant consciousness of all the space surrounding the dramatic action" that eliminated the importance of establishing shots.[28] But establishing shots traditionally serve *two* purposes—setting the scene, and setting up the spatial relations among the characters and their environment—of which the superfield can handle only the first.

Setting up spatial relationships requires the more fluid multichannel environment provided by digital surround and exploited by the ultrafield. Because the superfield provides a *consistent* ambient environment, it cannot tell the audience whether a character is moving around the room, or where people are in relation to that character. In other words, while the superfield can set up the *feel* of the diegetic environment, responsibility for conveying that environment's literal *space* still lies with the image track. An ultrafield-based soundtrack, on the other hand, can accurately place *all* the sounds of a space (ambient and otherwise) in their proper locations, taking the burden of explaining spatial relationships off the visuals.

Since the ultrafield fulfills *both* of the establishing shot's traditional responsibilities where the superfield addresses only *one* of them, establishing shots should be even less common today than they were in the Dolby Stereo era. And in fact, this appears to be the case. The D-Day sequence from *Saving Private Ryan*, for example, uses no master shot, and other scenes explored later will follow the same pattern. Midge Costin confirms this observation, remarking that "they do a lot fewer establishing shots [with digital surround] because sound is so much more effective."[29]

The second way in which the superfield affects the visuals is by providing the image track a greater degree of freedom. Traditional Hollywood soundtracks, as explained earlier, avoid noticeable cuts in part so that the fragmented visual track is countered by stability in the sonic realm; Žižek and Chion suggest that the superfield, by virtue of offering a continuous aural environment, pushes this freedom of the image track a degree further until it becomes (as Žižek poetically phrases it) "isolated fragments that float freely in the universal medium of the sound aquarium." The ultrafield, however, cannot offer the visuals the same sort of stable "sound aquarium." Its fundamental emphasis on *coherence* between image and sound means that the soundtrack becomes as disjointed as the image track, with cuts in both being equally noticeable.

This dual fragmentation *highlights* the visual cuts the soundtrack has traditionally functioned to hide. As Bondelevitch notes, movies today "tie the sound edits more to the picture edits, almost as though we *want* to point them out. . . . which is to me weird."[30] Gary Rydstrom takes a more ambivalent view. He suggests that quick changes in the soundtrack can be a useful tool for filmmakers but must be timed carefully to avoid bothering the audience: "You have to follow the visuals. You have to use a turning point, some key thing happening or a cut to an extreme close-up." Crucially, he takes issue with conventional thinking that the soundtrack has to be *continuous* to be effective:

> In *Backdraft*, where you're in the middle of a fire and everything's very hectic and very dangerous, you can shift focus on a cut instantly and it has the effect of a Godard jump cut. *There's something that shocks you and jumps you into the next sound.*[31]

Rydstrom's underlying principle that "you have to follow the visuals" is certainly in keeping with the continuous reorientation to the image track of the ultrafield. And his explanation of the *Backdraft* example calls to mind the image-driven shifts of the ultrafield, where each cut in the image track is accompanied by one in the soundtrack that "jumps" the audience "into the next sound."

At the same time, Rydstrom recognizes that this style of soundtrack "shocks you" rather than providing the audience with a continuous, stable environment like the superfield. Given this difference, one might expect that ultrafield-based soundtracks would not allow the image track the same flexibility as their superfield-based counterparts. Without the soundtrack as a consistent frame of reference—Chion's "stable place"—the digital surround era image track *should*, it would seem, rely on traditional continuity-based editing schemes. A quick look at recent movies reveals, however, that this is hardly the case. If anything, editing and shooting practices have grown even *less* structured in the digital surround era.

The explanation for this apparent paradox is that although the ultrafield does not offer the same *type* of continuity as the superfield, it still fulfills the *function* of creating stability. While the superfield guarantees the continuity of the overall environment as the visual track jumps haphazardly from one image to the next, it cannot reveal how the images fit together *in* that environment—each visual fragment "floats" on its own in the sonic aquarium, spatially unconnected to the shots before and after it. The ultrafield, on the other hand, sacrifices continuity of the *soundtrack* for continuity of the *space*. Repeatedly reorienting itself, the ultrafield-driven soundscape informs the audience of the spatial *location* and *orientation* of shots within the space, connecting each shot to the next through their implied relationship in the diegetic world.

Thus while the ultrafield in one sense draws attention to cuts in the image track, it simultaneously *hides* the constructed nature of the filmic apparatus by creating a tighter cohesion between image and sound; this in turn ties the fragmented image track together. Classic cinema offers a relatively consistent sonic environment coupled with frequently changing visuals; digital surround–era cinema replaces that scheme with one where aural and visual information "matches." This more coherent representation of the profilmic event serves as a new perceptual "anchor," negating the need for the aural continuity required of the pre-DSS soundtrack yet still granting the image track the ability to cut between *any* two shots.

NON-TRADITIONAL EDITING

In fact, the ultrafield offers the image track a significantly *greater* degree of freedom than the superfield. Chion asserts that the superfield establishes space while "the image selects viewpoints into it"—but these viewpoints must be carefully selected and *ordered* in a way that makes sense. The superfield cannot convey specific spatial relationships between different shots; responsibility for explaining how the shots fit together falls to the image track, just as it did in the monophonic era. This means that superfield-era visuals must by and large adhere to traditional continuity editing practices such as the 180-degree rule and concern for direction of movement or action across shots. The image tracks of ultrafield-era films, in contrast, can disregard these conventions and cut freely from any viewpoint to any other.

This distinction is best demonstrated through an example. Jay Beck cites the climactic sequence of Jonathan Demme's *The Silence of the Lambs* (1991)—where FBI agent Clarice Starling (Jodie Foster) searches the gigantic basement of a serial killer—as one of the best Dolby Stereo–based examples of sonic spatialization. In fact, the relationship between space and sound is the driving element of this scene. As Beck notes, it is the voice of Catherine Martin, the serial killer's hostage, that serves "the narrative function of guiding Clarice through the space while simultaneously acoustically rendering the spatial qualities of the basement."[32]

Yet while Martin's voice guides *Clarice* through the space, the limitations of the superfield prevent the film from similarly using her voice as a guide for the *audience*. Instead, the film relies on traditional continuity practices to serve this function. Beck points out that this sequence *does* diverge from traditional editing practices in a few places, and he traces this to the multi-channel soundtrack: "it is precisely Dolby Stereo's capability of rendering a three-dimensional diegesis that offered Demme and his team the ability to edit unstable images that break the 180° rule, jump from close-up to long shot, or rapidly cut between impossible perspectives onto a stable acoustic space."[33]

These deviations, though, are relatively minor. For instance, a few of the sequence's shots from Clarice's perspective fall *on* the 180-degree line; each of these, though, is both preceded and followed by a shot of Clarice looking around, and thereby clearly coded *as* POV (where the 180-degree rule is not generally applied). In fact, despite such minor deviations from classic continuity, each shot offers numerous visual cues explaining its relationship in space to the previous one—the construction is clear enough that the image track and the construction of space is perfectly legible even without the soundtrack.

The crucial point is that a Dolby Stereo or monophonic soundtrack *can* give the audience spatial information, but not the same *type* of information as a DSS soundtrack—true multi-channel *spatialization* should not be conflated with the spatial *cues* that any type of soundtrack can include. The key phrases in Beck's comment about Martin's voice are "acoustically *rendering*" and "spatial *qualities*"; he does not mention *placement* because Martin's voice, like all the important sounds in the sequence, remains firmly locked to the center channel. Hampered by the limitations of Dolby Stereo, the soundtrack can only give information *about* the space—it cannot provide any orientation *to* that space.

Digital surround sound systems, on the other hand, can precisely place sounds anywhere in the soundscape, allowing DSS soundtracks to provide both spatial cues *and* spatial orientation. Moreover, the ultrafield—by virtue of *not* being a stable acoustic space but rather one that depends on camera orientation—uses this capability to create exactly the coherent "three-dimensional diegesis" that Beck describes but that Dolby Stereo cannot actually render. Given this, the implication of Beck's claims about the effect of multi-channel sound on film visuals is that the ultrafield should allow contemporary films a relative freedom to violate traditional continuity editing principles. And in fact, many of them take advantage of this capability. *Saving Private Ryan's* opening, for instance, cuts shots back-to-back with little or no regard for screen direction or relative orientation.

A particularly salient example of ultrafield-driven editing is the lobby shootout scene in *The Matrix* (1999). Occurring about three-fourths of the way through the movie, this massive gunfight pits Neo (Keanu Reeves) and Trinity (Carrie-Anne Moss)—two of the film's heroes—against a large force of nameless guards as Neo and Trinity

attempt to invade a government building. The scene takes place in a large rectangular lobby with few obvious visual landmarks to denote specific locations. Visually, this scene breaks virtually every traditional shooting/editing guideline imaginable. As in *Saving Private Ryan*, the fact that the camera is pointing one way in one shot indicates nothing about where it will be pointed in the next—trying to identify a 180-degree line for even a short portion of this scene is futile. Neo, for instance, *often* seems to be moving left to right across the screen—but at other times he moves directly toward the camera, directly away from it, or from right to left. Sometimes he is onscreen, while at others he is offscreen to the right, to the left, or behind the camera. Shots of Trinity and the security forces exhibit the same disregard for directional continuity. Finally, despite featuring characters who move all around the space of the lobby, the scene does not provide an establishing shot until its very end, when the shootout has concluded and it is no longer crucial where each of the characters is.

This lack of order in the image track implies that this scene *should be* confusing to watch and difficult to follow—yet the 5.1 soundtrack keeps the spatial relationships among the various characters and the space quite clear throughout its entire length. Like that of *Saving Private Ryan*, the soundscape used in this scene is complex, featuring lots of sounds (primarily bullets) flying in different directions through the multi-channel environment. And just as in that film, the ultrafield "cuts" with the image track to maintain proper spatial orientation between picture and audio. In doing so, it creates for the audience a mental understanding of the lobby space without ever showing it. When,

3.2–3.3. Sequential shots from *Moulin Rouge* (2001). Classic continuity rules become less important in the digital surround era, as illustrated by the jump across the 180-degree line between these two shots.

for instance, Neo's bullets whiz through the theater from front to back, the audience knows that the camera is facing toward the building entrance even if this is not visually apparent; on the other hand, when the guards' bullets follow the same trajectory, it is clear the audience's (and camera's) orientation has been reversed.[34]

To be sure, Neo's onscreen movements also provide clues as to the camera's current orientation within the lobby space. Yet the usefulness of his motion (more or less toward the center of the building) for this purpose is limited. He is neither consistently moving nor always going in the same direction—and certainly when he is not onscreen, it is the ultrafield that guides the audience. The shots of Trinity make the value of the ultrafield clear. Despite having no consistent direction to her movements—she even goes back to a previous location at one point in the shootout—every time she appears onscreen the multichannel soundtrack makes her location within the lobby space clear. Ultimately, the point is not that in an ultrafield-equipped movie the visuals lose the *capability* to convey spatial information, but rather that the soundtrack frees them of the *responsibility* to do so. The effectiveness of this boundary-pushing interplay between image and sound was confirmed at the 2000 Academy Awards, which not only recognized *The Matrix* with Oscars for Sound and Sound Effects Editing over flashy competitors like *Star Wars Episode I, The Mummy,* and *Fight*

Club, but also awarded it the Oscar for Editing, a category where it was up against four of the five Best Picture nominees (including eventual winner *American Beauty*).[35]

QUICK CUTTING

These scenes from *The Matrix* and *Saving Private Ryan* reveal another common characteristic of digital sound–era editing: it is *fast*. Humphrey laments that "these days picture editors are like Ginzu choppers, they're sitting there doing three frames here, four frames there, I mean just stuff fast, fast, fast"[36]—the lobby shootout scene in *The Matrix*, for example, has an *average* shot length of about one second. Certainly one of the freedoms the ultrafield offers the image track is that of cutting more quickly; with the soundtrack providing an instantaneous frame of reference, the audience does not need the time required to process the visual relations between successive images. Yet the link between quick cutting in the visual track and the ultrafield is not strictly a causal one. Chion seems willing to assign multi-channel sound a good share of the blame (or credit) for the prevalence of what he calls "music video style" editing, meaning fast cutting with no regard for spatial relationships.[37] In contrast, sound designer Steve Flick notes that as the pace of picture editing has increased, it has fallen to the soundtrack to "glue together" the narrative. And because the multi-channel environment allows more sounds to remain in the soundtrack at once, it gives sounds a chance to *linger* even as it bombards the audience with new ones. Surround, in other words, makes it easier to "keep the resonance of the experience happening" no matter how fast the picture is cut: "[we] use surrounds to expand time and work against the contraction of time by the picture."[38] From Flick's point of view, the superfield and ultrafield are an *effect* of fast-paced visual editing rather than a *cause* of it.

Flick's and Chion's differing but logical arguments suggest a mutually reinforcing relationship between fast cutting and the ultrafield: the flexibility the ultrafield offers the visuals encourages faster cutting, which in turn forces the soundtrack to take even *more* responsibility for setting the space, which encourages the visuals to cut even faster, and so on. This relationship does, however, have a practical limit—the brain cannot process cuts in the soundtrack as fast as it can those in the image track. Part of the podrace sequence in *Star Wars I* presented precisely this challenge, as sound designer Ben Burtt (*WALL-E*, the *Star Wars* and *Indiana Jones* series) recalls:

> As the shots got shorter and shorter, the sound bites got shorter and shorter too, but became less distinctive even though they were different from one pod to another, just bursts of noise: *ing-onk-ook-eh*. There wasn't time for the pitch to be heard, sometimes only nine frames, so I really had to stretch things to develop distinctly different sounds.[39]

In these exceptionally fast cut scenes, the multi-channel environment is crucial *not* because it allows the soundtrack to reorient with each cut in the image track but because it gives sounds the ability—as Flick notes—to "linger" long enough for the audience to process them. Thus while the spatial freedom offered by digital surround *generally* favors the complex multi-channel soundtrack style of the ultrafield, in cases where the image track is cut extremely fast a simplified, consistent aural environment like the superfield may actually be more effective.

FRAMING AND CINEMATOGRAPHY

Digital surround sound's implications for the image track extend beyond the way shots are put together to those shots themselves. In exploring DSS's impact on cinematographic practices, the aesthetic effects of Dolby Stereo once more provide a useful starting point. Chion offers an explicit assessment of Dolby Stereo's visual ramifications, asserting that it has led to

> the multiplication of close-up shots of parts and fragments of dramatic space such that the image now plays a sort of solo part, seemingly in dialogue with the sonic orchestra in the audiovisual concerto. The vaster the sound, the more intimate the shots can be.[40]

Here he suggests that the superfield and Dolby Stereo changed shooting style in three distinct ways: the image track fragments spaces rather than showing them in their entirety, it employs a large number of shots relative to films of earlier periods, and it favors tight close-ups of people and objects over wide or long shots. Reexamination of the two sequences described earlier in this chapter indicates that these visual characteristics are also common to the digital surround era, perhaps even more so than to the Dolby Stereo period: the Omaha Beach sequence of *Saving Private Ryan* and the lobby shootout in *The Matrix* rely almost *exclusively* on short, close shots that each reveal only a fraction of the space.

It is certainly provocative that all three of the image-based trends identified by Chion are so strongly exhibited in these two sequences. To accept these changes in visual style as fundamentally tied to digital surround, however, requires considering how DSS and the ultrafield might actually *cause* each of them—or at least promote their use. Increased use of close-ups seems reasonable to accept as a logical outcome of multi-channel sound's enhanced capabilities for creating spaces. Because no camera or lens choice offers an infinite field of view or amount of detail, the choice of how wide or close a shot should be invariably involves a trade-off. As a shot's framing gets progressively tighter it offers a more detailed view of its primary subject—at the expense of presenting the *context* in which that subject exists. The close-up shot thus offers the audience intimacy with its subject but sacrifices any sense of the space or action around it. This is why in traditional editing schemes, the close-up is not used until after the environment around it has been set up by a wider shot. But if the *soundscape* can provide this contextual information, as the multi-channel superfield or ultrafield does, then close-up framings can be used more liberally. In fact, the ultrafield—with its robust ability not only to create *spaces* but also to convey the proper *relationships* among the various important elements *within* those spaces—should spur an even heavier reliance on close-up shots than the superfield.

The other two visual shifts mentioned above—that the number of shots used increases and that space is fragmented—can be explained in the DSS era via a combination of the ultrafield-based editing style and the use of close-ups. The increased number of shots is partly a predictable outcome of the quick cutting characteristic of movies with ultrafield-based soundtracks; if the image track is going to cut more quickly, it will necessarily fit more shots into a given period of time. This effect is heightened, however, by the increased use of close-ups. Important narrative elements are rarely limited to one small area of a movie's diegetic space. If the image track relies almost exclusively on close-ups that can each show only a small portion of that space, more shots will be required to convey all the story information. Similar logic offers a rationale for the fragmentation of space seen in multi-channel films: close-ups, by their very nature, cannot reveal a significant amount of the diegetic space or the action. If the image track has no establishing shot and relies principally on close-ups, the diegetic space is inherently split up into pieces.

All three of the visual trends identified by Chion as tied to surround sound can—regardless of their causes in the Dolby Stereo era—be justified in the DSS era as direct or indirect products of the ultrafield. What is intriguing is that this chapter's two example sequences seem to push those trends further than the above logic alone would dictate. In the case of *Saving Private Ryan*, Rydstrom notes that the close-up-heavy, quickly cut visual style dictated the ultrafield-based sound design, rather than the other way around: "The visuals were very close up and the way Spielberg shot, especially the opening battle, was very 'close' and confusing visually. . . . It was always shot from a very intimate angle and the soundtrack's job was to tell you the story that is going on all around us."[41]

The lobby shootout scene in *The Matrix* similarly pushes its use of close-ups and fragmentation to an extreme. For instance, the lobby is large enough that shots showing the full bodies of the actors would still reveal only a small portion of the overall space. So even if the filmmakers wanted to avoid the use of an establishing shot, they could easily have done so without relying too heavily on close-ups—they chose instead to make almost *every* shot a close-up. The image track offers tight shots of the characters' faces, floor-level shots of bullets hitting the ground and feet running, and other such shots. Wider shots appear infrequently, and seemingly only when necessary to show off the impossible acrobatics of Trinity or Neo—and even parts of these play in close-up.

To be sure, in some cases maintaining narrative clarity requires close shots given *The Matrix*'s quickly cutting image track. With shots only on screen for a second or so, the audience simply does not have time to search a wide shot for its most important elements—when Neo cartwheels across the floor, for instance, it makes sense to cut in a close shot of him picking up a gun since this action might not come across clearly in the wider shot. More often, though, objects and characters seem to be fragmented for the sake of fragmentation. The lobby scene's opening is telling: as Neo enters the lobby the film insistently refuses to show his whole body, instead offering quarter-body-length (or less) shots of his feet, his shoulders, and his face as he walks up to and through the metal detector.

This "excessive" reliance on close shots and fragmentation suggests that although the ultrafield liberates the image track from classical continuity practices, it does not truly "free" the visuals to employ any type and mix of shots at any time. Instead, it strongly biases the image track toward the specific visual traits listed above: quick cutting, lots of close-ups, and fragmented space. The explanation for this prejudice lies in a conceptual difference between the superfield and the ultrafield.

SHOOTING FROM WITHIN THE SPACE

Despite their differences in the aural realm, the effects on cinematic visuals of Dolby Stereo and the superfield proved a useful starting point for exploring those of DSS and the ultrafield—in general, the two systems encourage the same types of editing and shooting practices. Yet these broad similarities do not alter the fact that superfield and ultrafield differ on a fundamental level; it is this difference that explains why ultrafield-based films rely on *excessive* fragmentation and close shooting, where these visual traits were merely weak *tendencies* in the superfield era.

Specifically, the superfield and the ultrafield imply a different relationship between the audience and the narrative action: where the superfield places the audience at a *distance* from the onscreen world, the ultrafield situates the audience *in the middle of the action*. Consider first the superfield-based soundtrack. As a "stable place," it remains constant while the image quickly cuts from one close-up to another. The effect is that of someone scanning a scene erratically through a telescope or binoculars; as he moves his viewing device, his *visual* perspective jumps around but his *aural* perspective remains the same. Indeed, Chion suggests precisely this analogy in commenting that the superfield promoted a "surveillance-camera image" where "the image showed its voyeuristic side, acting as a pair of binoculars."[42] Using binoculars to watch an event, of course, requires remaining *at a distance from the action*.

3.4. Digital surround sound promotes camera placements
directly on the axis of action, as in this shot from *Transformers*
(2007) where a soldier fires straight at the audience.

In contrast to the stable place of the superfield, the ultrafield-
based soundtrack changes its orientation every time the image track
cuts, constantly reorienting itself to viewpoint implied by the onscreen
image. This creates the impression *not* of viewing the action from a
distance, but rather of being *in the middle of the action* and looking
around quickly. As the right-in-the-middle-of-it-all invisible auditor
shifts his visual attentions in different directions or to different areas
of the space, his head moves as well, reorienting his sonic perspective
to align with his visual one.

What makes this difference between Dolby Stereo–based "viewing at a distance" and DSS-based "viewing from the middle of the action" important is that it extends beyond the soundtrack, *to the images
themselves*. Both systems rely heavily on close-ups; those close-ups,
however, are not from the same *perspective* in both cases. Though the
superfield-based shooting style may eliminate the establishing shot,
it otherwise still relies principally on classical continuity rules about
camera placement. The camera is left outside the action, giving (like

the superfield) the impression of viewing the scene from an outsider's perspective. An ultrafield-based visual style, on the other hand, places its cameras right in the fray, situating the implied viewer *within* the boundaries of the scene.

This distinction is apparent in the visual contrasts between narratively similar scenes from the Dolby Stereo era and their digital surround–era counterparts. For instance, the superfield-based war scenes in *Apocalypse Now* (1979), *Platoon* (1986), and *The Thin Red Line* (1998) maintain a relative distance from the action, filming primarily from outside the principal battle arena; the ultrafield-equipped combat scenes of *Saving Private Ryan, Braveheart* (1995), and *Gladiator* (2000), on the other hand, frequently film from the middle of the battle.[43] A comparison of the lobby scene in *The Matrix* or the gunfights in *Terminator Salvation* (2009) or *Transformers* (2007) with similar shootouts in mono- or Dolby Stereo–based action films like *The Terminator* (1984), *Robocop* (1987), or *Die Hard* (1988) likewise reveals that the image tracks of the older films rely heavily on camera positions outside the main action, while those of the newer, DSS-era films often place the camera (and the implied audience) directly in the line of fire.[44]

Ultimately, this difference in camera (and audio) placement is why digital surround sound promotes a higher level of spatial fragmentation and greater use of close-ups than Dolby Stereo. Because the ultrafield-driven image track places the camera literally in the middle of the diegetic action, no one shot can reveal all the elements of that action—it can only be shown through a combination of shots, each of which includes only a portion of the space. In the same way, shooting from

3.5–3.6. Dolby Stereo–era cinematography differs from that of the digital surround era, both in shot scale and in camera placement relative to the action. An action scene from *Die Hard* (1988) employs a medium shot from outside the axis of action, while one from *Gladiator* (2000) uses close-ups taken from right *on* that line, between the two combatants.

in the middle of the action encourages the use of close-ups by literally placing the camera very near to the subjects being filmed—moving far enough away to get a wide shot requires leaving the space of the action.

THE COMPLEXITY OF AESTHETICS

The introduction to this chapter observed that it is difficult to draw direct *causal* connections between DSS and specific changes in visual style. A wide variety of factors influence cinematic aesthetics, and many of the image-based traits identified in this chapter can be linked not only to the advent of digital surround sound but also to cultural trends, changes in film industry practices, and the aesthetics of other media forms. Costin and Bondelevitch, for example, suggest that the increased use of close-ups in feature filmmaking may reflect the norms of television moving into the cinema, particularly as it has become common for directors and cinematographers to move back and forth between television and features.[45] Similarly, Tomlinson Holman and Walter Murch have cited the arrival of computer-based editing as one factor behind the increased pace of cutting in contemporary cinema.[46]

Perhaps the most compelling case that the adoption of DSS has worked in combination with other forces to encourage recent changes in visual aesthetics can be made for the diminishing importance of classical continuity practices. Digital surround sound and the ultrafield have certainly played a major role in this shift; as discussed earlier, the ultrafield's ability to provide spatial information eliminates the need for the image track to construct clear relationships between shots. The ease with which audiences accepted this move away from continuity editing, though, suggests a larger cultural change—today's audiences, who have grown up with music videos, personal camcorders, and user-friendly home editing systems like iMovie may simply be media-savvy enough to decipher inter-shot relationships without the help classical continuity offers:

> Audiences are hipper than they've ever been. The reason the 180 rule exists, and actually all stage direction rules exist, is so that you can explain three-dimensional geometry on a two dimensional screen. . . . Audiences now are used to seeing the stage line jump so much that it's not that much of an issue.[47]

A demonstration from one of Holman's classes is telling: after playing a film clip that obeys the 180-degree rule at first, then suddenly cuts across the line, he asks his students to identify what is odd about it. The fraction of the students who notice the violation of this fundamental continuity rule varies, but generally close to half of the students do *not* recognize it; as Holman notes, "it's amazing how they've been trained out of it."[48]

Holman's phrase "they've been *trained*" suggests that digital surround sound may have an impact even for film sequences (or entire films) still relying on monophonic or Dolby Stereo–era sound design— by exposing audiences to non-traditional editing practices, ultrafield-based films may have helped make the moviegoing public more comfortable with these practices in other places. *Moulin Rouge!* (2001), to offer one example, ignores traditional continuity rules in several early, ultrafield-driven scenes, then continues this visual practice in later sequences with more screen-centric soundtracks. And to demonstrate just how common violations of classical continuity have become, 2007's *Music and Lyrics*—a straightforward romantic comedy—freely jumps the 180-degree line in simple dialogue sequences.

As these examples show, no one cause can take sole blame or credit for the changes in visual style delineated in this chapter. What is clear is that the move to digital surround was a major factor behind these shifts and cannot be ignored in any consideration of contemporary cinematic style. When I showed several sound professionals a list of the traits discussed in this chapter and asked if they could accurately be tied to the adoption of digital surround, by and large they agreed, with David Bondelevitch the most concise in his assessment: "Quick cutting between shots, that's a given. Increased use of close-ups, fewer wide shots, and more shots, yes. Well, I would agree with all of these."[49]

This chapter and the previous one have together compiled an extensive list of aesthetic features—both visual and aural—linked to, if not all exclusively *caused by*, the transition from Dolby Stereo to 5.1 digital surround sound. Some of these stylistic features are clearly related to each other—for example, several of the shooting and editing strategies promoted by DSS are made possible by the ultrafield's ability to provide spatial information traditionally conveyed by the visuals. Others, however, have no obvious relationship; it is not immediately apparent, for instance, that DSS's enhanced low-frequency capability depends upon or itself encourages an increased use of close-ups. Yet all the traits discussed in these two chapters are frequently utilized together, suggesting an underlying commonality. The nature *of* that commonality, and specifically how all these stylistic elements work together to serve a single purpose, is the topic of the next chapter.

4

DECODING THE DIGITAL SURROUND STYLE

Certain Academy Awards like Sound and Visual Effects and Editing are sometimes referred to as technical awards. They're not technical awards. They're given for artistic decisions. And sometimes we make them better than others, and I guess we made a couple of good ones on this one.

RANDY THOM, ACCEPTING THE 2005 OSCAR FOR SOUND EDITING

Digital surround sound (DSS) has promoted a number of specific stylistic trends in the cinema. Some of these, such as movies' loudest sounds becoming even louder and their silences even quieter, derive specifically from the technical differences between DSS systems and their immediate predecessor, Dolby Stereo. Others result indirectly from this technological change. For example, filmmakers have always been *technically* able to ignore the 180-degree rule in picture editing, but their newfound ability to do so without confusing the audience is tied to the capability of DSS soundtracks to precisely place—and smoothly move—sounds around the theater.

That digital surround opened the door to changes in film style should not be seen as evidence of technological determinism; the shift to DSS has not *forced* filmmakers to adopt any new techniques or different stylistic approaches. Indeed, anything that could be done with a monophonic or Dolby Stereo soundtrack can still be done with a digital one, allowing filmmakers the *option* of continuing to employ Dolby Stereo–era sound design and shooting conventions. For those filmmakers taking this approach, the only tangible effect of the transition to DSS is that release prints of their movies now include a digitally encoded version of their soundtracks in addition to the standard analog one—a change that neither filmmakers nor audiences are likely to notice. In other words, the mere *ability* of digital surround to do certain new things has not meant that filmmakers have taken advantage of all those opportunities: a DSS soundtrack is perfectly *capable* of placing all dialogue in the left rear channel, but as yet no films have chosen to exploit this potential. Writing about the introduction of Dolby Stereo in the 1970s, scholar-filmmaker Michel Chion opined that "Dolby will become what we decide to make of it; it is not Dolby which should dictate what we should do with it";[1] the same is no less true of digital surround today.

As Randy Thom notes in this chapter's epigraph, making movies is about making artistic *choices*—and what digital surround sound did was give filmmakers more *choices* of aural and visual strategies. From this palette of options, filmmakers choose the strategies they believe will best serve a film's primary story concerns or the creative aims of a particular moment. The conclusion to chapter 3 mentioned that filmmakers often choose to deploy the DSS-linked aesthetic traits en masse—where one of them is used others tend to be as well. Since aesthetic choices are made to achieve particular creative or narrative goals, this adoption of a de facto "digital surround style" suggests these seemingly independent stylistic elements all serve a common purpose; the principal concern of this chapter is discovering that unifying aspect that underlies the "digital surround style."

A MUSIC VIDEO STYLE?

Extant frameworks for understanding contemporary film style may offer insight into the unifying element of the digital surround style's various components. For instance, several of the "new" techniques discussed in the past two chapters have gained notice by film scholars and critics *outside* the context of digital surround sound; of these, contemporary Hollywood's quick cutting and increased use of close-ups have probably garnered the most attention. Indeed, much popular discourse seems to take it for granted that current movies adopt an incoherent style based on music video aesthetics. This approach has even been given the (usually derisive) shorthand label of "MTV style."

Carol Vernallis, author of *Experiencing Music Video*, interrogates this alleged connection between music video and film and suggests that it runs deeper than mere visual similarities: "If we study music video closely, this 'low art' can tell us a great deal about contemporary media."[2] Rather than focusing on music video shooting and editing tactics themselves, Vernallis considers *why* music videos tend to rely on the particular stylistic traits they do—and whether the same rationale can explain those traits' increasing utilization by feature films. First, she notes that a given pop song can be paired with a wide variety of images—"the receptive soundtrack allows for a wide variety of audio-visual realizations."[3] Music cognition research supports this assertion. In one study pairing different images with the same music (and vice versa), the researchers found that several pairings could be perceived as equally good by audiences; as long as the audience could identify enough "accent points" where music and image somehow "matched," they were willing to accept the audio-visual combination as a logical one.[4]

Accent points only become salient through a specific *combination* of image and sound; pairing the same piece of music with different visuals will yield different accent points, as different elements of the image and sound will temporally "match." The implication of this result for music video is that *any* visual element (camera movement, color, flash frame, superimpositions, etc.) may draw attention to a particular aspect of the music at any given instant. Based on this logic, Vernallis argues that music video is about the *moment* and relies on ever-shifting, ephemeral connections between sound and image: "we're continually taken out of and back into the music, resuturing ourselves to the soundtrack, which produces a moment-to-moment mode of attention."[5]

Vernallis asserts that this moment-by-moment interaction between sound and image to create accent points is the defining feature of contemporary film style, and she uses as an example a scene from *The Bourne Ultimatum* (2007):

> *Bourne's* average shot length of 2 seconds nests within the music's tempo of roughly 120 beats per minute (one shot per measure). The characters'

sharply etched movements, the camera's rapid change of focus among them and the jagged editing can bring forward musical materials—a beat, a beginning of a musical hook. The electronic dance music's constant pulse means any beat, and any offbeat as well, can be brought to the fore. In this clip, the meter is changing, and the pulse is *jointly* constructed by image and music.[6]

Visually, the scene described here is not dissimilar from what others have described as the "MTV style"—it relies on a quick-cutting visual approach "based on dislocation, free-association, flux, color, and texture."[7] What distinguishes Vernallis's work is her claim that this visual structure is an *effect* of the accent point–based approach to filmmaking she dubs the "New Cut-Up Cinema."

Vernallis identifies a wealth of factors behind the prevalence of the "New Cut-Up Cinema," including the movement of directors between feature films and music videos, the introduction of new technologies allowing for more intricate manipulation of picture and sound, and the spread of high shooting ratios (where filmmakers shoot a lot of material, trusting that the right "pieces" can be found and fit together later) from short forms such as music videos and commercials to features. Curiously, though music video remains primarily a two-channel stereo medium even today, she also mentions 5.1 surround as a "shared technology" between cinema and music video that has enabled the former to adopt the style of the latter.[8]

This last assertion implies an affiliation between the digital surround style and the "New Cut-Up Cinema." To be sure, the constantly shifting sonic and visual spaces of DSS *do* fit with the fast-paced cutting and transience of music video. And some of digital surround sound's aural attributes—such as its capacity for intense low-frequency effects and its ability to incorporate more perceptible sounds at one time—could certainly be used to create accent points by highlighting specific elements of the image that might otherwise have gone unnoticed. Yet many of the stylistic traits of the digital surround style are, at a fundamental level, opposed to the aims of the "New Cut-Up Cinema." Vernallis points out that digital surround can be used to "place sound materials as points in space, or seamlessly meld them into immersive environments," but does not explain how these capabilities fits into the "New Cut-Up Cinema."[9] In fact, melding multiple elements into a cohesive environment suggests an *ongoing* consistency between the aural and visual worlds; this would be at odds with the *intermittent* sound/image intersections upon which the "New Cut-Up Cinema" centers.

Other components of the digital surround style not mentioned by Vernallis similarly demonstrate the incongruity between DSS-based aesthetics and those emphasized by Vernallis's model. The digital surround style, for example, relies heavily on close shots. Close-ups, though, are unnecessary in the "New Cut-Up Cinema" model—accent points between sound and image serve to draw the audience's attentions to elements of interest, without the camera needing to show those elements in close-up. In fact, wide shots, which by nature tend to include more visual elements, offer a greater number of possible sound/image "matching" opportunities and hence should be *more* prevalent, not *less*, in films relying on Vernallis's model. A similar argument can be made about the effect of the ultrafield. The "New Cut-Up Cinema" requires a wide variety of possible image/sound pairings, which are variously brought to the foreground by fleeting sound/image interactions; the ultrafield, on the other hand, asserts that for any given shot on the image track, only *one* orientation of the surround soundscape is a proper "match."

Aside from these stylistic differences between it and the digital surround style, the "New Cut-Up Cinema" model has a major shortcoming in explaining contemporary cinematic style: it fails to account for non-musical aural elements.[10] While Vernallis rightly chastises the many purveyors of the "film as music video" argument who ignore the soundtrack entirely, she only partially addresses their oversight. The bulk of her argument centers on rhythm and "pulse" as the crucial relation between image and sound, a contention that works well for music and for the heavily music-driven examples she cites. These terms quickly become less productive, though, when dealing with dialogue, sound effects, ambiences, and other sounds—all of which are just as important as music, if not more so, to DSS-based soundtracks. This music-centric view of film sound engenders another problem: a conception of the image/sound interaction as *singular*, with one sound and one image interacting at any time. Again, this works reasonably well for music video and even music-only film soundtracks, as a piece of music is usually *perceived* as a single entity. Film soundtracks, however, are notoriously *multiple*, with dialogue, effects, music, and other sounds all vying for attention—and digital surround encourages filmmakers to incorporate even *more* sounds, coming from even *more* places, into contemporary soundtracks.

Finally, one more subtle distinction between the "New Cut-Up Cinema" and digital surround's aesthetics should be addressed: the former's subordination of narrative to moment-by-moment image/sound pairings. Music videos nearly always emphasize spectacle and the *moment* rather than coherence or storytelling; audiences understand this and watch music videos under the assumption that they will receive fleeting moments of sound/image coherence, not necessarily a "story." Vernallis argues that when the music video style (the "New Cut-Up Cinema") is used in feature films, audiences similarly adjust their expectations and focus on the events of the moment rather than on the broader concerns of when, how, or even *if* a narrative will come together. They may still expect (thanks to years of watching movies) *that* the plot will progress somehow, but are less concerned with exactly *how* that might happen: "Do I care if Bourne meets Big Daddy Programmer, or Godzilla? No. The narrative pay-off is only a placeholder, a marker I know will be coming."[11] Narrative itself becomes a sort of MacGuffin existing merely to link the moment-by-moment sounds and images that are the movie's actual purpose—certainly this seems an apt description of some recent horror and action films where the story appears to have been considered little more than a necessary evil to link the individual gruesome or exciting scenes audiences really come to see.[12]

In contrast to this relegation of narrative to a secondary concern in the "New Cut-Up Cinema," the digital surround style *emphasizes* story. In the aural realm, the shifting ultrafield offers information about what is happening both on- and offscreen. The visual track, meanwhile, makes heavy use of close-ups to convey character emotions or plot points. In short, the various elements of the digital surround style work to clarify or enhance a film's story, not to wrest the audience's attentions *from* it. Indeed, every one of the film sound professionals I interviewed about the use of digital surround made a point to note that their sound design choices were driven by the *narrative*. As sound effects editor Suhail Kafity puts it, "Story, story, story, that is the bottom line."[13] These descriptions of narrative as a guiding principle sit in stark contrast to Vernallis's model, which subjugates narrative to the momentary play of music and image.

INTENSIFIED CONTINUITY

Ultimately, the principles of Vernallis's music video–based model do not mesh with those of the digital surround style. The specific differences between the two, however, suggest another possibly useful direction for the current investigation. In its emphases on narrative clarity and on guiding the audience's attentions to the "right" sound/image connections, the digital surround style actually follows long-standing Hollywood convention, in spirit if not in specific execution. In fact, David Bordwell has argued that recent shifts in visual aesthetics represent a new way of adhering to old norms rather than a fundamental shift in the way cinema operates. Responding to those who, like Vernallis, suggest that studio filmmaking has entered a "post-classical" era, Bordwell notes that in "representing space, time, and narrative relations (such as causal connections and parallels), today's films generally adhere to the principles of classical filmmaking."[14]

Bordwell's analysis draws on an extensive study of mainstream films from 1961 to 2000; it identifies four major differences in visual style between recent films and their earlier counterparts. In addition to two factors already cited as elements of both the "MTV aesthetic" and the digital surround style—a decrease in shot duration (i.e., faster cutting) and greater use of close framings (specifically in dialogue scenes, according to Bordwell's research)—it finds that contemporary films demonstrate a reliance on extremely long and/or extremely wide lenses and extensive camera movement.[15] While acknowledging these changes in shooting and editing practices form "the dominant style of American mass-audience films today," Bordwell asserts that this style is only a *new implementation* of well-established *principles*: "the ways in which today's films represent space overwhelmingly adhere to the premises of 'classical continuity.'"[16]

To situate the contemporary approach in the context of traditional practices, Bordwell dubs it "intensified continuity." He writes that "the new style amounts to an *intensification* of established techniques. Intensified continuity is traditional continuity amped up, raised to a higher pitch of emphasis."[17] In other words, intensified continuity does not represent a "break" from classic practices but a different way of adhering to established conventions. Today's movies may have more cuts and rely on closer shots than their earlier counterparts but, Bordwell argues, those cuts and shots still follow classic continuity principles.

As the move from "traditional" to "intensified" continuity came together over several decades, its roots are difficult to pinpoint. Bordwell finds its precursors in the work of innovative earlier filmmakers like Welles, Hitchcock, and Bergman,[18] and notes in addition that many of the most famous and influential scenes in classic films employ either the quick cutting—for example, the Odessa Steps in *Battleship Potemkin* (1925) and the shower scene in *Psycho* (1960)—or the free-roaming camera—for example, the opening of *Touch of Evil* (1958) and the party in *The Rules of the Game* (1939)—characteristic of intensified continuity.[19] Other factors leading to intensified continuity are more recent, such as the influence of television on audiences, the popularity of multi-camera shooting in feature films, and the ever-decreasing size of movie theaters. Bordwell also cites many of the same influences on feature filmmaking as Vernallis: movement of directors across media (feature film and music video for her; feature film and television for him), digital editing technology, and high shooting ratios.[20]

Although Bordwell does not mention DSS (or any other sound-related factor) as an influence on contemporary visual style, a logical question is whether the digital surround style fits into the rubric of "intensified continuity." In the visual realm, the two share a reliance on quick cutting and close-ups; eliminating establishing shots from the beginning of scenes, another part of the digital surround style, likewise meshes neatly with Bordwell's description of intensified continuity.[21] And on the aural side, an argument could be made that 5.1-channel surround sound represents a literal "intensification" of the soundtrack—it can include more sounds, they can be louder (or softer), and they can come from more places within the theater. Taking Bordwell's term "intensification" less literally, one could even point out that the LFE's low-rumbling effects and the constantly shifting sonic space of the ultrafield create a more "intense" experience.

Yet while the digital surround style and intensified continuity incorporate some of the same stylistic traits, they *deploy* these traits in fundamentally different ways. For instance, Bordwell asserts that the quick cutting and close-up shots of intensified continuity *reinforce* the 180-degree rule: "When shots are so short, when establishing shots are brief or postponed or nonexistent, the eyelines and angles in a dialogue must be even more unambiguous, and the axis of action must be strictly respected."[22] Yet this claim directly conflicts with the reality of DSS-driven editing, where close-ups, quick cutting, and missing establishing shots go hand-in-hand with a *disregard* for the 180-degree rule and visual establishment of the diegetic space.

This difference stems from a crucial shortcoming of intensified continuity as a model: it is based—as the subtitle of Bordwell's essay, "Visual Style in Contemporary American Film," acknowledges—on a purely visual conception of the cinema. By its very nature, intensified continuity cannot consider or account for the sound/image interactions crucial to the digital surround style. Consider Bordwell's assertion that intensified continuity's most obvious effect is

> to generate a keen moment-by-moment anticipation. . . . Close-ups and singles make the shots very legible. Rapid editing obliges the viewer to assemble discrete pieces of information, and it sets a commanding pace: look away and you might miss a key point.[23]

Here he convincingly describes how the four visual traits of intensified continuity work together to create an effect of continuous anticipation and attention, to make viewers believe they will "miss" something if their attentions ever wander.

Yet this proposed scenario depends on the cinema being an image-only medium, as Bordwell's own language—"*look* away and you might miss a key point"—reveals. With the digital surround style, "looking away" from the screen hardly deprives the audience of information about narrative events. The ultrafield-driven soundtrack continues unabated, its hyper-reality rendering even the smallest (onscreen *or* offscreen) actions audible. It even provides hints about what is happening in the image track, with the orientation of the soundscape explaining the camera's current perspective and abrupt shifts in that orientation indicating changes in camera angle and/or location. Where intensified continuity works "to rivet the viewer to the screen," digital surround expands the world of the movie *beyond* the screen.[24] In most cases, missing a shot or two of a film employing the digital surround style makes very little difference—perhaps this is why the shot sequences of contemporary films, in Vernallis's words, "resist memory."[25] Viewers do miss *some* information by "looking away" from the screen but would be more likely to miss *important* things by "listening away" (which is considerably more difficult to actually do).

It is this exclusion of cinema's aural component from Bordwell's analysis that explains why his model asserts the continuing importance of traditional continuity rules even though these rules have been called into question by contemporary practices and the digital surround style. The fundamental purpose of continuity rules is to make it clear for the audience how each shot relates to the next—because the *audience* is responsible for creating a coherent story out of the image track's succession of different shots. To borrow Bordwell's phrasing from above, continuity "obliges the viewer to assemble discrete pieces of information." In movies employing the digital surround style, on the other hand, the audience need not mentally assemble temporally *separated* pieces of information, as the information relevant to any shot is presented in the soundtrack simultaneously with that shot. Successive shots may obey the rules of continuity, or they may not—the *soundtrack*, rather than the preceding elements in the image track, provides the context for each new shot. If the effect of intensified continuity is to create attention through "moment-by-moment *anticipation*," then the digital surround style creates a "moment-by-moment *focus*," centered on a *continual present*.[26]

Ultimately, intensified continuity's dependence on a solely visual conception of cinema makes it an inadequate model for scenes employing the digital surround style. This does not mean Bordwell's paradigm is *never* a valid way of understanding contemporary cinema. In fact, quite the opposite is true: intensified continuity makes a lot of sense as an overview of the way visual style works in *many* films *much* of the time. But at precisely those moments where the digital surround style is in use—when the image track abandons the rules of classical continuity, when the soundtrack takes over responsibility for setting the space, when crucial information may emanate from anywhere in the theater—intensified continuity fails.

Moreover, intensified continuity's "failure rate" is liable to increase for the foreseeable future as more films employ the digital surround style. Bordwell developed his model based on a sample of 400 films from the years 1961–2000, including roughly the same number of films from each year—meaning less than a quarter of the movies he studied were released in digital surround. Moreover, relatively few of those likely utilized DSS's full capabilities; as discussed earlier, many film-makers were reluctant to fully exploit DSS's capabilities—lest their work not translate to all the venues in which they would be shown—prior to the standardization of 5.1-channel surround across theaters, home video, and television. Based on the limited use of DSS in his sample of films, it is perhaps not surprising that Bordwell's model does not reflect many of the elements of the digital surround style. But with DSS now virtually ubiquitous and use of the digital surround style increasing, intensified continuity might be more appropriately described as a "historical description" of late twentieth-century cinema than as a model for "contemporary" cinema.

Before abandoning the topic of intensified continuity, one more of Bordwell's contentions deserves attention: his claim that intensified continuity makes cinematic narration more apparent.[27] This is an intriguing proposal, since continuity shooting and editing practices normally help efface the constructed nature of cinema. It suggests that while obeying the *rules* of classical continuity, intensified continuity simultaneously works in opposition to one of the fundamental reasons behind its *use*. As Bordwell notes, stylistic

> gestures which earlier filmmakers would have considered flagrantly self-conscious . . . have become default values in ordinary scenes and minor movies. Interestingly, this more outré technique doesn't prevent us from comprehending the story. Having become accustomed to a new overt-ness of narration, we seem to have set the threshold for obtrusiveness higher.[28]

Whatever flaws the intensified continuity model might have, in this case Bordwell's logic can productively be expanded from the visual realm into the aural one, and more specifically to surround mixing practices. In the magnetic and Dolby Stereo eras, it was virtually forbidden (and often technically impossible) to place dialogue or other "spot effects" in the rear speakers of a multi-channel configuration. Even today, fears of the "exit door effect" linger, making some filmmakers reluctant to put spot effects in the surround channels. As aggressive use of the surround channels for *all* sorts of sounds becomes more commonplace, though, audiences will grow more accustomed to this "overt" narrational technique. For the next generation of filmgoers, the elements of the digital surround style some today find "obtrusive" will simply be the norm; a child who has grown up hearing entire conversations between offscreen characters mixed to the rear speakers (as in *Cars*) would likely find a filmgoer who turns around to look for the source of a sound from a surround channel as ridiculously naïve as the infamous title character of *Uncle Josh at the Moving Picture Show* (1902). Bordwell notes in the last line of his essay that "as styles change, so do viewing skills."[29] So, it should be added, do *listening* skills.

CLUES FROM A DREAMING EAR

While neither the "New Cut-Up Cinema" nor "intensified continuity" is an adequate structure through which the diverse aesthetic techniques associated with digital surround sound can be brought together, the ways in which the digital surround style *differed* from these other paradigms provide indications of its aims and effects. Comparison with Vernallis's momentary-interaction-driven model revealed that the digital surround style is tied to story and narrative; exploration in the context of Bordwell's visually centered model showed it relies on sound/image relationships to create a continual present. Taken together, these results imply that a legitimate unifying framework for the digital surround style must focus on the present moment while keeping at its core the film's story or narrative.

The final clues to unraveling this underlying structure come from Vivian Sobchack's essay "When the Ear Dreams: Dolby Digital and the Imagination of Sound," one of a very few scholarly works to give serious consideration to digital surround sound. Sobchack focuses her attentions on nine promotional trailers created by Dolby Laboratories to promote its Dolby Digital sound system. These short pieces (about thirty seconds each) were intended to be played before the main feature in Dolby Digital–equipped theaters; non-narrative in nature, each briefly plays some engaging visuals and sounds before ending with the Dolby Digital logo.[30] As these trailers are self-contained entities "eccentric to feature-length narrative cinema,"[31] the ways in which they use digital surround do not necessarily correspond to DSS's stylistic effects on feature filmmaking. Indeed, Sobchack is more interested in a phenomenological exploration of the way "seeing" and "hearing" function relative to each other and to the audience than in the specific aural and visual characteristics of either feature films or the Dolby trailers themselves. Nevertheless, her analysis of these trailers illuminates crucial principles underlying the digital surround style.

Two elements of Sobchack's essay deserve special attention. First, in discussing the sense of "space" the Dolby trailers create, Sobchack is struck by the paradox of its simultaneously "large" *and* "contained" nature:

> While the amplified, swelling sounds fill what seems like a vast space, that space seems nonetheless discrete, and doesn't precisely coincide with—even as it intersects with—the actual space of the theater in which we sit. The space of the sounding, particularly in its discrete elements, seems "deep" with a depth that has no discernable parameters and yet its breadth seems to have sharply defined edges. . . . Foregrounded in their clarity, the more isolated sounds and effects move from place to place (and speaker to speaker) around the listener and the theater but don't so much "fill up" the space continuously as "describe" it in a kind of discontinuous "mapping."[32]

Sobchack is particularly intrigued by the relationship between the theater itself and the space created by the soundtrack, noting that the experience of hearing the Dolby trailers is markedly different from that of the other common experience where audiences sit in a large room and are presented with sound, namely a musical concert. Writing that

> despite what can only be called the frequent "simulation" of echoes and reverberation, this is not the phenomenological sound of the concert

hall that one feels is palpably filled with—and inhabited by—the plenti-
tude of a sound gestalt in which one is immersed with others,[33]

she suggests the complex differences between these two types of encounters. Most apparently, the digital soundtrack attempts, through
carefully manipulated reverberation and resonance, to create its own
artificial space—to *replace* the acoustics of the venue with those of
its own design. Michel Chion, Sobchack notes, offered remarkably
similar observations after hearing a set of promotional trailers for the
THX certification system in the late 1980s, claiming that "the sound
feels very present and very neutral, but suddenly one no longer has the
feeling of the real dimensions of the room."[34]

This significant distinction between the Dolby Digital trailers and
a musical concert in part reflects the disparity between the spaces in
which they are heard. Tomlinson Holman observes that in terms of
functionality movie theaters *should* sound quite different from music
venues:

> There's a fundamental difference between a concert hall, which is a
> space for *production*, where the orchestra plays and interacts with the
> hall, and a movie theater, which is a space for *reproduction*—it's elec-
> tronically recorded, and you want to be able to do away with interacting
> with the space.[35]

That is, a concert hall is meant to be *heard* through the way it colors
a musical performance while a movie theater is expected to *hide* its
own presence and reproduce the soundtrack as "neutrally" as possible. High-end installations in particular—such as the THX-certified
theaters cited by Chion—are designed to be sonically transparent and
minimize reverberations; this design helps the same soundtrack play
back acceptably in a wide variety of theaters and maximizes the chance
that the soundtrack heard by audiences will be at least roughly what
the director and sound crew intended.

This approach to theater design is, however, a relatively recent
development. Well into the latter half of the twentieth century, movie
theaters were still constructed to be fairly "live," meaning that they
introduced significant amounts of reverberation. In the pre-surround
era, the theater-added reverb served to create a sense of envelopment;

as Holman points out, "in a really dead theater mono is just so obvious, so livening up those rooms was not such a bad idea in the mono era."[36] Not until magnetic multi-channel sound systems were introduced in the 1950s was this standard for movie theater architecture challenged, as multi-channel systems did not play well in "live" theaters—when sounds come from multiple speakers, each of which reverberate around the theater, the soundtrack becomes muddy and difficult to make out.

Given the relatively limited number of theaters with multi-channel systems at the time, this did not spark any industry-wide changes.[37] The widespread success of the multi-channel Dolby Stereo system, however, required less-reverberant theaters. "New movie houses whose acoustics are conceived or overhauled with luxury sound projection in mind," Chion observes, "have indeed mercilessly vanquished reverb through the choice of building materials and architectural planning."[38] In the digital surround era this trend has continued and even intensified; while loudspeakers and theatrical sound systems have grown more powerful, theater sound has gotten "drier," with the ultimate goal being an acoustically "transparent" theater that adds *no* acoustic color or reverberation of its own to the soundtrack.

That the Dolby trailers, as Sobchack observes, use digital surround to create a sonic space distinct from the space of the theater itself reflects a possibility available only *because* multi-channel sound forced a move to acoustically invisible theaters. This shift opened up new possibilities for sound design. Holman recalls recognizing this opportunity early in the Dolby Stereo era:

> If we make the theater dead, we can *afford* reverberation on the soundtrack, if we want. So we can put you in the basketball court. Or we could have, say, dry voiceover narration like Martin Sheen in *Apocalypse Now* and have it very intimate.[39]

But this newfound freedom was also a responsibility—with the sound of the theater itself eliminated, the *only* sense of space a movie can offer is that created by the soundtrack. Sobchack accurately notes that the Dolby trailers create their own sonic environment—what goes unsaid is that they *must* do so if any sort of space at all is to be perceived by the audience. In short, one lesson Sobchack's essay offers about the principles underlying the digital surround style is that the soundtrack must create its own spatial environment, located *in* but discrete *from* the (acoustically transparent) theater space itself.

The second element of Sobchack's essay deserving attention in the context of the current investigation is that the ninth and most recent Dolby trailer examined by Sobchack, titled "Stomp," differs dramatically from the eight that preceded it. Its most obvious difference is that it is the only one of the nine to use live-action footage; where the others rely on computer-generated visuals, "Stomp" showcases members of the dance/music troupe Stomp making sounds with their bodies and other objects as the Dolby logo tracks across the screen. More subtly, Sobchack recognizes that this trailer "constitutes sound/image relations that are quite different from its forebears."[40] Sobchack's essay centers almost exclusively on the eight "matching" trailers; indeed, virtually every step of her argument explicitly excludes "Stomp" from consideration.[41] Yet the reasons *why* "Stomp" differs from the other trailers suggest it may actually be the one that best speaks to DSS's use in feature filmmaking.

In the 1990s, when the first eight Dolby Digital trailers were made, digital surround was still new enough to be something of an attraction in its own right—thus these trailers aim primarily to "show off" what DSS technology can do. Sobchack notes that the trailers "promote the wonder, power, and difference that marks digital sound. . . . They present us with an audio-vision that is both objectively testing and subjectively dreaming its own possibilities and suspecting its own limits."[42] Her language is telling—the Dolby trailers demonstrate the new *"possibilities"* opened up by digital surround. Indeed, the mixers working on these early Dolby trailers noted that their goal was specifically to draw attention to the sound system by trying things they had *not* done before:

> It's important to have a modicum of surround subtlety while working on a full-length feature, but a handful of film sound mixers and editors had the opportunity to throw that philosophy out the window while working on logo trailers. . . . Teams packed channels with bird calls and swooshed and swirled effects, front to back, for brief logo trailers.[43]

As the quotation above acknowledges, these aggressive mixing practices were quite different from those employed by DSS-equipped features of the time. This makes sense given that the Dolby trailers fundamentally serve as *advertisements*. In the early and mid-1990s when these first eight trailers were created, a theater could show them to differentiate itself from the competition—"look, we have digital surround sound, and listen to the cool things it can do!"—and thereby convince moviegoers of its technological superiority over non-DSS-equipped cinemas.

By the time "Stomp" was created (four years after its most recent predecessor) in 2003, though, this sort of advertisement was pointless.[44] All recently built theaters had been constructed with DSS systems already installed, and virtually every older first-run venue had been upgraded to one of the digital surround formats—a DSS system had become a fundamental expectation of any decent movie theater, not a marketable selling point.[45] Conceivably, "Stomp" could have been used to advertise that a theater had *Dolby*'s version of digital sound rather than DTS or Sony Dynamic Digital Sound (SDDS);[46] this seems unlikely, though, since Dolby itself admits that the "three digital formats are virtually indistinguishable, even under carefully controlled listening conditions. In actual exhibition, any differences are far smaller than the differences between cinema sound systems and acoustics."[47]

"Stomp" ultimately seems designed to demonstrate not that a theater *had* digital sound, but that its sound system had been installed and set up *correctly*. While digital surround systems were ubiquitous by 2003, not all theater owners had the know-how, time, and/or inclination to properly configure them. As one mixer laments, "Most rooms or theaters are not calibrated correctly."[48] In this environment, showing a Dolby trailer (presumably in a theater where the Dolby system was properly set up) served as a pledge that the theater's sound system was working properly, and that moviegoers could expect the same high level of sonic performance during the feature as that demonstrated during the trailer.

This implicit promise explains why "Stomp" differs from its forerunners in style—using the same "look what digital surround can do!" aesthetic as the earlier Dolby trailers would have primed the audience for "packed channels with bird calls and swooshed and swirled effects" that the feature would not deliver. Instead, "Stomp" logically adopts the same stylistic approach that DSS-equipped features deliver, promising precisely the specific uses of digital surround that the ensuring movie will actually include. So while the earlier Dolby trailers showcase the novel capabilities of digital surround, "Stomp" illustrates the way those capabilities actually affected the aesthetics of feature filmmaking. In short, "Stomp" itself employs the digital surround style.

The differences between "Stomp" and the other Dolby trailers thus correspond to the distinction between DSS's *potential* effects and the *realities* of its use in actual feature film. Specifically, while digital surround technology introduced the *possibility* that the soundtrack would overwhelm the image, the digital surround style does not exploit this possibility. Sobchack observes that aside from "Stomp," the Dolby trailers give the soundtrack power over the image; they "begin only with sound and a darkened screen," after which "sound *calls the images into being* rather than emanating from them and then continues *to lead them* throughout."[49] In contrast, consider her observations about "Stomp": "the emergence of both sound and image are highly synchronized"[50] and "although sound is certainly foregrounded . . . it is not as acousmatically imaginative and generative as it is in the other trailers; rather, it appears generated from the physical action of the dancers seen on the screen instead of being their inaugural and driving force."[51]

Ultimately, "Stomp" adheres neither to the sound-driven paradigm of the earlier trailers, where sounds can "dream their own visible realization,"[52] *nor* to the traditional image-centric conception of cinema, where the soundtrack is "what goes with the image." Instead, it treats sound and picture as *equals*. Given that it is "Stomp" that says the most about how cinema functions in the digital surround era, Sobchack missteps a bit by ignoring this crucial implication of her passing comments on "Stomp" to focus her analytic efforts on the earlier Dolby trailers. Her essay's second lesson about DSS-era aesthetics is thus the one that Sobchack overlooks: the digital surround style utilizes a non-hierarchical relationship between sound and image. This explains why the two maintain tight synchronization: neither "leads" or "creates" the other.

A CINEMA OF IMMERSION

This chapter has now examined three extant ways of thinking about contemporary cinema. None of the three accommodated or accounted for *all* the aural and visual traits comprising the digital surround style uncovered in the previous two chapters; the ways in which each was found lacking, though, brought into focus several key structural characteristics of that style: it works in service of narrative, it uses interplay between sound and image to create a continual present, it uses the multi-channel soundtrack to replace the acoustic space of the theater with one of its own creation, and it relies on tight synchronization between sound and image, neither of which takes precedence over the other. Putting these elements together, a clear hypothesis emerges as to the organizing principle underlying the varied aesthetic traits of the digital surround style: they all work *to immerse the audience in the diegetic world of the film.*

Since "immerse" and "immersion" are grossly overused terms in work on film and other audio-visual media, it is important to clarify exactly what is meant in this case. This "immersion" is not the emotional or narrative involvement in a fictional world that can happen while watching a movie, nor is it a directly personal experience like virtual reality. It also does not equate to "realism"—films employing the digital surround style can and do manipulate sounds and images. Rather, the idea is that the audience is literally *placed* in the dramatic space of the movie, shifting the conception of cinema from something "to be watched from the outside"—with audience members taking in a scene *in front of them*—to something "to be personally experienced"— with audience members literally placed *in the middle* of the diegetic environment and action.

Considering the structural characteristics of the digital surround style listed above, it is apparent that this aesthetic of immersion fits all four. It creates a continual "present," keeping the audience's attentions on the moment at hand by placing them in the midst of the action *as it occurs.* It emphasizes the filmic narrative, putting filmgoers in the same world as the characters so as to experience the events of the story as those characters do. It "hides" the space of the theater itself, replacing it with the created space of the diegetic environment. Finally, it tightly synchronizes sound and image, with the picture providing one viewpoint on the diegetic environment and the soundtrack continually changing with the picture to present both the onscreen events and the (offscreen) rest of the story world as the implied audience would hear it, given the particular current spatial orientation revealed by the image.

4.1. This shot from *The Matrix* (1999) places the camera in the middle of the diegetic space, with action occurring on all sides.

Through all this, the cinematic experience shifts from being *presented with* a movie (to simply see and hear) to being *enveloped by* one.

The idea that digital surround works to immerse the audience in the diegetic world might seem at first a rather pedantic conclusion. Sound itself offers an intimacy and physical presence that image does not—in Walter Murch's words, it can "move us more deeply than the other senses."[53] Some have argued this is because humans begin life in the sonic environment of the womb, where they can hear but do not see,[54] while others note that hearing is literally a result of movements in the air around us, giving sound a physical presence implying both nearness and contemporaneousness that image does not have.[55] Both lines of reasoning suggest that "surround sound," which places more speakers around the auditorium (more physical presence) to envelop listeners with sound (as if in a womb), should enhance sound's inherently intimate nature and promote immersion.

In the production realm, many filmmakers intuitively understand sound's potential to bring the audience *into* the world of the movie. As director Michael Cimino explains it, sound "can demolish the wall separating the viewer from the film."[56] Several of the sound professionals I interviewed more specifically noted that directors and producers often assume this is the primary function of *multi-channel* sound systems.

Gary Johns, for example, said about surround sound that "everybody wants it to be immersion—they want you to really feel like you are in the movie";[57] similarly, Paul Massey described using 5.1 to "pull things away from the screen to allow the audience to be within the image, within the audio image."[58] On those rare occasions that surround has received attention from film scholars, they too have often assumed it serves principally to create "immersion." Yet perhaps *because* it seems so "obvious," this assumption has rarely been interrogated. In fact, pre-DSS claims that surround immerses the audience in the diegetic world generally do not mesh with actual cinematic practices. Matthew Malsky, for instance, asserts that 1950s widescreen cinema and its multi-channel soundtracks "promised total immersion of the senses—a complete transportation of the audience out of their Real and *into* the narrative of the film itself."[59] John Belton, though, has convincingly demonstrated that stereo sound in the 1950s was used as an "element of spectacle . . . associated for audiences not so much with greater realism as with greater artifice."[60] In other words, surround sound was designed to draw attention to itself, *not* to immerse the audience in the movie.

In his essay "The Sonic Playground," Gianluca Sergi argues that Dolby Stereo—DSS's immediate predecessor—works to create immersion, claiming that Dolby Stereo's multi-channel soundtrack "is directed to and orchestrated around the seats to put the spectator literally 'inside' the film, reducing the distance between audience and narrative world."[61] At the same time, however, Sergi acknowledges in *The Dolby Era* that Dolby Stereo soundtracks operate on "the 'one wall' narrative principle," which asserts that "audiences should be offered directional sound (i.e., sound whose direction could be easily identifiable) only from *one* wall of the auditorium, namely that where the screen is placed."[62] The contradiction here is that adhering to the "one wall" principle *and* placing the audience inside the diegesis requires the unlikely situation of a diegetic world where *no* localizable sounds ever occur anywhere other than where the audience happens to be looking at that moment. Sergi's language itself implicitly acknowledges this limitation, as he writes that Dolby Stereo *reduces* the distance between audience and narrative world, rather than that it *eliminates* it.[63] Ultimately, claims that Dolby Stereo placed the audience inside the diegetic world may reveal more about what people—including many inside Dolby—*wanted* it would do than about what it really *did*, as Benjamin Wright explains:

> That the listening subject experience the sound space of the diegesis in the space of the theater was perhaps the most fundamental goal of Dolby sound engineers and technicians . . . [but] these technicians developed a sense of "delocalization" that effectively limited the literal qualities of sound imaging. . . . As a result, [with Dolby Stereo] Dolby technicians pursued the idea of an *abstract* soundtrack that implied a sound space without *literalizing* its effects[64]

Unable to create a complete and accurate sonic *representation* of the diegetic world, Dolby Stereo instead settled for a soundtrack aesthetic that gave audiences a *sense* of that world, careful to keep their attentions focused on the screen in front of them rather than breaking down the barrier *between* them and that screen.

In short, multi-channel sound has historically *not* been used to create diegetic immersion, making it far from a self-evident conclusion that digital surround sound would be used in this way. Moreover, the digital surround style represents an *audio-visual* approach to diegetic immersion, something quite different from the audio-only forms others have described in relation to multi-channel. William Whittington, for instance, writes that "the use of surround sound offers a total sonic environment, which masks the real environment of the theater space to create a sonic space";[65] Richard Maltby similarly asserts that digital soundtracks offer "a three-dimensional extension of the screen's two-dimensional image in which the audience is surrounded by sound."[66] Both recognize the *power* of surround sound to create diegetic immersion but treat the soundtrack as if it operates in isolation.

The original aim of this chapter was to determine a unifying framework for the various aural and visual traits of the digital surround style. Based on its consistency with the structural characteristics of the digital surround style identified earlier in this chapter, "placing the audience in the middle of the diegetic world" is a strong candidate for that framework. For diegetic immersion to be a truly comprehensive paradigm for the use of DSS in contemporary cinema, however, it is crucial that *all* the individual elements of the digital surround style assist in the broad goal of immersing the audience in the movie's world. In other words, each of these traits should not only be *consistent* with diegetic immersion but should actually help *create* this effect. Each of these traits will therefore be examined in this context, beginning with the digital surround style's aural components.

CREATING DIEGETIC IMMERSION: SOUND

Chapter 2 identified three unique capabilities of DSS compared with monophonic and Dolby Stereo systems: a dedicated low-frequency effects (LFE) channel, a larger dynamic range, and five discrete, full-range channels; chapter 3 added the concept of the ultrafield, where the sonic space constantly shifts to match the spatial orientation of the onscreen shot. Three of these traits are easily linked to creating diegetic immersion. Most often used to add emphasis to powerful sounds like explosions or thuds, the bass effects provided by the LFE create sounds that the audience *feels* rather than *hears*; this physical power creates the very physical sensation of being *at* an earth-shaking event, not just *watching* one. As sound editor Hudson Miller explains, "the point-one [LFE channel] is . . . a pure gut, physical, straight-to-the-brainstem physical response."[67]

Similarly, the wide dynamic range and high signal-to-noise ratio of DSS mean that sounds at every loudness level—from virtually inaudible rustles to screams or booms near the sonic threshold of feeling—can be accurately portrayed with the full range of loudness with which they would be heard by characters in the onscreen world, allowing the soundtrack to convince audience members that they are really, physically *there*. And the ultrafield, by maintaining consistent spatial correlation between image and sound, conveys the idea that the filmgoers are actually *in* the world of the film: they hear exactly what they would hear, *where* they would hear it, based on their implied position in the diegesis indicated by the onscreen image.

The relationship between diegetic immersion and DSS's greater number of discrete, full-range channels is a bit more complex to explain. The most obvious outcome of the 5.1 format in this vein is that the five-main-channel configuration of DSS spatially surrounds the audience, shifting the soundtrack from "what's on screen" to "what's all around." Dolby Stereo and some other prior multi-channel systems did, of course, use speakers out in the space of the theater to create atmosphere, but their soundfields were ultimately always anchored to the screen as described in Sergi's "one wall" principle. Digital surround systems, in contrast, allow the soundscape to spread equally into the space of the theater, with no technical limitations restricting localizable sounds to the front speakers. This capability is crucial to the possibility of diegetic immersion—as explained earlier, Dolby Stereo's "delocalized" version of immersion implies that nothing with a localizable sound can be happening anywhere other than onscreen, a severely limiting and unrealistic view of the world. Systems that allow "more precise positioning of all sounds" are, as Dolby Laboratories itself claims, "more like real life."[68]

DSS's discrete, full-range channels support diegetic immersion in another way as well. Michel Chion notes that Dolby Stereo accentuated sonic *details* of the onscreen world that had gone unnoticed—or been left out of the soundtrack entirely—in the monophonic era:

> The appearance of high frequencies in the sound and of fine layers of ambient sound and details behind the voices have produced a sharper sense of the micro-present. Breaths, squeaks, clinks, hums—a whole noisy folk has patiently awaited its day, the minor denizens of sound. In certain cases they have perhaps won . . . they have pulled the cloth toward them without moving what was on the table.[69]

But as chapter 2 showed, the large number of full-range, independent channels that digital surround systems provide allows those systems to play a greater number of simultaneously perceptible sounds than Dolby Stereo ever could. Thus digital surround can refine the sonic subtleties described by Chion even further than Dolby Stereo, creating a more *complete* aural environment. If Dolby Stereo *reduces* the distance between audience and diegetic world—Sergi's earlier assertion, which Chion's phrase "pulling the cloth toward them" recalls—then digital surround sound takes the next step and moves the audience *into* that world.

This argument for the value of DSS's discrete, full-range channels in creating diegetic immersion relies on an implicit assumption: that digital surround's 5.1-channel configuration offers *enough* channels to create a reasonable facsimile of the onscreen world. As shown in chapter 1, 6.1- and 7.1-channel configurations provide audible benefits

4.2. EVE's arrival on Earth in *WALL-E* (2008). Since much of this scene is shot from camera positions in between WALL-E and EVE, the ultrafield is responsible for letting the audience know what is happening with the offscreen character. Here the surround channels convey EVE's actions while the camera faces WALL-E.

in comparison to DSS's standard 5.1 configuration, and the 10.2 (and up) configurations of next-generation sound systems suggest that adding even more channels has additional advantages. In fact, acoustics and spatial imaging expert Jens Blauert has suggested that creating a completely believable sonic impression of a space might require up to *thirty* channels, a number that makes "5.1" channels seem surprisingly inadequate.[70]

The crucial distinction here is that while it may take up to thirty channels to create a "completely believable" sonic space—that is, one indistinguishable from a real-world environment—diegetic immersion does not set the bar so high. Rather, it requires merely that a sound system have enough *envelopment* and *imaging* (placement of sounds in space) capabilities to create an environment (however limited, relative to a "completely believable" space, as it might be) that the audience will *accept* as an accurate representation of the diegetic world. In the case of envelopment, research suggests that the minimum number of full-range, discrete channels required to create a feeling of envelopment is *five*—precisely the number included in digital surround's 5.1 configuration.[71]

The case of imaging is a bit trickier. Gianluca Sergi observes that digital surround systems privilege the screen by placing more channels in front of the audience than behind it (though he acknowledges that 6.1-channel designs such as Dolby Surround EX and DTS-ES challenge this model). Sergi cites this fact as evidence that DSS must keep important sounds onscreen, a claim that the digital surround style's use of the ultrafield—which places important sounds throughout the soundscape—easily refutes. But his initial observation raises an intriguing concern: given that 5.1 uses only two surround channels but three front channels, it may not provide enough spatialization capabilities to create diegetic immersion. Tomlinson Holman, however, suggests that front/rear symmetry is unnecessary in cinematic sound systems:

> If you're always associated with a picture in your system, you're always going to want more channels in front of you to organize with the picture. You want better correspondence between sound and the picture image with the picture, than you care exactly where a sound effect in the surrounds appears in the theater.[72]

In other words, sounds coming from offscreen require less precision in localization since they do not need to match an onscreen image.

The channel arrangement of DSS's 5.1 configuration thus represents a compromise of sorts: it places discrete channels in all four corners of the room to allow for placement of sounds all around the theater, while placing an extra channel on the front wall in recognition that the screen is a "special" site requiring more precise localization— yielding the five channels needed to create envelopment. In short, while DSS's five discrete, full-range channels are a far cry from the thirty required to create a "completely believably" aural environment, they still offer the capabilities needed to create diegetic immersion.

CREATING DIEGETIC IMMERSION: IMAGE

The previous chapter identified a sizable number of image-based traits as part of the digital surround style: limited use of wide or establishing shots, fragmentation of space, heavy use of close shots, shooting from within the space of the action, quick cutting, and disregard for classical continuity editing practices. In that discussion, these traits were all tied to the "freedom" given to the visual track by the ultrafield. Reexamining these traits through the lens of diegetic immersion reveals another commonality: they all serve to literally place the audience *in the middle of the diegetic action.* This is self-evident in the case of one trait—"shooting from within the space of the action"—but equally true for all the others.

Master shots, for instance, by definition provide an overview of the complete action in one shot. The digital surround style limits their use for precisely this reason—they define the boundaries of the action, and place it all in *front* of the audience, providing the perspective of outside observers watching from a distance rather than that of people actually *in* the space where the story is taking place. Just as marching band formations can be seen only by those in the stands, not by those actually in the band, once the digital surround style has placed filmgoers in the middle of the diegetic world it is impossible for them to get a view of it all at once.[73]

The digital surround style's free-form editing, particularly the violation of traditional continuity rules, similarly heightens the sense of being *in* the space. The 180-degree rule that underlies much of continuity editing establishes a line through the diegetic space and requires that all shots be taken from the same side of that line.[74] This practice implies that the action can be confined to one area, that the space "behind" the camera (that is, on the same side of the line as the camera) contains nothing of any interest. Like a master shot, it suggests that the viewer is not "in the world" of the film but rather slightly "outside" it, positioned in such a way as to take in all the important action, with nothing worth seeing ever happening anywhere other than in front of the audience. The digital surround style, by violating the 180-degree rule, implies that the camera simply cannot capture all the action without turning around to shoot "behind" the audience; it places the implied filmgoer quite literally in the middle of the film's events, with action happening both in front of and behind him or her.

While the digital surround style tends to avoid master shots and traditional continuity shooting and editing because these techniques imply that the audience is outside the action, it makes heavy use of techniques that *do* place the audience right in the midst of the action. Close shots signify nearness to the objects, people, or actions shown onscreen, better mimicking what a viewer would see if he or she were actually *in* the onscreen space. In fact, in this way diegetic immersion helps explain not only the digital surround style's heavy use of close-ups but also another contemporary trend noted by Bordwell: the demise of ensemble staging and the resultant privileging of the face.[75] Ensemble staging generally utilizes wide shots where several actors can all be seen in their entirety—a viewpoint that, like a master shot, implies being at a distance from these people. In contrast, close shots, especially those of *faces*, imply being in close proximity to the actors—this mimics real-world experience, where humans generally focus on people's faces in everyday interactions, only seeing their full bodies from head to toe when watching them from a distance.

The last two stylistic traits of the digital surround style, quick cutting and the fragmentation of space, might superficially seem opposed to the strategy of diegetic immersion, as they both suggest a spatial discontinuity that runs contrary to the everyday experience of space as roughly continuous. In the digital surround style, however, it is the ultrafield-based soundtrack, not the onscreen images, that provides stability and continuity to the audience experiencing a film; with the soundtrack guiding the audience, the image track can *be* discontinuous without creating a *sense* of discontinuity. Instead, its fast-paced cuts and fragmented views of the diegetic world suggest that important events are happening on all sides, and that the camera is "looking around" as quickly as possible trying to catch it all. In other words, they locate the audience in the *middle* of the action—precisely the aim of diegetic immersion.

THE DIGITAL SURROUND STYLE CONFIRMED

That each of the aural and visual traits of the digital surround style clearly serves the goal of placing the audience in the middle of the diegetic world confirms diegetic immersion as the unifying framework of the digital surround style. As a final "real-world" test of this paradigm, I asked filmmakers themselves to summarize what they felt the effects of digital surround sound on filmmaking practices had been. The first thing that became clear was that while actually working on films, these artists rarely think about the abstract principles (such as diegetic immersion) that may influence their decisions. In part, this is because the tight timelines of post-production (discussed more in the next chapter) simply do not give them much time during a job to think about these more abstract issues.[76] At a deeper level, though, this reflects the fact that filmmaking is an artistic endeavor, and "overthinking" can be detrimental to the creative process; as Richard King put it, relying on specific ideas about how "cinema" works "kind of paints you into a corner . . . you sort of limit yourself creatively because you go on a preconception."[77] Randy Thom neatly summarized this fact, noting,

> Most filmmakers, whether they are directors, composers, or sound designers, are minimally analytic about their own world. . . . Storytellers tend to live and work on gut feelings, intuition, and their own raw nerve endings.[78]

Yet regardless of how they may work "in the moment" of *doing* their jobs, film sound professionals can be quite perceptive about their work and its effects. And in support of this chapter's conclusions, many of their comments about digital surround's effects alluded to creating a complete world and/or bringing that world into the space of the theater, precisely the objectives of diegetic immersion. Sound designer Erik Aadahl, for instance, said that digital surround made a movie "more of a realistic experience" for the audience; his use of the word "experience" certainly suggests something quite different than just sitting in a theater watching an onscreen world.[79] Similarly, sound editor Suhail Kafity cited *Crimson Tide* (1995) as an example of excellent surround sound usage because "it made you feel like *you* were in a sub."[80]

In fact, some of their comments reflected precisely the elements of the digital surround style identified in the previous two chapters. Midge Costin, for instance, explained that part of the challenge in putting together 5.1 soundtracks was keeping track of offscreen action and following through on what was happening in the world even when it was not being shown:

> We actually had to start cutting and thinking in that way, definitely taking the screen apart and saying what would be coming from here? . . .

Now I have to follow that through. You're only seeing the close-ups, but then this goes on to do this and that goes on to do that. You're supposed to be *immersed* in this. . . . We were the reality. We would keep the reality going.[81]

The sonic result of this editing work to "keep the reality going" is, of course, the ultrafield. Sound designer Glenn Morgan, meanwhile, gave an explanation of surround sound that comes close to articulating the concept of diegetic immersion itself:

Surrounds are really beneficial for when they support you in the environment in terms of filling it out, turning it into three dimensions. . . . *Harry Potter* is a good example. When you're in the dungeons or the caves, the castles, you really want to feel like *you are submersed* inside the basement or as far down as you can go. And so all of a sudden, now, the surrounds become part of the environment because you hear creaks, and wood, and things that really engulf you and give you claustrophobia.[82]

Statements like Costin's and Morgan's suggest that even if sound designers, editors, and mixers may rarely have to articulate the goals underlying their aesthetic decisions, they do have very clear ideas about the consequences of those choices. Thus in a second round of interviews, I asked my interviewees for their comments on a set of theoretical conclusions about digital surround sound's impact, assuming that even if they themselves rarely spelled out the rationale underlying their work, they would recognize whether specific ideas about DSS's effects meshed with their own experience or not. Most importantly, I explained that my work on digital surround sound suggested that it encouraged a particular aesthetic style and asked them what they thought about the conclusion that "Cinematic experience shifts from *watching* a movie to *being immersed in the diegesis* of one."[83]

The word "diegesis" elicited a complicated reaction; perhaps due to the same reluctance of filmmakers to overthink their own work mentioned above, filmmakers do not like to use it. Randy Thom, for instance, argues that diegesis "is a term more appropriate for *analyzing* a film than for *making* one."[84] Tom Holman is even more direct: "I don't use [the word] 'diegesis' because it's an academic term, not a production one. . . . 'Diegetic' and all that stuff makes Hollywood people very nervous."[85] The term itself aside, my interviewees' overall response to the notion of diegetic immersion was very positive. Richard King's take on the use of surround sound and immersion was representative: "Whatever makes you feel like you're part of the experience is helping. . . . The image is there, but whatever can bring it off the screen—and feel coherent to the film, to the image, is great. More and more films are obviously doing more and more of that."[86] Others were more concise: "Yeah, I would agree, surround sound is definitely more immersive."[87]

One major objection to this conclusion was raised—but one that actually bolsters the argument for diegetic immersion. Former Motion Picture Sound Editors president David Bondelevitch suggested that throughout cinema history, there have *always* been films that attempted to immerse the audience in this way, and DSS has simply increased filmmakers' ability to achieve that effect. As he put it,

> movies have always been designed around getting the audience to feel like they are in the universe of the film as much as possible. Because of technology, we now have more ability to do that with sound than we ever have before. . . . In the past only the picture had been able to do that. Now it's more obvious that the sound is able to do it because we can create a 360-degree universe instead of just the flat screen that the picture could do. So I don't know if I'd say it's *shifted*, I'd say sound is definitely *used* in that manner.[88]

My interviewees did make one caveat very clear: while new technology has increased the cinema's capabilities for diegetic immersion, and more films are taking advantage of that capability, not every moment of a given film will follow this approach, and indeed not every movie will even deploy it at all. Steve Flick, to cite just one reaction, was quick to point out that "it's dramatic choices in how you use surround. . . . It's so difficult to have an axiom."[89] With the aesthetic elements and foundational principle of the digital surround style now in hand, Flick's comment suggests the next crucial question to ask about the effects of DSS: when is diegetic immersion the "correct" dramatic choice? That is, *where* and *how* is the digital surround style actually *used* in contemporary films?

5

USING THE DIGITAL SURROUND STYLE

What you can do is you can envelop people, but the gimmick
of just because it's there, do you have to be obligated
to put stuff in the surrounds? Absolutely not.

MARTI HUMPHREY, RE-RECORDING MIXER

I should be pulling [the audience] into the movie. If they're sitting there
and it's a night scene and they're in the countryside and there's a gust of
wind and a dog barks way off in the distance back here [in the surrounds],
there's got to be a *reason* that the dog barks back there. There's got to be
a payoff for that, like a car comes down the road from that direction or
something threatening is going to happen from that direction. It can't
be random things [just] because it's cool to have a sound back there.

RICHARD KING, SOUND DESIGNER/SUPERVISING SOUND EDITOR

Humphrey and King speak for the community of film sound professionals in recognizing that just because surround sound makes particular stylistic options available does not mean those options are always
the right ones to *use*. The digital surround style of diegetic immersion
is no different from any other filmmaking strategy: it is appropriate in
some places but not necessarily in others.

Earlier chapters identified what new aesthetic elements digital surround sound (DSS) brought to the cinema and how those traits served
to bring the audience into the diegetic space of the movie, immersing
them in the heart of its three-dimensional world. As acknowledged at
the end of chapter 4, these chapters offered a broad, somewhat abstract
view of digital surround sound's use. This chapter moves the discussion
of the digital surround style into a more concrete realm by exploring
the question raised by Humphrey and King in their comments: where
and when should that style actually be *deployed*?

DETERMINING WHEN TO USE DIEGETIC IMMERSION

For sixty years the screen-centric design of monophonic sound (as well
as Dolby Stereo) dictated how sound and image are used; that history
cannot and should not be discarded lightly. DSS enables the cinema
to move away from this long-standing practice, but it is hardly surprising that this transition has progressed cautiously. Anything that could
be done with a monophonic or Dolby Stereo soundtrack can still be
done with a digital one, and frequently filmmakers will make *some*
use of DSS's multi-channel environment without embracing the novel
strategy of complete diegetic immersion. In practice, use of the digital
surround style thus spans the spectrum from *Transformers: Revenge of
the Fallen* (2009), which deploys the style's full complement of aural
and visual traits in almost every scene, to *WALL-E* (2008), which combines heavily immersive sequences with more conventionally shot and
mixed segments, to *Traffic* (2000), which was mixed largely in mono for
a "documentary" feel and not surprisingly adheres almost exclusively
to a traditional screen-oriented aesthetic in other aspects of its visual
and aural design as well.[1]

This mix of approaches does not negate the significance of DSS's
effects any more than the fact that films today may still include black-
and-white segments diminishes the importance of color to film. Rather,
it shows that the cinema remains in a time of transition—one the
reverse of the late 1970s shift Jay Beck explores in "A Quiet Revolution," where the introduction of Dolby Stereo sparked a *regression*. In
that case, filmmakers who had been experimenting with new ideas
were encouraged to return to more traditional practices; in the current

transition, filmmakers have the opportunity to explore new strategies but always have the safety net of Dolby Stereo–era practices on which to fall back.

The specific degree of this shift to the digital surround style is difficult to gauge given that the same movie will often employ full-on diegetic immersion at one point and a screen-centric approach at another. When asserting that the adoption of Dolby Stereo led to changes in cinematic visuals, for instance, Michel Chion admitted that the editing style sparked by this new technology "is only tendential, rarely present in a pure fashion, and in most films it is combined without difficulty with the customary rhetoric of shot-division."[2] The same can be said for the digital surround style: it does not *replace* the options already available to filmmakers, it merely *expands* the palette of possibilities. Used in the wrong places, this new style may even cause more problems than it solves—as Dolby consultant Thom Ehle (*Forgetting Sarah Marshall, Red Dragon, Collateral Damage*) dryly notes in reference to early DSS-era movies that took digital sound's enhanced dynamic capabilities as a license to simply be consistently loud, "just because we *could* doesn't mean we *should*."[3] Similarly, re-recording mixer Paul Massey explains that extended use of the full complement of digital surround's effects "gets very tiring on the audience and in the end doesn't achieve a great deal if it is for a prolonged scene, because there is nothing new about it and there is nowhere to go with it."[4]

If Massey hints that one reason not to employ the digital surround style at all times is that it puts too much strain on the audience, he is not alone. Walter Murch echoes this assumption, arguing that the way our brains work makes multi-channel effects important for "embodied" sounds like music and ambiences but unnecessary (and perhaps overwhelming) for "encoded" sounds like dialogue.

> We are able to tolerate—even enjoy—the mixture of mono and stereo in the same film. Why is this? I believe it has something to do with the way we decode language, and that when our brains are busy with Encoded sound, we willingly abandon any question of its origin to the visual, allowing the image to "steer" the source of the sound. When the sound is Embodied, however, and little linguistic decoding is going on, the location of the sound in space becomes increasingly important the less linguistic it is.[5]

Tomlinson Holman succinctly sums up current thinking on usage of DSS's multi-channel capabilities: "You don't have a movie that's all surround sound or a movie that's all direct sound. . . . It depends on the degree of involvement that the filmmaker wants moment to moment and if you did it all the way, it would probably be boring."[6] This logic helps explain why movies rarely employ diegetic immersion for their entire length—though as filmmakers and audiences become more comfortable with the digital surround style, such use may become more prevalent.

Filmmakers agree that the decision on when and where to employ the digital surround style should ultimately be driven by the *story*. Filmmakers have a lot of aesthetic options at their disposal, and from those choose the tools they believe will best tell the story of the film at hand—those points where diegetic immersion is the best fit for a movie's narrative are the times the digital surround style will be utilized. Virtually every sound professional I interviewed noted that ultimately the *story* is the determining factor in their surround usage. Sound editor Hudson Miller's viewpoint is typical of others in the field: "I approach sound in a three-dimensional world as related to the characters, story, and their conflicts and adventures . . . my responsibility is to help the director and editor tell the *story*."[7] Suhail Kafity offers a similar perspective, explaining that "If the storyline allows [for surround] then you should utilize it, if the storyline isn't allowing it then I think you're putting it to waste, you shouldn't be forcing something into it. . . . I am all for using surround as much as possible—if not further than that if you can—depending on the storyline more than anything else."[8] Midge Costin is more succinct: "We'd do all kinds of work. Sometimes, that [surround] would be there and sometimes that wouldn't. It all comes down to, depends on, the story."[9] And Walter Murch neatly summarizes the guiding principle of sound design by noting that "The bottom line is that the audience is primarily involved in following the story . . . the right thing to do is ultimately whatever serves the storytelling."[10]

Since the creators of film sound always try to focus on what would best serve the *story*, occasionally they must sacrifice effects that might *sound* great, or creative ideas about multi-channel usage, when those elements do not serve the best interests of the film as a whole. As Glenn

Morgan puts it, "the one thing that can drive a [director] crazy is to have a craftsperson focus on what they've done and not how it supports the film."[11] In a character-focused, dialogue-driven scene, for example, aggressive use of surrounds may not be appropriate even if it would assist in creating envelopment. One sound designer cites a moment from *The Green Mile* (1999), where a bird chirp unexpectedly pops out of the left surround channel, as just such a *misuse* of surround. As he remarks, "you're watching the movie and it's totally filled with drama, not expecting a big action movie or anything like that, and then they do an effect like that, it's kind of distracting."[12] Alan Parker, director of *Angela's Ashes* and *The Life of David Gale*, concurs: "It's pretty great what you can do now with that (sixtrack) spread. On the other hand, it depends on the kind of movie, and for the *kind* of movies that I do, surround has to be used very judiciously."[13]

For other types of movies a surround-intensive, immersion-driven approach might be the ideal style. Consider as one example *Last Action Hero* (1993), the first movie released in the Sony Dynamic Digital Sound (SDDS) digital surround format. This film's narrative centers on a boy who, while watching the latest Schwarzenegger action film, finds the border between the onscreen world and his own magically eliminated. A bomb thrown by an onscreen villain, for instance, flies out of the screen and rolls down the theater aisle, blowing the young protagonist into the middle of the onscreen car chase he was just watching. For a movie whose story is quite literally *about* a breach in the boundary between the real world and the onscreen one, the digital surround style—which places the audience in the middle of the diegetic world—is a perfect fit. Indeed, from an aesthetic perspective, Sony chose exactly the right film to debut its new digital surround sound system; the film's one-sheet, showing Schwarzenegger flying off the movie screen into a watching audience, perfectly illustrates the aim of diegetic immersion.

Critics generally praised the concept of *Last Action Hero* but found fault with its particular execution. Roger Ebert described *Last Action Hero* as "more like a bright idea than like a movie that was thought through";[14] the *Austin Chronicle*'s Marc Savlov called it "a film with so much promise, you just want to hunt down everybody involved when you realize it doesn't deliver the goods";[15] and the *Washington Post's*

Desson Howe wrote that "Even if this intermingling of kid fantasy (meet PG-13 hero Austin O'Brien) and adult shoot'em-up, Hollywood insider jokes and cheap Arnold puns, doesn't completely bowl you over, it's clever and intriguing."[16] These mediocre reviews (and the film's lukewarm reception at the box office[17]) highlight the importance of story: problems with the film's script were given most of the blame for *Last Action Hero*'s shortcomings. Tellingly, critics and audiences did not mention the film's aggressive multi-channel mixing and DSS-based visual style, despite *Last Action Hero* likely being the most surround-intensive film that audiences at the time had ever seen. This suggests that its use of the digital surround style did not prove a distraction to filmgoers even at that early stage in the DSS era—probably because diegetic immersion *did* seem the appropriate aesthetic choice for a story about blurring the line between audience and screen.

INDUSTRIAL IMPEDIMENTS: MORE WORK IN LESS TIME

Despite the importance of story and narrative as a determining factor in deciding whether the digital surround style might *fit* a given movie, story is not the ultimate determinant of whether that style is actually *used*. Often aesthetic choices—particularly those in the aural realm—are limited by logistical and practical concerns. Schedule and budget constraints, for instance, invariably restrict the realm of aesthetic possibilities. Unfortunately, sound often seems to bear more than its fair share of this burden, probably because sound is *perceived* as easier to "fix in post." As one sound editor explains, "most [directors] are on such a tight leash, budget-wise, that they would rather spend the extra $10,000 over here to get the shot they want, or the costume they want because they know even if it sounds terrible now, we can make it sound good later."[18] Between this attitude and the fact that sound editing and mixing are nearly the final steps of making a movie (when other departments may have already gone over budget), frequently the sound department ends up with less time and money available than it would take to make the best soundtrack possible. This is at least part of the reason that some films for which diegetic immersion might have been an appropriate choice for the story material have *not* employed the digital surround style.

Since the aim of this chapter is to explain where and why the digital surround style is used, it is crucial to understand the complex factors that can *keep* filmmakers from using it by limiting their ability to use surround sound as fully or creatively as they would like. To be sure, the digital surround style is an *audio-visual* aesthetic incorporating a range of aural and visual tactics. It might seem, therefore, that these other elements could be utilized even in cases where DSS's multi-channel capabilities were not fully exploited. This is, however, not the case. Many of the digital surround style's key features—the ultrafield, non-traditional editing patterns, reliance on close shots, and so forth—are only made possible by the soundtrack's multi-channel capabilities. This means any factors that prohibit a film from employing the full range of DSS's surround abilities simultaneously hamper implementation of the *other* aspects—visual and aural—of the digital surround style. Put more simply, although surround sound is only one aspect of the digital surround style, it is the *foundation* upon which that style is built. Thus while the following discussion focuses specifically on obstacles to using DSS's multi-channel capabilities, any elements impeding use of *this* facet of diegetic immersion simultaneously inhibit adoption of the *rest* of the digital surround style.

Time and money, as mentioned above, are probably the two most significant elements constraining what can be done in *any* aspect of filmmaking—and these two factors are tightly tied together. Given that studios see no return on any money invested in a movie until it is actually in theaters, it has always been beneficial for the industry to keep overall production timelines as short as possible. This imperative has only been strengthened by the rising costs of producing and advertising a movie; the result is that filmmaking schedules overall have gotten tighter, as Richard King notes: "They want to shorten the time from the moment they pull the trigger on making the movie to the moment the movie's released. Every day that the movie's in process, a meter's ticking."[19]

These tight schedules increase the odds that shooting will run over schedule, pushing the start of post-production back. But with feature release dates usually set by studios "before they ever start shooting,"[20] post-production does not have the same luxury of running over—indeed, this phase must often actually be shortened even further than it otherwise would have been to "make up" time lost in production. This compression affects the sound department the most. Many sound design decisions—particularly those related to surround—cannot be finalized until the picture edit is done, as they depend upon what is onscreen at a given moment, where the cuts come, and what direction the camera is facing with respect to the various sound sources in the diegetic world. Yet the time between picture lock and release date is precisely where post-production time frames have tightened the most. Thanks in part to the compressed time between production and release, films are still being test-screened and picture edited almost until their release dates, requiring the sound department to devote time and effort that otherwise could have been spent on the creative aspects of sound design to conforming their work:

> There's more work to do in less time because they have test screenings all the time. With test screenings, the crew's job much of the time now is just keeping up with picture changes. So you don't have the creative time that you used to have to try different things. . . . Instead, you're sitting at your computer getting the new version of the picture and reconforming all the sound effects that you cut in the first time.[21]

Sound designer Ben Burtt neatly summarizes the effect of shortened schedules on sound design, lamenting that "tradition now is to do things faster than we were doing ten years ago—to deliver the film in a much shorter time. Therefore the people doing sound design really suffer more because they get hardly enough time to do anything other than throw stuff in the film and get out of there."[22]

One way to partially address the tighter post-production schedules is to hire the sound crew earlier in the process so they have more time to work before the release date. Sound designer Erik Aadahl points out that he was brought onto *Superman Returns* (2006) while the movie was still shooting, over seven months before it was released, and that "directors who have some clout, or movies with bigger budgets, are seeing extended [sound] schedules with smaller crews."[23] This approach can only do so much to combat the problem of compressed schedules, though, since making final decisions on things like surround usage requires seeing the final picture edit.

Most of the time, Aadahl goes on to say, this problem is addressed simply by hiring more sound editors. Sound editor Frank Warner (*Rag-*

ing Bull, St. Elmo's Fire) echoes this assertion: "Somebody gives a release date not thinking about anybody on the way up, so everybody has to follow. So they say, 'Go out and hire an army.'"[24] In practice, this makes it difficult for a sound crew to develop an appropriate overall aesthetic and agree on how various elements will be handled, especially given their limited time together: "Generally most sound editors are on a maximum of about twelve weeks before a release date, sometimes it is eight to six weeks before, depending on the schedule,"[25] and if this is turns out not to be enough, then the producers "just throw enough people at it in the next four weeks to get this done."[26]

Throwing more bodies at a soundtrack generates enough "person-hours" to get all the "necessary" sounds edited into the movie, but at the expense of creativity. Maintaining any sense of consistency when thirty or forty people are frantically cutting effects necessitates placing fairly severe limitations on each editor's creative freedom. On one movie, for example, each editor was responsible simply for spotting in one or two specific effects through the entire movie, with no control over the design of those sounds or how they would relate to any others.[27] Not surprisingly, sound editors do not like working this way—one described it as

> just a train wreck . . . when I cut I like to be very specific like you are telling a story with it. So each shot you are featuring something that you want to draw the viewer's eye and ear and attention to, and it is ridiculous having more than one person working on a scene, it is just crazy.[28]

TECHNICAL IMPEDIMENTS: THE CHALLENGES OF 5.1

Advances in technology have, to a degree, enabled sound editors and mixers to work more quickly. Powerful hardware and software systems such as Pro Tools (the film industry's standard tool for audio editing and mixing) make it easy to edit sounds together, try out different ideas, and automate things like volume changes—tasks that took much longer in decades past when all sound work was done on mag stock (35mm strips of magnetic tape, which had to be manually cut and spliced to edit sounds). Yet while audio post-production technologies have improved, sound designers, editors, and mixers have simultaneously been asked to do more with them. Even monophonic feature soundtracks have grown steadily more complex over the years, and digital surround sound compounds this problem by requiring sound crews to construct 5.1 different channels of audio. This increased workload tends to counterbalance any time savings from technological improvements.

Moreover, the technologies used in post-production have not fully accommodated the move *to* digital surround—much of the post-production process still occurs in monophonic or two-channel environments. Picture editing, for instance, usually occurs in a small room with one or two speakers of indeterminate quality that likely cannot reproduce the full dynamic and frequency range of DSS and certainly cannot reproduce its surround effects. Sound designers and/or editors may work in 5.1-equipped suites—though this has only recently become common—but the temp tracks they send the director and picture editor are heard in the (mono or stereo) picture editing suite. The complete soundtrack is generally not heard in a 5.1 environment until the movie makes it to the mixing stage. At this point, near the very end of the filmmaking process, the picture edit has been locked and all the elements of the soundtrack already created; what remains is to put these sonic pieces together and mix them into a coherent whole. Overall, this process makes it difficult for directors (or anyone else) to consider the multi-channel environment ahead of time, much less to think about how surround usage might affect the picture edit (or any other aspects of the soundtrack).

Even when 5.1 technology is used across the entire post-production workflow, it is unclear whether this ultimately saves time. Editors working in 5.1-equipped Pro Tools suites can do some surround panning throughout the process and deliver 5.1-channel automation to the dub stage (another name for the mixing stage), where it can be used as is or altered if necessary.[29] This has enabled sound designers to start playing with surround usage much earlier in the post-production process and even to get feedback from directors early on about their "taste" in this area[30]—shifts that make it easier to integrate surround effects into not just the soundtrack but the movie as a whole. At the same time, doing sound editing in 5.1 requires more *time* than doing so in mono or stereo, for two distinct reasons. First, as Steve Flick explains, "You're either editing or you're mixing. I mean, you can edit and mix, but if you're editing, you're not mixing." In other words, despite the obvious advantages to being able to work with surround in the editing suite, any time spent panning effects is time *not* spent recording, creating, editing, or synching new sounds. Second, to facilitate the creation of an immersive multi-channel environment, sound editors must plan ahead what is going to be in the various channels and give the re-recording mixer enough sounds to build different elements of the world in each.[31] This requires significant additional work on the editing side, notes David Bondelevitch:

> There are people that record in the field in 5.1 using various different formats . . . but frankly it's very cumbersome [to record and edit] that way. So what most people do is record in stereo, and then in the process of preparing it for the dub stage, "surround-ize" it by mixing multiple elements together and panning them different ways or let the mixer turn a bunch of stereo tracks into surround[32]

Regardless of the technical capabilities of modern audio editing suites, the bulk of multi-channel mixing, especially the creation of an enveloping soundfield, *has* to be done on the dubbing stage (where the final mix is created) for practical reasons related to the way sound behaves in different-sized spaces. Erik Aadahl elaborates:

> Things that require real precision like something very quick, like a bullet fly-by, those sorts of things I will do in my studio, but for the most part everything else will be done on the mixing stage. . . . Doing surround sound mixing in a small room is going to translate very differently to a big theater, so that sort of stuff I want to leave to the big theater mixing stage. Because you are pushing a certain amount of air and there are delays coming from the screen, and you really want to optimize it for the theatrical experience. I have found that stuff that sounds great in my room, when I move it onto a stage and listen to it there things are just a little different.[33]

To be sure, industrial practices and the traditional separation of mixing and editing also play a role in pushing surround decisions to the mix stage—sound editors do not want to be perceived as telling mixers "how to mix"—but even if these considerations did not exist, simple acoustics dictate that most surround mixing decisions would have to be left for the theater-sized dubbing stage anyway; in Aadahl's words, "it's just physics."[34]

Mixing well in surround inherently takes more work than mixing in mono or Dolby Stereo—there are more channels that need to be mixed and more decisions to be made about sound placements. Given that many of these decisions need to be made on the mixing stage, one would expect that movies today spend more time at the mix stage than their pre-digital-era predecessors. Yet even as the demands of the mixing process have grown, the time allotted for it has decreased. In some respects this is a logical development: the replacement of mag stock and film-based mixing stages with digital ones has reduced down-time and allowed for making quicker changes (including the ability to easily fix isolated problems in the mix without remixing an entire reel of film). These technical improvements certainly *do* save time during parts of the mixing process—but those small time-savings do not seem enough to offset the *increases* in mixing time that 5.1 requires. Even so, mixing schedules have continually shrunk in the years since the adoption of digital surround sound: "Now, you get six weeks to do the picture," notes Thom Ehle. "It used to take twelve weeks."[35] Indeed, the twelve-week schedule that used to be the norm is now considered "generous even by blockbuster standards,"[36] according to sound editor Andy Kennedy (*Batman Begins*, the *Harry Potter* series, *Hotel Rwanda*)—and that time must now include premixing, mixing, *and* the preparation of multiple foreign language versions. These tight schedules make it extremely difficult for mixers to implement the detailed panning and spatialization necessary for a complex surround scheme.

OPERATIONAL IMPEDIMENT: NON-LINEAR WORKFLOWS

Paradoxically, the same technologies that are used to justify shorter mixing schedules can actually *slow down* the mixing process. Just as mixing and panning can now be done in editing suites, today's mixers have access to the same range of editing capabilities as audio editors. Sometimes this can save a lot of time. In the era of mixing on mag stock it could take minutes or even hours to replace one sound effect with another if a director decided in the mixing stage that he wanted to do so; today, this can be done in seconds with a few clicks of the mouse. The downside to this increased flexibility, however, is that while in the mag stock era everyone avoided changing decisions about sound editing and design on the mix stage except where absolutely necessary, the enhanced capabilities of digital systems means that today the mixing stage frequently becomes an edit room:

> You will find that the entire dub screeches to a halt routinely now while they look for an alternate ADR [Automated Dialog Replacement] line or an alternate dialogue line or an alternate music cue that you had three weeks ago. And you'll just grind to a halt over these things that should have been taken care of in the editing room before you even got to the dub stage.[37]

Steve Flick's comment that it is impossible to simultaneously edit and mix is as true on the dub stage as in the editing suite. The more of a film's allotted mix time on the dubbing stage is spent doing this sort of work, the more the mix suffers, as this re-recording mixer attests:

> I'm sitting here on the clock, effects mixer sitting here on the clock, sound supervisor sitting on the clock; they have a sound editor, a dialogue editor, a music editor, a music supervisor, associate producer, a director, and producers . . . all sitting here while one person does something because they didn't communicate, and drags everything down to a grinding halt. . . . And what happens is the [movie] suffers . . . there's not enough time to do the stuff in the surrounds.[38]

The overall compression of the filmmaking process has exacerbated this problem by promoting parallel workflows: sound design, picture editing, and visual effects all take time but must all be handled in the same limited post-production window, meaning they must proceed concurrently. As the release date nears, the logistics of coordinating these parallel processes can become unwieldy, such as when a late-arriving visual effects scene limited the ability of one interviewee to tweak the soundtrack to match picture:

> I remember getting picture for it on a Friday at like 5 in the afternoon and we had premixing on it at 8 A.M. the next day, so I was working through the night getting that thing done, and then the music had length issues and so everyone was working, and it hits the final stage the day after that.[39]

Parallel workflows can also inhibit creativity in another way: "The director's focus is really split now. And you're lucky if you can get the director to pay attention when you need him."[40] Mixer Paul Massey notes that the last few years have seen

> increasing demands on directors at the end of their production periods . . . they could be on the scoring stage because the music is still being written, they could be catching up on ADR sessions that are coming in late, and they could certainly be doing color timing for the picture.[41]

Ultimately, this multi-tasking means that directors "usually show up at the final dub not having seen anything yet. . . . And at this point they're saying no to things that should have been handled in the editing room weeks ago."[42]

Even once the final mix begins, the sound crew must often work without the director present, meaning that if the director does not like some of the decisions made in his absence even *more* of a film's limited time on the mix stage may be taken up by changing work that has already been done. "I want the director there from Day One," opines mixer Richard Portman. "I can't tell you how many times I've made a mix where the director comes in three weeks after we've started and says he doesn't like any of the birds."[43] This problem affects all aspects of the mix, including surround usage:

> A lot of times we get asked to increase what we are putting in the surround and make the surround more of a ride . . . you try it again, and then typically they will say, "Oh, that's not quite working, is it? Maybe we were better off where we were before, or somewhere in between." And you go back there, and that happens a lot.[44]

Directors obviously *should* have a say in creative decisions like surround mixing; the issue is that modern post-production workflows make it increasingly difficult for them to be available for aesthetic discussions. The end result is an inefficient process that limits the creative potential of the soundtrack and the movie. Indeed, some directors themselves see the folly in this setup, as Richard King recalls:

> I'm working with an Australian director on another project and he was just confounded by this notion of me being on while they're still cutting the picture. He said, "Well, in Australia, we lock the picture and then the sound crew comes on and we're able to completely focus on the sound and work with the sound guys."[45]

Ultimately directors, sound designers, editors, and mixers all want to make each film as strong as it can be, but time frame, budget, and technical factors all conspire to make it quite difficult to give the soundtrack, and particularly surround sound, the attention it deserves. This is particularly true in the case of surround mixing—with tight time frames that do not allow for detailed panning, and directors not always around to discuss how they would like to use the surround channels, mixers often end up relying on traditional screen-centric practices regardless of what they feel would be best for the story: "When you are in that sort of a situation the mixers are going to be as conservative as possible just to not make any ripples in the water."[46]

PERSONAL AND PSYCHOLOGICAL IMPEDIMENTS

Not all the factors limiting the use of surround sound—and by extension the digital surround style—originate in post-production schedules, technology, or other such institutional factors: the individuals involved in making a movie play an important role as well. Directors with a television background and actors-turned-directors, for example, are perceived by many film sound personnel as being generally less interested in surround than directors coming from other areas. On a broader level, many directors and producers worry about the potential of surround effects distracting the audience and therefore choose to be less aggressive with their surround mixing than they otherwise might.

Historically, technologies intended to "put the audience in the movie" have often had precisely the opposite effect. 3-D is an excellent example: the polarized or two-color glasses needed to create 3-D images constantly remind viewers that they are only spectators in a theater.[47] Similarly, most audiences experiencing Sensurround would have been paying *more* attention (not less) to the space of the theater as they enjoyed the ride-like Sensurround rumblings. Given digital surround sound's analogous status as a new technology designed to "immerse" the audience, it is only natural for filmmakers to worry that surround effects may distract audiences from the cinematic experience as these earlier technologies did. DSS differs from 3-D and Sensurround, though, in an important way: it does not physically foreground itself as an apparatus. It neither requires filmgoers to don special gear (i.e., 3-D glasses) nor submits them to unusual physical sensations (i.e., perceptible shaking). To the conscious minds of audience members DSS goes largely unnoticed—they are already used to hearing sound in movies and are even moderately accustomed to surround sound.

Filmmakers' rational concerns about surround sound distracting the audience thus center not on the idea of multi-channel sound *itself* but on a particular *use* of it. Specifically, they worry about the "exit door effect," where one of the surround channels suddenly plays a recognizable, loud sound and the audience mistakenly believes it to come from the *space of the theater*. In other words, the exit door effect is a situation where—like 3-D or Sensurround—the apparatus calls attention to itself. Concerns over this effect can be traced back to the very first cinematic use of surround sound: supposedly some audience members ran screaming from *Fantasia* when, late in the movie, sounds suddenly appeared in the rear of the theater.[48]

It is crucial to recognize that the exit door effect is caused not by hard effects in the surrounds per se but rather by the audience's *reaction* to these. In everyday life, humans are accustomed to hearing sounds from all directions; Gary Rydstrom asserts that because of this, hard effects in the surrounds are not *inherently* problematic:

> My strong feeling about it is that since we are predators, the way we perceive the world is that we see up front, we see up front very well, and we hear all around us. We hear 360 degrees, we are always hearing 360 degrees, so why shouldn't movies reflect that reality when it's dramatically appropriate? I don't think audiences will be distracted, if you design the soundtrack properly, by a world that is going on behind them and offscreen.[49]

That some films *have* used the surround channels aggressively without distracting the audience confirms Rydstrom's suspicions; hard effects *can* be placed in the surrounds and remain unobtrusive "if you design the soundtrack properly."

The exit door effect may have been a legitimate concern in decades past, when surround sound—and especially the ability to put spot effects in the surrounds—was a rarity and hence drew audiences' attentions, but this is hardly the case today. William Whittington notes that "the introduction of sound technology often *recalibrates audience expectations* so that the newest advances—whether in the area of noise reduction or digital presentation—immediately become the standard."[50] With digital surround sound now nearly two decades old, audiences should have grown accustomed to movie soundtracks with spot effects in the surrounds, and the exit door effect should no longer be a concern. Tomlinson Holman points to precisely such a shift in audience expectations, noting that he cited the exit door effect as a key mixing concern in his 2000 book 5.1 Surround Sound but has since seen audiences grow more comfortable with surround: "the audience is trained today to accept that and to be less distracted by it; the 'exit sign effect' [an alternate name for the exit door effect] I talk about is not the problem it once was."[51]

But if contemporary audiences are accustomed to surround effects and the exit door effect need no longer be a major concern, then the fact that the industry does not take advantage of DSS's capabilities to the degree that audiences are ready to handle them suggests something deeper than a simple concern over distracting audiences. Casual comments such as "directors usually, by the way, don't like the surrounds"[52] and "a lot of [how you use surround] is the taste of the director and a lot of directors don't like stuff in the surrounds"[53] by sound personnel suggest that directors—at least in the view of their crews—often exhibit a surprisingly pervasive aversion to surround usage. One possible explanation for this bias is simply that many directors (like many film scholars) ascribe to an screen-centric model of cinema. Richard King, for instance, recalled working with a director who opposed putting *anything* in the surrounds, arguing "Well, the movie's on the screen. I'm hearing all this sound out here, but the movie's on the screen. I want to focus on the screen."[54]

The hesitancy of some directors to use surround sound to its fullest capabilities may also stem from more fundamental gaps in the way they think about sound *in general*. Most directors come from a writing, acting, or visual arts background; very few come out of sound departments.[55] As a sound designer candidly puts it, "a lot of directors don't have that much of an education in sound."[56] This makes the area of sound understandably scary for directors, who are expected to be in charge of *every* aspect of production and are ultimately responsible for the quality of the finished movie. Many directors, explains one sound editor, don't understand it at all and are afraid of it and don't react very well to the whole post-production process because they feel like the movie is getting out of their control. . . . And then they don't understand any of the technical aspects of it. They don't understand how creative it can be.[57]

Consequently, as a way to maintain some sense of control over the process, they emphasize the aspect of sound they understand, which is ensuring that the sound design matches what's onscreen: "The directors are all so literal, you just cover everything that they see and they're happy."[58] Sound editor Richard Anderson (*Raiders of the Lost Ark, The Lion King, Batman Returns*) describes this mentality: "Some directors are big on just hearing what they see visually, what we call, 'See a dog, hear a dog.' . . . It drives some directors nuts if there's a bark but they don't see the dog, even if it's played at a low level in the background."[59] The end result is sound design that is not as creative as it could be, particularly in terms of how it uses surround sound.

Obviously if many directors are—as some members of the film sound community feel—unwilling to use surround sound extensively, this significantly limits the number of films in which the digital surround style will be employed. But perhaps more important than what directors *actually* believe is that sound professionals have the *perception* that directors will only use surround (and sound in general) conservatively. Sound editors and mixers, as discussed earlier, work under tight time frames and hence endeavor to use their time as efficiently as possible. If they *think*—correctly or not—that more creative or aggressive uses of surround will not be deemed acceptable by a director or producer, they are unlikely to take the time to even *try* those uses. Thus surround use depends not only on a particular director's own proclivities but on a sound crew's beliefs *about* those proclivities. As the ways film sound personnel perceive directors' attitudes toward sound and surround change—sound designer Erik Aadahl comments that "directors and picture editors are getting a lot savvier about sound, how cool it is and how important it is for storytelling"[60]—DSS's multichannel capabilities will be utilized more extensively; at the moment, directors' perceived aversion to active surround channels significantly limits the way the 5.1 surroundscape is utilized.

DISTRIBUTION IMPEDIMENTS

The discussion above highlighted obstacles to utilizing surround sound during the production process. A significant additional problem, though, arises *after* production: the same soundtrack will sound strikingly different in different theaters, due to variations in exhibition spaces and setups. Walter Murch notes that "it used to be possible to imagine an average movie theater, but now with various-sized multiplexes and DVDs and in-flight films, etc. it is simply impossible to prefigure an ideal mix."[61] Even seemingly identical theaters can sound strikingly different, since many theaters do not have their sound systems installed and/or calibrated correctly. What audiences actually *hear*, then, may or may not be what the filmmakers heard on the mixing stage; "all bets are off [as to what audiences hear] because the exhibition end of it, that is just the one part of the chain that we just don't have control over," comments Aadahl.[62]

Even though all creative decisions have been made before a movie hits theater screens, exhibition-related concerns are a major factor in determining stylistic practices. When filmmakers cannot be sure that the exhibition end of the production chain will accurately reproduce their work, they *change* that work in an attempt to preemptively avert problems on the exhibition end. Chapter 2 offered a typical example, noting that many filmmakers intentionally mix their films "too loud" precisely to compensate for the fact that most theaters play soundtracks "significantly quieter than the films' directors intended them to be played."[63]

Exhibition problems affect surround mixing even more than other aspects of the soundtrack, simply because surround speakers are one of the most difficult parts of a sound system to set up properly—speaker placements, wiring, and volume levels all need to be calibrated correctly. Director Alan Parker laments that poor surround reproduction is common and has a negative impact on the audience experience:

> When you're irritated by strange sounds that are coming from behind, it probably isn't the fault of the mix, it's the fault of the quality of the speakers in the cinema, and how they've been balanced. . . . You never know if the surround speakers are turned down, or if they're too loud.[64]

Exhibitors, meanwhile, are often not even aware of problems with their sound systems; Walter Murch recalls having carefully remixed *American Graffiti* (1973) in surround for its 1978 re-release, then going to see it in a theater that "had no sound coming from their surrounds, and when I talked to the manager about it he assured me that this was because the 'director wanted it that way.'"[65]

Filmmakers have in some cases tried to alter the ways in which they use surround to minimize the impact of such exhibition shortcomings. Unfortunately, the only foolproof way to do so requires making the surround channels essentially superfluous to the mix—audio engineer Stephen Julstrom, for example, recommends that if particular sounds in the surrounds "are important to the movie, they [should be] mixed at a lower level in the front to guard against the unpredictable nature of surround reproduction in theaters."[66] Ben Burtt takes this principle a step further. After attending public screenings of *Star Wars* and *The Empire Strikes Back* and finding

> that due to poor equipment and managerial disinterest the narrative sound events he had carefully placed on the surround channel were simply not being properly played in theaters . . . Burtt initiated a new strategy, soon emulated by other sound designers. All narrative information would henceforth emanate from the front speakers, with the surrounds used for spectacular (but *nonessential*) enhancements.[67]

This strategy obviously prohibits using the surrounds in the active, integral-to-the-experience manner required by the digital surround style.

The exhibition situation today is somewhat less dire than that experienced by Burtt. Increased educational efforts by companies like Dolby, the THX certification program, and higher expectations from audiences (who often have 5.1-channel home systems) have helped decrease, if not eliminate, differences in surround reproduction across theaters. Yet exhibition concerns remain a factor in surround mixing—as Richard King explains, "I tend to go to theaters just to check them out when movies I've worked on are released and you know, the right surround speaker is out, or they're horrible. So that scares filmmakers [to want to] keep everything in the front and keep it safe."[68] Even in cases where theaters are correctly set up, differences in the sound systems themselves can cause some headaches. King notes, for example, that in certain situations there can be a major difference between 5.1-channel Dolby Digital and its 6.1-channel successor Dolby Surround EX:

> If you've got a number of sounds that you're placing in the back—like in *Master and Commander*, when you've got 500 pieces of shrapnel coming over your head, all that would just be a blur in 5.1. But in EX, you can actually place those things very specifically. It makes you duck much more than in 5.1. Unfortunately, the translation between 5.1 and EX is not good, and the movie doesn't sound as good in 5.1 as it does in EX because we mixed it in EX . . . we would've mixed it differently, I think, if we'd mixed it [in 5.1][69]

Sound editor Christopher Reeves succinctly sums up the dismal reality of exhibition: "If you're not on the actual mixing stage, the odds that you'll hear exactly what they want you to hear are very slim."[70]

With so many possible sources of errors in reproduction—translation from mixing stage to theater, incorrectly set up or calibrated theater sound systems, channel configuration discrepancies among even correctly installed and calibrated sound systems—filmmakers are pushed to be more conservative with surround mixing than they might wish, despite their conscious efforts to do "what's best for the film and what plays best in the best theaters."[71] Until filmmakers can have confidence that what they hear on the mixing stage will be what the audience hears in the theater, exhibition concerns will continue to inhibit aggressive use of DSS's multi-channel capabilities.

FACTORS PROMOTING SURROUND USE

The preceding discussion examined how production budgets and schedules, technical obstacles, industrial practices, fears of distracting the audience, visual-centric notions of cinema, and concerns about exhibition all serve to hinder experimentation with surround sound. Taken together, these diverse problems perhaps suggest a hopeless situation where it is nearly impossible to do anything creative with surround sound. But such a view underestimates the creativity and talent of the many filmmakers who find ways to push the boundaries of their art even in the face of all these difficulties. When interviewing sound designers, editors, and mixers, it is difficult not to be struck by how strongly they all *care* about making the best films possible, despite the numerous constraints that can make it difficult to do so. The creativity apparent in the best contemporary soundtracks indicates that when given the chance to use surround—or indeed *any* element of sound design—in whatever way works for the story, film sound professionals are eager to do so.

The above list of factors *inhibiting* the use of surround can in some ways be turned around to suggest situations or elements that *encourage* creative sound design and surround usage. For instance, a director who *does* understand the power of sound and encourages sound design that goes beyond what's onscreen should promote greater experimentation; in fact, several interviewees suggested that having such a director is the single biggest asset for which a sound team could ask. This type of director seems to take one of two forms. On one side are directors like James Cameron who will be engaged with the soundtrack through the whole process, will "sit through all the premixes," and are "very clear on what surround sound can do for them and what dynamic range can do for them in storytelling . . . Cameron will literally, for all practical purposes, grab your shoulders and pull the mixers up and down, he's so engaged in the process."[72] On the other are those like Steven Spielberg who hire talented, creative people and then

> sort of recede . . . they let their crew do what they do best. . . . [These directors] make really good movies, and they let probably everybody in their own departments do that. They're not afraid of it. They're creative in some ways, and then they bring in people who bring their ideas too.[73]

Intriguingly, interviewees did not indicate that one of these approaches was more effective than the other; the key is the fact *that* the director makes it clear he cares about sound, not *how* that care is manifested. As Midge Costin puts it, "it's important, I think, to have creative people *either* be interested at the start of the process, like early, really early, *or* to let people like me do their thing."[74] Of course, it is also possible for a director to incorporate elements of both methods. A couple different interviewees singled out Tony Scott (*Crimson Tide, Spy Game, Days of Thunder*) and Jerry Bruckheimer (*Pirates of the Caribbean, The Rock, Top Gun*)—the latter a producer, but one who maintains a lot of creative control on his films—as powerful filmmakers who communicate clear ideas about how they want to use sound without being as "hands on" as James Cameron.[75]

The other crucial element promoting creative sound design and surround use is *time*. If condensed schedules limit surround use, the reverse is true as well. The films interviewees cited as having the best surround design, and those they were the most excited to have worked on, were often those where the sound crews had more than the usual amount of time to try things out and really *design* the soundtrack. The classic example is *Apocalypse Now*, which famously spent years in post-production. But more recent examples show that this extended schedule is not unique, particularly for films with complex sound design schemes—the post-audio crew for the *Matrix* series, for instance, had over a year to work on each film.[76]

These two factors most frequently cited by interviewees as promoting creative surround use—sound-aware directors and longer sound design schedules—are not surprisingly often found together: a director who cares deeply about sound will try to allocate enough time and money for the sound crew to do their best work. On *Jurassic Park* (1993), for example, Spielberg brought on the sound crew months before shooting even started so they could develop the film's signature dinosaur sounds,[77] an approach also adopted by *Transformers* (2007; executive produced by Spielberg).[78] Similarly, the crew for Terrence Malick's *The New World* (2005) spent several months on audio post,[79] and Michael Mann spent almost seven months working on the soundtrack for *The Last of the Mohicans* (1992);[80] Malick and Mann are directors known for their attention to detail in all aspects of filmmaking, so it is hardly surprising that they take the time to carefully construct soundtracks for their films.

AMBIENCES

Recognition that multiple factors inhibit or encourage heavier use of surround sound—and thereby, indirectly, diegetic immersion—helps explain why some movies use the digital surround style more than others but does not answer the fundamental aesthetic question of where and why filmmakers may *want* to use this style in the first place. As noted earlier, the universal feeling among the filmmakers I interviewed was that surround sound and the digital surround style should be used where "appropriate" to the story. The remainder of this chapter will consider the practical implementation of that abstract notion, examining *how* diegetic immersion functions to serve the narrative in actual films. Obviously it would be impossible to offer a comprehensive catalog of all possible uses of the digital surround style; instead, this survey will focus on several of the most *common* ways in which films deploy it.

The spread of the diegetic world's ambient sounds throughout the multi-channel sound space into the space of the theater is perhaps the simplest version of diegetic immersion, literally enveloping the audience in the sounds of the onscreen world. It is also considered a relatively "safe" use of surround sound, as ambient sounds tend to be unobtrusive and contribute to the audience's sense of envelopment without drawing attentions to the multi-channel apparatus itself. Indeed, Tomlinson Holman observes that surround ambiences are often so subtle that the audience doesn't even know that the surrounds are doing anything unless they suddenly shut off and the soundfield collapses back onto the screen: "Most people do not recognize that fact, that [the surrounds] are doing a lot, even when they're 'silent.'"[81] Echoing Holman's point is Marti Humphrey, who points out that "some of the best movies out there are things that, if you went ahead and you muted the surrounds, you'd go, 'What's missing?' But they're not beating you over the head that they're playing all the time."[82]

Precisely *because* multi-channel ambiences so often go unnoticed, they seem a somewhat "boring" use of surround. Ambiences are, however, one of the most important elements of sound design, and as highly constructed as any other component of the soundtrack. As re-recording mixer Richard Portman (*The Pelican Brief, The Hand That Rocks the Cradle, The Deer Hunter*) puts it, "I know that I can never play the real ambience in a movie. They always want it to be real, but you can't."[83] And as part of this construction, at one point or another nearly all contemporary films deploy some of DSS's unique abilities. Steve Flick even comments that to him, surround sound is much more valuable for its capacity to create an environment around the audience than for its capability to place "spot effects" in the surrounds.[84]

This reaction hints at one reason for the ubiquity of surround sound ambiences: they take advantage of the multi-channel environment without noticeably straying from the traditional "one wall" principle. Indeed, even those who seem the most wary of more "obvious" uses of surround appreciate its ability to create fuller background atmospheres. "I think the 5.1 environment still is centered at the screen," Mike Knobloch opines. "The reason there are speakers around you is to create this *environment* around you [even while] the focal point is still in front of you."[85] David Bondelevitch likewise argues that ambiences "work well in the surrounds" because they do not draw the audience's attention away from the screen.[86]

Multi-channel ambiences ultimately form the foundation of diegetic immersion—after all, the easiest way to start making audiences feel they are in the diegetic world is through creating the right ambient space. For example, Richard King explains how much *Signs* (2002) relied on precise, deliberate use of atmospheric sounds: "The ambiences were very carefully laid out with the goal that they wouldn't feel like they were carefully laid out; they were natural. You were just *in* a cornfield, or *in* a small town in Philadelphia, or whatever."[87] And because ambient sound so often goes unnoticed, it has the power to affect audiences without them noticing. Continuing with *Signs* as an example, King describes how minute changes in ambience can subtly alter the mood of a scene:

> Some scenes at night there would be crickets and some scenes there wouldn't be crickets, and the absence of crickets might not be obvious or cause noticeable alarm, but would maybe make you a little uneasy. . . . It's night, it's summer, and there's no crickets. You're not really thinking about that, you're thinking about the scene, but it makes you uneasy.[88]

To be sure, background ambiences were an important part of sound design long before digital surround sound arrived. Since the dawn of sync sound, films have always employed *some* sort of ambient sounds, even if sometimes only those as consciously unnoticed as "room tone" (the usually unheard sounds present in any space, even a seemingly silent one). But surround sound offers the key ability to expand these

5.1. 2002's *Signs* carefully places ambient sounds in the multi-channel soundscape to create a complete, immersive environment that subtly changes with the mood of the film. This seemingly normal cornfield becomes an eerie, threatening place when the sounds of insects and birds disappear.

background sounds beyond the onscreen world into the space of the *theater*, implying that the audience is *in* the diegetic world, not outside watching it through a window (i.e., the screen). "What surround really does most effectively is allow you to paint the environment the story's going to be told in," sound editor Hudson Miller notes.[89]

Christopher Reeves offers an example from the television world. To convey the sense that the lawyers in a courtroom drama rented cheap, grungy offices, the sound crew simultaneously played three separate exterior backgrounds during scenes in the office, suggesting that the walls were thin and the wider offscreen world was leaking in. But, Reeves noted, "if you watched it on a stereo TV, almost all of that disappeared" since the surround information was missing.[90] Suhail Kafity recalls that even the single rear channel of Dolby Surround (the home version of Dolby Stereo, used for standard-definition television broadcasts since the 1980s) offered possibilities for ambient sound design far beyond what would have been possible without surround:

Hill Street Blues is a primary example—there was so much going on that if you did that show in mono it would lose seventy percent of the sound that was in it. . . . When you were in that stationhouse you were surrounded with sound. And while you don't always see a whole lot of people, it gave you the impression that this was a very busy area.[91]

In real life sound is all around us, Kafity remarks, and the creation of a believable diegetic environment thus virtually *requires* surround sound: "You stand in the middle of a park and close your eyes and pay attention to the sound, there are all sorts of things happening all over the place. So on a movie or a television show you can get the same results [with surround sound]."[92]

The *Hill Street Blues* example poses the question of the difference between digital surround sound and its predecessor Dolby Stereo when it comes to ambiences, since a version of the latter system proved effective in that show. In considering the distinction between the two, it is noteworthy that many of those interviewed for this project specifically mentioned the discrete stereo surround configuration of DSS (i.e., its dual surround channels) as a significant improvement over Dolby Stereo's single surround channel when it comes to creating ambiences. One reason is that the capabilities of 5.1 allow filmmakers to be more exact in the environments they build. To once more cite Richard King on the ambience-driven soundtrack of *Signs*, "the goal was to be very precise because Night [M. Night Shyamalan, the film's director] is very precise in his writing and the way he makes his films. . . . I would literally work with him on placing a bird in a specific spot or a kind of cricket."[93] The limitations of the Dolby Stereo matrix simply preclude this level of precision in placing sounds. *Aliens* (1986), a Dolby Stereo–era release, builds some complex ambient spaces for the windswept surface of planet LV-426 and for the alien "nest," but these environments do not feel as "enveloping" as those in *Signs*, since hard effects originate only from the screen and the mono surround channel cannot move sounds—even background noises—around or through the audience.

DSS also allows ambiences to offer more information about the diegetic world than was possible with Dolby Stereo. When the drilling crew arrives on the surface of the meteor in *Armageddon* (1998), for instance, offscreen winds moving through the sound space "establish a character—it sounds like the meteor is chomping on something in the background,"[94] giving the environment a personality of its own. The same principle applies in more realistic environments as well. Steve Flick notes that

> in *Predator* they did a lot of surround work specifically cut for the surrounds. . . . A couple [scenes] are in a river, a couple are in a village, but they all have active surrounds, and you wanna fill up the space left and right to see that they're in a place. And the shape of the place changes with the distance that you place the birds or the events or whatever squealing in the distance.[95]

This method of implying spatial information through multi-channel environments is a crucial part of how ambiences fit into the digital surround style, and it requires more than the pseudo-four-channel Dolby Stereo system can provide. As one example, *Se7en* (1995) builds its soundtrack on the foundation of an omnipresent "sounds of the city" background. Accosting us with different sounds from all sides when outdoors (and from whichever sides are near windows when indoors), the inescapable, enveloping city ambience creates a feeling of being literally hemmed in by people on all sides. On the other end of the population spectrum, the background ambience of the deserted island in *Cast Away* (2000) uses a limited palette of wind, water, and rustlings; this sparse soundtrack serves as a constant reminder of the absence of humans. The discrete 5.1 mix also orients us to the space, with the channel placement and perceived distance of the ocean waves providing bearings in an environment with few obvious landmarks—here the ultrafield is clearly at work, using the background sounds to orient us better than the visual track alone can. Finally, through an ever-shifting mix of its few elements the soundtrack does at least as much as the visuals to keep us apprised of the upcoming weather that dictates many of the main character's decisions, often alerting us to upcoming storms well before we can see them.

Perhaps the best proof that DSS's multi-channel capabilities are crucial to building immersive ambiences is simply that filmmakers spend the time and money to create unique sounds for each channel. Occasionally sound crews will actually record five-channel ambient spaces like those used in *Master and Commander* (2003) and *The End of the Spear* (2005).[96] More often, individual recordings are combined to build up multi-channel ambiences, as Christopher Reeves explains: "When you talk surrounds, absolutely, we cut surrounds, we cut backgrounds for surrounds. . . . When it comes to walla groups, we'll cut four groups of walla for surround—walla doesn't usually go into the center channel."[97] It is not enough to simply spread the same sound to all the speakers: building complete sonic environments requires using subtly different sounds in each channel. If filmmakers did not believe strongly that the soundtrack (and film) ultimately benefited from this careful construction of multiple unique channels of audio, they would hardly devote significant effort or time to it.

Digital surround sound offers more than just increased channel separation, of course, and some of these capabilities also aid in the creation of sonic environments. DSS's large dynamic range and low inherent noise, for example, allow for very quiet, very subtle ambiences. *Signs*, as discussed earlier, relies for much of its eerie atmosphere on just-barely-noticeable ambient sounds that are only possible because of these technical capabilities. Other horror/suspense films also provide excellent examples of the application of digital surround sound technology to ambiences. *What Lies Beneath* (2000), for instance, employs both ends of the dynamic spectrum, with scenes (such as that where one character finds a bathtub in her home inexplicably filled with water and then sees a ghost) juxtaposing subtle, barely heard room ambiences with loud score music, effects, and screaming. The careful play of silence and sound in *Joy Ride* (2001) are similarly only possible in a digital 5.1-channel environment. Non-horror films also take advantage of DSS's unique capabilities in creating their environments; the ambiences of *Finding Nemo* (2003), as one example, are founded on a "bubbly" sound that pervades the underwater world, with the bubbles in each channel differing slightly to subconsciously hint at different things in each direction. Depending on the onscreen action, the bubbling alternately increases to signify activity and life, or disappears entirely (like the aforementioned crickets in *Signs*) to suggest danger. The bubbling throughout is subtle and low in the mix—only the high signal-to-noise ratio of DSS enables it to stay audible even at its lowest volume.[98]

A final way in which DSS systems enhance filmmakers' ability to create environments is that the discrete 5.1-channel configuration can reproduce *multiple* ambiences—that is, more than one diegetic space—simultaneously. This is a technique impossible to achieve with Dolby Stereo.[99] *American Beauty* (1999) demonstrates this strategy in a scene near the film's end. Carolyn Burnham (Annette Bening) is sitting in a parked car and rolls down the driver's side window to reveal the front of her house. Initially our aural and visual positioning is inside the car with her—in particular, the soundtrack is dominated by rain beating down on the car's metal roof. The image track then cuts to Carolyn's point of view as she rolls down the driver's side window. As the window comes down, the front center channel suddenly provides sound from outside the car—we now hear the rain directly (rather than muffled through the window). On the surface this seems a rather pedantic example of sound mixing; it ties the sound space directly to the image space, revealing the "outside" sounds only when a window is open so these sounds could be heard from the camera's position. Yet the non-center channels remain "inside" the automobile (playing the "rain on roof" sounds), matching our aural perspective with Carolyn's—like her, we are enclosed in one space with only one opening through which to experience whatever may be outside, so we hear the outdoor space from one channel and the indoor space from the others.

With five discrete full-range channels, up to five spaces could theoretically be simultaneously presented in a digital sound system. Mike Figgis's semi-experimental *Timecode* (2000) does not go quite this far but comes close with *four* distinct spaces. The film is designed around a visual gimmick: the narrative plays out in four ninety-minute continuous shots, each in one corner of the split-four-ways screen. At any given time up to four different scenes may be present visually— and at moments Figgis takes the novel approach of including all four in the soundtrack, with each assigned to a different audio channel. That is, at one point in the film the sounds associated with the lower left image play out of the left surround channel, those from the upper left image out of the front right channel, and so on, with no apparent organizational system dictating which image is associated with which audio channel at any given time (the pairings change). This configuration keeps the audience aware of the variety of scenes playing out at once; additionally, it gives the audience members freedom to choose where to focus their attentions. The end result is a curious blurring of the line between filmmaker and audience, as the decision about which of the four images is most important at a given moment shifts back and forth between the audience and the director. *Timecode* is an admittedly unusual film, but one whose style is only made possible by DSS's capacity for presenting multiple spaces at once.

SETTING UP THE SONIC ENVIRONMENT

Of course, digital surround sound's ability to build a complex ambient space—or even multiple spaces—does not mean that it is always a good idea to make environments as "full" as possible. In particular, filmmakers stress the need to remain aware of the possibility of distracting the audience with "unexpected" sounds. Steve Flick explains:

> You have to understand immediately what is coming in the surrounds to have something that you're not going to turn and look at . . . it has to be a conventional sound, or associated with a vector that comes to and from the screen. Like the sounds of rain or birds offscreen—we all know what that is and can accept them in the surrounds as an ambient element. They just have to be immediately identifiable to an audience in order to have them accept it as part of an ambient sequence.[100]

In other words, while audiences will almost always readily accept certain recognizable sounds as part of the ambience and will accept others *if* they have already been introduced as part of the diegetic world, sounds not fitting into either of these two categories can prove distracting. With ambient sounds, this concern is relatively minor—most of the time the background sounds of a space are immediately apparent as just that. But some movies aggressively place *all* kinds of sounds in the surrounds—including hard effects and even dialogue—without any problems.

This recalls Gary Rydstrom's comment that "I don't think audiences will be distracted, if you design the soundtrack properly, by a world that is going on behind them and offscreen."[101] He was speaking about the exit door effect specifically, but his remark more generally suggests ("design the soundtrack *properly*") that particular sound design approaches permit more aggressive uses of both surround sound and diegetic immersion ("a world that is going on behind them and offscreen"). The key here is that just as audiences learn over time how to understand movies, and can even gradually adapt their viewing practices to new filmmaking styles, each individual film also trains them about how to watch and listen *to that film*. Using the same hard effect in the surrounds late in two different movies, for instance, could be perfectly effective in one but pull the audience completely out of the story in the other. Flick offers the hypothetical example that

> you could have unmotivated abstract sounds coming out of the surrounds, which would exist for the reason of their own being rather than in service of any kind of linear story. And *once you've got an audience accustomed to that*, then you could use the surrounds abstractly and non-synchronously all the time.[102]

Ultimately, in other words, whether the audience will unthinkingly accept a given multi-channel effect or be distracted by it depends on what has come before.

Utilization of the digital surround style at *any* point in a movie thus requires establishing at least the possibility of doing so early in the film. In a sense, a film's opening minutes create a contract with the audience about the "palette" of stylistic tools the movie might employ, and going outside this palette later can be jolting. As one sound editor explains, the first reel of a film is where you "find the sound of the picture."[103] This way of thinking about sound design actually mimics other areas of production—screenwriters, for example, are taught that they need to grab the reader's attentions in the first ten or fifteen pages of a script, as it becomes nearly impossible to captivate the reader later. The same holds true for sound design, and indeed virtually all aesthetic elements of filmmaking; Walter Murch has written, for instance, that "if the amount of music in a film's first thirty minutes is beyond some critical threshold, you create expectations in the audience that require you to keep going, adding more music."[104] Thus if the surround channels will see significant use late in a movie, they should be used early on as well so the audience gets, in Aadahl's words, "tenderized to the surrounds."[105]

Cluing the audience in to a film's sonic palette can take a number of forms. The most basic of these is using multi-channel ambiences to immerse the audience as discussed above. Ambience "is where you create your base," Glenn Morgan explains. "In the 5.1 setup, you need a good solid base to start from. After that, everything else is different—you can enhance on that."[106] For films that plan to make more extensive use of surround than ambiences and the occasional fly-by, proportionately more aggressive surround effects are required early on. As Paul Massey notes, "If you have a fairly flat film that is fairly upfront on the screen and then suddenly you go crazy in the surround, it is all out of proportion, or all out of whack";[107] Midge Costin echoes Massey's point, commenting that "you don't want to be pulling everybody away and have those hard effects [later] unless there are a lot of backgrounds that have hard effects."[108]

Surround-intensive 5.1-channel environments, isolated hard effects, or a combination thereof can all work to set audience expectations for aggressive surround usage when used early in a movie. *Harry Potter and the Half-Blood Prince* (2009), for example, opens with a lengthy tracking shot following several evil characters as they fly across London, burst through a wall, and finally land in a small shop. Throughout, the soundtrack aggressively pans effects around the 5.1 soundscape—pieces of the blown-up wall fly from the front to the rear of the theater, wind whooshes by in the narrow city streets, and so on. By the time this first shot is completed, the audience is conditioned to the complex surround mixing later scenes will employ. The first shot of *Terminator 3: Rise of the Machines* (2003) uses the multi-channel soundscape equally aggressively: a missile flies from the right rear channel through the right front one and into the center channel before exploding, creating a sonic shock wave that expands out through the entire soundscape. With its active multi-channel soundscape thus established from the start, the film is able to aggressively mix sounds around the 5.1 soundscape throughout its length without ever drawing the audience's conscious attentions to the surround channels.

A slightly more subtle, but equally effective, mixing strategy is demonstrated by the opening of *Transformers: Revenge of the Fallen*. During the Dreamworks and Paramount opening logos, the soundtrack plays mechanical-electronic sounds (matching the sonic style of the film's signature "transforming" effects) that move throughout the 5.1 soundscape. More specifically, they spatially track visual elements, moving in correlation with the clouds of the Dreamworks logo and the flying stars of the Paramount one. Even before the movie proper

5.2. The opening shot of *Terminator 3: Rise of the Machines* (2003) reveals a city at night about to be hit by a missile streaking in from screen right. By smoothly panning the sound of the missile to match its image as it flies by, the movie immediately accustoms the audience to hard effects moving throughout the 5.1 soundscape. After the missile hits its target, the resulting blast wave reinforces this aggressive multi-channel mixing strategy by spreading out from the screen into the surround channels.

begins, this mix has already accustomed the audience to a full, active surround environment tightly tied to the visuals but extending their world beyond the screen—and the film exploits this acclimatization by utilizing an ultrafield-driven, heavily spatialized soundtrack in nearly every scene.

A film planning intensive surround use must not only establish audience expectations for this at the beginning but also follow through *on* those expectations with some consistency. Otherwise it risks undoing that setup work, as *Million Dollar Baby* (2004) demonstrates. The film begins with fairly aggressive surround usage, but after the opening scenes goes long stretches with almost no use of the surrounds for anything other than subtle ambient sounds. This extended segment of limited surround usage "re-trains" the audience *not* to expect noticeable sounds in the surrounds. Then, near the film's end, the movie suddenly uses a "hard effect" (a door slamming) in the right surround speaker, which takes the audience right out of the movie—many people mistake it for the sound of someone actually entering or leaving the theater itself in a literal "exit door" effect.[109] Had this door slam occurred in the first half of the film when the multi-channel environment was more continually activated, or had the film maintained its aggressive use of the 5.1 soundscape beyond the opening scenes, this sound would have been immediately understood as part of the soundtrack; the reason the effect is distracting here is that audience expectations have been re-calibrated to a screen-centric mix.

The argument here is not that major aesthetic shifts *cannot* take place after the opening scenes of a film, but that such changes are likely to distract the audience. A few films have successfully altered their *visual* aesthetics over the course of a film: *Brother Bear* (2003), for instance, abruptly changes the screen aspect ratio when its protagonist is transformed from a human into a bear, and in the most famous shift of all *The Wizard of Oz* (1939) transitions from monochromatic sepia to full-spectrum color when Dorothy reaches the land of Oz. In both of these examples, though, there is a major narrative shift occurring at the point where the visual aesthetic changes. The same holds true in the aural realm. *The Matrix* (1999) is a good example in this category, as its soundtrack is more surround-intense for scenes inside the Matrix than for those in the "real world"; *Last Action Hero* follows a similar strategy in differentiating the "movie world" from the "real world." Both of these films, notably, *begin* in the world where surround effects are more intense to prepare the audience for the same effects later—it is much more difficult to begin with a screen-centric mix and move to a fuller soundscape.

An exemplary example of how to "tenderize" the audience to aggressive surround mixing is the beginning of *The Rock* (1996), which takes a simple but effective approach to setting up the sonic environment and the feeling of immersion. It begins with the Hollywood Pictures and Simpson/Bruckheimer Productions company logos; each of these is accompanied by a continuous 5.1-channel mix of the musical score (which bounces a guitar beat around the front three speakers) and the sounds of a military skirmish. The Simpson/Bruckheimer logo also includes its customary thunderstorm sound effects, which nicely play out in all five main channels. After these logos, the visual track uses four brief shots to run a couple of opening credits, then cuts to its title, spelled out in capital letters and filled with flames. During the four shots prior to the title, the 5.1-channel music and battle sounds continue unabated and even increase: more instruments are added to the score, the battle comes to include explosions (all around) and radio chatter (front center channel), and the LFE channel gradually gets louder and louder. The score and battle sounds continue as the title appears but are drowned out as the title rushes out through the audience, to the back of the theater, and the soundtrack momentarily engulfs us in a 5.1-channel fiery roar. Thus from its very beginning, the film accustoms us to the surround environment, with the image and sound of the title itself making clear promises about what *The Rock* will offer: excitement, fire, and total immersion (in both the movie and the soundtrack).

Surround sound and immersion are not reserved for action movies alone, of course. The opening of *Cars* (2006) sets up the digital surround style even better than that of *The Rock*, employing virtually all the visual and aural elements of this aesthetic in its opening minutes. The film opens in blackness, with a faint whisper of engines and an indistinct, distant-sounding crowd in the surrounds—already the movie is using subtle sounds in the surrounds to build out an environment around the auditorium and hint at an expansive world outside the immediate space portrayed at the moment. Out of this almost-silence comes the first sound demanding conscious attention: Lightning McQueen's pre-race pep talk to himself, mixed to the center channel (like most dialogue) while the screen remains black. That a *sound*, rather than an *image*, opens the movie is a telling sign that the soundtrack will bear a significant share of the storytelling responsibilities. As Lightning's monologue continues, the blackness and voiceover alternate with brief flashes from a race; each of these visual flashes is accompanied by equally brief car sound effects that whip around the space of the theater to match the onscreen action. These shots are, in keeping with the digital surround style, close shots not revealing much of the background or space around them and are cut so quickly that they would be hard to identify as an auto race without the associated aural clues.

Having already established the centrality of the soundtrack and blatantly panned sounds around the multi-channel environment in its first minute, the movie finally offers a visual of its main character as Lightning's dark transport trailer opens up and he starts rolling into the light. Here again, close shots are used to reveal details of Lightning before we get a brief view of him in his entirety as he exits the trailer; the soundtrack opens up at the same time, with the sounds of racing and cheering now noisily surrounding us on all sides, no longer muffled by the walls of the trailer. As the movie continues with the opening race scene, it makes aggressive use of the ultrafield, with sound effects panned throughout the auditorium and the soundtrack as a whole cutting with each new shot in the image track. Visually, meanwhile, the movie holds to all the visual traits of the digital surround style. We see the race in a quick succession of close-up shots, mostly taken from right in the middle of the action as cars drive over, around, or even *through* the implied camera position. To be sure, the movie does include a few wider shots to establish the scale of the space (a huge stadium), to make jokes (as when the "wave" is performed by the cars in the stands turning their headlights on and off in unison), or to get exposition out of the way (i.e., showing the lead cars together in one shot to establish their relative positions in the race). But the bulk of the shots of the race itself are taken from within the action. As these shots are cut together, little attention is paid to traditional continuity rules—a shot of cars whizzing from left to right, for example, may be immediately followed by the same cars moving right to left.

In only its first few minutes, *Cars* has already deployed virtually all the stylistic elements—aural and visual—of the digital surround style, surrounding us with the world of the story and accustoming us to the diegetic immersion aesthetic, including heavy use of multi-channel panning and hard effects in the surrounds.[110] The race that begins the movie is an action-packed event and thus a relatively easy place to introduce these elements. But the promise of diegetic immersion offered during the race is met throughout the film, which employs DSS-based stylistic traits even in simple dialogue scenes. And precisely because the film's opening "tenderizes" the audience to an active, all-around-the-theater soundscape, the rest of the film can freely mix any and all sounds to anywhere in the theater. In fact, as noted earlier, *Cars* even frequently pans *dialogue*: Lightning's trial, for instance, features dialogue panned to match both characters' movements—for example,

Doc Hudson making his way to the judge's podium—and their positions in the diegetic world, as when the (offscreen) citizens of Radiator Springs are heard in the surrounds cheering for Lightning to "fix the road." Throughout the movie, these effects all work together to create the perception of being *inside* the diegetic world, not just watching it.

POINT OF VIEW AND POINT OF AUDITION

A few minutes into the opening race scene of *Cars*, a collision between two racers quickly cascades into a massive accident. Dozens of cars spiral out of control or crash; the track is soon littered with disabled vehicles and clouded with smoke. Throughout this sequence, the film's use of the digital surround style continues: cars hurtle through the air right past the camera; the image track rapidly cuts between many angles, with no regard for the 180-degree rule; and the visuals are matched by screams and other sounds whipping through the theater. Lightning, who was near the back of the pack, must now make his way through the carnage. And here the movie introduces a different filmic device: *point of view* (POV). Suddenly we see and hear what Lightning himself would see and hear. Onscreen, the crowded track races toward us, Lightning's red hood barely visible at the bottom of the screen and stationary in our field of view, as if we were looking out the front windshield (the location of vehicles' eyes in *Cars*). In the aural realm, sounds whiz by and around us from Lightning's perspective as he weaves through the crowded mess—in film studies parlance, we experience his "point of audition," or POA. These POV/POA moments are intercut with wider shots showing Lightning making his way until he has safely navigated the wreckage, at which point the movie abandons the character's literal perspective in favor of its previously established third-person viewpoint.

The brief moments here (and later) of literally seeing and hearing things just as Lightning would are among the most immersive of the entire movie. In fact, the use of point of view and/or point of audition is a doubly immersive technique, one that goes beyond putting filmgoers inside the world of the story to putting them in the perspective of a specific character *within* that story world. This suggests point of view serves the same underlying *goal* as previously discussed elements of

5.3. A literal point-of-view shot from the opening race of *Cars* (2006). The camera presents Lightning McQueen's perspective as he tries to make it through a pileup on the racetrack; the front of Lightning's hood can be seen at the bottom of the frame.

the digital surround style but offers a more "precise" form of diegetic immersion. As Benjamin Wright notes, POV/POA "transforms the listening subject into a surrogate perceived, and a participant in the diegetic audiovisual space";[111] similarly, Rick Altman writes that "point-of-audition sound always has the effect of luring the listener into the diegesis not at the point of enunciation of the sound, but at the point of its audition. . . . Instead of giving us the freedom to move about the film's space at will, this technique locates us in a very specific place— the body of the character who hears for us."[112] POV/POA, then, pushes the digital surround style to its extreme, placing the audience not just in the onscreen world but at a single and singular location within it.

While POV/POA sequences may lock the audience into a very particular position within the diegesis of a film, they conversely offer filmmakers the perceived freedom to be more experimental, particularly in the aural realm. Filmmaker and Northwestern University Radio/TV/Film professor David Tolchinsky observes that many of the most "interesting" uses of sound in movies—that is, those places where the soundtrack does something unusual or provocative—seem to occur during point-of-view sequences.[113] Sound editor Midge Costin agrees, saying that "the most wonderful opportunity to do something interesting [with the soundtrack] is point-of-view sequences"[114] The idea that POV sequences spark interesting uses of sound makes sense: if "interesting" sounds are those that violate standard practices, then logically POV scenes should have "interesting" sound since point of view is not the "normal" mode of filmmaking but rather a specialized technique that, as in the scene from *Cars* described above, is generally used only for brief portions of a film. Directors, as discussed earlier, are sometimes hesitant to break with conventions of "what has worked before" unless given a specific reason to do things differently, and POV sequences offer just such a reason: for a POV scene to be read as such, it *must* use a style distinct from the rest of a movie. With POV scenes necessarily shot and edited differently from the surrounding sequences, it is not surprising that their soundtracks function differently as well. Furthermore, many standard production practices have become adopted as such because over the years they have been proven to "work"—that is, they help make films easily legible to audiences. Since a given character's worldview may *not* make perfect sense, legibility is less of a necessity in POV scenes than in other parts of a film.

Because POV/POA sequences are inherently both immersive *and* aesthetically non-traditional, they are a perfect fit for the digital surround style. Often, as in the *Cars* example, a movie that has already adopted the visual and aural techniques of that style for its non-POV segments simply continues exploiting them during POV sequences. In other films, those stylistic elements are exploited more freely during POV scenes than during the rest of the movie. A typical example is the abortion clinic sequence in *Juno* (2007), where the title character (played by Ellen Page) sits in the waiting room a few moments before becoming annoyed and leaving. Though this scene is not *shown* through Juno's POV, the soundtrack clearly presents her psychological *perspective* on the scene. As Juno sits, the sounds of the various people around her begin to build up and spread through the 5.1 environment, gradually surrounding both her and the audience. Heard in a monophonic or Dolby Stereo environment, the perceived effect here would be one of increasing volume, intimidating enough in itself. The discrete 5.1 configuration of DSS, however, allows for each sound to maintain its unique character and for the audience to empathize with Juno; the feeling of claustrophobia is overwhelming and becomes too

5.4. The title character of 2007's *Juno* waits in an abortion clinic. As the noises of the other people in the waiting room get louder and spread out into the surround channels, the audience, like Juno, becomes overwhelmed. It is a relief for both Juno and the audience when she runs out of the clinic and these sounds abruptly disappear. This sound design strategy intentionally draws attention to the multi-channel environment.

much to take, just as having an abortion is ultimately more than Juno feels she can handle. While it can be risky to use the surround channels so aggressively in a film that employs a screen-centric soundtrack, in this situation it works perfectly since the enveloping soundscape is *supposed* to draw attention to itself.

Just as DSS enables filmmakers to create detailed multi-channel ambiences that were simply not possible with earlier systems, its unique capabilities can communicate complex POV/POA scenarios beyond the abilities of monophonic or Dolby Stereo soundtracks. One exceptionally "complex" perspective making use of digital surround's multi-channel capabilities is the in-Malkovich's-head scenes of *Being John Malkovich* (1999).[115] Visually, the image track is matted to provide a roughly elliptical image, showing exactly what Malkovich himself would see through his own eyes. Aurally, the soundtrack simultaneously places the audience inside *two* people's heads: Malkovich's and that of the person "inside" him. The film distinguishes between these two through miking and mixing differences. Specifically, the "person in Malkovich" is closely miked, as in a voiceover, and mixed to all five main channels; Malkovich's voice is also miked closely—though with reverb added—but is kept out of the front center channel; and "outside" sounds are miked normally (with reverb) and mixed in the five-channel sound space to correspond with where they originate relative to Malkovich. This aural configuration allows filmgoers to, without conscious effort, distinguish the three simultaneous sound sources—and would not have been possible with a pre-DSS soundtrack.

It also reminds us *whose* perspective we are actually experiencing. As we are "inside" Malkovich, it would be easy to assume the movie offers us Malkovich's visual and aural point of view, but the audio-visual design makes it clear that we are actually experiencing the POV of *the person inside him*. On the aural side, the soundtrack (with its multiple spaces and voices) foregrounds the voice of the character inside Malkovich, which sounds the closest to the way we "hear" our own voices by being "everywhere"; the character inside Malkovich is also heard with a normal frequency range. Malkovich's voice, on the other hand, is given the same sonic treatment as all the other sounds coming from "outside" the character: its frequency range has been flattened a bit, some "reverb" makes it sound a bit more distant, and it is mixed to correspond with its location in space—around Malkovich's head but *not* in front of it. The relative volume levels of the two voices is telling as well: the character inside Malkovich is high in the mix, while Malkovich's own voice is relegated to more of a "background noise."

The image track similarly encourages identification not with Malkovich but with the person inside him. Its most striking feature during these sequences—the matte—indicates that we are looking out *through* something, in this case another person's eyes. Films most often use mattes when a character is looking through binoculars; the matte's use here recalls that more common scenario. It conveys the voyeuristic

5.5. *Being John Malkovich* (1999) uses the multi-channel soundscape
and a visual matte to create a very specific perspective: that
of being a person *inside* John Malkovich, seeing and hearing
through his eyes and ears without actually *being* him.

pleasure these characters take in being inside Malkovich, reminding
us that they have not actually *become* Malkovich but are instead looking out from *inside* him. Between the complex sound space and the
matted visual track, these scenes ensure that the audience identifies
with the proper character perspective and hence shares the experience
of being *in* John Malkovich's head instead of simply *being* him as the
film's title promises.

A movie does not need to use quite as strict an interpretation of
"point of view" as *Being John Malkovich* to have the audience share
a character's experience. In *Daredevil* (2003), for instance, audience
identification with a character facing off against Elektra (played by
Jennifer Garner) is heightened through a clever bit of surround mixing. Elektra spins a pair of blades (one in each hand) around as she

faces her adversary, and the sound of the blades quickly whips around the audience as if "you are standing right where the other character is and she is standing right there—it's a stretch, but it's cool," explains Erik Aadahl.[116] Here, similarly to the *Juno* scene discussed earlier, diegetic sounds and panning are exaggerated to suggest the focus of a character's attention and provide insight into his or her mind; both examples demonstrate the enhanced possibilities multi-channel sound offers POV to convey not just location but *psychology*. As William Whittington points out, surround sound serves not only "to locate the listener within the diegesis [but also] sometimes within the *minds* of the characters in the diegesis, adjoining them with thoughts, speculations, and possibilities."[117]

"Psychological POV" scenes, like the more literal point-of-view segments of *Cars* or *Being John Malkovich*, rely on diegetic immersion. They place the audience in the middle of the narrative action—except in these cases, that "action" is what is happening inside a character's head. The *Lord of the Rings* trilogy (2001–2003), for example, uses the tactics of the digital surround style to place the audience in the "shadow world" with Frodo (Elijah Wood), one of the series' hobbit heroes, for scenes where he is wearing the One Ring. For portions of these sequences, Frodo is visible onscreen—clearly we are not literally seeing "through his eyes." Nevertheless, we are seeing/hearing in the same *way* he is; we are placed *experientially* with him even if not literally in his physical position.

The "shadow world" experiences are visually marked by indistinct borders, with everything blurred and constantly moving—the best description might be that the edges of objects are "smudged," like semi-erased chalk. Additionally, the full-time denizens of the shadow world, such as the normally black-cloaked Nazgul, are revealed in their "true" forms. Aurally, the shadow world is completely different from the "real" world. High-pitched, electrical-sounding "whooshes" continually zip around the five-channel sound space. A constant rumbling, windy noise suggests thick fabric whipping around; this sound effect perceptually fits with the visual aesthetic of unclear borders, creating the sonic impression that everything onscreen is wrapped in a noisy, moving fabric. The "stormy" effect is heightened by the LFE channel playing a low, thunder-like rumble throughout the films' shadow world segments. A couple of other effects (aural and visual) are scene-dependent: any scene with the Nazgul, for instance, includes the high, whispered, almost wheezing-like sounds of the Nazgul mixed to all five speakers. Finally, while *Lord of the Rings* generally uses a highly present musical score employing all 5.1 channels, music disappears entirely for the "shadow world" sequences to heighten the contrast between this environment and the "real world."

Several of the shadow world scenes include the giant red eye of the evil Sauron. The first of these occurs at the Prancing Pony tavern and includes Sauron speaking to Frodo: amidst some other unintelligible dialogue, he clearly says, "I see you!" For this scene, the film breaks from its normal mixing practice of keeping dialogue mainly in the front center channel. Instead, Sauron's voice starts in the front of the theater (primarily in the center channel but also present in the left and right channels) but spreads out to all five channels for the word "you." The result sounds something like, "I see YOU!" with the added implication that Sauron is *everywhere*. For the remainder of Sauron's (again indecipherable) dialogue, the main sound of his voice returns to the front channels, but he can still be heard saying different things in the surround channels. Perceptually, the effect of this strategy—which would not be possible using Dolby Stereo—is to reinforce the feeling that Sauron is omnipresent.

Although sound and image work together to place us in Frodo's psychological position, the two modalities do so in different ways. The soundtrack presents a stormy, highly active, and enveloping environment; "whooshes" whip around the multi-channel soundscape seemingly at random, and incomprehensible dialogue and whispering are thrown in for good measure. The result is a complex and disorienting space. The image track, meanwhile, is sparse—with the "real world" visible neither to us nor to Frodo, the few objects the visuals do include here take on a heightened importance. Indeed, the objects seen in the shadow world (i.e., the Eye of Sauron in the Prancing Pony scene, or the Nazgul on Weathertop) are those crucial to the narrative. Thus while the soundtrack serves to literally immerse us in Frodo's bewildered state of mind, the visual track correlates this with "we see what he sees" images. Taken together, they clearly present Frodo's *perspective*, though not his exact *view*.

The same conceptual approach is utilized in *I, Robot* (2004) for a scene after protagonist Detective Spooner (Will Smith) has been in a massive car wreck. Visually, as Spooner climbs out of his vehicle and walks away from it, the movie keeps Spooner onscreen (with slightly canted angles) rather than presenting his *literal* point of view. When Spooner first gets out of his car, all the film's diegetic sounds are semi-muted and processed to seem distant. As he tries to walk away, a piercing high-pitched sound builds up in all five channels, simulating tinnitus. The net effect is that the audience shares Spooner's sense of mild disorientation even though it is not put in his exact spatial perspective. Notably, the audience's disorientation results in part from the elimination of the ultrafield-based surroundscape that would otherwise provide spatial guidance; with all five channels playing the same sound (muffled noise and a ringing), the soundtrack here offers no spatial markers. Sound designer Erik Aadahl recalls that "originally that wasn't the approach" planned for the sound design, but that the visuals suggested it as a possibility: "the way they shot it, it's just off kilter enough for [the ubiquitous ringing] to be justified and not seem wrong."[118]

The opening sequence of *Saving Private Ryan* (1998) uses somewhat different techniques to convey the temporary shell shock of Captain Miller (Tom Hanks). As he scans the beach, the picture edit alternates between close-ups of Miller's face and (literal) POV shots of whatever he is seeing at the moment. Meanwhile, the sound design muffles the bulk of the surrounding action, foregrounding only those objects to which Miller is paying close attention at the time. Here the film presents what his brain *thinks* it's hearing rather than what he actually *is* hearing, since it becomes clear soon after that his ears are working fine. In some way, though, this is even more powerful a device than a more traditional point-of-view approach, as it literally ties our *perceptions* to Miller's—sound designer Gary Rydstrom explains that these sorts of effects "work remarkably well to help the audience identify with the character even more, because they feel like they've been in his head for a short period of time."[119]

The same sequence also employs a more complex psychological point-of-view device shortly before Miller and his men reach the beach. As boatloads of soldiers prepare to land, the filmmakers place the battle sounds in the rear of the theater. Here placing the explosions and gunfire in the surround channels not only matches the visuals spatially—the cameras remain pointed away from the beach—but also helps the audience share in the soldiers' experience. Like the GIs, we hear a battle raging but cannot see it (their view is blocked by the landing craft walls) or do anything about it at the moment. We, like them, have no choice other than to sit and wait—and as horror filmmakers have known for years, what we (and the soldiers) imagine in this lull is more frightening than anything the film could actually show. By presenting a visual and aural perspective *facing* the soldiers, the filmmakers sacrifice potential *spatial* identification with the characters to offer *psychological* and *emotional* identification: neither the audience nor the soldiers can see the approaching danger.

When the soldiers finally reach the beach, the movie continues to provide their psychological perspective but does so in a different way. Now the soundtrack, as discussed in the last chapter, deploys all the elements of the digital surround style. The ultrafield immerses us in gunfire, explosions, and bullets whizzing by on all sides; the image track uses shaky camerawork and jumpy edits to engender a sense of disorientation. Like the soldiers, we want to make it to a safe place but have no clear sense of where that might be—the beach, ocean, and boats all seem equally prone to the German fire. In this case we identify not with any one particular soldier but with the *feelings* all of them share of what it is like to be part of this attack; "You took to the scene as though you were this unnamed soldier experiencing the landing at Normandy," as Rydstrom puts it.[120]

As a final example of the use of digital surround techniques to convey psychological point of view, 2002's *Spider-Man* makes brilliantly simple use of the multi-channel environment to let us into Norman Osborn's head. In a key scene Norman is seemingly alone in his home when he (and the audience) hears the voice of his alter-ego-to-be, the Green Goblin. As it speaks, the Goblin's voice moves quickly around the sound space, always remaining tantalizingly out of sight. Because the film has previously set up the aesthetic of diegetic immersion, including aggressive surround mixing, this is not distracting—we are accustomed to being "inside" the diegetic world and initially assume, as does Norman, that someone else must be in the room with him.

As it darts around the multi-channel sound space, the Goblin's voice demands that we search for it visually; the camera takes on this task, repeatedly cutting to shots showing the space where the voice *should* be given its location in the sonic environment. Each time a new shot yet again reveals the Goblin's absence and the Goblin's voice jumps to another audio channel, we share Osborn's increasing frustration—like him, we *want* to locate the voice but cannot see its source.

This game of cat and mouse between sound and image forces us inside Osborn's mind, so that when we eventually realize he has gone insane—the Goblin's voice exists only in his head—we feel *pity* rather than the dislike/fear/hatred we would generally muster for a super-villain. The sound design of this sequence relies primarily on DSS's multi-channel capabilities for its effectiveness, but these capabilities are only effective in conjunction with its visual style of quick cutting between tight shots to create the initial assumption that the voice could be coming from someone offscreen.[121] And as one more reminder how valuable it is to have the time in post-production to try new ideas, *Spider-Man* sound designer Steve Flick notes that the movement of the Goblin's voice around the multi-channel space, like the tinnitus effect in *I, Robot*, was not planned ahead of time but instead an idea suggested by the way the image track was shot and edited.[122]

A FUTURE-PROOF STYLE?

The aim of this chapter was to uncover where and why the digital surround style of diegetic immersion is (and is not) used. This investigation began with a look at factors complicating the use of that style, as well as those promoting such use. It continued by examining a few of the ways in which filmmakers have deployed diegetic immersion; this included consideration of the different *extents* to which the digital surround style can be deployed, all the way from its use across entire movies to employment by select segments of a film (such as POV scenes). As this work has shown, DSS's multi-channel capabilities and the digital surround style are today utilized by all sorts of movies, and their importance to cinematic aesthetics is only growing. Yet the speed at which technology and media change begs the question of how accurate the stylistic trends discussed in this and the preceding chapters will be in the future. This section on film aesthetics thus concludes with a brief look at the future of diegetic immersion as an organizational principle for cinematic style.

One trend suggesting the continuing importance of the digital surround style is that some of the previously discussed impediments to surround sound usage are disappearing or diminishing. With digital surround sound now well into its second decade as a presence in theaters and homes, contemporary audiences and filmmakers have grown comfortable with it and indeed are paying more attention to the quality of soundtracks in general. The growth of home theater has been a crucial factor here, as Midge Costin explains:

> It's really what everyone's listening to it on. Before, when it was coming off these little speakers, it didn't matter anyway. You just couldn't get everything you wanted onto it—you couldn't hear it at all. Now with so many people having surround at home, it makes a huge difference.[123]

With 5.1 surround the current norm not just for theatrical exhibition but also for television and home video (DVD and Blu-Ray), audiences have grown to expect quality multi-channel soundtracks out of all their media. As their expectations have grown, the bar has been set higher, and the general belief among sound personnel is that this has led to a marked increase in the quality of film and television soundtracks: "Everybody's demanding it or expecting it, and you can hear it."[124]

Studios and producers, too, now better recognize the possibilities offered by digital surround sound and are increasingly willing to spend time and money to create the best soundtracks possible. Not enough data about audio post-production budgets or timetables is available to draw useful conclusions about the specific effects of dollars and days put into sound. Using awards as a *very* rough approximation of the "quality" of a finished soundtrack, however, does reveal some provocative correlations.[125] For instance, in five of the first ten years of the 2000s the movie that has won the Academy Award for Best Picture has also won the Award for Best Sound, indicating that the overall "best" movies also tend to be those that take the necessary time to polish the soundtrack. Given the choice, studios would rather make money than win awards, so probably of even more importance is that there does appear to be a correlation between good sound work and high box office revenues. Of the seventeen movies that won Oscars for Best Sound, Best Sound Effects Editing, or both in the past decade, *ten* landed in the top ten in domestic box office receipts for their respective years, and all but four were in the top twenty. As a group, they averaged close to $177 million in domestic receipts off an average budget of $100 million, for an average return of $77 million per film even before counting any international, television, or DVD revenue.[126] In contrast, during the same time frame only three of the ten Best Picture winners finished in the box office top ten—and all three of these also won Best Sound. Of the Best Picture winners that did not also win Best Sound, *none* was among the top ten domestic earners for its year. Obviously a lot of factors affect box office receipts and Oscar wins, and a correlation does not imply a cause-and-effect relationship, but this data does at least show that quality soundtracks strongly correspond with strong box office performance. Perhaps this is why, as mentioned before, some high-profile movies are now bringing on sound crews earlier in the process and giving them more time to develop their sound design ideas.

This broad cultural shift toward greater awareness of and appreciation for sound suggests that filmmakers may in the future have greater freedom to exploit the full capabilities of digital surround sound and diegetic immersion. Even today, aural and visual traits of the digital surround style that were rarely employed a decade ago—hard effects in the surrounds and violations of the 180-degree rule, for example—are common enough to often go unnoticed. With audiences and filmmakers alike having grown accustomed to diegetic immersion, the factor most likely to necessitate a major move away from this style would be a change in exhibition technology. After all, the introduction of digital surround systems heralded a shift away from the long-standing "one wall principle"; another major shift in cinema technology could conceivably do the same to the "digital surround style." Yet in this case that appears unlikely: the new technologies on the horizon seem likely to *encourage* diegetic immersion.

In the visual realm, for instance, the industry is currently contemplating the potential of 3-D.[127] Filmmakers like Steven Spielberg and James Cameron are betting that 3-D projection is here to stay, with Cameron vowing "every film I'm planning to do will be in 3-D";[128] others are more skeptical, noting that 3-D is in at least its eighth distinct bout of popularity in what seems to be a cycle.[129] As Roger Ebert points out, although the new 3-D technology "hailed by honcho Jeffrey Katzenberg as the future of the cinema . . . is better than most of the 3-D I've seen," it still suffers from the same fundamental failing as its predecessors—it draws attention to itself as an effect: "It's a constant nudge in the ribs saying never mind the story, just see how neat I look."[130]

But even if 3-D's future is uncertain, it does seem clear that 3-D filmmaking meshes neatly with the digital surround style. This style is founded on the aim of *diegetic immersion*, which 3-D's proponents claim is the major reason to use the new technology: "We want you to feel more like you are *in* the movie," says *Avatar* (2009) producer Jon Landau about the decision to film the movie in 3-D; moviegoers apparently embraced this approach, as *Avatar* is now the highest-grossing film of all time thanks in part to the large fraction of its audience who deemed it worth the extra cost to see the movie in 3-D.[131] Jeffrey Katzenberg uses similar language to explain Dreamworks Animation's plan to release all future projects in 3-D, stating that 3-D is about "bringing the audience into the experience—immersion."[132] James Cameron goes a step further, suggesting that 3-D projection convinces the brain that it is really *experiencing* the onscreen action rather than just *watching* it.[133] Given this commonality of effect, it comes as no surprise that 3-D and DSS seem to feed off each other: since 3-D offers cinematic visuals the same capability of spreading into the theater that the soundtrack already possesses, it promotes a more active use of multi-channel sound to match this more enveloping visual environment. Certainly recent 3-D movies tend to rely heavily on surround effects, and Katzenberg confirms that Dreamworks Animation has found 3-D visuals to require "more immersive" sound design and more aggressive use of the surround channels.[134] Thus if 3-D does become a mainstream cinema technology, its use will easily fit into the established digital surround style, *heightening* the experience of diegetic immersion rather than fundamentally *altering* it.[135]

The prospective nature of technological change in the aural realm is more complicated, as the exact direction technology will evolve is less clear. Chapter 1 demonstrated that 5.1-channel-based configurations are likely to remain the home theater standard for the foreseeable future. Some households will expand their systems (or already have done so) to take advantage of the 6.1 and 7.1 soundtracks available on some Blu-Ray discs. 6.1 and 7.1, though, merely add additional surround channels to 5.1 configurations; it is unlikely that even widespread adoption of these expanded configurations would significantly alter the digital surround style of diegetic immersion. Indeed, their capacities for more precise rear imaging and better envelopment make them even *better* than 5.1 at putting the audience in the middle of the action—Dolby Surround EX, the first 6.1 system, was originally created so that the podracers of *Star Wars Episode I* could fly directly *through* the audience in a way 5.1 did not permit.

Given that television and home video are lucrative aftermarkets for feature films, the fact that home systems will remain 5.1 based indicates that theatrical systems will probably do the same. Even if theaters universally adopted more advanced sound systems, it would simply not be worth the added time and money for most filmmakers to produce significantly more complicated mixes for those venues knowing that none of the effects beyond those possible in a 5.1 system would be heard by the home market. This scenario would be identical to that of DSS use in the early and mid-1990s, when most filmmakers were reluctant to make DSS-based aesthetic elements crucial to their films' stories lest the home audience miss important information. In the short term, then, diegetic immersion should remain the key effect of digital surround sound.

As to the longer term, Walter Murch suggests that digital surround sound has conquered most of the limitations of earlier systems: "We've kind of reached the limit of a certain progression of technical advances—frequency response, dynamic range, distortion, etc.—so there will have to be a different *kind* of change if we're going to move forward."[136] The one remaining avenue for significant technological advancement is the number of audio channels available; as Tomlinson Holman explains, "We've reached the end of one era, which is the era of ever-expanding frequency and dynamic ranges. Now we're looking at the spatial dimension a little more."[137] Chapter 1 suggested Holman's "10.2" system as a possible successor to 5.1-based systems; this system adds eight new channels—seven full-range discrete channels and a second LFE channel—to the 5.1 configuration.

As with 3-D on the visual side, it is uncertain whether this system will ever become the standard for theatrical exhibition but clear that its adoption would only *promote* diegetic immersion. Building on the 6.1 configuration of Dolby Surround EX, each of the new channels 10.2 adds is designed specifically to increase the system's ability to create the illusion of a complete world around the audience. The front channels of a 5.1 or 6.1 theatrical setup, for example, span only the width of the screen; 10.2 adds "wide right" and "wide left" channels to the left and right of the screen so that the sonic environment can be literally wider than the edges of the frame. In the same way, it addresses the fact that all the channels of current DSS systems are in the same horizontal plane by adding "upper left" and "upper right" channels— these not only make vertical imaging possible (sounds can move up and down) but also mimic the "first reflection" sound wave humans subconsciously use to determine the size of indoor listening spaces.[138]

As noted in chapter 1, some 5.1 setups reproduce each surround channel through a *single* speaker while others use an *array* of surround speakers—each configuration has its advantages, but the same sound mixes do not play equally well over both. 10.2 alleviates this discrepancy by adding two new surround channels for a total of four: left and right "point" source channels, for instances where a precisely localized sound is desired, and left and right "diffuse" channels, for surround effects that spread around the audience but are not supposed to be identified with a single point in the space. This ability to use both "point" and "diffuse" surround elements obviously makes it possible for 10.2 to create more complete and believable environments around the audience. Finally, the second LFE channel allows mixers to put bass sounds out of phase to create the impression of very large spaces. Holman explains that the motivation behind the second LFE channel in the 10.2 configuration was that "if we hear differences between the low frequencies in our two different ears, we hear that as 'big space.' You walk into Notre Dame, you *hear* that it's large."[139] In other words, the second LFE channel serves the sole purpose of allowing mixers to create soundtracks that give a stronger impression of a space *different* from that of the theater itself.

All the ways in which 10.2 expands 5.1, then, are specifically aimed at improving its capacity for diegetic immersion. These additions have been effective: those who have heard the system in use tend to notice precisely its ability to create a sense of being *in a different space*. The response of Michael Riggs, an editor at *Audio* magazine, is typical:

> I found it very easy to believe that I was hearing live sounds taking place in a space much larger and very different in configuration from the one I was sitting in. The vividness of the acoustical representation was simply astonishing.[140]

Tellingly, both the twelve-minute official "demo" of 10.2 and *Seven Swans* (2005)—the first (and so far only) film mixed in 10.2—focus on enveloping the audience in created spaces. *Seven Swans*, in fact, stages its action all around the audience, a strategy Holman likens to "theater in the round" turned "inside out."[141] In the end, if 10.2 were to succeed 5.1 as the standard format for film soundtracks, it seems certain that diegetic immersion would remain the guiding principle of surround-driven sound design. In fact, given the system's design it is difficult to imagine a rationale for adopting 10.2 *other* than enhancing cinema's capacity for diegetic immersion.

A SCHOLARLY DISCONNECT

For the foreseeable future at least, the fundamental principle of the digital surround style appears secure. Changes in industrial practices and the continuing growth of home theater suggest that the use of diegetic immersion will only increase; as it does, audiences will continue to grow better conditioned to envelopment and surround sound, enabling filmmakers to experiment further with the limits of DSS-driven aesthetic strategies. And potential changes on both the visual (3-D) and aural (10.2) sides of exhibition technology are designed specifically to enhance the cinema's capacities for diegetic immersion.

With a solid understanding of the past, present, and (possible) future effects of digital surround on cinematic aesthetics in hand, this book now turns its attentions away from film production and style to film scholarship. Exploring filmmaking practices and the ways DSS is used in actual films has made it clear that the adoption of digital surround sound had a significant impact on the aural and visual strategies used in contemporary cinema. Extant film scholarship's capacity to handle these new strategies, however, is limited. The long dominance of cinema studies by visually oriented work has left the field ill-equipped to deal with films' sonic components or the sound/image relationship—a major shortcoming in relation to the digital surround style, which relies heavily on surround usage and the sound/image relationship.

The remaining chapters of this work seek to remedy that gap in current scholarship. The book's third and final section explores the ramifications of DSS and the digital surround style on theoretical concepts related to the ontological question of how "cinema" ultimately works, thereby demonstrating the centrality of the changes already discussed to contemporary cinema. These explorations of the way cinema as a whole functions in the digital surround era, though, require the ability to *study* films from that era. And this, in turn, necessitates developing textual analysis strategies capable of handling the complex multi-channel mixes and shifting sound/image relations of the digital surround style. The next section of this book tackles precisely that task.

2

ANALYSIS

6   STUDYING MULTI-CHANNEL SOUNDTRACKS

Textual analysis has been remarkably impervious to all things sound.

GIANLUCA SERGI IN *THE DOLBY ERA*

Formal analysis is one of the fundamental tools of cinema scholarship. Meticulous examination of a film's images, sound, and story reveal how it functions and can even suggest more universal truths about cinema in general. The analysis process is detail oriented, requiring close attention to the intricacies of a film's construction. Prior to the advent of home video, such in-depth study was difficult; scholars needed either to rely on memory and the rare screenings of classic films or to obtain a print of a film and study it on a flatbed. The former approach had obvious shortcomings in terms of the level of detailed study possible; the latter required access to expensive equipment and film prints. The introduction of videotape made the analysis process much easier; although tape contained only a fraction of the visual detail of a film print, its visual shortcomings were offset by its ability to easily pause, rewind, and fast-forward movies, all while watching them on a home television. Laserdisc and then DVD improved upon the VHS format (not least by accustoming audiences to presentation of films in their original aspect ratio), and today Blu-Ray and downloadable movies continue to push forward the quality and/or accessibility of home formats. Today scholars may write on movies without ever seeing them in a theater, relying instead on details gleaned from repeated screenings on a home television set or a laptop. For exploring many aspects of cinema—editing patterns, production design, and performance, for example—this methodology is generally effective, and the ready availability of all sorts of movies (Hollywood and otherwise) on home formats has unquestionably benefited film scholarship.

In terms of film sound, though, analyzing films based on television or laptop screenings rather than theatrical exhibitions is problematic. Without a good home theater system, any multi-channel effects go completely unheard and unremarked upon. To revisit an example from the previous chapter, a scholar examining *Juno*'s (2007) abortion clinic scene this way might notice the soundtrack get louder or more dense but would miss the way the sonic environment gradually *envelops* the audience with annoying noises. Any television- or computer-based analysis would therefore have a difficult time explicating this scene; its multi-channel mixing plays a crucial role in conveying Juno's thought process, helping the audience empathize with her feeling of being hemmed in with no escape from the problem facing her.

Those scholars who *do* employ a 5.1-channel setup when conducting close analyses face a different problem: film scholarship to date offers little guidance about how to incorporate multi-channel concerns into their work. Virtually all published analyses, as Sergi's epigraph suggests, focus on the image—and even those that incorporate the soundtrack generally ignore issues related to stereo or surround sound. The goal of this chapter is to address that gap in scholarship by providing guidelines for determining where over the course of a film multi-channel effects might require closer investigation, strategies for listening to these sequences, and suggestions for analyzing the results. Lest this analytic approach seem abstract, divorced from the reality of film practice, the chapter will conclude with a case study demonstrating its methodology in action.

CRITERIA FOR AN ANALYTIC MODEL

Aural analysis is an inherently more difficult and more subjective endeavor than image-based analysis. The transient nature of sound itself, the fact that a soundtrack can include multiple elements at one time, and the lack of standard vocabulary for describing sounds all make it impossible to neatly break down soundtracks into the aural equivalent of the shot lists common to image-based analysis. Due to this complexity, designing a comprehensive model for soundtrack analysis is too large a task to tackle here. Instead, this chapter will focus on the particular component of aural analysis that is of the most importance to the current project and least studied elsewhere: use of the multi-channel soundscape. The digital surround style is ultimately built on DSS's multi-channel capabilities; even its visual traits (quick cuts, fragmented space, disregard for traditional continuity) derive largely from the ultrafield's placement of important sounds all throughout the soundscape. Enabling textual analysis to handle diegetic immersion-driven films therefore necessitates developing a procedure for examining how films utilize the multi-channel environment.

To maximize the value of such a multi-channel analysis methodology to the field of film studies, three criteria must be satisfied. First, it should focus on the filmic *text* itself—the images, sounds, and script. Second, it should be flexible and *robust* enough to be employed on a wide variety of films. Third and finally, it should be *accessible* to any film scholars who may wish to use it. Beginning with the first of these stipulations, requiring focus on the actual *text* does not mean that analyses cannot be tied to theoretical concerns, nor that interview-based or historical work should not be employed alongside textual analysis. But it does assert that they should *begin* with the cinematic text itself lest the analyst's perceptions be skewed by a particular theoretical agenda.

A focus on the text also means that it is not enough to note that a film *has* a multi-channel soundtrack; the analysis should incorporate its actual *use* of the multi-channel environment. In what little work has been done on multi-channel sound, too often the specifics of actual surround mixing are either ignored entirely or are not integrated into the rest of the analysis. Jay Beck's essay on the construction of diegetic space in *The Silence of the Lambs*, cited earlier, demonstrates the way even a thoughtful argument can fall into the latter trap. Beck's argument is that as Clarice explores Buffalo Bill's basement, she uses *sound*—first diegetic music from a stereo system and then the kidnapped woman's screams—to guide her. This is an insightful comment about the underlying structure of this climactic scene, supported by specific observations about how the music from the stereo system and the woman's screams change as Clarice moves through the basement.

Moreover, Beck even pays attention to the way the sounds are mixed within the multi-channel environment, noting that sounds do *not* move around the four-channel Dolby Stereo surround configuration to match Clarice's perspective:

> If the shot depicts her point of view, the sound carries over from her spatial position in the previous shot and does not change in volume or reverberant qualities. . . . Despite the fact that Clarice's breathing occasionally is heard from a position away from the location of her body, the combined impact of the other sound sources (diegetic music, dialogue, and crucially ambience and sound effects) adds up to mark the point of audition as Clarice's.[1]

Yet even as Beck takes the crucial step of considering the way sounds are placed within the surroundscape, the last sentence of this quotation suggests the disconnect between his overall claims about this scene and what he uncovers about its use of the multi-channel environment. On the one hand, the essay asserts that the soundtrack offers Clarice's point of audition (POA), claiming that diegetic sounds are "each carefully *positioned* to coincide with Clarice's point of audition."[2] On the other, it recognizes that the sequence's *surround mixing* does not match Clarice's POA, with the simplest example being that Clarice's breathing originates from a different place than her body. This distinction does not negate the essay's fundamental point about the soundtrack guiding Clarice. But *not* interrogating this conflict between multi-channel use and narrative structure is a notable oversight in an essay ostensibly about Dolby Stereo's ability to "create and *spatially* deploy effects."[3]

That said, many textual analyses ignore multi-channel mixing entirely; Beck's essay at least *considers* the placement of sounds in the multi-channel soundscape, even if it does not integrate those observations into its arguments. A truly effective multi-channel analysis methodology must do more than either approach, providing for the careful study of films' multi-channel use *and* for the incorporation of the findings into broader analytic arguments.

The second criterion for a multi-channel analysis strategy, flexibility, means for one thing that this approach should work with *any* multi-channel soundtrack format, from Dolby Stereo to the present 5.1-channel digital systems to whatever the future has in store. Additionally, a robust analytic approach should be *capable* of functioning with any *type* of film, not just those of a particular genre, era, or style. For a counterexample, consider William Whittington's work on surround sound (specifically Dolby Stereo) and the science fiction genre. Drawing on John Belton's claim that surround "is not meant to heighten realism at all, but just the opposite, to denounce it,"[4] Whittington suggests that surround sound has a particular affinity with science fiction, since both emphasize "artifice and a self-reflexive awareness of it by filmgoers."[5] This logic makes sense in the context of sci-fi and Dolby Stereo and even suggests a strategy for multi-channel analysis—searching a film for places where surround is used to heighten artifice or spectacle.

Yet for much of contemporary cinema this approach to analysis would not be very useful. The digital surround style uses surround principally to create immersive, believable environments that envelop the audience but go consciously unnoticed, not to create artifice or "awareness of [surround] by filmgoers." A truly robust multi-channel analysis model must avoid a priori assumptions about the ways surround is used. Significantly, this means that it should be able to handle movies using surround for artifice or spectacle *and* those using it for diegetic immersion—as well as those adopting any other strategies in their use of surround.

The final criterion for an analytic methodology is that it should be *accessible*; that is, it should require neither specialized training in sound, nor unwieldy technology, nor extensive technical expertise. One of the advantages of image-based scholarship is that it requires little specialized training; any film scholar can watch a segment of film and make observations about the image track. For sound scholarship to flourish it should remain equally "open," even if this means focusing on macro-level perceptions at the expense of some mixing subtleties. Certainly it can be *useful* to recognize tiny shifts in surround mixing over the course of a movie, and a robust approach should not prohibit integration of these observations with those noting more obvious elements of the mix. A truly accessible methodology, however, cannot *require* expert listeners able to pick up on these nuances.[6]

THE REPRODUCTIVE FALLACY

The criteria discussed above *describe* an ideal analytic methodology but offer little guidance in how to *develop* such an approach. Extant textual analyses focusing on sound might provide a starting point—except existing work in cinema studies offers few guidelines for closely studying film sound. More precisely, little work exists on examining the *entirety* of a motion picture soundtrack. Film soundtracks include a wide variety of sounds: diegetic music, (non-diegetic) score music, voices speaking dialogue, background voices, ambient noises, Foley (i.e., clothes rustles or footsteps), and sound effects may all be present at any given moment. Yet much writing ostensibly on *sound* ignores the vast majority of these, instead focusing on a specific *subset* of the soundtrack—without distinguishing between the particular component being examined and the soundtrack as a whole.

Not all possible subsets of the soundtrack receive equal attention. Analyses of "film sound" only rarely touch on elements other than the dialogue and the musical score; indeed, the latter component is often described simply as "the soundtrack," with the attendant implication (intended or not) that all the other sounds on the soundtrack are unimportant. While such conflation of the two ideas by the general public is understandable, it is surprisingly pervasive among scholars as well; as Gianluca Sergi observes, "reviewers and scholars also routinely identify the music score as the soundtrack to the effect that the distinction between the two terms becomes invisible."[7]

Nancy Newman's essay on *The 5,000 Fingers of Dr. T* (1953) typifies the way much cinema scholarship excludes sound effects, ambient sounds, and other non-music, non-dialogue elements from "the soundtrack." The essay's introduction makes the promising claim that the piece will examine "the various elements of *The 5,000 Fingers'* soundtrack"[8]—the piece then focuses almost exclusively on that film's use of music, with the only deviation being occasional references to the words of the dialogue. Another telling example is the analysis of *Letter from Siberia* (1957) presented in Bordwell and Thompson's *Film*

Art, a textbook widely used in "introduction to film" courses. In this case study, the authors explain how several different voiceovers impart strikingly disparate meanings to the same series of shots—*without* any mention of the *sound* of the voiceovers.[9] This example is part of a section titled "The Powers of Sound" but is about *words*, not sound; pairing the text of the voiceover as onscreen titles with a silent screening of these shots would produce exactly the same effect.

Obviously it is not fair to expect every piece of film scholarship to deal fully with the soundtrack, or to ask everyone writing about cinema sound to consider all elements of the soundtrack equally. Every article or book necessarily sets limits to its scope. But the fact that the soundtrack is so often equated to the score and/or dialogue raises the question of *why* this should be the case. The answer lies in what Rick Altman dubs "The Reproductive Fallacy," the assumption that the seemingly "natural" sounds in a soundtrack—for example, a car drives by onscreen and the soundtrack includes the sound of a car driving by—are *reproductions* rather than *representations*.[10] That is, these sounds are so "obvious" that they appear unworthy of study; music and dialogue, on the other hand, brazenly declare themselves "intentional" elements demanding attention. Someone had to *write* the words spoken onscreen, and someone had to *compose* the music, but effects and ambiences often seem as if they were "already there." It is not coincidental that when sound effects *have* drawn scholarly attention, it has generally been in the context of science fiction or fantasy films like *Star Wars* (1977) or *WALL-E* (2008) where it is clear that many of the sound effects had to be *created* since their onscreen sources do not exist in the real world. The otherworldly sound of a lightsaber has clearly been painstakingly *designed* and hence draws scholarly attention, even as the Reproductive Fallacy asserts that more "everyday" sounds are just natural parts of the background captured on set and can be ignored.

Even for those who consciously set the Reproductive Fallacy aside, it is often difficult to overcome the mindset of sound as a technical skill rather than a creative art. "I think there's a thinking that sound is fairly obvious: you see something, you put a sound in, and you are done," laments sound designer Gary Rydstrom. "The main attitude people have to change is that sound is a technical part. People think about it as negative cutting, it's the technical step at the end where you put the door slams, the cat meow, and the traffic in—then you have a finished film."[11] In truth, as film sound personnel are quick to point out, *all* the elements of a Hollywood feature soundtrack are intentional; each element is carefully crafted, recorded, edited, and mixed to work as a whole. If the completed soundtrack gives the impression that every one of its sonic elements obviously belongs and nothing is missing, this only testifies to the caliber of the filmmakers who strive to make the soundtrack *seem* natural regardless of how much work it takes to create this illusion.[12] A robust analysis method must move beyond this impression to critically examine *every* element of the soundtrack.

IDENTIFYING KEY MOMENTS

Critical dissection of an entire movie is a monumental undertaking, and most close readings (image based or otherwise) instead focus on individual scenes or short sequences that can be exhaustively analyzed. The question this practical reality raises is *which* segments should be analyzed. One way to identify potentially "interesting" uses of surround sound is to look for places where the multi-channel usage deviates from traditional practices. As shown in previous chapters, the "standard" approach to sound mixing has long been to keep most sounds on the screen. In the monophonic era, obviously all sounds came from the single (front center) speaker. With the advent of Dolby Stereo, the screen-centric mix was expanded slightly: dialogue and most effects remained in the center channel, but two-channel stereo music (as well as occasional simply panned effects like screen drive-bys) spread out to the left and right to provide a broader "stereo" experience. Any time a movie violates this established convention, its mixing is worth examining.

This guideline can be taken a step further: it is generally the places where a film most fully adopts *all* the principles of the DSS-driven style—including, though not limited to, deviating from screen-centric mixing principles—where it is most important to consider the effects of the multi-channel soundscape. In a recent study examining the effect of different sound presentation modes, film excerpts were screened in either two-channel stereo (L/R) or 5.1-channel surround, then rated by audience members in a variety of categories. The results showed that for excerpts primarily employing Dolby Stereo–based aesthetics (both visual and aural), the sound presentation mode had no significant effect on audience ratings. For those clips adopting major elements of the digital surround style, however, ratings varied significantly depending on whether the excerpt was screened in surround or stereo. In fact, this effect on audience ratings appeared to be stronger the *more* of the aural and visual traits of the digital surround style a clip exhibited.[13] This confirms that when conducting aural analysis, it is crucial to study multi-channel effects at those places where the sound and/or image tracks most completely adopt the digital surround style.

If virtually an entire film aggressively uses the whole multi-channel soundscape, then searching for moments where it does so is hardly useful in winnowing down the film to key moments to study. The study cited above suggests that in these cases the entire film's soundtrack may be worth examining closely. Yet paradoxically, of particular interest may be those few moments where the film deviates from its normal mixing strategy and adopts a screen-centric approach instead. Knowing that all decisions about where and how to move sounds around the 5.1 environment are intentional makes those moments where filmmakers violate their own established patterns all the more intriguing. By their very nature these are not the sections that are most representative of the film as a whole, but like a black-and-white scene in the middle of a color film, they do signify that something interesting—and likely worthy of close study—is happening.

LISTENING AND ITS CHALLENGES

The first step in analyzing a film's multi-channel use is to screen it all the way through and determine its overall surround aesthetic using two basic questions. First and foremost, does the film rely mainly on a screen-centric mix that rarely puts spot effects in the surrounds, or does it have an aggressive mix where the surrounds are heavily active? Second, what sort of relationship does it create between soundscape and image? That is, does the former often reorient itself to match the latter (à la the ultrafield), or does the soundtrack instead remain consistent within scenes regardless of what the image is doing (à la the superfield)? Together, the answers to these two questions offer a good overview of the film's approach to multi-channel.

From here, the next step is to screen the movie again, stopping, re-winding, and rewatching portions as necessary to identify—and closely study the multi-channel use in—key scenes or sequences. As a group, the scenes investigated in this way should include both "representative" scenes that follow the movie's primary mixing style and those scenes where the film deviates from its general surround style. The former must be carefully examined to ensure that the overall aesthetic has been correctly determined, and the latter dissected to determine *why* their aesthetic approach differs from the film's "normal" mode. The initial screening will likely have suggested some segments that fall into each category, but re-screening the entire film *after* determining its general mixing style invariably reveals additional points deserving study.

Here a practical problem arises. Detailed study of a film's multi-channel mixing requires a dependable way to determine which sounds are in which channel. Even in an ideal listening environment it can be difficult to tell exactly what sounds are playing through what chan-nels when the entire 5.1 soundtrack is blaring. Sounds played through the subwoofer *may* have originated in the LFE channel, but they also could be the low-frequency components of one or more of the main channels, routed to the subwoofer through the bass management cir-cuitry included in most home theater setups. More subtly, loud sounds in one channel may prevent a listener from consciously noting quieter sounds in that or other speakers. In many mixes, for instance, dialogue dominates so much that the only way to hear the subtleties of what is happening in the surround channels is to mute the center channel so that the dialogue disappears and the rest of the soundtrack can come to the foreground.[14]

This phase of analysis thus requires a system where each of the six channels of the 5.1 soundtrack can be individually turned off (muted) or heard on its own (soloed, in audio parlance). Unfortunately, few home theater systems come with such capabilities. The ideal way to achieve this functionality is to run a DVD player through a professional-style

5.1 audio mixing console, a setup offering the additional advantage of real-time level meters that indicate at a glance when sound is present in a given channel. These systems, though, can easily cost several thousand dollars, making such a setup prohibitively expensive for those without ready access to such hardware through their institutions or personal connections. On the other end of the spectrum, it is *possible* to analyze a film's multi-channel usage by intermittently disconnecting various speakers from the amplifier, but this is extremely time consuming and often impractical. A marginally less cumbersome option is to move around the space and listen to each speaker individually, but this quickly grows tiresome and still offers no way to distinguish between the LFE channel and other sounds routed to the subwoofer.

For most people, then, the best overall solution is to create a makeshift 5.1 console, which allows for quick and easy soloing and muting of channels as needed. Technically, this is a fairly straightforward process, involving running the 5.1 analog outputs from a DVD player to an inexpensive six-channel mix board (or multiple two-channel boards), then connecting the outputs of this board to a home theater system with 5.1 analog inputs. Assuming one already has a DVD player and a 5.1 home theater setup, the necessary hardware can easily be purchased for under $200; even including a DVD player, a 5.1 receiver, and decent speakers, the total cost is under $1,000, still a relatively small investment.

Admittedly, its hardware requirement may be seen as a "failure" of this analytic approach; one of the stated criteria for this analysis strategy was that it be "accessible" to a wide range of scholars. I would argue, however, that arranging *some* sort of mute/solo-capable 5.1 setup is simply a cost inherent to studying cinema in the digital surround era. Scholars studying film have always needed access to specific technologies, whether those be the expensive Steinbecks used for shot-by-shot analysis in the pre-video era or the commonplace color televisions and DVD players used in the same way today—few, if any, venues would publish a close analysis of a color film conducted on a black-and-white television. Multi-channel sound is a crucial aesthetic component of contemporary cinema, and it is not unreasonable to suggest that today, access to a 5.1 system for research purposes is a requirement, not a luxury.

BREAKING DOWN SEQUENCES

The practical concern of finding suitable hardware on which to analyze multi-channel soundtracks aside, the major issue when studying individual sequences is identifying which sonic elements are noteworthy. This is, to a degree, a subjective question dependent on the focus of a given study—when analyzing *Fight Club* (1999) for the case study on the voice/body rift presented later in this book, for instance, I obviously paid special attention to the placement and mixing of voices. But a few general principles will serve any analysis well. To begin, for each sequence closely scrutinized it is important to note whether the multi-channel design used adheres to the film's general surround aesthetic—and if not, *how* it does not. It is also valuable to note what was happening immediately before the sequence in question, and what happens immediately after—specifically, whether the mixing strategy changes, and if so how.

The earlier step of determining a film's overall aesthetic greatly simplifies the process of making specific notes on sound placement. For example, if a movie mostly places dialogue in the front center channel, then dialogue need only be specifically noted in places where it moves elsewhere in the 5.1 environment. In the same way, if a film largely adheres to ultrafield-based editing principles, where sounds move around with each cut in the image track, it is not necessary to list every sound that appears in each speaker for each shot; noting the places where sounds are *not* mixed to match the spatial orientation suggested by the image will suffice.

The goal of this process is not to create a detailed mapping of where every sound is at every moment but to foreground *patterns* and *shifts* in multi-channel usage. Since in most cases identifying every tiny detail in every speaker is not crucial, it is rarely necessary to listen to each audio channel individually. Some changes, such as the jump from a center-only mix to a full surroundscape, are readily apparent when the entire 5.1 mix is playing, and even more subtle ones can be recognized without listening to the same sequence six times (once with each channel soloed). Changes in multi-channel usage tend to be roughly symmetric. That is, when a film with a screen-centric mix suddenly activates the surround channels (or a surround-intense film folds down to the screen), the changes tend to affect *both* the left and right surrounds at the same time. Similarly, when the breadth of a mix changes—for example, when a center-heavy mix broadens out to emphasize the front left and right channels or vice versa—it expands or contracts roughly equally from the center.

These observations suggest a practical shortcut of sorts: rather than listening to each channel on its own, channels can be *paired*. Soloing both rear channels gives a good impression of what the film is doing in terms of surround usage; soloing the front left and right indicate how "wide" the front stereo field is. This approach is usually no less effective (and is certainly much faster) than listening to each channel individually. It also provides plenty of information about what is in *each* of the two channels playing, since the brain is fairly adept at separating the sounds heard from two different locations once the distraction of the other four channels has been eliminated. And individual channels can still be soloed as necessary to clarify differences between two similar-sounding channels.

In summary, key segments should first be played with the entire 5.1 soundscape active to glean an overview of the soundscape. Another couple screenings with just the surround channels active, and one or two more with just the front left and right soloed, will generally reveal the important information about which sounds are where. Depending on the specifics of the mix, a separate screening with the center channel only may help, but most of the time it is fairly easy to identify what was in the center channel by noting what from the 5.1 mix does not appear in the surrounds or front left/right channels. And since the LFE channel includes little semantically meaningful content, it is not usually necessary to screen a whole segment with just this channel active; briefly soloing it during any screening will reveal whether it contains any significant audio content.

The above analytic methodology allows for the main note taking on a film to be done in a reasonable time frame; including the initial screening of the movie straight through from beginning to end, the total work time is roughly four to five times the movie's duration, depending on the particulars of the film. This takes into account that the second screening will take significantly longer than the length of the movie itself, as it will include multiple replays of the key segments being studied. It also recognizes that taking careful notes on these segments takes time and is crucial to the process—a detail that seems irrelevant at first may prove important later in the analysis, and any extra time spent recording information that later turns out not to be unimportant is far outweighed by the time it would take to go back and re-study segments where key details were not documented.

This technique for studying multi-channel usage is complex, but effective. A seemingly easier approach, in comparison, would entail screening the film straight through multiple times with different speakers turned on and off each time (i.e., one screening with just the surrounds, one with just the center, etc.). From a technical standpoint this would alleviate the need for a mixing console—speakers could simply be connected and disconnected manually, since the active speaker configuration would change only every two hours rather than at every key sequence. But the more complex strategy described above offers the crucial advantage of providing necessary *context* for the sounds heard in each channel. Watching an entire movie with only certain speakers turned on diminishes awareness of how the sounds being heard in one channel fit together with those in the others. As a simple example, such an approach may reveal that a gust of wind appears in all five main channels at one point in a movie but would make it difficult to tell whether this gust appeared in all the channels at once or traveled through the soundscape (and if so in what direction). The admittedly more complicated approach of studying key segments in detail one at a time while slowly progressing through the movie's length, on the other hand, makes it easy to tell at all times how the sounds in each channel fit into the overall soundscape, as well as how each sequence's multi-channel mixing relates to that of the rest of the movie.

MAKING SENSE OF PATTERNS AND SHIFTS

The multi-channel analysis tactics presented above address the practical issues of how to examine a film's surround mix and determine what portions of it are most important to study in detail, as well as the aesthetic question of what features of the mix should be noted during this process. But the critical step of *using* the information gleaned from this work in an actual filmic analysis remains to be discussed. Even the most comprehensive set of notes on a film's surround design is of little value merely as a list of what sounds were mixed to which channels throughout the movie; filmic analysis requires not only closely reading a text but also making sense of the details discovered through that reading.

This most important phase in any type of textual analysis is also the most difficult one about which to provide any concrete rules. Obviously the goal is to put the data revealed through close study into some sort of broader framework, but exactly *how* to do so will vary from one movie to another, and possibly even from one sequence to another in the same film. The surround aesthetic of one film might best be explained through the film's narrative structure, while that of another is better discussed through the lens of a historical moment. Indeed, any number of critical frameworks could help explicate a given movie's multi-channel usage: that film's visual style, its relationship to other films within a particular genre, the mixing strategies used in previous works by its director or sound crew, a broader theoretical concept from film studies, and so forth. Indeed, if a film is doing something truly *interesting* with its multi-channel design, it is likely not doing exactly the same thing as any other film—ultimately, the onus is on the analyst to draw on his or her knowledge, insight, and judgment to determine the most useful construct to employ.

The reliance of this final step of the process on the analyst's ability to determine the "right" analytic structure for a given sequence is not unique to soundtrack-based analyses. The image-based analyses of Raymond Bellour's seminal *The Analysis of Film* all use the same approach to breaking down the film—shot-by-shot close study—but frame these in different ways. For example, in Bellour's analysis of a sequence from *The Birds* (1963) he uses three binary oppositions to categorize each shot (seeing versus being seen, static versus moving, and close versus distant) and largely ignores components of the image outside this framework.[15] His dissection of the cornfield scene of *North by Northwest* (1959), meanwhile, maintains the distinction of "seen" versus "being seen" but discards the other two oppositions in favor of criteria such as symmetries between shots, interruptions in regular alternations, and the directions of arrival and departure of various people and vehicles within the diegetic space.[16]

The analytic model proposed in this chapter mirrors Bellour's shot-by-shot approach in merging rigor and freedom. On the one hand, it offers a specific process through which to discover the details of a text's multi-channel sound design. On the other, it does not dictate a single structure through which to interpret these details, leaving room for the analyst to determine the optimal framework. This combination of a heavily prescriptive initial mode of attack with an open-ended inter-pretation phase make this investigative approach flexible and robust enough to deal with all types of films in a variety of analytic contexts.

The limited guidance on the crucial interpretation phase given here may leave the prospective multi-channel analyst wanting more. For the reasons explained above, it is impossible to provide specific rules about this step of the analysis process. This book will, however, offer additional guidance through sample analyses. Each chapter from here forward will conclude with a case study investigating a single film's multi-channel strategies in the context of that chapter's central theme. While these analyses will not cover *all* the possible lenses through which multi-channel mixing might be examined, they will provide a sampling of the diverse issues around which multi-channel analyses can be structured. This chapter closes with an examination of multi-channel's use in the 2007 thriller *Disturbia*, using as its explanatory framework the distinction between remaining *outside* the onscreen world—the aesthetic of cinema's traditional "one wall principle"—and being in the *middle* of it, as the digital surround style suggests.

CASE STUDY: *DISTURBIA* AND VOYEURISM IN SURROUND

Perhaps no film is a better exemplar for discussing the relationship of viewer to onscreen world than Alfred Hitchcock's 1954 masterpiece *Rear Window*, which countless scholars have invoked as a metaphor for the cinema or television. The plot of the film involves a home-bound protagonist who takes to observing the lives of the neighbors visible from his windows (as if viewing them on television or a movie screen). Eventually he comes to believe that one of those neighbors is a murderer and strives to prove it even though he has no hard evidence. Aided by two companions—one of whom is his love interest—he is eventually proven correct, but not before the murderer tries to kill him.

As distinctive as this plot description might seem, it describes not only *Rear Window* but also the 2007 thriller *Disturbia*. *Disturbia*'s credits list no source material for its screenplay, but audiences and critics quickly identified it as a loose remake of *Rear Window*. Not all the details of the two films are identical, of course. For example, the protagonist of *Rear Window*, L. B. Jeffries or "Jeff" (James Stewart), is an adult temporarily in a wheelchair due to injury, while *Disturbia*'s hero Kale (Shia LaBeouf) is a teenager under house arrest. And while Jeff lives in an apartment and watches his neighbors in their *apartments* across the courtyard, Kale lives in the suburbs and watches his neighbors in their *houses*. But these minor plot changes ultimately seem "immaterial variations or transparent rephrasing to produce essentially the same story," as the copyright holders to the short story on which *Rear Window* was based asserted in a lawsuit against *Disturbia*'s producers.[17]

Disturbia, like *Rear Window*, can be considered a metaphor for filmgoing or television viewing. Kale himself suggests this parallel when he remarks to his friend Ronnie (Aaron Yoo) that people watching is "reality TV without the TV." But though both films may function as metaphors for the moviegoing experience, they represent different conceptions of what that experience *is*—thanks to the different *tools* they use to tell "essentially the same story." Specifically, *Rear Window* employs a mono soundtrack while *Disturbia* uses a 5.1 DSS mix. Given that one of the principal effects of digital surround has been to reconfigure filmic space from "what's on the screen in front of us" to "what's happening all around us," this shift results in a major difference in how the two films conceive of the cinematic experience.

The most obvious evocation of this difference is that Kale is literally *surrounded* by neighbors. In *Rear Window*, Jeff watches his neighbors through a single wall of windows in his apartment. In *Disturbia*, meanwhile, Kale finds interesting people to watch on *all* sides of his house. When first explaining his voyeuristic hobby to Ronnie, he virtually drags his friend from room to room throughout the house—no *one* room offers a view of everything he wants to see. Like a multi-channel soundscape, each direction offers something different and each provides someone (or something) worth watching or hearing.

This literalization of the multi-channel environment is only one surround-related facet of *Disturbia*. More subtly, the storyline demonstrates the erosion of the barrier between spectator and film that DSS and diegetic immersion promote. In both *Rear Window* and *Disturbia*, this barrier is narratively realized as the separation between the voyeuristic watchers and the world they see outside. In *Disturbia*, this is hardly a rigid boundary. For instance, when Ashley—the girl next door who is originally an object of Kale's voyeurism—catches Kale and Ronnie watching her, she comes over to join their stakeout of neighbor and suspected killer Mr. Turner (David Morse). Ashley (Sarah Roemer) easily transitions from the "exterior world" to the "safe" world of Kale's house, as well as from an object of voyeurism to a voyeur herself.

This same fluidity applies to the perceived distance between the teen voyeurs and Turner. From one perspective, a less-rigid separation is a good thing: it means that Kale and his friends do not have to content themselves with merely *watching* Turner. On several occasions, they leave the safety of Kale's home to investigate Turner and collect information not available through the simple voyeurism of *Rear Window*'s Jeff. Kale himself enters Turner's house twice, while Ronnie goes into Turner's house once and into his car another time. Ashley, meanwhile, tracks Turner when he leaves the house, following him around a hardware store and into a parking garage.

The blurring of this boundary, though, also has a darker side. It allows Kale and his friends to further their investigations by venturing into the world they're watching, but the reverse is true as well—that world can intrude on their own. This is made abundantly clear when Turner shows up in Kale's house the morning after he has caught Kale spying on him. Ostensibly, he is there because he gave Kale's mother a lift home after she had a flat tire; the not-very-hidden message to Kale is that Turner slashed her tire in the first place. This serves as a demonstration that he can easily affect Kale's world—including getting to his family and friends—if Kale's spying continues. Later, when Turner catches Ashley following him, he unexpectedly gets in her car with her. Though he makes no explicit threat to her, as with Kale his actions themselves carry an implicit message: by crossing a supposedly "safe" boundary (the security of one's home in one case, the privacy of one's car in the other), he shows that in this world it is impossible to simply "watch from a safe distance." The space between watcher and

6.1. Collapsing the distance between inside and outside, voyeur and object, in *Disturbia* (2007). Ashley catches Kale watching her through a window; soon she will join him in spying on the neighbors, becoming a voyeur herself.

watched can *always* be crossed, and danger is no longer localized to a specific place (i.e., onscreen)—it can be *anywhere*.

To be sure, the voyeurs and the object of their voyeurism interact in *Rear Window* as well. In one case, Jeff's girlfriend, Lisa (Grace Kelly), breaks into Thorwald's apartment; later, Thorwald (Raymond Burr) comes to Jeff's apartment and attacks him. What differentiates the two movies is that in the original film, these dual crossings—Lisa to Thorwald's apartment and Thorwald to Jeff's—occur at the story's climax. They are suspenseful *because* they are unusual—the distance between voyeur and object is not *supposed* to be traversed, and these crossings reveal the ultimate fragility of the distinction between the exterior world and the seemingly safe distance from which the voyeur observes it. Until the film's climax, Jeff feels safe watching Thorwald from his apartment. In *Disturbia*, on the other hand, the distance between exterior world and voyeur is not crossed, it is *collapsed*. Kale and the people he watches continually interact. Even minor characters like the children next door are both objects of Kale's voyeurism *and* agents who violate his safe haven by hitting him with water balloons and placing dog feces on his front stoop.

In other words, where *Rear Window* maintains a clear separation between Jeff's apartment and the rest of the world that can only be breached at the climax, *Disturbia* offers an environment where anyone and anything can and does cross between Kale's house and the outside world. *Disturbia's* climax thus cannot be just *any* bridging of the distance between watcher and outside world—that space has already been repeatedly crossed. It must be *Kale's* traversal of this boundary, since he was the one character who was limited, by his ankle monitor, to a particular space. More specifically, the climax must involve his recognition of what the rest of the characters already know, that *there is no separation* between his world and the outside one. There is no "safe zone" to stay inside. *Rear Window* climaxes with Thorwald invading Jeff's space, but *Disturbia* can only be resolved by Kale turning that confrontation on its head and himself invading Turner's house.

In this context, a close study of the multi-channel mixing of *Disturbia* is revealing. The film adopts two distinct strategies for its use of the surround channels, one from the beginning of the movie up to the climax and a different one from that point forward. The initial approach keeps most effects and dialogue in the front channels, using the surround channels primarily for music and subtle ambient sounds. Spot effects are placed in the rear channels only when they represent a dangerous potential collision between outside forces and Kale's life—a rupture of the barrier between his controlled and contained world and the dangerous world outside. The movie's first spot effect in the surrounds, for instance, comes during the early car crash scene as a speeding truck barrels toward Kale and his father. With the camera facing them, we hear the truck in the rear channels just as the characters spot it, a split second before it hits them.

Kale's father is killed in the crash. Thus only a few minutes in, *Disturbia* has set up a stark association between surround effects and danger. Or, to be more precise, it has associated surround effects with danger from *outside forces*, like the truck that comes from nowhere to kill Kale's dad. Subsequent instances of effects in the surrounds fit the same profile: they signal threats from outside Kale's seemingly "safe"

world. The most notable use of the surrounds in this way is their association with Turner; in several scenes the surround channels are initially almost silent, then blare to life when Turner appears. The same
"outside threat" motif applies to a couple of electronic noises mixed to
the surrounds, including a camcorder beep (when Kale starts taping
Turner's actions) and the click of Ashley's cameraphone (as she takes
pictures of Turner at the hardware store). In both cases, the specific
action represented by the rear-mixed sound effect directly leads to a
confrontation between the teens and the suspected killer. As a final
example, several times in the film Kale's doorbell rings. When he is
expecting someone the ringing is mixed to the front and center like
other effects. When he is *not*—and the ringing therefore represents
a potentially dangerous intrusion of the outside world—the ringing is
mixed to the surrounds.

The threat signified by surround use does not have to be *physical.*
Take, for instance, the scene where Kale is about to show Ronnie the
primary object of his voyeurism (before he has any suspicions about
Turner), Ashley swimming next door. As they enter the study from
which they can see her pool, a quiet "splash" in the surround channels
signifies that Ashley is, in fact, outside in her bikini. The danger represented by this surround effect is that of Kale getting caught playing
peeping Tom by the person he most wants to impress. And in fact, Ashley *does* catch him, though (luckily for him) she seems unperturbed by
his spying. Later, during Ashley's party, a similar "emotional" danger is
symbolized by the placement of sounds from the party in the rear channels. Her party has drawn the "popular crowd" Kale despises, and the
fact that their sounds are placed in the surrounds indicates that at least
for the moment the prospect of losing his friend to this outside group
is no less threatening than the potential murderer next door. Indeed,
Kale abandons his surveillance of Turner to watch the party, apparently
deeming the possible loss of Ashley the more pressing threat.

Tellingly, plenty of effects throughout the movie *could* have been
panned into the surrounds to spatially match the visuals, but the only
ones for which this is done are those that suggest a definite threat—
emotional or physical—to Kale. This mixing strategy changes, though,
at the brief lull near the end of the film's second act, when it appears
Turner was innocent all along. With the exterior threat apparently

toothless, the soundtrack has folded down to the front channels alone, with not even music or ambient sound in the surrounds. Then, very subtly, thunder effects come into the surrounds as Kale absentmindedly plays back a videotape Ronnie shot while trying to escape Turner's house. As Kale gradually realizes that there is something odd on the tape, the thunder in the surrounds grows louder and the score spreads back into the rear channels. Kale clicks to enlarge the picture, and as he zooms in, the clicks spread through all the channels, until finally we are enveloped by them as he clicks one last time to reveal a dead body hidden behind a grate. Simultaneously, a cross-cut scene shows Turner attacking Kale's mother (Carrie-Anne Moss) and taking her hostage.

A dead body and an attack on Kale's family being linked to a surround effect is consistent with the film's established paradigm of rear channel sounds symbolizing danger. But this point marks a key transition in mixing strategy, since the entire 5.1 soundscape is now integrated into a single immersive environment. As the thunder and mouse clicking rise in volume and spread from the front channels through the whole theater, the movie reveals that *no* place is safe. The dangers of the exterior world, to this point only implied, now reveal themselves as *everywhere*, with Turner taking away the person most symbolic of the safety of home—Kale's mother. Tied to this narrative shift is an aesthetic one: the sonic environment grows much more spatialized. All sorts of sounds—even voices—now spread throughout the theater, and the soundtrack's orientation adjusts to the onscreen images, helping us keep our bearings in the now completely immersive world. The to-this-point screen-centric soundscape, in other words, now embraces the fully immersive sonic possibilities of 5.1 surround and the ultrafield.

Kale himself is the beneficiary of this newly spatialized sonic environment. When he enters Turner's house to find his mother, he has no idea where she is being held. It is her muffled cries for help that guide him through the house to a secret passage and ultimately into a makeshift dungeon beneath. In keeping with the ultrafield-based style, her screams are carefully mixed to correspond with the onscreen camera angle and guide Kale to the appropriate location. When the camera is looking toward Kale as he walks through the house, the screams are behind us; when it shows him in profile, they are offscreen to one side only, and so on. It is literally the spatial orientation provided by

6.2. When Kale enters Turner's house in search of his mother, the placement of her voice in the multi-channel soundtrack guides him. At this point her cries for help come from the right surround channel.

the multi-channel environment that allows Kale to find and rescue his mother.

Specific differences between *Disturbia* and *Rear Window* cannot be pinned to the move from mono sound to digital surround sound— too many factors are at play in any filmmaking decisions to draw this sort of direct *causal* link. One might argue, for instance, that *Disturbia* differs from *Rear Window* primarily because the newer film accommodates personal communication technologies such as cell phones and camcorders that did not exist in the fifties. Yet 1998's made-for-TV remake of *Rear Window*, which exploits virtually all of the same technologies as *Disturbia*, follows the lead of the 1954 film in maintaining distinct borders between the protagonist's apartment and the suspected killer's until the climax. It also employs the same spatial geometry as the original film, with its voyeur watching the outside world through windows on a single wall rather than being surrounded by them. The crucial difference between the 1998 *Rear Window* and *Disturbia* is that the former, like Hitchcock's original, does not have a 5.1 surround track;

made for standard-definition stereo television, it follows the screen-centric sound model of mono and Dolby Stereo. Even if no direct cause-and-effect relationship between style and sound format can be asserted, it is clear that the *ways* in which *Disturbia's* story differs from *Rear Window's* are symptomatic of the move from screen-centric mono sound to the diegetic immersion of the digital surround style.

This close analysis of *Disturbia's* plot and its surround mixing explains how and why the film substitutes a full three-dimensional geography for *Rear Window's* unidirectional one and eliminates the boundary between voyeur and object. Perhaps most importantly, it explains why Kale is able to rescue a potential victim, where Jeff is not. It is worth noting that *Disturbia* was critically and financially successful, in sharp contrast to the negative critical reception and poor box office performance of Gus Van Sant's ostensibly shot-for-shot remake of *Psycho* (1998) from a few years earlier. Together, these results suggest a general truth of no small importance in an era when remakes and "reimaginings" form a sizable portion of Hollywood's output: when remaking a monophonic film, it is crucial to account for shifts in technology and audience expectations in the intervening years. The 1998 version of *Psycho* (largely unsuccessfully) pairs a monophonic-era visual style and script with a 5.1 soundtrack; *Disturbia*, on the other hand, uses the 5.1 environment to complicate the relationship between watcher and watched, reflecting the intermingling of audience and diegetic space promoted by digital surround–based aesthetics. *Disturbia*, in the final analysis, succeeds not *in spite of* its differences from *Rear Window* but *because* of them—its makers understood the ramifications of 5.1 surround and integrated them into its plot to create the right movie for the time.

7

STUDYING IMAGE/SOUND INTERACTIONS

The mental effort of fusing image and sound in a film
produces a "dimensionality" that the mind projects back
onto the image as if it had come from the image in the first
place. . . . We do not see and hear a film, we *hear/see* it.

WALTER MURCH

Cinema is an audio-visual medium and must be studied as such. While much film scholarship has neglected the soundtrack in favor of the image, it is equally inappropriate to do the reverse and focus exclusively on the aural component of cinema. The strategy outlined in the last chapter for analyzing multi-channel usage is thus incomplete: to be productive, any multi-channel-inclusive analytic approach cannot treat the soundtrack as if it exists in isolation but must incorporate interactions *between* it and the image.

This is particularly true for movies that adhere to the digital surround style, which often shifts narrative and thematic burdens from the image to the soundtrack. In this style of filmmaking, image and sound are tightly tied together, each influencing the other, and neither makes complete sense outside the context of the sound/image pairing. This two-way influence is perfectly illustrated by an anecdote from sound designer Erik Aadahl about his work on the movie *I, Robot* (2004). For the scene described earlier where Detective Spooner has just emerged from his battered car and the soundtrack simulates tinnitus, Aadahl notes that the "spacey" feel of the soundtrack was suggested by the fact that the camera angles were slightly canted. As it turns out, the director and picture editor had not intended for Spooner to seem "totally out of it" as this sound design suggests; once they heard it, though, they let the scene run longer than had been intended so that the sound design had time to progress from muffled sounds at first, through the tinnitus effect, and finally back to normal.[1] A sound design decision originally evoked by the image, in other words, itself affected the picture edit in turn.

While this particular example relies on knowledge of I, Robot's production process, close study of the film itself reveals similar collusions between image and soundtrack. As Spooner is about to leave a robot junkyard, for instance, sound effects in the surrounds lead him back into the site—where the old robots are now being viciously destroyed by new ones, an event propelling the movie toward its climax.[2] The point is that the relationship between sound and image in the real world of film production is complex; textual analysis methods that fail to address image, sound, and their interactions are at best incomplete and at worst a catalyst for inaccurate conclusions. The goal of this chapter is to reformulate the text-driven but soundtrack-focused analysis method developed in the previous chapter into an analytic approach that recognizes—and provides a framework for addressing—the bidirectional importance of the picture track to the soundtrack and vice versa.

SHOT-BY-SHOT ANALYSIS

The conventional way to study a film sequence is through shot-by-shot analysis; as the analytic approach with which film scholars are most familiar, this is a logical launching pad for the development of a more comprehensive method. As its name suggests, the shot-by-shot approach generally ignores the soundtrack—other than perhaps to note the lines of dialogue accompanying each shot—and is therefore ill suited for studying sound/image interactions, at least in its traditional form. The methodology of conventional shot-by-shot analysis, as de-

7.1. Detective Spooner emerges from a car wreck in *I, Robot* (2004).
The canted angle of the image track and the multi-channel ringing
noise in the soundtrack work together to convey his disorientation.

scribed in Bellour's landmark *The Analysis of Film*, is to examine every
shot in a sequence, then try to explicate the sequence's structure and
meaning through commonalities or oppositions between those shots.

An example will demonstrate this methodology and provide a common "proving ground" for each analytic approach considered here.
The opening of the 1996 action film *The Rock* makes an excellent
test case—in the span of under three minutes this sequence offers
significant visual and aural fodder for discussion, employs several different types of interaction between sound and image, and aggressively
activates the 5.1 soundscape. The specific segment considered here
begins after the two production company logos (Hollywood Pictures
and Simpson/Bruckheimer Productions) and ends with a close-up of
a tombstone just before General Hummel (Ed Harris) speaks his first
line. It includes thirty-nine cuts, yielding a total of forty shots.

Twenty-one shots are of General Hummel alone, with the first
seventeen of these in his home and the remaining four at a cemetery.
Twelve shots are of a group of soldiers burying a fallen serviceman at

the same cemetery. Two more shots feature Hummel *and* the soldiers at the cemetery. Four of the remaining five shots are the film's title, a fireball that fills the screen, and two shots of helicopters. The last of the forty shots, both in description here and in the sequence itself, shows Hummel's wife's gravestone from his point of view (POV).

Applying a traditional shot-by-shot approach to this sequence exposes both linkages and oppositions between the shots of Hummel and those of the soldiers. On the one hand, both have the same blue lighting tint and portray a ritualized, highly ordered activity: Hummel puts on his military uniform piece by piece, while the four soldiers perform a military burial ceremony. At the same time, a contrast is drawn between Hummel as a single figure and the four soldiers as a group. The sequence highlights this distinction with a formal shift in motion and direction over the course of the opening. At its start, there is not much movement either from Hummel or from the soldiers. In the middle of the sequence Hummel and the soldiers are moving in the same direction within each frame. And by the end they are moving in opposite directions, a fact made clear when they pass each other on a road in the cemetery.

This duality of the relationship between Hummel and the soldiers summarizes the movie in microcosm. At its start, Hummel and the soldiers are linked by their military service, and both have a keen respect for their dead comrades. But where the other soldiers are still following the closely prescribed rules of the military (symbolized by the burial ceremony), Hummel has already planned to break the established rules of that organization and set himself against its hierarchy. The visual contrast between a tightly integrated group and a loner opposing that group also foreshadows the primary plot of *The Rock*, which sets a pair of outcasts (Nicholas Cage's FBI agent and Sean Connery's convict) against the highly organized group of ex-Marines who capture Alcatraz and function as a cohesive unit.

Shot-by-shot analysis has remained a valuable tool of film scholarship precisely because it is so useful, and this case is no exception—the shot-by-shot approach does an excellent job explaining how the shots of Hummel and the burial ceremony foreshadow the film's plot and themes. Yet at the same time it fails in at least one regard: it offers no explanation for the four shots *not* falling neatly into the Hummel/soldiers framework. These four shots (title, fireball, and two of helicopters) are visually linked by their strong orange tones, which contrast with the blue tones of the rest of this sequence. Yet it is unclear what this difference in color scheme implies. These shots, moreover, do not seem to be part of the diegetic world. They are clearly not from the same time and place as the other thirty-six shots and cannot even be read as visualizations of the past events suggested by the radio chatter on the soundtrack, which specifically indicates that *no* helicopters were sent in for Hummel's trapped soldiers. In short, these shots defy easy explanation when the image track is considered alone. This shortcoming highlights the need for a way of considering the interaction *between* sound and image.

A MODEL FOR SOUND/IMAGE INTERACTION: COOK'S TRIPARTITE SCHEME

A significant body of experimental work in psychology and musicology seeks to explain how image and sound work together in audio-visual media. Several studies, for example, take up the question of how the musical score draws attention to particular elements of an audio-visual work during a screening[3] or influences which elements are remembered afterward.[4] Other research investigates what makes a pairing of music with images seem more "effective" in transmitting meaning.[5] Such experimental work has been productive—indeed, the useful concept of "accent points" discussed earlier in relation to the "New Cut-Up Cinema" was drawn from one of these studies on how image/music pairings function. But because good experimental practices require minimizing the number of variables examined in any given study, this branch of work has of necessity been so narrowly focused as to yield little broadly applicable information about sound/image interactions. All of the aforementioned studies, for example, are based on pairing images and music (non-musical portions of the soundtrack have received considerably less attention) in tightly prescribed ways rather than on searching for a broader, more all-encompassing model of how visuals and sounds might relate.

That scholars working from a humanities-based perspective have gone further in developing comprehensive sound/image models than their colleagues relying on experimental work comes as no surprise given the necessary practical constraints on the latter approach. Nicholas Cook and Michel Chion have independently proposed models for the relationship between aural and visual elements in audio-visual works. While the experimental studies mentioned above rely for their conclusions on viewers' *perceptions* of audio-visual interactions, Cook and Chion instead approach the problem from a more abstract perspective, considering the possible ways sound and image media *might* interact to create new meanings. Examining their models for sound/image interaction—as well as the analytic concerns those models raise—will identify the parts of these frameworks that may be of use to the analytic methodology being developed in this chapter, as well as specific missteps it must avoid.

In his book *Analysing Musical Multimedia*, Cook suggests that at any point in a multimedia work the relationship between music and image falls into one of three categories: conformance, contest, or complementation.[6] In a nutshell, "conformance" refers to instances where the images and music present essentially the same information, "contest" to situations where music and image apparently contradict each other, and "complementation" to a middle ground in which the two neither have identical meanings nor directly interfere with each other. Cook explains that any music/image interaction can be put into one of these categories using a two-question binary tree. First in this tree is a "similarity test," which considers whether the relationship between the two elements can be inverted: if it is equally accurate to say that the music projects the images or to say that the images project the music, then their relationship is categorized as *conformance*.[7]

When the similarity test establishes that the images and music do not feature *equivalent* meanings, the issue becomes one of the *type* of difference between the two. The second half of Cook's binary tree is a "difference test," which asks whether the music and visuals each try to present their own meaning as the dominant one, with the meaning of one mode of media apparently "contradicting" that of the other. In essence, the difference test is designed to separate cases where picture and music are working on different *levels* from those where they are actively "vying for the *same terrain*."[8] Those in the latter category fall into the category of *contest*, and those in the former are labeled *complementation.* The categories of conformance and contest thus sit at opposite ends of a spectrum—with direct conflict between music and image at one end and complete agreement between them at the other—with complementation offering a middle ground in which the two modalities neither have identical meanings nor directly interfere with each other.

Key to Cook's model is that these categorizations depend not on sound or image individually but on their *pairing.* As a demonstration of how his three-part system functions—and an example that broadens Cook's approach beyond *music* to sound in general—consider the sound of a harsh wind. This sound could work in *conformance* with an image of a desert plain: using the "inversion" formulation of the similarity test, it seems that the wind suggests the desert image as much as the desert image suggests the wind. This same sound paired with images of a downtown cityscape and a family room filled with happy people, on the other hand, could represent *complementation* and *contest,* respectively.[9] Applying the difference test, in the former case the wind suggests another layer of meaning to the city while not actively opposing the image, while in the latter, the bleak wind sound insinuates precisely the opposite meaning of the image track's seemingly happy family.

The *function* of Cook's systematic categorization scheme is to provide a structure through which to identify points in a work that deserve close audio-visual analysis. It does this partly through eliminating those places where close analysis is *not* necessary: in cases of conformance, where image and sound offer the same meaning, an image-only (or sound-only) analysis should be sufficient. Furthermore, Cook explicitly asserts that while the vast majority of multimedia works throughout history have tended to operate in the *conformance* mode, it is *contest* that best allows for the creation of new meanings through the interaction of images and music.[10] Given this, searching a longer piece like a feature film for points of contest or complementation provides an excellent starting point for analysis, especially in cases where conducting a close reading of the entire text may prove too time intensive to be practical.

Cook is not the first scholar to argue that opposition between image and sound is more productive than coherence between them. Both this claim and his acknowledgement that most sound/image pairings employ conformance recall writings by leading Soviet filmmakers in the 1920s, who feared that sync sound would be used simply to match the image rather than to provide "an orchestral counterpoint of visual and aural images."[11] Where Cook advances this line of thinking is by explaining precisely *how* image and sound can combine to create an affective impact present in neither alone. He proposes that a "gap" in one modality leaves room for the other to transfer meaning. In the case of the example mentioned above, an image of an empty city street is emotionally "gapped"—the audience does not know how to feel about it without any other information. This gap is what allows the soundtrack to change the image's perceived meaning. The addition of an up-tempo, major key score would give the street a happy, cheerful mood, while a harsh wind sound would suggest something more sinister.

Application of Cook's approach to the opening of *The Rock* yields insights into the way mood and emotion are created that shot-by-shot analysis did not reveal. For example, the shots of Hummel getting dressed are ambiguous as to tone, especially in relationship to the burial scene with which they are intercut. It is difficult to tell from the images alone whether the soldier being buried is someone for whose death Hummel feels responsible, or someone he tried to save, or someone with no relation to him at all. Operating in complementation to the image, the soundtrack transfers meaning into this signification gap in two ways. The melancholy musical score explains Hummel's state of mind, and the radio chatter, clearly from Hummel's past, clarifies *why* he feels this way—he is sad because he is remembering the men who have died under his command. Audio clips from congressional hearings also suggest a reason why Hummel might choose to go against the military (as indicated in the shot-by-shot-based analysis above): the military power structure has refused to acknowledge these dead Marines. Together, these interactions give the opening a very personal sense of sorrow and loss, tying the funeral of an unknown soldier to specific losses felt by Hummel and engendering sympathy for his later decisions.

Though it offers advantages over shot-by-shot analysis, Cook's model has its own limitations. For one, his assertion that important meanings are created when image and sound are *not* in conformance downplays the importance of conformant relations. As Cook admits, historically *most* multimedia has been of the conformant variety. A model purporting to address sound/image relationships should speak not only to the "most interesting" of those relationships but to the rest of them as well. Even if conformant relationships do not have the capacity to produce as strikingly *different* meanings as those resulting from complementation or contest, they nevertheless retain a potent capability for *amplifying* meanings. Conformant non-diegetic music, for instance, has long been used in films precisely because it has the power to heighten emotion beyond that provided in the images alone.

The opening of *The Rock*, in fact, clearly demonstrates the value of conformant relationships. At two points during this sequence, onscreen objects in Hummel's room create sound effects—his dog tags jingle against each other as he puts them on, and his wedding ring clinks as he places it atop a dresser. Simply by virtue of being the *only* two sound effects heard in this space, these sounds seem to be of significance and deserve attention. Cook's scheme, though, would identify these sounds as being in conformance with the image, and hence not of particular importance. The sounds clearly match onscreen sources and are only heard when those sources are shown in close-up, making even the "scale" relationship conformant (bigger image of object equals bigger sound of object). But Cook's scheme says nothing about what (if any) meaning this tight pairing might create.

This points to a deeper limitation of his model: its three-part categorization scheme is useful at suggesting moments worthy of closer study but does not provide guidance as to *how* to analyze those moments. That is, even if the ring and dog tag sounds operated in *contest* with the image, Cook's model would suggest only that meaning likely is *created* by this pairing—not what that meaning *is*. Consider again the helicopter shots for which shot-by-shot analysis offered no clear explanation. Cook's binary tree would identify these as being in *contest* with the musical score: the shots suggest action and movement, while the score is slow, downbeat, and repetitive. According to Cook, contest is the mode of interaction best suited to the creation of meaning, and thus this pairing should result in some type of new meaning. Yet it is unclear *what* meaning might be created by this particular aural/visual conflict—no ready "gap" exists in either modality.

AN ALTERNATIVE MODEL: "ADDED VALUE"

In *Audio-Vision*, Michel Chion presents an alternate model for audio-visual interaction with two advantages over Cook's. First, Chion reaches further than Cook by explicitly setting out to create a theory for *all* image/sound interactions, not just those involving music—though as shown above, Cook's model *can* in some cases be expanded to encompass non-musical sounds. Second, Chion's approach avoids Cook's excess of new terminology (complementation, difference test, and so on), instead introducing only one major new term: *added value*. As defined by Chion, this is "the expressive and/or informative value with which a sound enriches a given image, so as to create the definite impression (either immediate or remembered) that this meaning emanates 'naturally' from the image itself."[12] In other words, "added value" is the information that *seems* to come from the image even though it really originates in the soundtrack.

Like Cook, Chion believes it is the interaction *between* sound and image that creates new meaning. But unlike Cook, whose categorization scheme is designed to suggest places where new meanings *might* be formed, Chion focuses on *finding* these new meanings first, *then* unpacking how they occurred. Specifically, he suggests using a "masking method," where the aural and visual components of a work are screened first in isolation, *then* together, to identify places of "added value." The masking method gives the analyst the opportunity to "hear the sound as it is, and not as the image transforms and disguises it" and "the image as it is, and not as sound recreates it."[13] By first taking note of salient features in each modality without knowing how the two relate, then viewing the film with both images and sound, the analyst is primed to be "open to the surprises of audiovisual encounters."[14]

Ultimately, Chion condenses much of the sound/image relationship into two questions: "What do I see of what I hear?" and "What do I hear of what I see?"[15] The inverses of these same questions ("What *don't* I hear of what I see?" and "What *don't* I see of what I hear?") are equally useful, as they identify places where image or sound *alone* creates a particular meaning. These questions point out a key difference between Cook and Chion's models: where Cook emphasizes that points of contest or complementation are more worthy of analysis than those of conformance, Chion recognizes that added value can work in a variety of ways and remarks that "no situation is ever 'neutral' or 'normal,' and thereby unworthy of consideration."[16]

Returning to the dog tag and wedding ring sound effects from *The Rock*, added value offers a clue as to the significance of these sounds. Hummel defines himself in large part *by* his association with the Marines, even after he defects, and the dog tags being the first thing he puts on is a crucial symbol of that identification. Similarly, the wedding ring is another strong signifier of identity—one many men *never* remove—making Hummel's choice to leave it behind on the dresser a highly meaningful act. Adding specific sound effects *only* to these two items creates an "added value," drawing our attentions to the particular onscreen items making noise and confirming their importance to the scene. That both are metallic sounds also subtly ties together dog tags and wedding ring in a clever pairing; taking off a wedding ring before leaving home generally signifies the intention of breaking a vow of fidelity, and the dog tags indicate that it is Hummel's pledge to the Marines and the U.S. government that he plans to break.

The masking method reveals further elements of added value in this sequence. Most notably, it highlights that the main plot element of this sequence, Hummel's backstory, is not *seen* at all. It is only *heard* through his congressional testimony and his soldiers' radio messages. The perception, watching this scene with image and sound together, is that Hummel is reflecting on his country's failure to save his soldiers and is deeply saddened by the situation—the same meaning Cook's approach suggested. Yet the masking method makes it clear that the visuals *alone* are inconclusive about Hummel's perspective and *could* even be read as implying that it was *Hummel's* decisions that resulted in soldiers' deaths. Hummel's face, viewed without the soundtrack, portrays an intriguingly unclear emotion: he may be sad, or thoughtful, or regretful, or angry. When image, music, and the explanatory radio chatter and congressional testimony are combined, however, the face becomes infused with a deep sense of loss and pain in a sonic version of the Kuleshov effect. A true case of "added value," these emotions are *perceived* as intrinsic to the image track.

As with shot-by-shot analysis or Cook's tripartite model, the "added value" approach has its own limitations. Like those approaches, it offers

7.2. General Hummel dons his uniform. While he will soon set himself against the military hierarchy, the reverence with which he puts on everything from his dog tags to his officer's cap indicates that his military career is a defining part of his life. *The Rock* (1996).

no explanation for the helicopter shots or the way these images interact with the soundtrack. And though the masking method is rooted in study of a film's visual and sonic elements, its underlying principle relies heavily on *perceptions* of these elements to identify where value has been added. This reception-based approach can, if not used carefully, result in conclusions only tenuously tied to the formal elements themselves.

LIMITATIONS OF THE COOK AND CHION MODELS

Perhaps the biggest drawbacks to Cook's and Chion's models as originally formulated are those they share. Despite their stated intentions to explain various types of audio-visual interactions, both assume that the multimedia experience is primarily a *visual* one, with the auditory features of a work making important contributions to its perceived meaning but going largely unnoticed. Chion, for instance, defines "added value" specifically in terms of transferring meaning *from* sound *to* image. While allowing for the *possibility* that the image might similarly affect the audio, Chion emphasizes that it is still the image that dominates the audience's impressions: "For all this reciprocity the screen remains the principal support of filmic perception."[17]

Cook's model has an apparent advantage in this area, as his formulation seemingly allows for bidirectional interactions between music and image—the similarity and difference tests give equal weight to the two modes. All the same, Cook ultimately subscribes to an image-centric argument similar to Chion's. Noting that music generally goes consciously undetected by the audience, he indirectly brands the image as the *primary* locus of meaning. Indeed, his assertion that "music . . . participates in the construction of meaning, but disguises its meanings as effects"[18] recalls Chion's claim that the soundtrack contributes "added value" perceived as coming from the image.

Another issue is that both Chion's and Cook's approaches fundamentally assume sounds already have their own *intrinsic* meanings. Cook is explicit about this assumption. His model focuses only on music/image interactions in part because music—at least according to his model—already carries clear meaning on its own, allowing for the transference of parts of that meaning to signification "gaps" in the image. Chion does not expressly state that the sonic or visual components of a multimedia work must contain inherent meaning, but his definition of "added value" implies that sounds, at least, must have intrinsic meaning, since it is this "expressive and/or informative value" that is transferred to the image.

Neither model strictly defines the "meaning" of a sound. In some cases it refers to something concrete, such as the denotation or connotation of a song's lyrics;[19] in others it is more abstract or subjective, such as the "liveliness and precision" Cook associates with the Mozart piece played during a car commercial he discusses.[20] The unclear nature of the sonic "meaning" required by both Cook and Chion results in analyses based not on the filmic *text* itself, but on subjective *perceptions* of it. In his analysis of the car commercial cited above, for example, Cook argues that the "liveliness and precision of Mozart's score . . . become the liveliness and precision of the ZX 16v [car]";[21] that is, by pairing images of the car driving with this particular piece of music, the commercial creates the impression that the car is lively and precise (whatever those adjectives may mean for automobiles) like the music.[22] Whether a particular sound is "lively and precise," though, is certainly debatable, and depends on the context: lively and precise in comparison to *what*? Moreover, Chion and Cook both suggest a direct correlation of descriptors (such as "precision") across modalities.[23] This assertion sidesteps the fundamental question of whether particular descriptors are used the same way in different contexts; a "hard" sound might not mean the same thing as a "hard" image.

Compounding this uncertainty is that not all sounds or images possess clear meanings. To once more return to the helicopter shots from *The Rock*, one reason it is difficult to determine their function is that they suggest several possible "meanings." For example, helicopters are generally fast, so these shots *could* signify speed—but they are shot in slow motion, so they could also signify lack of speed. Considered through another binary, they could be read either as symbols of power and strength (as armed military helicopters) or impotence and weakness (as the shot sequencing suggests the helicopters may have exploded). In short, the ambiguous nature of "meaning" in Cook and Chion's models makes them so flexible as to only be useful on sounds and images with straightforward, objectively clear "meanings."

INCORPORATING MULTI-CHANNEL

Neither Cook's model nor Chion's offers a clear way to handle multi-channel soundtracks, or even addresses the possibility of multiple competing sounds existing at the same time. Both treat the soundtrack as a unified object in the traditional pattern of the image track, with only one sound (shot) present at a given time.[24] This assumption implies that at any moment sound and image relate to each other in a single, specific way. In reality, the soundtrack is plural, including multiple distinct channels behind the screen and in the space of the theater, any or all of which may include several sounds, each relating to the image in a different way.

The multi-channel analysis approach explained in the previous chapter is perfectly capable of handling the soundtrack's plural nature; applying this method to the opening of *The Rock* reveals some telling relationships among the soundtrack, image track, and narrative. The beginning of the film is dominated by order and tradition. Intercut scenes of a military burial and of Hummel putting on his uniform emphasize these elements narratively; the opening shots' screen-centric mixing practices and somber blue-tinged visuals do the same aesthetically. Only a few shots in, though, the movie provides a clue that the order portrayed in these scenes will be disrupted: the film's title, represented as an orange fireball (contained within the letters of "The Rock") sweeping sonically and visually out through the theater space. This shot's color scheme breaks with the movie's established blue-colored visuals, and its activation of the full 5.1 surroundscape (including the LFE channel) deviates from the screen-centric mix used up to this point.

Immediately after the title the movie's original mixing strategy and color scheme return, but as the sequence progresses these elements are increasingly challenged; this shift in style foreshadows the plot of the movie, in which order, tradition, and discipline are gradually tossed aside. The musical score in particular begins this sequence with a screen-centric mix—direct sound comes from the front, reverberations from the surrounds—but eventually spreads to be loud and direct on all sides. The soundtrack also includes a number of explosion and gunfire sound effects throughout. Only when the orange-colored shots (title, explosion, helicopters) are onscreen, though, do these "battle" sounds spread out into the space of the theater; for the burial/Hummel scenes they remain within the screen. This marked difference in mixing suggests that the orange-colored shots somehow represent a "different" reality than the shots of Hummel and the burial ceremony. That the dominant sounds in this sequence, particularly the radio chatter and the congressional testimony, are *past* sounds now existing only as memories provides a clue as to what this space is: the orange shots place us briefly inside Hummel's head, showing what he is thinking. This is confirmed by a closer look at the shot sequence—each of the helicopter and explosion shots is preceded or succeeded by a shot of Hummel's eyes staring into space, apparently remembering. Significantly, these memories are the spark that cause Hummel to break with the military and take Alcatraz. In other words, the movie's first shots to fully utilize the immersive 5.1 environment are precisely those portraying the narrative *cause* of the break with order and tradition, which is formally represented by the move from screen-centric practices to an immersive surround mix.

TOWARD A COMPREHENSIVE APPROACH

Neither shot-by-shot analysis nor the Cook and Chion models so clearly establish these connections among Hummel, the orange-tinged images, the musical score, and the disruption of military (and cinematic) order as this cursory examination of the sequence's surround mix. Yet these approaches do have value. Shot-by-shot analysis remains an excellent, detail-centric way to discover patterns in cinematography, editing, and production design. Both Cook's and Chion's models reveal interactions shot-by-shot study does not; their emphasis on sound/image pairings is a useful supplement to that detail-oriented visual approach.

The ultimate goal of this chapter is an analytic methodology for examining sound/image relations in a multi-channel environment. A logical way to develop such a model is to build off the strengths of the extant analytic strategies already examined while finding ways to counter their shortcomings. Shot-by-shot analysis, for example, excels at picking up small details and patterns in the visuals, a key component of any analytic model. To build off this strength and counter its attendant limitation (the exclusion of the soundtrack), this approach could productively be expanded to encompass the soundtrack. Although creating a sound-by-sound map of a sequence is necessarily a less-clear process than listing the shots in the image track, due both to the subjective nature of sound and to the fact that multiple sounds can be present at the same time, it is a way of adopting shot-by-shot analysis into a truly audio-visual approach.

The models proposed by Cook and Chion likewise have useful elements to contribute to a more comprehensive analytic approach. Their greatest strength is that they offer frameworks for transference of information, emotion, or meaning from one modality to another; their primary weaknesses are that they are image-centric and that they rely on a conception of "inherent" meaning. Two alterations can neutralize these limitations without sacrificing the use value of the Cook/Chion models. The first of these is to broaden the concepts of added value and signification "gaps" to include a wider range of multi-modal interactions. Added value, for instance, could describe not just sound transferring meaning to the image but also an image affecting our perceptions of a sound, one image changing how we view another image, or one sound (or one portion of the 5.1 soundscape) altering our impression of another. Notably, this expansion necessitates considering the possibility of added value effects between non-simultaneous images and/or sounds—one shot may affect perceptions of the shot following it even though the two do not occur at the same time.

As an example of this expanded view of "added value," one common case of "added value" is the use of a low rumble in the LFE track to make a "big" sound (such as an explosion) feel more powerful. The LFE channel is rarely used on its own; most sounds it makes are paired with higher frequency sounds placed in another audio channel. The impression created by this pairing (as demonstrated in chapter 2) is that of a powerful sound effect *located in the channel with the high-frequency sounds.* Meanwhile, the de-localized LFE rumble *responsible* for this perception of power goes unnoticed. More complex types of interactions between the various audio channels are also possible—as one example, perceptions of the spatial characteristics of dialogue in the center channel are highly influenced by that dialogue's presence and reverberant qualities in the other channels. Indeed, perhaps because audiences are less consciously focused on the soundtrack than on the image, "added value" between two sonic elements is particularly effective.

The second change to the Cook/Chion models relates to the first: the concept of *meanings* should be expanded to incorporate anything about a sound or image that might relate to another sound or image. Cook's category of contest, then, could include not just two audio-visual elements with different emotional or formal connotations but also two media that differ in semantically "meaningless" ways. In *The Rock,* for instance, the explosions mixed to all 5.1 channels could be considered to be in *contest* with those mixed only to the front channels, since the presence of the former forces the analyst to interrogate the latter: why are *these* explosions placed in the front channels alone while others are mixed to both the front channels and the surrounds? Likewise, the sound effects of Hummel's wedding ring and dog tags may not be in contest with their corresponding *images*, but they *are* placed in opposition to the notable absence of sound effects (other than these two) in Hummel's house. As this example demonstrates, a broader definition of contest and added value can incorporate changes *over time*. If a movie's sonic or visual style is different at one point than at another—as with the shift in *Disturbia*'s surround mixing discussed in the previous chapter—then awareness of this change changes audience perceptions of both the original style *and* the new one, creating a meaning not present in either alone.

A HYBRID MODEL FOR MULTI-CHANNEL ANALYSIS

Combining all the above-described changes yields an analytic model that draws on the strengths of the three original textual analysis models discussed but avoids many of their shortcomings. To summarize, this methodology involves three steps. First, a "masking" approach is used to break down a film sequence shot-by-shot, both visually and aurally. Though creating a "sonic shotlist" is an inherently subjective project, the goal is not to create a *perfect* map of the image and soundtracks but to provide an overall guide and reveal the salient features of each on their own.y

Second, chapter 6's multi-channel analytic approach is employed to supplement this overall map with more specific details about the film's use of the surround environment. With a general sense of the soundtrack already in hand, the emphasis in this phase is singling out the places where something interesting is happening in the multi-channel mix and/or the mixing strategy markedly differs from the established norms. Any new sounds that were not perceived when playing the soundtrack as a whole are also noted at this point.

Third and finally, the analysis itself is conducted through a bimodal process. One-half of the analysis follows the traditional shot-by-shot methodology of noting patterns and structures and deciphering their meaning and function—with the difference that now these patterns may be found in the image, in the sound design, or in some combination of the two. The other half of the analysis identifies and examines places of *contest* within the sequence, recalling that if contest is defined as loosely as possible then any meaningful interactions between elements should fall under this category. Determining all the possible points of contest can be a complex task, since *any* two components of the sequence may be in opposition—a sound and an image, two sounds, two images, or an image (or sound) and an established pattern are all possibilities. Once these points are identified the concepts of added value and signification gaps can be employed to determine the meaning of this opposition.

The procedure outlined above does not specify whether Cook's model of sound/image interactions or Chion's is best suited to this comprehensive textual analysis strategy—in fact, it freely commingles elements and terminology from each. Both models ultimately rest on the principle that features from one element of a multimedia work associate themselves with—and are perceived as intrinsic to—others, even if they assert different principles for exactly *how* this transference occurs. From a practical standpoint, then, components from both models can be adopted where appropriate. Chion's masking method is a logical and straightforward way to recognize the salient features of the soundtrack (whether one channel or the whole thing) and the image track; Cook's categorization scheme can be used to consider the data obtained from the masking method and identify the interactions most worthy of close analysis. Added value and signification gaps can similarly each be employed where they seem most productive in elucidating a cinematic text.

I should note that the multi-channel-specific analysis approach developed in the last chapter is actually a stripped-down version of the more comprehensive approach described here, using essentially the same methodology minus the image-related portions. In fact, the analysis model developed in chapter 6, which requires listening to various subsets of the 5.1 soundscape, is also a variation on Chion's masking method, which is designed to foreground aspects of one of a film's components (soundtrack, image, or even a particular channel of the surround soundtrack) that might be hidden when that component is experienced in combination with the others. Chion writes that the masking method allows one to "hear the sound as it is, and not as the image transforms and disguises it";[25] this multi-channel analytic strategy could be said to help the analyst "hear the audio *channel* as it is, and not as the *rest of the soundscape* transforms and disguises it."

7.3. Harry with the winged Snitch in hand at the end of the Quidditch match in *Harry Potter and the Chamber of Secrets* (2002). "Added value" explains why the Snitch seems to fly around quickly and erratically despite not moving very fast when actually onscreen.

A simple example will help illustrate the functioning of this comprehensive analytic strategy. Consider the Quidditch scene in *Harry Potter and the Chamber of Secrets* (2002), specifically its presentation of the winged golden orb known as the "Snitch." One of several flying "balls" in the aerial game of Quidditch, the film's characters describe the Snitch as fast and therefore difficult to catch. In an initial screening of this scene, the Snitch indeed seems to zoom around the space of the theater at lightning speed. But while the *perception* is that we *see* the Snitch moving quickly, the masking method reveals that it only intermittently appears onscreen and is generally stationary or moving slowly when it does so. Using Chion's terminology, the impression of the Snitch's quick visual movements is "added value" from the soundtrack. This effect, moreover, encompasses two distinct elements: the high-pitched buzzing sound of the Snitch implies speed in the image, and the fact that this sound zips quickly all around the multichannel soundscape when the ball is *offscreen* leads to the impression that it continues this high-speed motion when it is *onscreen*. Cook's model could equally well explain the same effect: the Snitch's limited (and brief) appearances onscreen leave a signification gap since the audience does not have time to form a strong visual impression of it, and the speed of its movement in the soundtrack "fills" this gap to create the impression that the Snitch is speeding around the screen although it actually is not. Regardless of which set of terminology is used, it is clear that the sequence creates a structural opposition (contest) between the continual presence of the Snitch in the soundtrack and its relative absence in the visuals. This imbalance allows for a transference of meaning from the former to the latter.

CASE STUDY: HIDDEN MEANINGS IN *JOY RIDE*

This chapter initially set out to develop a comprehensive analytic strategy; it will conclude by deploying that newly developed strategy on a complete cinematic sequence. An action scene (like the Quidditch scene referenced above) that aggressively uses the multi-channel environment is an obvious candidate for this project. In the digital surround era, however, multi-channel effects are important in an wide range of movies and sequences, not just in those whose surround use is the most apparent. For this case study, therefore, I have selected a sequence from a movie that generally adheres to the digital surround style but does so more subtly than films like the *Star Wars* prequels or other action-adventure movies.

Specifically, this analysis will examine a scene from the 2001 suspense thriller *Joy Ride*. This movie does include some action sequences that noticeably activate the multi-channel environment, but the particular segment discussed here, occurring about twenty-five minutes into the film, is a dramatic scene in a hotel room that does not use any attention-grabbing surround effects. In a previous scene, brothers Lewis and Fuller (played by Paul Walker and Steve Zahn, respectively) have set up a prank, using their CB radio to convince a trucker—known only by his CB handle "Rusty Nail"—that a lonely woman is waiting for him in a hotel room that is actually occupied by an obnoxious businessman. Now, Lewis and Fuller wait in the room next door to hear the results of their prank.

Adopting the analysis process delineated above, the first step to parsing this scene is to use the masking method to break down the image and soundtracks. Rather than list each sound and each shot in the image track here, I will summarize them and describe the most important observations. The image track is comprised of forty-five shots, all taken from within Lewis and Fuller's room. Two shots (numbers six and forty-three) are literal point-of-view shots showing what the characters see as they look out their room's window; none of the other shots present a character's exact visual perspective. Overall, the picture edit adheres to traditional continuity rules and provides a good visual map of the small space of their room as Lewis and Fuller move around it. What it does not offer, though, is much in the way of narrative material. Essentially the image track shows Lewis and Fuller moving around the room and growing progressively more tense but gives little explanation for their actions or their perceived state of mind. The only real *actions* they take are turning off the television early in the scene, making a phone call a few minutes later, and receiving a phone call shortly after that.

The soundtrack offers somewhat more information but, like the visuals, is narratively unclear. Its major components are ongoing rain and traffic sounds, intermittent but somewhat regular thunder, occasional dialogue, and basic Foley. Individually perceptible sound effects are limited; those of note include a couple of low thuds and multiple phone rings. Significantly, not all the phone rings sound the same—some of them are loud and present while others are quieter and sound muffled, or at least less direct (the high frequencies appear to have been rolled off). Just before the first of the loud, present rings, the soundtrack drops off almost to total silence, which makes the ensuing ring seem louder than it otherwise would. Aside from these effects, one long stretch of the scene includes a series of muffled noises and voices, which are present enough in the mix to draw conscious attention but low enough— and processed enough—so as to be indecipherable. Music, seemingly non-diegetic, is used sparsely and consists mostly of brief electronic tones. The scene includes only one actual melodic cue (a descending chromatic scale), which is placed low in the mix twice, then swells into the foreground at the end of the scene.

Combining these observations with those from a third screening of the image and soundtrack together clarifies several relationships. Most importantly, the lack of information in the visuals is explained: the bulk of the scene is devoted to Lewis and Fuller *listening* to what they (and we) cannot see happening next door. The more "distant" sounds—including the muffled phone rings and the indecipherable voices—are those originating in this offscreen space; we, like Lewis and Fuller, cannot hear them distinctly. Even if most of the visuals are not explicitly coded as point of view, this sonic treatment makes it clear that we are in the same diegetic space as the characters, hearing what they hear—a key point in a sound-dominated scene like this one. The soundtrack also explains why the brothers move around the room at various points in the scene—at first they try to eliminate any indications that their room is occupied, then they strive to better hear what is happening next door, then they use the phone to report the disturbance, and at the end they check what is happening outside, making sure their own room is secure.

Channel masking reveals a highly complex approach to surround mixing. Overall, the film exploits the 5.1 environment to create the tight image/sound matching characteristic of the digital surround style, with an ultrafield-driven mix that specifically places sounds where the onscreen image indicates they would be in the offscreen diegesis. This holds true both for spot effects—such as the thunderclaps outside and the truck door slamming in the parking lot when Rusty Nail first arrives—and for ambient sounds like the rain heard through the windows. The mix also uses processing and volume changes to signify spatial relationships. The sounds from the next room are obviously processed and lowered in volume to sound as if they're heard through a wall, but even background effects like the ever-present rain are altered to correspond to the image—these get louder and more present for camera angles closer to a window and are loudest during the POV shots looking directly out the window. In short, the soundtrack carefully places and mixes sounds to match the image track.

But a channel-masking analysis reveals other, less expected sonic strategies as well. Perhaps most intriguing is that when listening to the center channel on its own, the voices from the next-door room can be heard much more clearly—indeed, we can follow the dialogue between Rusty Nail and the businessman. Their words, it turns out, are not *inherently* incomprehensible. Rather, when heard in the context of the entire soundscape, the noise from the rain and traffic in the other channels makes them *seem* unhearable, just as a conversation between two people several feet away may be perfectly clear when heard with no distractions but is difficult to understand if the two are surrounded by a crowd of other speakers.

The other audio channels, then, contribute an *added value* to the center channel by making us perceive its sounds as something other than what they actually are. This raises the question of why the filmmakers took the difficult approach of carefully balancing the mix so as to make the next-door conversation *audible* but not *legible*, when it would have been much easier to achieve the same result simply by processing that dialogue. The visuals offer a clue to their rationale. During the muffled conversation, the image track holds a single shot for a full thirty seconds (out of a four-minute scene). Initially this shot is a two-shot with Lewis and Fuller on opposite sides of the frame. Between them, on the wall separating them from Rusty Nail, hangs a painting. As they try to hear what is happening next door, the brothers move closer to the wall and eventually press their ears against it. While they are listening, the camera begins to track forward, gradually pushing Lewis and Fuller outside the frame; when it stops, the painting fills the entire frame, and the camera holds here for about ten seconds before cutting away (to an over-Fuller's-shoulder medium close-up of Lewis).

The joint effect of this shot and the surround mix described above is to further align our perceptions with those of Lewis and Fuller. Like them, we feel like we *should* be able to understand the sounds coming from the neighboring room—as indeed we could *if* the pouring rain and loud thunderbolts were not masking them. Even if we cannot consciously make sense of the sounds heard through the wall, subconsciously we recognize that they *could* be made out; they have not been processed beyond recognition. And just as Lewis and Fuller move closer to the wall to hear better, the camera acknowledges our sense that we can *almost* hear what's happening next door, pushing in toward the wall to offer that closer perspective.

As one might expect from a film adhering to the digital surround style, the soundscape shifts as the camera tracks toward the wall. This change, though, does not precisely reflect the camera's new position. To be sure, the rain gets quieter in the surround channels, matching the visual suggestion that as we move closer to the sounds coming from next door we should hear less of the sounds from other directions. But the absolute level of the sounds from the next room in the mix does not change (even if they seem *relatively* louder as the surrounds drop in loudness), and the rain sounds from the other speakers remain strong enough to continue prohibiting us from understanding the muffled voices. Meanwhile, another change occurs in the surround channels. Throughout the scene to this point, the soundtrack has included intermittent splashes, logically associated with passing cars on the rain-soaked highway outside. These have been mixed to whichever channel was closest to the road, in this case the left surround channel. Now, those irregular splashes spread into *both* surround channels and morph into regular *waves*. This is a subtle change, not consciously perceptible in the context of the complete 5.1 soundtrack but clear when listening to the surround channels alone. A sound effect that had previously matched the sound of tires driving through puddles changes, taking on a distinctly different sonic characteristic reminiscent of the roar of the ocean and the crashing of moving water against a rocky shore.

On their own, these waves seem out of place for a scene in a hotel room. The image track, though, offers a clear candidate for their source: by this point the entire screen is filled by the hanging painting, which features an ancient sailing ship asea in a rocky cove during a nighttime storm. The wave sound effects match the painting's visible waves, which are crashing against several large rocks near the ship. As if to confirm this association of the surround channels' wave effects with the painting, the thunder sounds shift as well. To this point all thunderclaps have been present in four of the main speakers (all but the center channel), though mixed to be loudest in the speaker closest to the outside. Now, though, some of the thunder is heard *only* in the surround channels. Specifically, when lightning flashes *across the painting*, lighting it up (and visually suggesting that lightning is flashing *within* the painting itself), simultaneous thunderclaps are heard in the surround channels; in contrast, those peals of thunder not associated with any visible lightning continue to be heard in the front channels. Between the thunder and the waves, the sound mix clearly associates the painting with the surround channels.

This association, though, is in conflict with two key facts. First, the painting is an inanimate object and should not be generating *any* sounds, regardless of where they are panned. Second, the painting is onscreen—in fact it is *all* that is onscreen—so it seems odd that its sounds would be mixed to the rear channels. Both of these concerns can be explained by noting that in the context of the full 5.1 soundtrack the sounds "from" the painting are not consciously perceived. The wave effects are subtle, and most viewers are unlikely to notice exactly which bursts of thunder come from which speakers. More importantly, at this point in the scene we are not focused on the painting or on the storm sounds but rather on the muffled sounds coming through the wall. Like Lewis and Fuller, our aural attentions are busy trying to reconstruct the events next door without a visual referent. This allows the "painting's sounds" to work on us unobtrusively, as long as they remain in the surround channels and hence do not interfere with the center-channel-based sounds from next door.[26]

The sounds associated with the painting are not placed in the rear channels solely to keep them from intruding on the center channel; this placement also allows the filmmakers to take advantage of DSS's ability to present multiple spaces simultaneously. The literal effect of these sounds is to surround us with the sonic world suggested by the painting. This fantastical space in the rear channels is kept distinct both from the space of Lewis and Fuller's room (diegetic sounds in the front left and right channels) and from the offscreen space of the room next door, whose sounds originate in the center channel. The result is three distinct spaces, each of which represents different aspects of where Lewis and Fuller *are*. Physically, they are in their own room. Their mental energies, meanwhile, are devoted to the room next door. But the surround channels present a third space suggested by the painting. To understand its meaning, consider that this particular scene is a turning point in the film—more specifically, it is *during this specific shot* that the brothers' seemingly harmless prank goes horribly wrong, making Rusty Nail seek to kill them (the main narrative line of the movie) and turning their simple road trip into a battle for their lives.

What the metaphoric space of the painting indicates, then, is Lewis and Fuller's position of *peril*. Like the onscreen ship about to crash into rocks, they are in dangerous waters and unlikely to survive the now inevitable sequence of events. In the same way the painting takes up the entire screen, its sounds spread out into the theater, making the danger it visually portrays a tangible entity all around the brothers.

7.4. The start of a lengthy shot in *Joy Ride* (2001). Fuller and Lewis listen at the wall, while the camera slowly tracks in toward the painting. Though the conscious attentions of Lewis, Fuller, and the audience are all focused on the sounds coming from next door, the multi-channel soundtrack actually portrays three distinct spaces by the time the camera has tracked close enough that the painting fills the frame.

Placing these sounds in the surround channels keeps us from identifying the danger Lewis and Fuller will face; it remains an unknown and unseen power that cannot be tied to the screen. Notably, this is not the first time we have seen the surround channels associated with danger—surround effects in the first two-thirds of *Disturbia* always signified threats to its protagonist. This parallel use is no coincidence; the surround channels are particularly well suited to representing danger precisely because they portray the unseen, a connection that will be further explored in chapter 10.

Much more could be said about this scene and the way it uses the multi-channel environment and the image track together to convey things neither alone could. The shock value of Lewis and Fuller's phone ringing late in the scene, for instance, derives primarily from the fact that visuals and sound design just prior to this moment are constructed to focus our aural attentions on the room next door; as we strive to hear these muffled sounds, the loudness and presence of this "local" sound is such a shock to our ears that we are just as startled as Fuller and Lewis. But even on its own, the short segment analyzed above demonstrates just how important interactions between the image track, the soundtrack as a whole, and the various channels of the 5.1 soundscape are to the overall effect and meaning of this scene.

Joy Ride is hardly unique in making multi-channel effects crucial to its design. Indeed, in every film to which I have applied the analytic methodology developed in this chapter, that approach has revealed hidden structures or important sound/image interactions that would not have been uncovered by more traditional practices. This result confirms that surround sound is today a significant component of film aesthetics—even in films like *Joy Ride* that may seem to the casual moviegoer to be relatively subtle in their use of the multi-channel environment—and any scholars studying contemporary cinema should employ analytic methods that can account for its use.

Textual analysis can, as shown with *Joy Ride*, be employed to explicate how a film's aesthetic components work together to serve narrative or other themes. As explained at the conclusion of chapter 5, though, textual analysis is also valuable to film scholarship for the broader ideas about cinema it can reveal, validate, or even contradict. With a surround-inclusive approach to analysis now in hand, it is time to put that methodology to use in the more abstract realm of cinema theory. This book's third and final section turns its attentions to the ramifications of digital surround on the way the cinema functions. The comprehensive analysis methodology developed in this chapter, though, will not be left idle. Each of the remaining three chapters in this book will incorporate a case study in which this new analytic approach is used to illustrate that chapter's particular theoretical concept in the context of a specific film.

3

THEORY

8

BODY AND VOICE

The transition from monophony to multitrack overhauls the rules of the game. The voice may be contained in a space that is no longer defined solely in visual terms, but also auditory ones. Its real positioning in a three-dimensional auditory space, in the middle of other sounds, takes away its imaginary place. The voice wishing to dominate must do so in a changed kind of space, which voices can no longer "contain" in the same way.

MICHEL CHION IN *THE VOICE IN CINEMA*

The relationship between body and voice is a fitting topic with which to begin exploring the ramifications of digital surround sound (DSS) for film theory and scholarship. After all, the ability to synchronize human voices with their onscreen images is perhaps *the* defining characteristic of sound cinema. Sound effects and music often accompanied silent films, but dialogue and voices directly associated with the onscreen characters could not. Lecturers offered verbal enhancement to some films, but it was clear in these cases that the voice heard and the bodies seen onscreen had two distinct sources. The triumph of sync sound technology was the ability to record voices and play them back *matched* to the bodies that created them.

Cinema has changed much since the dawn of sync sound, but its reliance on codes of synchronization—particularly on the matching of body to voice—has not. To this day Hollywood works hard to ensure that this pairing of image and sound is done correctly lest audiences note that the film has gone "out of sync." Films may play with this convention—pairing a child's body with a demonic voice in *The Exorcist* (1973) or switching the voice/body pairings of two stars when a movie premiere in *Singin' in the Rain* (1952) runs into technical problems—but even these "false" pairings demonstrate the effectiveness of synchronization in asserting that a particular voice and a particular body belong together.

Yet the cinema's "synchronization" of voice and body has always remained incomplete. The two are *temporally* synchronized but occupy different *spatial* positions. Voices nearly always emanate from the screen while the bodies ostensibly tied to them freely wander the diegetic world, sometimes appearing in the image and sometimes leaving it even as their voices continue to come from the same onscreen place. Digital surround sound offers at least the *possibility* of rectifying this dichotomy. For the first time in cinema history, filmmakers have a standardized system in which voices not only can be *placed* in a variety of places around the theater but can actually be *heard* in that configuration in nearly all theaters and even in many homes. Indeed, this book has already noted a few films (*Spider-Man*, *Kinsey*, and *Girl, Interrupted*) that achieved specific aesthetic or emotional effects by violating the long-standing tradition of keeping all dialogue in the front center channel.

Even in the digital surround era, deviations like these remain relatively unusual. Most films, most of the time, continue to mix dialogue front and center. But the mere *possibility* that voices can now move around the theater alters the dynamic of the voice and body pairing. Just as silence can exist only in relation to sound, mixing all voices to the center channel has a different connotation in a world where they *could* be placed elsewhere than in one where they can *only* reside in the center. This chapter will explore exactly *how* the relationship between voice and body changes once the former is no longer restricted to a single locale.

THE VOICE

The human voice has long been a, perhaps *the*, fundamental point of interest in film sound. At the dawn of synchronized sound the newly sync-sound-equipped movies were commonly labeled "talkies" or "talking pictures" rather than "sound films," a signal that what really fascinated audiences was the opportunity to hear *voices* coupled with the onscreen images. As one scholar puts it, "In actual movies, for real spectators, there are not *all the sounds including the human voice. There are voices, and then everything else.*"[1] Filmmakers follow the same principle: dialogue is always considered the key element of the soundtrack, with the primary concern of any mix being legible dialogue. Common production practices that in the abstract seem strange and intrusive—such as "dipping" the musical score down in the mix when characters are speaking—go unnoticed because they allow the dialogue to be heard. "We've got to remember, it's all about words," explains re-recording mixer Marti Humphrey. "First and foremost, I always want to make sure that I can hear every word."[2] Dolby consultant Thom Ehle is more succinct: "You've got to hear the dialogue to hear the story."[3] Michel Chion highlights the unique place of dialogue by comparing it to film visuals; while moviegoers are content to have objects come into and fade out of view through lighting, framing, and focus, "We must always hear *every word*, from one end to the other."[4]

As sound recording equipment of the early sync era did not allow for much "remixing," the principal job of early production recordists was to ensure all the dialogue could be clearly understood. Despite their job's emphasis on *words*, these technicians noticed that the *way* in which those words were spoken was equally important. Drawing on the French Impressionist filmmakers' term *photogénie* (the notion that filmed objects reveal something different on the screen than they do in the profilmic world),[5] those working in early sound media coined the term *phonogénie* to reflect the real-world experience that certain voices "recorded" better than others.[6] In part, *phonogénie* arose from limitations of early recording media—voices with too much or too little resonance actually would not record well. But *phonogénie* also carried a more inexpressible weight: some voices simply *sound* better recorded than others for no obvious reason. These first film sound technicians thus already recognized dialogue as both a conveyor of semantic meaning and a *sound*.

While the concept of *photogénie* has remained common and has even bled into everyday use through the term "photogenic," its aural equivalent has not. Interest in the human voice, it seems, is driven primarily by its value for transmitting meaning. Even the common soundtrack breakdown scheme of music, effects, and dialogue subliminally reinforces this thinking, with "dialogue" inherently suggesting not just characters' words but the place of those words in a language-based conversation. To convey the fullness of human speech as a *sound*, "voice" seems a better term than "dialogue." Both imply the ability to convey meaning, but "voice" adds an implicit focus on the *aural quality* of those words. And given the unique characteristics of each person's voice, this term also ties the words being spoken *to a specific person*.

SYNCHRONIZATION

The assignment of each voice to a single person is crucial to the success of synchronized sound. As Mary Ann Doane and others have persuasively argued, cinema is inherently heterogeneous. That is, its combination of sound and image is not "natural," and audiences must therefore be "tricked" into accepting it. The soundtrack always "carries with it the potential risk of exposing the material heterogeneity of the medium,"[7] and classic practices of sound editing and mixing are designed specifically to avoid this revelation.[8] Most important among these practices is "synchronization," the temporal matching of a voice (sound) with an onscreen person (image)—specifically, the matching of each voice to a *unique* onscreen body.

The need for temporal synchronization between (visual) body and (acoustic) voice has roots in the monophonic technology of early sound films. While characters' *bodies* could be anywhere—not just *within* the image but also offscreen—the single speaker system meant that *voices* always came from the center of the screen. Alleviating this discrepancy necessitated synchronizing body and voice. Yet synchronization was not a means of truly unifying body and voice but merely a *code* through which to hide the true disunity between them. Consider the comments of a viewer experiencing a sound film for the first time:

> Right at the start the general effect is rather disconcerting. Since the loudspeaker installed behind the screen never changes its locus of sound propagation, the voice always comes from the same spot no

matter which character is speaking . . . the concordance of lip movements and spoken syllables strengthens our demands for credibility and
forces us to locate the sound in space—in fact, makes this absolutely
indispensable.[9]

Audiences today do not experience the same "disconcerting" effect as
this early filmgoer only because they have become so accustomed to
cinema's spatial separation of body and voice that they no longer notice
it—the code of temporal synchronization hides this incongruity, and
filmgoers play along with the deception.

Digital surround sound's spatialization capabilities *could* hold the
potential to remedy the body/voice separation—if, as the sync sound
neophyte above asserts, the difficulty in matching the two originated
solely in their spatial disunity. The roots of cinema's split between body
and voice, however, lie deeper than mere spatial incoherence. The ability to edit sound and image separately—to "match" any body with any
voice—means the rift between the two can never be completely eliminated. While the code of synchronization encourages the *acceptance*
of mismatched pairings (i.e., *The Exorcist* and *Singin' in the Rain*), it
simultaneously serves as a reminder of their illusory nature; awareness
of synchronization's ability to create "false matches" means even seemingly "correct" pairings cannot be completely trusted. Additionally,
as audiences grow more movie-savvy (through DVD supplemental
features and the like) and learn about production sound practices like
ADR (Automated Dialog Replacement, the process of re-recording
dialogue in a studio in post-production to obtain cleaner recordings),
they become even less likely to believe in *any* sort of unity between
body and image. With the rift between body and voice fundamentally
entwined in the technology of cinema, merely adding "spatial matching" to the code of synchronization can hardly reunite the two. As film
scholar William Johnson puts it, "There is *always* a gap between the
image track and the sound track."[10] Chion concurs, arguing that the
split between body and voice is *not* a technological shortcoming but a
foundational characteristic of the cinema: "It's clear that if voice and
body do not hang together in the sound film, the problem does not
lie in some technical lacuna. Adding relief, smell, or touch wouldn't
change anything, nor would higher-fidelity recordings or *a more scru-
pulous localization of sound*."[11]

But while the rift between body and voice is not *healed* by multi-channel sound, it is *altered*. Where filmmakers previously could manipulate only the *temporal* synchronization of image and sound, they can now play with *spatial* synchronization as well. The decision by *Timecode's* (2000) filmmakers to sometimes temporally synchronize *offscreen* sounds with *onscreen* sources is a perfect example of this. Screened using a monophonic system, this movie *seems* to adhere to the classic code of tying voices to bodies through temporal synchronization. Heard in a 5.1-channel environment, on the other hand, the film clearly undermines the code of synchronization by emphasizing the separation between onscreen bodies and their voices.

Conceptually, *Timecode* follows in the footsteps of the aforementioned scene from *Singin' in the Rain*, using the "material heterogeneity" of the cinema to foreground the (normally unnoticed) code of synchronization. But in this example it is spatial rather than temporal synchrony that reveals the *disunity* of sound and image. The incongruence between *Timecode's* mixing aesthetic and its visual style further highlight this split. In the image track, the whole story unfolds in four simultaneously present, unbroken digital video shots. Between its reliance on continuity and its use of low-end digital video, the film's image track conveys a sense of "naturalism." Yet *Timecode's* soundtrack, which separates actors' voices from their bodies, subverts this impression. By pairing an *apparently* "unconstructed" image track with an *obviously* highly constructed soundtrack, the film ultimately reminds audiences that no matter how "natural" or "unified" a film may seem, cinema is by nature a heterogeneous medium. Its codes are *always* at play, even when—perhaps *especially* when—they appear not to be.

ONSCREEN/OFFSCREEN

Most films, of course, do not employ multi-channel voices in as incongruous a way as *Timecode*. Voices usually remain in the center channel in adherence to monophonic and Dolby Stereo practices; less frequently, they move around the theater to maintain an "accurate" spatial match between diegetic body and voice. But even in these cases, multi-channel has a significant impact on the relationship between image and sound. Consider one of the most basic distinctions about the relationship between image and sound: whether a sound is "onscreen" or "offscreen." Tomlinson Holman sees this question as the principal concern of sound engineers, saying the job "boils down to a few aesthetic choices that apply to the engineering. The biggest one is the difference between on-screen sound and offscreen sound . . . the aesthetic question is not only what you do, it's what kind of sounds you put *in the surround versus the screen*."[12]

Holman observes that in multi-channel, sounds can literally move "off" the screen; *Timecode*, for instance, features a person's body on the screen while his voice is played in a surround channel. In traditional usage, this voice would be labeled "onscreen," as its source is shown in the image. But this seems a clear misnomer, since the sound emanates from outside the plane of the screen. The problem is that despite being used to describe *sounds*, the onscreen/offscreen distinction is really about the *visuals*.[13]

In a monophonic environment, with a single speaker located behind the screen, this usage makes sense—sounds are *never* really offscreen. Rather, an "offscreen sound" is one understood to come from some object or person not currently visible in the image. In a discrete 5.1 environment, however, relying on the image track to determine whether a sound is "onscreen" or "offscreen" is insufficient. The onscreen/offscreen binary of the monaural world splinters into several fragments in the new multi-channel environment. Even ignoring non-diegetic sounds like the musical score,[14] a diegetic sound object may be onscreen visually but offscreen aurally (as in the *Timecode* example above), onscreen aurally but offscreen visually (the traditional meaning of "offscreen"), onscreen both visually and aurally (the traditional meaning of "onscreen"), or offscreen both visually and aurally. And even this schemata does not include all the possible ways in which an aural object could be *partially* matched with its visual counterpart, for example, showing a man on the right side of the screen and placing his voice in the left front speaker instead of the right.

Other scholars have also noted that surround sound has implications for the onscreen/offscreen distinction. In his discussion of Hollywood's flirtation with magnetic multi-channel soundtracks in the 1950s, for instance, John Belton notes the possibilities of a truly offscreen space for sounds: "For the first time in film history, offscreen dialogue was literally offscreen, emanating from surround speakers on either side of the auditorium."[15] Filmmakers of the magnetic era did not make much use of this possibility, largely returning to monophonic-era mixing practices by the mid-1950s, but Dolby Stereo's introduction two decades later again challenged the onscreen/offscreen binary. As Chion writes, "Multitrack sound and a wrap-around 'superfield' . . . problematize older and simpler notions of onscreen and offscreen."[16] Like Belton before him, though, Chion has little to say about this issue. Instead, he sidesteps it with the assertion that mixing important sounds outside the center front channel is "disconcerting" to the audience[17]—a contention that may have been accurate in the 1980s (though Chion presents no evidence that it was) but is, as discussed in chapter 5, of questionable validity today.

THE ACOUSMÊTRE

The classification of sounds as "offscreen" or "onscreen" takes on par-ticular importance in the context of the voice/body rift. Once multi-channel sound gives voices the same power as bodies to move around the theater, the possible distinction between the two becomes even greater. Traditional synchronization has relied on temporal matching of voices with bodies. Even in the monophonic era, though, simple time-based synchrony was not enough to provide a convincing impres-sion of voice/body unity: the 1920s moviegoer cited earlier mentioned that it is the "concordance of *lip movements* and spoken syllables" that sells the illusion of synchronization. Pairing voices with *bodies* is not enough—it is specifically the pairing of a voice with a *mouth* that con-vinces us of the unity between image and sound. This observation has a crucial consequence for the concepts of onscreen and offscreen: it suggests that any time we hear a voice while its accompanying *mouth* is not visible, we are actually experiencing an "offscreen voice"—in the traditional, image-driven sense of offscreen—regardless of whether any other parts of the speaking character are onscreen or not.[18]

The existence of "offscreen voices" reveals a loophole in the code of synchronization. While requiring films to establish a temporal match between image and sound, it does not dictate that voices must *always* be paired with mouths, or even bodies. As long as *some* voices and bodies are correctly paired, others may remain unmatched—in fact, "offscreen voices" have been used as a storytelling device throughout sound cinema's history. They have also attracted significant scholarly attention; Michel Chion devotes the largest portion of his book *The Voice in Cinema* to "offscreen voices," focusing on those that remain offscreen until far into a movie or are never matched to a body *at all.* He labels a disembodied voice—one that has not yet been attached to an onscreen body (that is, an onscreen *mouth*) an *acousmêtre.* Acousmêtres, Chion claims, have special powers deriving from their position "outside" the traditional cinematic code of synchronization, which dictates that voices and bodies must be tied together.

These powers, moreover, are enhanced by the move to multi-channel sound. In a monophonic or Dolby Stereo soundtrack, the front center channel is inherently "multiple." It contains a mix of sounds, some of which are "offscreen" (as it is traditionally defined) and others of which are "onscreen." In particular, all *voices*—including the acousmêtric voice—are contained in this channel. The acousmêtre is thus hardly *unique.* It shares the space of—and is forced to compete with—the rest of the soundtrack, including onscreen voices, and on- and offscreen sounds. In the fully spatialized environment of the digital surround style, though, the situation is markedly different. Here *most* sounds are carefully placed in the multi-channel soundscape to ensure that the aural environment created matches the visual one suggested by the onscreen images. But the disembodied voice of the acousmêtre retains the unique power to *choose its own location.* With no physical body to tie it down, the acousmêtre is free to roam from channel to channel throughout the theater. It can choose to be in the plane of the screen—where it becomes the *only* such sound with no corresponding image—or out in the space of the auditorium. It can even occupy multiple channels simultaneously, a power generally withheld from sounds whose sources *are* or *have been* visible in the image track.

Spider-Man's (2002) Green Goblin, already encountered in chapter 5, is an excellent example of a multi-channel acousmêtre. When Norman Osborn first hears the voice of his evil alter ego, the Goblin is a textbook acousmêtre, literally a voice with no body. This is why Osborn cannot locate the *source* of the voice—it *has* no physical source. During Osborn's search, the Goblin demonstrates the multi-channel acousmêtre's power over the cinematic image itself. His spatialized voice guides the visuals as the camera repeatedly cuts to where the Goblin *should* be based on his voice's location. Each time, however, it finds nothing, and the voice reappears elsewhere. The Goblin literally exists outside the camera's purview: he not only *has not* been seen but *cannot* be seen, even when we look in the "right place." 1995's 12 *Monkeys* uses an acousmêtric voice in much the same way. In one scene Cole, the film's protagonist (played by Bruce Willis), is locked in his prison cell and hears a voice questioning his sanity. The voice swirls around the five-channel soundscape and is never tied to an onscreen body, leaving the audience forever unsure whether the voice was real, perhaps piped in by the prison authorities, or existed only in Cole's (insane) mind.[19]

PSYCHO AND THE VISUALIZED ACOUSMÊTRE

The code of synchronization suggests offscreen voices should not be able to remain unvisualized for long, as the audience *wants* to match voices with bodies: "It is the law of every offscreen voice to create this desire to go and see who's speaking."[20] Acousmêtres can, however, retain their power by exploiting the fact that "real embodiment" of a voice requires pairing the voice with a *mouth*. Randolph Jordan's provocative analysis of 2001's *Donnie Darko,* for instance, shows that the supernatural rabbit Frank continues to function as an acousmêtre even after numerous onscreen appearances because the character wears a mouth-covering mask in those scenes. In a reversal of the *Spider-Man* scene, where the Goblin's voice emanates from a specific location but its visual source cannot be located, Frank's voice in these early scenes issues from all five main channels even as his body appears in a single place onscreen. Only when Frank finally removes the head of his costume to reveal his mouth does his voice fold down to the center channel, finally tied down to a body.[21]

Hitchcock's *Psycho* (1960), which will serve as a productive point of comparison in the upcoming case study, relies on a similarly visualized acousmêtre. At first, the film is driven by a perceived need to find Mrs. Bates's body and "match" her voice with it. This desire is rooted in the code of synchronization—we have *heard* Mrs. Bates's voice but have

8.1. Frank, the spectral rabbit of *Donnie Darko* (2001), is a visualized but masked acousmêtre. Until he removes his mask, his voice cannot be tied to a *mouth* and hence plays through all five main channels of the 5.1 soundscape.

not *seen* her speaking. In Chion's words, "the story is propelled by the obsessive idea of getting into the house in order to see the mother. . . . Entering the house equals finding the source of the voice, bringing the mother onscreen, attaching the voice to a body."[22]

The camera does eventually make it into the house, but even then it does not allow the audience to see Mrs. Bates's body and hear her voice *at the same time*. Repeatedly *Psycho* teases us with the *possibility* of this pairing while never providing it. The lighting and cinematography in the shower attack, for instance, are designed to prevent a clear view of Marion's attacker. Later, Norman carries his mother down the stairs as she speaks to him. This would seem the perfect opportunity to at last tie Mrs. Bates's voice to her body, yet the carefully choreographed camerawork and blocking reveal her body but not her *face*, prohibiting us from tying down the acousmêtric voice to a *mouth*. Even after the "mother" personality wins out over the "Norman" one, the movie fails to provide "real embodiment" of her voice: it concludes with "Mother" speaking in voiceover as Norman's unmoving face remains on the screen. A psychologist has explained that Norman has both personalities inside him, and hence her voice *should* emanate from his body, but the movie forever withholds the temporal pairing of a moving mouth with a voice that would definitively confirm this pairing. The desire for synchronization remains unfulfilled, and the mother's voice remains forever an acousmêtre.

Chion finds in *Psycho* exposure of "the very structure of sound film, based on an offscreen field inhabited by the voice, which is the inevitable corollary of the onscreen field."[23] With its plot clearly rooted in the cinema's fundamental split between body and voice, this assessment makes sense. But *Psycho* is a monophonic film, and if "the very structure" of sound cinema is tied to the offscreen/onscreen dynamic as Chion indicates, then the film might not be so revealing about the way contemporary *multi-channel* cinema functions. Chapter 6 noted that one problem with Gus Van Sant's 1998 remake of *Psycho* was its grafting of monophonic-era visuals onto a multi-channel sound design. More important than this mismatch is that *Psycho*'s plot is intrinsically tied to the acousmêtre. With the acousmêtre significantly altered by the advent of multi-channel sound suggests remaking *Psycho* in 5.1 would require completely rethinking not just the film's aesthetics but also its plot—a task Van Sant and his crew did not undertake.

CASE STUDY: *FIGHT CLUB* AND THE "UNIFIED" ACOUSMÊTRE

1999's *Fight Club* employs a narrative device virtually identical to that of *Psycho*: a main character controlled by another voice that we eventually realize is part of him. Also like *Psycho*, the film plays with cinema's material heterogeneity through the voice/body split. In doing so, though, it seems to postulate a more positive resolution to this split than its forerunner: where *Psycho*'s Norman is finally *destroyed by* his acousmêtre (his mother's voice eventually takes over his body), *Fight Club*'s protagonist is ultimately able to *defeat* his. Since the rift between body and voice is inherent in cinema's nature and cannot be remedied by multi-channel sound or any other technology, *Fight Club*'s main character is no more capable of reuniting body and voice than was

Norman Bates. That the outcomes of the two stories are nonetheless so different is a result of the changed status of the acousmêtre in the multi-channel world of digital surround.

In *Fight Club*, "Jack"[24] (played by Edward Norton) is unsatisfied with his life until he meets, and is befriended by, a flamboyant soap salesman named Tyler Durden (Brad Pitt). The bulk of the film is spent on Jack watching the seemingly omnipotent Tyler start an underground organization. Eventually, Jack recognizes that Tyler is a creation of his own psyche; the ensuing battle for supremacy between the two halves of Jack concludes the film. Both *Fight Club* and *Psycho* depend for their suspense on the audience not realizing too soon that their central characters have split personalities. And both achieve this deception by adhering to a modified version of André Bazin's rule that "when the essence of a scene demands the simultaneous presence of two or more factors in the action, montage is ruled out."[25] Bazin, writing about cinematic fights between man and animal, observed that "creating" a fight by editing together shots of each creature on its own is ineffective; the audience must see at least one shot containing both man and animal to believe they are in the same space.

Psycho and *Fight Club* extend this logic to split personalities—for the audience *not* to realize that Mrs. Bates is part of Norman or that Tyler is part of Jack, the movies must show both members of each pair together. Thus we see Norman carrying his mother down the stairs, and Jack fistfighting with Tyler. The ways the two films *use* the onscreen bodies of their acousmêtres, however, sharply differ. *Psycho* relies primarily on Mrs. Bates's offscreen voice and only shows her body enough to convince us of its existence. *Fight Club* takes the opposite approach—rather than *hiding* the body of Jack's alter ego, it foregrounds a "Tyler" embodied (and voiced) by Brad Pitt, who is frequently onscreen interacting with Jack and others.

The treatment of Tyler in *Fight Club* raises the question of whether Tyler should be considered an acousmêtre like Mrs. Bates. In the initial moments of the scene where he and Jack first meet, he is clearly a true acousmêtre. We hear his voice—significantly, over an image of Jack—but do not have a face or mouth to which we can attach it. Two shots later, though, the camera reveals Brad Pitt, and we see his mouth onscreen as we hear his voice coming from the screen; for the rest of the movie, this body and voice will remain tied together. Now linked temporally and spatially to an onscreen body, Tyler's voice *should* lose its acousmêtric nature. This is not the case, however: Tyler retains his acousmêtric powers even after his body is revealed.

Chion lists as the four "powers" of the acousmêtre "the ability to be everywhere, to see all, to know all, and to have complete power. In other words, ubiquity, panopticism, omniscience, and omnipotence."[26] Tyler maintains all four of these powers throughout *Fight Club*. First off, he is ubiquitous: as Jack learns when trying to locate Tyler after his friend disappears without a trace, Tyler has been every*where* and has talked to every*one*. Later his omnipresence grows even more power-ful—by the film's third act, Tyler can instantly pop up anywhere he wants, regardless of physics or logic. Secondly, Tyler is panoptical: he sees what Jack is doing even when the two are separated, and often Jack, despite thinking he is alone, suddenly finds Tyler watching him. Thirdly, he is omniscient: Tyler always knows what Jack is doing, to whom Jack has spoken, and what Jack's goals are. And, finally, Tyler is omnipotent: he can do *anything he wants*. The very existence of Fight Club (the organization in the film, not the film itself), based solely on Tyler's ability to bend hundreds of people to his will, is a testament to his omnipotence.

Since Tyler behaves as an acousmêtre throughout the film, it seems curious that *Fight Club* matches his voice with a body so early on. The rationale for doing so lies in the 5.1-channel environment of-fered by DSS. In a monophonic or Dolby Stereo environment, the acousmêtric voice originates in the same place as all other voices: the front center channel. In the fully spatialized diegesis of the digital surround style, however, the acousmêtre can go *anywhere* while other voices and sounds remain spatially tied to their sources. This creates a problem for a movie like *Fight Club* that depends on the audience *not* recognizing that two voices are really part of the same person. Were the filmmakers to avoid *showing* Tyler so that his voice would not be "nailed" to a body, where would that voice originate? If it came from the screen, it would either be linked with the onscreen Jack, the only visible *source* of a voice, engendering suspicion that Tyler was merely a voice in Jack's head. Locating Tyler's voice out in the space of the theater would be equally ineffective. Not only would this mislead the audience by artificially separating Tyler's voice from its true source (Jack), it would inevitably cause the audience to wonder why Tyler was always offscreen.

Paradoxically, preserving Tyler's power as an acousmêtre thus *necessitates* attaching his voice to a unique body. Of course, this strategy presents its own problems. Most notably for *Fight Club*, Tyler's voice *has* no real body of its own. Tying it to Brad Pitt could therefore be considered an unfair "trick" that prevents the audience from discovering the truth about Jack and Tyler only by "cheating." A close look at the film's aesthetics, though, reveals that the choice to attach Tyler's voice to a separate body is part of a larger strategy employed by the filmmakers, one based on presenting the audience with Jack's point of view (POV) from its very first moments all the way through its end. In this framework, the audience sees Tyler as a real, separate person *since this is how Jack sees him.*

Visually, the fact that *Fight Club* offers Jack's POV is conveyed in several ways. For instance, it includes single-frame flashes of Tyler before his "official" introduction into the film, signifying the "Tyler" part of Jack's psyche bubbling toward the surface. In the same vein, it shows Jack's inner thoughts as he meditates and visualizes the catalog ads that rule his life literally surrounding him in his apartment. The film's visuals even "freeze" when Jack wants to share some information, demonstrating that the image track is *entirely* driven by his thoughts. Perhaps the single most telling visual cue that we are "inside Jack's head" comes in the opening credits, which place us *literally* in the middle of his brain—the filmmakers would have been hard pressed to find a more literal way of signifying that what is happening in Jack's brain is the key to the film.

Fight Club's script similarly offers clues that it is being told from Jack's perspective. Jack's ability to manipulate the movie itself, moving backward and forward through time as he recounts his story, serves as one clear hint that the entire experience of the film reflects what is in his head. That Jack speaks directly to the audience in voiceover also suggests his point of view. Interestingly, in one extended narration about Tyler, what would in most films be a voiceover by Jack is instead presented as a direct address by Jack to the camera with Tyler in the background. That Jack speaks straight to the camera fits with the film's

8.2. Rather than pair a voiceover by Jack with images of Tyler, *Fight Club* (1999) places Jack *in* the diegetic space of the scenes he is describing and has him address the camera directly as he explains Tyler's various odd jobs. This strategy helps maintain the illusion that Jack and Tyler are two separate people.

overall strategy of making it clear we are getting *Jack's perspective* on events, not necessarily the literal truth. But this formal strategy also derives from another factor—if Tyler were instead left alone onscreen during a long voiceover by Jack, the audience might begin to associate his body with Jack's voice and hence spoil the film's surprise.

Like its visuals and script, *Fight Club*'s approach to multi-channel mixing hints that we are seeing and hearing from Jack's perspective. In the scene where Tyler leaves Jack, Tyler's dialogue appears—clear and distinct—not only in the center channel but in all four of the other main channels. Significantly, this is the only time in the film this dialogue mixing strategy is employed. Narratively, the effect is to place us in Jack's *aural point of view*; having just survived a major car wreck, he is drifting in and out of consciousness and is having difficulty spatializing the acousmêtric voice he is normally able to "nail down" to his imaginary friend. No longer tied to a body, Tyler's voice—like that of the masked Frank in *Donnie Darko*—envelops us, simultaneously coming from everywhere (all five main channels) and nowhere (since it cannot be tied to a body). Even after Tyler has ostensibly left, his acousmêtric voice remains with Jack—since it does, in fact, *come from* Jack. In the very next scene, as Jack wanders the house largely oblivious to the frenetic work of Tyler's Project Mayhem recruits, Jack's voiceover in the center channel dominates the soundtrack. But the apparent stability of his persona is undercut by the other channels, in which various voices subtly repeat Tyler's aphorisms.

Understanding that *Fight Club* keeps us in Jack's perspective throughout its length explains why attaching Tyler's voice to a separate body meshes neatly with the film's overall aesthetic. It does not, however, explain why *Fight Club* ends so differently from *Psycho*. Both feature protagonists in conflict with acousmêtres. But where Norman is consumed by his acousmêtre, Jack is able to defeat Tyler. Viewed more generally, where *Psycho* foregrounds the essential inability of nailing down the acousmêtric voice to a body, *Fight Club* seems to posit the opposite prospect—Jack destroys Tyler, his voice-in-the-head, and thereby correctly links his *own* body and voice. For comparison, a *Psycho*-esque ending to *Fight Club* would feature the voice of Tyler completely taking over Jack's body and the "Jack" persona disappearing entirely.

The key to their different endings is that *Jack himself* realizes that Tyler is his creation. In *Psycho* quite the opposite occurs—indeed, it is a psychiatrist who must finally explain the situation, as Norman is never able, and never *will* be able, to do so. Because Jack ultimately recognizes that he has two voices inside him, he has the opportunity to try to save himself from his acousmêtric alter ego. And, crucially, he knows what he has to do to accomplish this. In Jack and Tyler's final scene "together," Jack says to Tyler, "I want you to really listen to me. My eyes are open." He then sticks a gun in his mouth and shoots himself. This last line—"my eyes are open"—carries dual meanings. On the surface, Jack is saying that he is fully aware of what he is about to do—shooting himself is not merely the suicidal act of an insane person. But on a deeper level, "my eyes are open" means that Jack understands the truth of his relationship with Tyler and *sees* what he has to do to end it.

What Jack understands, what he *sees* now, is that *Tyler is a voice.* And in the cinema, the source of the voice is the *mouth.* Tyler's voice can only be destroyed by attacking it at the mouth—precisely what

Jack does. He is ultimately able to kill Tyler's voice, in other words, because he realizes *where* that voice is located—and it is here that multi-channel sound gives Jack a crucial advantage over Norman Bates. In the monophonic world of *Psycho*, voices could never be traced to a specific place. *All* voices came from the same site—the center of the screen—regardless of the actual location of their sources. DSS-based multi-channel, though, provides not only spatial cues to the diegetic world but also an *orientation* to that world. Voices diegetically originating in different places actually *come from* those different places, allowing specific voices to be tied to specific locations. In this spatialized environment, Jack is able to locate the wandering voice and, ultimately, destroy it.

In doing so, he apparently recreates the consonance between body and voice destroyed by the advent of the sound film. But since the rift between sound and image is intrinsic to the cinema and *cannot* be rectified through surround sound, this perception of unity must be illusory. Understanding what Jack *really* does when he "kills" Tyler requires remembering Tyler's structural position in *Fight Club*. Despite being seen—from Jack's perspective—as a "real" person who appears on screen and has a voice synchronized with his mouth, Tyler is actually a figment of Jack's imagination. He exists in the "real world" only as a voice—and hence remains an *acousmêtre*. As such, what Jack *really* accomplishes at the end of *Fight Club* is not the reunification of body and voice it might appear to be. Truly unifying body and voice would entail irrevocably "nailing down" the acousmêtre to its own unique body. What Jack does instead is *destroy* it. He prevents the acousmêtre from wandering *not* by attaching it to a body but by killing it, prohibiting it from doing anything at all.

If the end of *Fight Club* leaves the impression that Jack has managed to reestablish the imagined original unity of body and voice, this is because the film has pulled a subtle bait and switch. Where the conventional code of synchronization seeks to *hide* the split between body and voice, *Fight Club* instead *foregrounds* it. It does so, however, through a specific example, the duality of Tyler's voice originating in Jack's body. The audience thus comes to associate Tyler (the acousmêtre) with the voice detached from the body *in general*. When this *single* split between Jack and Tyler is remedied, this conflation results in the *feeling* that the larger sound/image split inherent to sync sound cinema has been rectified.

It is no accident that issues of cinematic technology and the voice/body split are raised in *Fight Club*; the movie expressly concerns itself with film technology and with the relationship between sound and image. This is best illustrated by the final scene, which finds Jack reunited with Marla (Helena Bonham Carter), his semi-girlfriend. They watch out a high-rise window as buildings explode and crumble to the ground. As this happens, Jack says a couple of last lines to Marla and grinding rock music slowly fades in on the soundtrack. Right before the final fade to black, the film appears to jump in the gate, and a few frames of a penis flash in before the image track returns to the two-shot of Marla and Jack.

This pornographic insert recalls an earlier sequence where Tyler, working as a projectionist, spliced single frames of pornography into family films. It also reemphasizes that film is a constructed, technological medium that can be easily altered. Significantly, the sound design of the spliced-in shot at *Fight Club*'s end differs from that of the spliced-in shot from the earlier scene. In that scene, the soundtrack included a split second of pornographic moaning timed with the on-screen flash of the inserted frame; this time, the shot comes *without* a break in the sound, even though actual film splicing *has to* affect the soundtrack.[27] As the image track presents a "splice" but the soundtrack does not, the film forces its audience to recognize that the two have been constructed separately—to acknowledge the material heterogeneity of the cinema once more before the movie ends. The soundtrack is not merely "whatever matches the picture" but rather an entirely separate construction that, at any given time, may not have *anything* to do with the image.

This final scene's surround design also foregrounds its "constructedness" by aggressively differentiating the sounds coming from each group of speakers. The overall soundtrack to this scene includes direct (i.e., clean, or without noticeable reverb) dialogue, ambience, spot effects, reverberations of the dialogue, and other diegetic effects. No music—diegetic or otherwise—is used until the rock music appears at the very end. Prior to this point all types of sounds, save dialogue and a few deliberately placed spot effects, have been included in all four non-center speakers. Music, ambiences, and reverb have invariably spread throughout the whole soundscape. Here, though, this pattern in broken—and as discussed in chapter 6, such deviations from established mixing strategies are usually significant. Reverb, ambience, and effects gradually fade out of the front left and right channels, leaving those speakers playing only music; the rear channels, conversely, continue to include reverb, ambience, and effects but do *not* include any of the music. The resulting mix—which places dialogue in the center, two-channel stereo music in the left and right channels, and ambient/reverb sounds in the surrounds—follows Dolby Stereo norms rather than the immersive digital surround style the rest of the movie employs. Like the inserted penis shot, the effect of this sonic shift is to highlight the inherently constructed and mutable nature of film itself.

Emphasizing its own heavily manipulated nature, the conclusion of *Fight Club* forces a retroactive reassessment of the entire movie's emphasis on separating sound and image as an intentional decision. Though the film does not—and *cannot*—remedy the body/voice split introduced with sync sound, it shows how this split is altered by the spatialization of the digital surround era. In doing so, it lays the groundwork for new ways of thinking about the voice and body in the multichannel world, and it demonstrates that despite the challenges posed by surround technology, the acousmêtre remains a viable cinematic device in the DSS era.

9

APPARATUS THEORY

Surround for film, for my taste what it does is it takes away
the two-dimensionality of the screen. It opens up the room
and it gives you more of a realistic experience.

ERIK AADAHL, SOUND DESIGNER

I think the 5.1 environment still is centered at the screen . . . the
reason there are speakers around you is to kind of create this
environment around you but the focal point is still in front of you.

MIKE KNOBLOCH, UNIVERSAL PICTURES EXECUTIVE

In their introduction to the 2008 essay collection *Lowering the Boom*,
editors Jay Beck and Tony Grajeda argue that despite assertions of
cinema studies having entered a "post-theory" era, classic film theory
deserves to be reexamined in light of the soundtrack it has so long
ignored:

> The study of film sound theory, historically marginalized and thus
> underdeveloped in cinema studies, has only recently started to evolve,
> and it offers numerous possibilities for advancing, revisiting, and revis-
> ing current feminist, Marxist, psychoanalytic, queer, and apparatus
> theories. . . . We recognize work on sound as a clarion call for a *return
> to theory*, one that allows for a number of innovative and original ap-

proaches to theoretical perspectives that have otherwise been regarded as defunct.[1]

The last sentence of this plea concedes that the grand theoretical constructs that once dominated film scholarship have largely gone out of fashion. What Beck and Grajeda wisely recognize, though, is that many of these theories were developed with little, or more often *no*, consideration for the cinema's aural component. As one scholar writing in the late 1980s put it, "Theories can and do flourish without acknowledging sound as an integral part of film—in some cases, almost without acknowledging its existence."[2] Even those models of film theory that are now considered obsolete offered useful insights in their day; they may yield further revelations into the workings of cinema when reinterrogated from an *audio*-visual perspective.

This and the next chapter offer bidirectional examinations, considering two strands of classical film theory in the light of digital surround sound and vice versa. That is, they examine both how these models illuminate the functioning of multi-channel cinema *and* how digital surround sound partially rehabilitates these theoretical constructs. Together, these approaches confirm Beck and Grajeda's supposition that even obsolete elements of film theory can be productively reappraised from a sound-aware perspective and demonstrate the importance of including multi-channel considerations in that perspective.

WHY APPARATUS THEORY?

One of the specific theories mentioned by Beck and Grajeda as deserving reexamination is apparatus theory. This is a logical first element of classical theory to consider in the context of digital surround sound (DSS) for two reasons. First, as a construct closely tied (as its name suggests) to the *technology* of cinema, apparatus theory would seem likely to be affected by, and say something about, a technological change such as the adoption of DSS. James Lastra contends that apparatus theory represents a kind of technological determinism;[3] if so, then a significant shift in cinematic technology should certainly impact the theory and its conclusions.

Second, apparatus theory focuses specifically on the *screen* as the locus of the movie. In deeming cinema a primarily visual medium, apparatus theory is hardly alone. Unlike most other theories of film, though, apparatus theory makes the physical movie screen the literal focus of its argument. Rick Altman may have had apparatus theory in mind when he observed that "generations of film theorists have assumed that the whole of the cinema may be reduced to the screen."[4] Yet as the quotations that opened this chapter hint, the role of the screen as the lone "place" of the movie is in flux in the digital surround era. While Knobloch asserts that the screen remains the "focal point" of the theatrical experience, Aadahl's claim that surround "takes away the two-dimensionality of the screen" and "opens up the room" implies that the screen may no longer be the *sole* focus of the audience's attentions. This latter viewpoint is supported by the adoption of the digital surround style, which expands the diegetic world of the movie beyond the screen into the rest of the theater, making the movie not just what is *in front of* us on the screen but what is *all around* us.

Briefly, apparatus theory encompasses several related arguments that the cinema can be understood through the technologies it employs. One branch of apparatus theory, for instance, focuses on the apparatus of production, linking the specific perspective provided by the camera lens to a particular humanist ideology.[5] The specific version of apparatus theory to be examined here is that put forth by Jean-Louis Baudry in his 1975 essay "The Apparatus," which focuses on the apparatus of exhibition (the arena where digital surround is deployed). Baudry's argument has three parts. First, he compares the cinematic apparatus (projection, screen, and theater) to Plato's allegorical cave, writing that "the allegory of the cave is the text of a signifier of desire which haunts the invention of cinema and the history of its invention."[6] From there, he makes a similar comparison of the exhibition apparatus to the dream state. Third and finally, he uses these previous claims to link the pleasure of cinema to that of regression to a primitive (i.e., infantile) state.

PLATO'S CAVE AND MOBILITY

In the first phase of Baudry's argument, he draws a number of connections between Plato's cave and the movie theater: the space is dim/darkened, images are projected onto a blank space (wall/screen) in front of the "audience," the projection apparatus is above and behind the "audience" so as to remain hidden, and those watching remain immobile. While the first three of these seem reasonable descriptors of the theatrical experience, the validity of his final claim—that the audience remains immobile—is less certain. To be sure, Baudry does not assert that the cinema viewer is literally *forced* into immobility like one of Plato's prisoners; he acknowledges that the viewer can always leave the theater, change his seat, and so on, but argues that audiences generally remain still. Yet even this more "limited" claim of immobility is inaccurate. Writes Noël Carroll,

> Unlike Plato's prisoners, the film viewer can move her head voluntarily, attending to this part of the screen and then the next. . . . Even if there is a sense in which we might say that movement [in the cinema] is "inhibited," it is certainly not a matter of motor inhibition, but a voluntary inhibition promoted by respect for conventional decorum.[7]

Indeed, anyone who has sat in the front row of a large theater can attest that not only *can* filmgoers move their heads, they *must* in some situations. Carroll's argument thus makes sense when considering the relationship between the spectator and screen (where, in the monophonic era when Baudry was writing, both sound and image resided).

Carroll's idea of a "mobile" audience, though, is more troublesome in the age of digital surround sound and diegetic immersion. Spectators listening to a monophonic film hear essentially the same soundtrack no matter where they sit, but once different sounds are being sent to various channels around the theater, the aural experience of hearing becomes heavily dependent on the point of audition. Even in a well-designed theater where everything possible has been done to minimize the acoustic differences between seats, noticeable differences remain and seem to increase as the number of discrete channels does. Those listening to a 5.1 film from different seats in the same theater may hear substantially different soundtracks. An example from my own experience: I saw *Moulin Rouge!* (2001) twice in the same theater, once in the far right rear corner and later in a prime seat roughly in the center of the auditorium. The difference between hearing a right-surround-heavy mix in the former case and a properly balanced one in the latter was astonishing, and it fundamentally altered the moviegoing experience: in the first case I had to constantly fight to make out the narratively "important" sounds over the background noise, while in the latter I was able to sit back and enjoy the movie more passively.[8]

The digital surround style ultimately works to immerse the audience in the movie's diegesis. This illusion, however, only works for *stationary* filmgoers. If a spectator moves, what had seemed to be a coherent, complete environment is suddenly revealed as an artificial representation clearly composed of multiple independent sources. In the "real world," moving around *does* change what we hear, but in a subtle and continuous way—though the details of the aural environment may shift, the soundscape remains perceptibly "whole." A seemingly cohesive 5.1 theatrical soundscape, however, quickly collapses into a limited number of point sources once filmgoers begin moving around the theatrical space, or even moving within their seats; simply cocking one's head back and forth can briefly collapse the sound field and reveal the location of each speaker.

In the digital surround era, then, movement by the spectator can destroy the illusion of diegetic immersion. This challenges Carroll's assertion that cinemagoers are immobile only out of "respect for conventional decorum." In "The Apparatus," Baudry introduces the concept of a "reality test," as a way to tell whether a perception is of something in the exterior world ("real") or of something created within the mind ("fake"), such as a hallucination. The reality test depends on mobility, since "a perception which can be eliminated by an action is recognized as exterior."[9] Baudry's argument implies that audience immobility is a crucial factor in the cinema's ability to "fool" audiences into believing the reality of what they are seeing onscreen. Since they cannot move, they cannot execute the action-dependent reality test, and hence they cannot be sure whether the images onscreen are real or not. Like both Plato's cave and the dream state, the cinema lacks a "reality test."

But Carroll objects to Baudry's formulation, pointing out that whatever impression of reality the cinema creates is *not* destroyed by motion:

> If there is such a phenomenon as the impression of reality, then it should be an empirical matter to establish whether it disappears when the spectator is in movement. In my own case, I have found that I can back out of a movie theater while watching the screen or return to my seat from the beverage bar with no discernible difference in the impressions I derive from the screen than when I am seated.[10]

From Carroll's image-centric, monophonic-based perspective, this may be correct. In the multi-channel era, however, quite the opposite is true: for films using the digital surround style, the impression of reality *is* destroyed by movement. This illusion is shattered, the spectator becomes consciously aware of both the space of the theater and the constructed nature of the film, and the immersive aesthetic of DSS fails in its efforts to create a new environment that hides the space of the theater.

What this means is that even though cinema spectators are not *literally* immobilized like the prisoners in Plato's cave, in the digital surround era they lose the ability to move *without disturbing the impression of reality*. Baudry suggests, and Carroll does not dispute, that cinema audiences come to the movies seeking the "impression of reality." If cinemagoers choose immobility, this is not simply because they are adhering to "social convention"[11] as Carroll claims, but because this is the requirement of receiving the "impression of reality" they desire from the moviegoing experience. For the immersive digital surround style to place viewers *in* the diegetic world, those viewers must choose to remain immobile.

Both the digital surround style and Plato's cave thus function only through the spectators' immobility. But the two also differ—significantly, in a way tied to sound. Plato hypothesizes that his prisoners can hear the puppeteers. He assumes, though, that what they hear are not the *direct* sounds created in the back of the cave but rather the *echoes* of those sounds off the front wall. Since these sounds would thus seem to originate from the wall, Plato reasons, the prisoners would associate them with the shadows projected on the wall.[12] This situation is similar to that of the monophonic cinema, where all audio comes from (and is associated with) the screen. The cinema of Dolby Stereo fits the cave model even better; here "important" sounds are tied to the screen while ambient sounds, like reverberations of the sounds around the cave, come from all around. 5.1 digital surround, though, operates much differently: *all* types of sounds come from *all* directions, constantly shifting and panning not only across the screen but also into the space of the theater.

This active, immersive aural environment differentiates the cinema from Plato's cave in an important way: it encourages belief in a world *beyond* what is visible onscreen. We are *not* meant to assume that the world ends at the boundaries of the screen but rather to consider the visual elements present at any given time in the larger context of *what we hear from outside the screen.* The prisoners in Plato's cave, in contrast, believe that all of reality is what they can see (and hear) in front of them on the wall.

By reminding us that a world exists beyond that in front of us, and that we are getting only a limited perspective of the situation at hand, the DSS soundtrack might seem to fulfill the role of the prisoner from Plato's cave who has seen the outside and returns to tell the others. Yet the soundtrack of a DSS-equipped film is, like the onscreen image, part of the constructed illusion of cinema. And the "extended world" it suggests is not that of the "real world" but that of the offscreen parts of the illusory diegetic environment. The true function of the multichannel soundtrack, then, is to *confirm* that the onscreen world is the *only* reality, strengthening the cinematic illusion rather than betraying it.

DREAMS AND REPRESENTATIONS AS PERCEPTIONS

On the whole, Baudry's analogy between Plato's cave and the cinema may be *more* accurate in the immersive digital surround era than in the monophonic era in which he devised it. Both DSS cinema and Plato's cave immerse the audience in a simulated world that is believed to be the actual world in which the audience is seated. The contemporary moviegoer, of course, is not a modern-day Uncle Josh, literally deluded into believing that the diegetic world seen onscreen is "real." But once the digital surround style eliminates all perceptions of the actual auditorium, filmgoers can allow themselves (for the sake of enjoying the movie) to "forget" that they are in a movie theater and, for the space of two hours, "believe" in the onscreen world.

Baudry hypothesizes that cinema itself is a realization of a latent desire for this effect of mistaking *representations* for *perceptions.* "It is this wish," he writes, "which prepares the long history of cinema: the wish to construct a simulation machine capable of offering the subject perceptions which are really representations mistaken for perceptions."[13] In support of this claim, he links the cinematic experience to dreaming, a situation where exactly that misidentification occurs. Like viewers of an immersive movie, dreamers may sometimes recognize that they are "in a dream," but that does not make their experience seem any less real. In fact, quite the opposite: representations interpreted as perceptions can offer a sense of reality that is somehow "more real" than the real world itself. As Baudry explains,

> Something of a desire in dream unifying perception and representation—whether representation passes itself for perception, in which case we would be closer to hallucination, or whether perception passes itself for perceived representation, that is, acquires as perception the mode of existence which is proper to hallucination—takes on the character of specific reality which reality does not impart, but which hallucination provokes: *a more-than-real.*[14]

The "more-than-real" applies not merely to dreams but to the *cinema,* which "is different from the usual impression which we receive from reality, but which has precisely this characteristic of being more than real which we have detected in dream."[15]

Here again Carroll reasonably objects to Baudry's argument, specifically to his linking of *all* motion pictures to the "more-than-real." Carroll notes that the "more-than-real impression of reality" is an apt descriptor of some films, but not all. Explaining that "in dream, this impression appears to refer to imagery charged with affect. In film, we are told that this impression is one that diverges from our ordinary encounters with mundane life," he argues that while many films *do* fit this model, "not all films bestow comparable affective results. Home movies, or bank surveillance footage, especially of persons unknown to us, may appear affectless, flat, and lackadaisical."[16]

The examples Carroll chooses here are unfortunate in that they undermine his own argument. Clearly, the apparatus of bank surveillance video and home movies is *not* the same apparatus as that of feature film at either the production or exhibition levels. Setting aside that the former media are rarely projected in a theater, their soundtracks are entirely different. In particular, the highly constructed surround soundscape played in the contemporary film theater is a far cry from the silent (or possibly monophonic) and usually unmanipulated soundtrack that accompanies home movies and surveillance videos.

Nevertheless, Carroll's underlying point does hold some weight. He observes that while Baudry "claims that the more-than-real impression of which he writes is a consequence of the cinematic *apparatus*,"[17] not every theatrically exhibited movie offers the same "more-than-real" impression of reality as dreams. As in the case of Baudry's analogy between Plato's cave and the cinema, though, DSS at least partly blunts Carroll's argument. The digital surround style places the cinemagoer in the middle of the onscreen action, encouraging a sense of personal engagement and affect. When we hear and see what *seems like* a complete environment surrounding us, our natural reaction is not to think that we are hearing a constructed *representation* of a space, but that we are actually hearing the space itself—in other words, to mistake representation for perception. The diegetic immersion–driven style offers close-ups of details we "realistically" might not be able to see, emphasizes quiet sound effects that "realistically" would not be heard, and aggressively pans sounds all around us to foreground the 360-degree nature of the world around us. All these aesthetic traits certainly contribute to a sense that we are experiencing something "*more*-than-real."

The fact that diegetic immersion–based cinema *does* offer a more-than-real impression of reality may not seem sufficient to counter Carroll's objection. His point is that apparatus theory should depend *on the apparatus*, not about the specifics of how that apparatus is stylistically deployed. He explicitly notes that many films *do* promote an intense affective response, but that it is the narrative structure of those films, rather than the technological apparatus itself, that creates this effect.[18] The same argument could be made in the case of the digital surround style; creating diegetic immersion is an aesthetic *choice*, not a *requirement* of theatrical exhibition—hence any affective response it engenders derives from the structure of a specific film, not from the cinematic apparatus itself.

As demonstrated in the first section of this book, though, it is precisely the *technological apparatus* of digital surround sound that *promotes* diegetic immersion. Since it is exactly those films *using* the digital surround style that best create a more-than-real impression of reality, the more-than-real effect is, indirectly at least, an effect *of the apparatus*. This recognition also counters Carroll's other major objection to the dream/cinema parallel, that "the dreamer does not have the same experiential awareness of a darkened room that the film viewer does."[19] He is, again, broadly correct. But it is precisely this "awareness of the darkened room" that the diegetic immersion–based style—a result of the apparatus—causes viewers to ignore, thereby placing the audience in the same experiential state as the dreamer.

THE PRIMITIVE STAGE

The final phase of Baudry's argument builds on the connections between Plato's cave and the cinema and between dreaming and cinema, specifically their common theme of mistaking representations for perceptions. He suggests that confusing representations with perceptions corresponds to a return to a "primitive stage" in which perception and representation *are the same thing.* This primitive stage is that of being in the womb—where "self and environment are said to merge and where perception and representation are believed to be undifferentiated."[20]

The sonic environment created by multi-channel sound has an obvious connection to the sounds heard while in the womb. A number of scholars have described the soundscape heard by the unborn baby as a "sonorous envelope," dominated by the mother's voice surrounding the child on all sides.[21] Without pushing the connection too far—clearly there is a major difference between being surrounded by sounds in a theater and being surrounded by sounds in the womb—both can be described as *immersive.* Though few have explicitly tied the sonorous envelope to multi-channel sound, it is telling that theories connecting the cinema to the womb gained traction in the wake of Dolby Stereo.[22] The connection grows even tighter in the era of digital surround sound, where *all* types of sounds, including voices, can surround the audience. And, to push this comparison one step further, DSS's addition of the LFE channel allows it to emphasize low-frequency sounds—which make up the bulk of the sounds heard by a child pre-birth.[23]

If the all-around-you soundscape of multi-channel cinema mimics in form the aural space of the womb, the immersive design of the digital surround style also matches the primitive stage in other ways. Baudry describes the primitive stage as "a mode of relating to reality which could be defined as *enveloping* and in which the separation between one's own body and the exterior world is not well defined."[24]

He could just as well be describing the digital surround style, which is one of *envelopment* in the diegetic world of the film. More specifically, the digital surround style aims to visually and aurally place the spectator *in the middle of* the onscreen action, perceptually hiding the real distinction between the audience member's place ("one's own body") and the filmic ("exterior") world.

Just as importantly, the digital surround style serves to conflate representations with perceptions, the key effect of the primitive stage. Writing about audio recording in the early 1980s, Mary Ann Doane asserts that "technical advances in sound recording (such as the Dolby system) are aimed at diminishing the noise of the system, concealing the work of the apparatus, and thus *reducing the distance perceived between the object and its representation.*"[25] In the DSS era, further advances in sound recording and reproduction technology have essentially eliminated system noise. If the "distance perceived between the object and its representation" has therefore become *imperceptibly small*, then representation and perception have become unified, and the audience is returned to the primitive stage.

Baudry explicitly locates the pleasure of cinema in this return. Suggesting that all people harbor a subconscious wish to again be in the primitive stage, he writes that

> the cinematographic apparatus brings about a state of artificial regression. It artificially leads back to an anterior phase of his development—a phase which is barely hidden, as dream and certain pathological forms of our mental life have shown. It is the desire, unrecognized as such by the subject, to return to this phase, an early state of development with its own forms of satisfaction which may play a determining role in his desire for cinema and the pleasure he finds in it.[26]

Intriguingly, Baudry here locates the pleasure of regression in an *unrecognized* desire. As noted in chapter 4, sound can work on the subconscious more directly than image. This suggests that the digital surround style, which relies heavily on the soundtrack to convey information other aesthetic approaches assign to the visuals, may work more directly on this desire than other forms of film.[27] Whether or not it is better than its predecessors at assuaging the *desire* for regression to the primitive stage, the cinema of the digital surround era has a definite advantage in *promoting* that regression. Its enveloping aesthetic strives to make the spectator ignore the theatrical apparatus and become "part" of the movie; its "sonorous envelope" provides the appropriate atmosphere for a return to an infantile state; and its essentially noise-less audio coding and reproduction minimize the distance between audience and diegetic world.

In fact, recent work in neuroscience suggests that the cinema may indeed induce a return to a primitive stage, if not necessarily that of be-ing in the womb. One study, for example, found that adults engrossed in a movie exhibit brain activity patterns similar to those of babies.[28] Specifically, activity in the prefrontal cortex—an area of the brain largely undeveloped in infants—is suppressed during a movie. This portion of the brain is largely responsible for the ability to direct atten-tions; the prefrontal cortex difference between baby and adult brains thus partly explains why adults are good at focusing their concentra-tion on a single aspect of the environment, while infants are not. In-fants, in other words, pay attention to the world around them, but they maintain an awareness of *everything* happening around them rather than ignoring the elements an adult would deem "background" or "distractions."[29] From this perspective, the immersive environment and 360-degree soundfield of the DSS-era cinema mimics the childhood mode of experience—and perhaps promotes a return to a "primitive stage"—better than the more traditional aesthetic approach of locating all a movie's aural and visual information within the narrow confines of the screen.

All this suggests that Baudry's formulation of apparatus theory may actually be more applicable to the contemporary DSS-equipped cinema than to the monophonic cinema of the time he conceived this theory. To be sure, plenty of valid criticisms of his particular claims can still be raised, and large questions remain about the role of apparatus theory as a whole in the DSS era. For instance, if the perspective of the camera lens is a reflection of Renaissance humanism (as some apparatus theorists assert), what does the changed visual style of di-egetic immersion—heavy use of close-ups, fast cutting, fragmentation of space—mean?[30] The fundamental *question* of apparatus theory is an important one—what does the technology of cinema tell us about the ideology of cinema?—and deserves to be considered in light of such a significant change to cinematic technology as the adoption of digital surround sound.

This broad question I will leave open. The aim here has been neither to systematically discount all the objections to Baudry's work nor to suggest that the tenets of apparatus theory should be unreservedly accepted as a valid model for cinema in the multi-channel era. Rather, it has been to confirm the proposition set out at the start of this chapter, that even out-of-fashion theoretical models can be productively reexamined in the light of digital surround sound; the fact that DSS complicates arguments both for and against Baudry's formulation of apparatus theory clearly demonstrates the value of such work. To move this investigation into a more concrete realm, the conclusion of this chapter explores Baudry's claims in the context of an actual film.

CASE STUDY: THE MATRIX AND REGRESSION

Perhaps no recent film would be a better vehicle through which to investigate Baudry's claims about the cinema as agent of regression than *The Matrix* (1999). The film's narrative offers several parallels to Plato's allegory of the cave, which provided the foundation for Baudry's argument. The Matrix (the construct within the film, not the film itself) is of course reminiscent of Plato's cave—like the prisoners in the cave, the humans whose minds are in the Matrix have been imprisoned since childhood and are presented with a constructed illusion that they take as reality. Other elements of the film's plot are similarly reminiscent of the cave allegory. In Plato's story, for example, one person gets out of the cave to see the real world outside; in *The Matrix* a limited number of prisoners are able to free themselves from the Matrix and live in the "real world." After leaving Plato's cave, this man's eyes hurt from suddenly being exposed to the sun; upon waking up in the real world, Neo remarks that his eyes hurt from the light. And in perhaps the most fundamental parallel, both tales describe the human reluctance to recognize as "false" a world believed to be "real." Plato's story explains that the prisoners do not want to hear from the man who has seen the outside world and beat him when he tries to share his experience; *The Matrix* gives us Cypher, a character who chooses to kill his friends rather than give up the illusion of the Matrix.

Given these similarities between *The Matrix* and Plato's cave, it is not surprising that a number of writers have explored the relationship between the two.[31] These works, however, have tended to focus on the film's plot as an entry point into deeper philosophical issues. Understanding this movie in the context of Baudry's apparatus theory requires going beyond the level of narrative *content* to the film's *form*. The above exploration of DSS's ramifications for Baudry's model suggested that the diegetic immersion–based digital surround style *should* produce a regression to the "primitive stage." This case study will test that hypothesis through *The Matrix*.

Since not all contemporary films adopt the digital surround style, the first point to establish is that *The Matrix* actually *uses* this aesthetic approach. One piece of evidence suggesting that it *does* is its aggressive use of the multi-channel environment. For several years early in the DVD era, *The Matrix* was *the* DVD people used to show off their new home theaters. With bullets zipping all around the soundscape during action scenes, the LFE channel providing throbbing bass in others, and a bevy of other in-your-face uses of the 5.1 environment, the film provided a showcase for what digital surround sound could do. As William Whittington observes, "The first *Matrix* film became *the* DVD that all home theater owners had to have."[32]

Of course, active surround design *alone* does not create diegetic immersion. The digital surround style includes a wide variety of visual *and* aural characteristics that work together to place the audience in the diegesis. As shown in chapter 5, one crucial component of the digital surround style is setting up diegetic immersion from the very beginning of the film; a close examination of *The Matrix*'s opening will thus prove instructive. From the moment the production logos begin, the multi-channel soundscape is active, with the musical score employing all six of the 5.1 system's channels. As the Warner Brothers logo floats onscreen and maneuvers itself into its final position on the center of the screen, a series of electronic noises match it, both in moving from the back of the theater to the front and in eventually collapsing from the whole width of the screen to the center. The Village Roadshow production company logo follows the Warner one, with the soundtrack reusing the same mixing pattern.

The logos are followed by a black background awash in the green text of what we will later learn is the encoded Matrix. The music component of the soundtrack is still a full 5.1-channel mix; the clicking sound of the streaming text, meanwhile, is primarily spread across the front screen but leaks a bit into the surround channels. One by one the text streams stop, leaving the title "THE MATRIX" alone onscreen; the LFE and front channels chime in with a loud thud as each of the title's letters lock into place.

By this point the only plot information we have about the film is its title, yet the filmmakers have already introduced several aesthetic elements they will employ throughout *The Matrix*—an active soundscape encompassing all five main channels, low-frequency sounds played through the LFE channel, and rigid spatial matching between image and sound—all of which are characteristic of the digital surround style. The movie proper begins with nothing on the empty black screen except a cursor; aurally, the score music drops to a whisper (exploiting DSS's excellent dynamic range) but remains present in all five main channels. As the cursor prints out a couple lines of text onscreen, the sound of the printing moves (in concert with the text) across the front three channels. The text informs us that a telephone "trace" is beginning, and the screen fills with lines of digits that slowly resolve into a telephone number.

Roughly at the same time, two characters begin a voiceover conversation. Their voices are spread across the three front channels, breaking the convention of mixing all dialogue to the center. Thus with its very first dialogue, *The Matrix* primes us for an unconventional and heavily multi-channel soundtrack. The "trace" continues during this conversation, and (as with the opening title) the visually changing digits are accompanied by a "clickety" sound. As the trace runs, the camera tracks in on the ever-changing digits; paralleling this move, the clicking sound shifts around the soundscape. Originally based in the front center while the entire trace is onscreen, the clicking spreads out (both across the width of the screen and into the surround channels) as the camera tracks in far enough that the trace program is still running beyond the edges of the screen, then closes back in to the front center when only one digit is still changing. As it reaches the center of the screen, this final digit locks in as a zero.

From here the camera tracks *into* the digital green "o," which expands in depth to create a tunnel. The sound mix parallels this, *surrounding* us with electronic noise as we move into the zero. Here

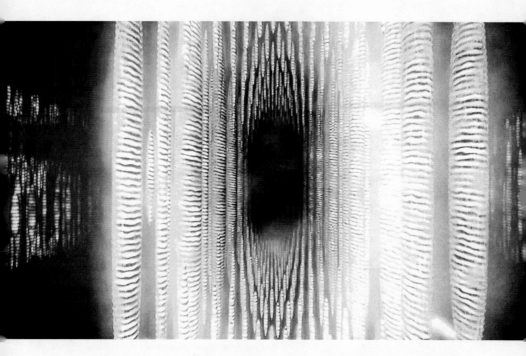

9.1. Near the beginning of *The Matrix* (1999), the camera travels *into* a digital zero, which becomes a sort of tunnel. This movement suggests going *inside* a computer system, and when the camera comes out the far end of the tunnel to the first live-action shot of the movie, we are in fact inside the Matrix.

again the discrete channel configuration of the 5.1 system is utilized, as the noise comes from all around us but the specific sounds in each channel differ slightly. Finally, as we come to the end of the tunnel, the tunnel sounds move to the rear channels only, then quickly fade away. We track speedily into a bright light, then pull back to reveal that it is a flashlight being held by a police officer. The quick push in and pull back are accompanied by "whooshes" in the audio that are perceived as the sounds of air flying by as we move quickly with the camera. As the first live scene begins, everything but the ambient sound of the onscreen space fades out.

From a sonic perspective, this opening has demonstrated all the technical capabilities of 5.1 digital surround in setting up a carefully spatialized and all-around-us environment. More importantly, though, both sound and image have been used to blatantly place the audience *within* the film. The end of the opening sequence has us traveling through a tunnel whose opening was an onscreen digit of a computer program. By entering this tunnel, we have moved narratively and literally inside the digital code—that is, *inside the Matrix itself.* And just as we are pulled into this space visually by the movement into the zero, the soundtrack follows suit by *surrounding us* with the electronic noise of the Matrix as we move through the tunnel. Significantly, this electronic noise moves to the rear of the theater as we come out of the visual tunnel, indicating that the boundaries of the Matrix are now somewhere *behind* us. We, as well as everything we see onscreen, are situated firmly *inside* the Matrix.

Only a minute and a half into the movie, it is abundantly clear that the aesthetic approach of *The Matrix* is the DSS-driven one of diegetic immersion. This criterion settled, the central issue is *how* that style promotes regression to Baudry's primitive stage where, as Carroll puts it, "perception and representation are believed to be undifferentiated."[33] From a narrative-driven perspective, it is noteworthy that putting people into the primitive stage is, succinctly, the function of the Matrix itself. Its prisoners are provided with *representations* of a world, but these representations are piped straight into their brains *so as to be treated as perceptions.* As far as the brain knows, the signals it receives from the Matrix *are* reality. Asleep in their fluid-filled "wombs" and unable to distinguish between representations and perceptions, the vast hordes of people trapped in the Matrix are in a perpetual primitive stage. If a fundamental human desire is to *return* to this stage, as Baudry claims, it is no surprise that not everyone "freed" from the Matrix is happy about it.

Filmgoers, too, crave a regression to the primitive stage; *The Matrix* promotes this feeling through two strategies. First, from nearly the beginning of the film, we are encouraged to identify with Neo. Initially, this is done through making the world inside the Matrix seem slightly "off." For example, the "whoosh" sound effects that accompany camera moves and many character movements are strikingly out of the ordinary, suggesting that as much as the onscreen world *seems* like the one we know, it is not. *Matrix* sound designer Dane Davis (*Speed Racer, 8 Mile*) recounts that one early idea he had about creating the feeling that "this wasn't really real" was to exactly repeat

9.2. Neo wakes in the "real world" for the first time. Emerging from his fluid-filled pod, he sees millions of other artificial "wombs," each holding a human stuck in the perpetual "primitive stage" of the Matrix. *The Matrix* (1999).

common sound effects, as if the Matrix itself had only a limited sound library on which to draw. Ultimately he and the directors decided this would more likely be perceived as bad sound design, and the plan was scrapped, but this shows that they were consciously working to differentiate the world inside the Matrix from real-world experience.[34] The result is that when Morpheus confirms Neo's suspicions that something is "not right" with the world, we understand what he's saying—as an audience, we have shared this impression.

This psychological identification with Neo continues through the rest of the film. As each new contortion in the plot occurs, we encounter it—and are surprised by it—with him. Often we are confused by what we see onscreen; Neo, however, is confused right along with us, which only strengthens our identification with him. At the same time, these strange occurrences are made believable because *Neo* believes in them. We ultimately perceive his world as "real"—however odd it may be—because *he* does, and because we have been through the same journey with him.

Neo's driving ambition by the second half of the movie is to become "The One," the person who can manipulate the Matrix as an extension of himself. Put another way, "The One" is the person who has eliminated any boundary between himself and his environment (i.e., the Matrix itself). The position of "The One" forcefully echoes Baudry's formulation of the primitive stage as "a mode of relating to reality . . . in which *the separation between one's own body and the exterior world is not well defined*."[35] Neo's ultimate goal, then is to regress to the primitive stage. From this perspective, the only difference between him and Cypher is the method by which he chooses to pursue this aim. As we have identified with Neo throughout the film, we have come to share in his ambition: we want to see him become The One and, like him, seek to regress to the primitive stage.

This desire is met by the film's immersive nature. It opens, as we have seen, by literally pulling us into its space, placing us physically *inside* the world of the movie. It *envelops* us and *erodes the separation* between us and the filmic environment—a description that recalls once more Baudry's description of the primitive stage. Additionally, *The Matrix* uses the quick cutting characteristic of the digital surround style. Watching and listening to the film, we barely have enough time to process its quickly changing images and sounds *as they seem*, much less to *analyze* them as the second-generation "representations" they ontologically are. Thus we are forced to conflate representations with perceptions—precisely what happens in the primitive stage.

Finally, *The Matrix* goes beyond the "normal" aesthetic elements of the digital surround style to cause us to mistake representation for perception. It does so through a shrewd strategy reminiscent of *Fight Club's apparent* reconciliation of the voice/body split through the destruction of a *particular* acousmêtre. In *The Matrix*, the "immersive" characteristics of the digital surround style—in particular aggressive panning around the multi-channel soundtrack and fast cutting—are used much more aggressively for scenes *within* the Matrix than for those outside it in the (film's diegetic) "real world." Over time, we subconsciously come to associate "immersion" with a "constructed world." This association is the precursor to a *Fight Club*–esque bait and switch, as it suggests that when the immersive style of the film disappears for the scenes in the "real world," *we ourselves* are no longer experiencing a "false world." Secure and perhaps a bit smug in being "in on" the secret that everything we see *inside* the Matrix is only an illusion (a representation), we forget that as an *audience* we are experiencing a constructed world regardless of whether the film's characters are inside the Matrix or not. The Matrix and the "real world" are *both* representations disguised as perceptions; that the film foregrounds this in the former case makes it no less true in the latter.

At its core, *The Matrix* is about a deep-seated human question: are our perceptions "real" or merely some sort of dream? While its plot literalizes this uncertainty, its use of the digital surround style engages with the same question in a subtler fashion. Our situation as audience is different from that of the slumbering people still trapped in the Matrix—but perhaps not as different as we might think. We are not immobilized in pods—but to experience the full measure of DSS-driven immersive style requires us to remain stationary. We do not have a data port feeding an artificial world directly to our brains—but our eyes and ears nonetheless present us with one every time we go to the cinema. We do not spend our entire lives in a womb—but for the space of two hours we too can blur the boundaries between ourselves and a world, treat representations as perceptions, and revert to the primitive stage Baudry suggests we all subconsciously desire.

10

THE REAL AND
THE SYMBOLIC

The close relationship between cinema and our psychic life emerges
not only from the way in which a subject is modeled, but also
from the trends and themes that films repeatedly introduce.

FRANCESCO CASETTI

The introduction to the previous chapter argued for reexamining no-
longer-fashionable branches of film theory in the light of digital surround sound (DSS), given that many theoretical models for cinema
say little or nothing about the soundtrack, much less about multi-
channel. Because apparatus theory relies directly on the *screen* as sole
locus of filmic meaning, it was a logical candidate for DSS-driven
reexploration; in the last chapter, just such an analysis demonstrated
that even this often-dismissed vein of film theory offers useful insights
about contemporary cinema when considered in the context of today's
multi-channel soundtracks.

That investigation's necessary focus on the specific details of apparatus theory forced it to neglect psychoanalysis, the broader theoretical
framework of which apparatus theory is a part. Baudry's invocation of
the unconscious and his description of the primitive, narcissistic state
(where perception and representation are united) rely explicitly on
Freud's work;[1] moreover, the fundamental argument in Baudry's formulation of apparatus theory is itself a psychological one: that cinema

functions in the same way as dreams, and thus watching a movie affects us the same way dreaming does. This final chapter complements the preceding one by examining psychoanalysis itself through the lens of digital surround sound.

While several areas of psychoanalytic film theory deserve DSS-oriented reconsideration, any attempt to tackle all of them would fill several books. Psychoanalysis is invoked by a broad range of scholarship, including everything from models for how cinema functions (i.e., Baudry's work on apparatus theory or Christian Metz's *The Imaginary Signifier*) to feminist work on the voice (Kaja Silverman's *The Acoustic Mirror*) to analyses of individual films and filmmakers—Hitchcock's works alone have spawned several books grounded in psychoanalytic theory.[2] This chapter's explorations will focus on a single concern of psychoanalytic theory particularly relevant to surround sound: the relationship between the Real and the Symbolic in Lacan's reformulations of Freudian theory.

VARYING APPROACHES TO PSYCHOANALYTIC FILM THEORY

As the above examples demonstrate, vastly dissimilar types of cinema scholarship fall under the general label of "psychoanalytic theory." To help distinguish these varying uses, Francesco Casetti outlines three distinct branches of psychoanalytic film studies; these provide a useful way to categorize individual psychoanalysis-based works. The first of Casetti's branches is perhaps the most radical application of psychoanalysis. In works based on this approach,

> cinema is seen as directly modeled on our psychic apparatus. Rather than being a means to reach certain secret nodes or the equivalent of certain unconscious manifestations, cinema emerges as a phenomenon that extends and encompasses the structures and dynamics that are the object of psychoanalysis. . . . Thus, the procedures behind films reproduce the mechanisms that construct dreams, mental lapses, and hallucinations.[3]

In other words, this category of psychoanalytic scholarship assumes elements of the psychic apparatus have analogs in the cinema. Baudry's work on apparatus theory, which ties cinema to dreaming and to the "primitive stage," can be placed squarely in this category.

Casetti's phrase "certain unconscious manifestations" also hints at a second category of psychoanalytic film theory, the application of psychoanalysis to *filmmakers*. Here films are treated as "symptoms" that, when analyzed, reveal hidden truths about their makers. Casetti summarizes this method as "a spontaneous extension of the analyst's couch: the director becomes the patient, the film the discussion, and the critic (and the astute spectator) the analyst."[4]

The third and final of Casetti's categories involves close filmic analysis, like the second. But instead of analyzing what movies can reveal about their makers, work in this category explores movies *in and of themselves*: "In this case it is not filmmakers who are analyzed through their work, but cinema itself [which] lies on the analyst's sofa."[5] Though this branch of psychoanalytic work, like Casetti's first one, aims to explicate the nature of cinema, it does not claim cinema correlates *directly* to the "psychic apparatus." Rather, it seeks ways in which the two may be *related* and uses those to exploit psychoanalysis's understanding of the unconscious in explaining how parts of cinema work.

Two factors recommend this third methodological approach as the most appropriate for a DSS-related investigation. First, its objective is understanding the way cinema works, which the last chapter suggested has been altered by the adoption of DSS. Second, it tackles that question through close analysis of actual films, a tactic that can—through the tools developed in this book's second section—explicitly incorporate multi-channel considerations. Thus the current investigation will explore *parallels* between DSS and the psychic apparatus, and what those say about the cinema, without claiming a one-to-one correspondence between the two.

THE REAL, THE SYMBOLIC, AND THE SUPERFIELD

Much psychoanalytic film scholarship—including apparatus theory—emphasizes the desire of those within the Symbolic order to return to the Imaginary realm. In the context of sound, the Imaginary is best exemplified by the "sonorous envelope" discussed earlier; as Sean Griffin notes, music in particular has the potential to erase the perceived boundary between listener and world, recreating the sense of unity characterizing the Imaginary.[6] The digital surround style could easily be read as promoting this sort of return to the Imaginary, since it seeks to eliminate the distance between the audience and the onscreen world. Yet this seemingly obvious conclusion masks an underlying gap in logic: while diegetic immersion places the audience in the middle of the diegetic world, it does *not* recreate the imagined unity of the womb "in which the individual has no sense of separation (or even sense of self)."[7] In fact, quite the reverse occurs: the constantly shifting soundscape and images typifying diegetic immersion emphasize that the environment around the audience moves and changes *independently* of the spectator. The audience is *in* the diegetic world but not *united with* it.

In fact, the psychoanalytic ramifications of DSS are best understood not through the relationship between the Symbolic and the Imaginary but through a different tension: that between the Symbolic and the *Real*. As Slavoj Žižek explains in the introduction to *Looking Awry*, "What we call 'reality' implies the surplus of a fantasy space filling out the 'black hole' of the real."[8] The crucial question this observation poses in the case of cinema is what part of the DSS-equipped cinema is the "real" and what is "reality." A vital clue to the nature of this distinction, at least in the Dolby Stereo era, is the superfield. As noted earlier, the superfield consists of *noises* and *ambient sounds*—precisely those sounds that exist *outside* the purview of the Symbolic realm of signs and signifiers. In other words, the superfield foregrounds the *Real* at the expense of the structured Symbolic order that *dialogue* and the *image track* represent.

This reverses the traditional hierarchy of image over sound. Chion notes that the multiple aural layers—dialogue, music, and most importantly *noises*—made possible by improved sound technology like Dolby Stereo take precedence over the visuals, leaving the image track "to float like a poor little fish in this vast acoustic aquarium."[9] Žižek takes Chion's argument a step further, drawing a parallel between this reversal and *psychosis*. In psychoanalytic terms, reality posits the Real as a "lack" or hole in the Symbolic order; disruption of this arrangement creates a psychotic state. By allowing the Real to take precedence over the Symbolic, the superfield-equipped cinema creates just such a state:

> We have here the "aquarium of the real" surrounding isolated islands of the symbolic. In other words, it is no longer enjoyment that "drives" the

proliferation of the signifiers by functioning as a central "black hole" around which the signifying network is interlaced; it is, on the contrary, the symbolic order itself that is reduced to the status of floating islands of the signifier.[10]

Through the superfield, Dolby Stereo cinema literally surrounds the Symbolic order (dialogue and the image track) with the sonic aquarium of the Real—a deviation not only from the normal Symbolic/Real relationship but also from traditional, image-focused conceptions of the cinema.

THE RESTRUCTURED REAL AND THE ULTRAFIELD

In Dolby Stereo, the Real surrounds the Symbolic. But digital surround sound may activate a *different* relationship between the Real and the Symbolic than its predecessor. One possibility would be that DSS *reverses* Žižek's Dolby Stereo–based formulation of the screen as "reality" and the soundtrack as "real," instead surrounding the Real of the *screen* with the (Symbolic) "reality" of the *soundtrack*. Indeed, some of the digital surround style's aesthetic components suggest just such a situation. For example, its image track abandons the highly structured shooting and editing patterns associated with the Symbolic in favor of quick cutting, close-ups, and unclear spatial organization. Having abandoned any sort of "code" or "language," the image now presents a series of individual impressions that *could* be viewed as more reminiscent of the Real than of the Symbolic. The ultrafield-driven soundtrack, in this framework, would be read as consisting of *signs* that serve to explain and corral the visuals. Continually reorienting itself to provide a narrative space *around* the image, the soundtrack assumes the role of the Symbolic order, containing the unstructured Real of the image.

This formulation is, however, ultimately unsatisfying. Descriptions of DSS-era practices offered in earlier chapters strongly suggest that the multi-channel soundtrack represents the realm of the *Real*, not that of the Symbolic. The ultrafield, for instance, includes all the noises and ambient sounds of the superfield—these are renderings of the Real, not signifiers. And the DSS soundtrack, reproduced in an acoustically dry theater, effaces all traces of the listening space itself and replaces them with the sounds of the narrative world. Žižek describes the Real as a presence "that 'seizes' us immediately, 'renders' immediately the thing" and, in doing so, "suspends external reality"[11]—a perfect description of a cinematic soundtrack that substitutes a complete but created environment for the "external reality" of the actual theater.

That the soundtrack represents the Real in both the 5.1-equipped, ultrafield-driven cinema and its Dolby Stereo–based, superfield-driven counterpart does not mean the two function identically—they rely on starkly divergent models for the sound/image relationship. In the case of the superfield, a consistent sonic environment is paired with an ever-changing visual image; the result is that "the space defined by the sound is not the same as that once constructed by the image."[12] The ultrafield's soundtrack, on the other hand, employs quick cutting and shifting sounds to maintain a continuous spatial match with the images onscreen; this tight correlation implies that the spaces represented by the ultrafield-based soundtrack and the image track are the *same*, not *different* as in the superfield-based cinema.

Since the soundtrack of the digital surround cinema represents the Real, its image track must therefore *also* represent not the everyday space of reality but the fantastic space of the Real. Or, to be more precise, the image track must at least *sometimes* portray the Real. As explained in chapter 5, few films adopt the digital surround style for their entire lengths; most movies at least occasionally employ a more traditional Dolby Stereo–era style, with the image track as the Symbolic. But the crucial point is that in the DSS era, the Real sometimes intrudes into the image. And therein lies the difference between Dolby Stereo and digital surround sound: where the former maintains the Symbolic as "floating islands" of image in the sonic aquarium of the Real, the latter allows the Real to expand into what had been the last safe haven of the Symbolic. It is no accident that, as detailed above, the DSS-driven image track in some ways fits Žižek's description of the Real even though the image is generally associated with the Symbolic—sometimes it is one, and sometimes it is the other.

Indeed, at its core diegetic immersion functions to blur both the boundary between theater and diegetic world *and* that between Symbolic and Real. Žižek points out that "external objects" like those onscreen at the movies are normally viewed as "fundamentally 'unreal,' as if their reality has been suspended."[13] When the border between viewer and object is breached, what erupts is a "grey and formless mist, pulsing slowly as with inchoate life . . . the Lacanian real, the pulsing of the presymbolic substance."[14] Diegetic immersion represents exactly this breach of the Real into the Symbolic, eliminating the difference between the *interior* of the auditorium (the audience's position) and the *exterior* of the onscreen world.

PSYCHOSIS THROUGH IMMERSION IN THE REAL

Of course, the Symbolic and the Real are not *supposed* to mix. The Real is a powerful force, and "reality"—that is, the Symbolic order— can exist only when a barrier is maintained between it and the Real.[15] When this barrier breaks down in the human mind, allowing the Real to overflow or be incorporated into "reality," the result is a psychotic state. In the cinematic context, a similar failure to preserve this boundary allows the Real to seep into the ordered structure of the film itself. A "psychotic" film is thus one where "the content, far from being simply 'depicted' is immediately 'rendered' by the very form of the film—here, the 'message' of the movie is immediately *the form itself*."[16] This is exactly what the digital surround style of diegetic immersion achieves: a rendering of the *experience* of a movie's events. A perfect example is the Omaha Beach sequence of *Saving Private Ryan* (1998): the film's soundscape, cinematography, and editing "render" for us not the actual *battle* itself, but the soldiers' *fear* and *confusion*. It is little wonder that filmmakers frequently deploy the digital surround style for literal and psychological point-of-view scenes; the formal characteristics of this style are *inherently* geared toward creating a "rendered" sense of experience rather than a literal reproduction.

Saving Private Ryan is hardly unique in employing an aesthetic form that "renders" narrative or thematic content—many DSS-era movies could similarly be described as "psychotic." In fact, several of the films used as case studies in previous chapters not only are *about* cracks in the barrier between the Symbolic and the Real but *literalize* this rupture through their form. *Disturbia* (2007), for example, centers on the distinction between inside and outside, between the safety of the home order (the Symbolic) and the lawless murderer (the Real) who cannot be kept outside it. Kale lives on an "island" of the Symbolic, its boundaries established by the law through his electronic ankle monitor, surrounded by the aquarium of the Real. He behaves as if the neighbors he watches through his windows are fictional—echoing Žižek's assertion that "behind the closed windows, the external objects are, so to speak, transposed into another mode. They appear to be fundamentally 'unreal'"[17]—but ultimately this barrier between inside and outside cannot hold. The Real erupts into Kale's ordered space when his mother is kidnapped and he himself is attacked.

Disturbia's multi-channel soundtrack aurally renders the danger of breaking down this barrier, exactly as Žižek suggests the form of a "psychotic" film should. Throughout most of Disturbia, the surround channels are used to signify threats to Kale, specifically threats *from the outside*. Since surround sound represents the Real, this sound design literally embodies the threat of the Real intruding into reality—put another way, it serves as the "aquarium of the real" lurking just outside the Symbolic. The film's third-act embrace of the digital surround style and diegetic immersion signifies that the Real, which had only intermittently broken into Kale's world before, has now fully breached the barrier keeping it out.

The analysis of Disturbia's ending in chapter 6 centered on Kale's realization that the boundary between inside and outside no longer exists. From a psychoanalytic perspective, his newfound knowledge is that the power of the Real has usurped the Symbolic, rendering it impotent. The symbolic "law," in fact, is explicitly revealed as helpless when the lone police officer sent to Turner's house near the film's end is quickly dispatched by Turner. With the "law" of no assistance, the only way for Kale to reestablish the necessary boundary between inside and outside is to abandon the order it represents and battle Turner on his own turf. Kale leaves his island (whose borders have already been breached by the Real) and enters Turner's house to retrieve his mother. He finally finds her in an area *not* included on the house's official blueprints—an area that is without name, outside the world of signifiers—using as his guide the multi-channel soundtrack.

The Matrix (1999) can likewise be read as a story about the inability of the Symbolic to withstand the power of the Real in a multi-channel world. What is the Matrix if not the Symbolic order itself, papering over

10.1. Neo's point of view at the end of *The Matrix* (1999). He finally sees the world of the Matrix for what it is: merely a construction of symbols and signs.

the "real" with an ordered and structured but ultimately false "reality"? This is why Morpheus and his crew generally do not expose people to the "truth" after a certain age—people must be pulled out of the Matrix before they have been completely indoctrinated into its Symbolic order, lest their inability to accept the truth about their "reality" lead to madness, as it does in the case of Cypher. The Matrix works unceasingly to eliminate those who have escaped its Symbolic order, but the Real *cannot* be contained. At the end of the film, Neo calls the Matrix itself to announce his intention of replacing its false reality with "a world without rules and controls, without borders or boundaries." The Matrix attempts to trace his call, but instead of finding Neo's phone number, the trace program offers only the response "system failure." The system in question is of course the Symbolic order, and the failure is that of its attempt to contain the power of the Real.

As in *Disturbia*, *The Matrix*'s form renders this breach, through its groundbreaking "bullet-time" cinematography and other visual effects. Repeatedly, the rules of "reality" are violated by gravity-defying wirework, characters morphing into new people, and cameras and characters that move faster than the laws of physics allow—each of these represents an intrusion of the Real into the ordered world of the Matrix. Perhaps most significantly, when Neo realizes he is "The One," his new worldview is shown as the scrolling *code* of the Matrix—he at last sees that the Matrix literally consists of nothing but *symbols* incapable of affecting The One, who *is* the *Real*.

Fight Club (1999) offers, at least on the surface, a somewhat more optimistic take on the Symbolic's capacity to contain the Real. Jack develops dual personalities because his psychological barrier between the *Real* and *reality* has disappeared—precisely the definition of madness. Tyler is the *Real* that invades Jack's nicely ordered, catalog-purchased world—but at the same time he *is* Jack. When Jack tells Tyler, "You're a voice in my head," Tyler's truthful response is "And you're a voice in mine." Asking which is the "true" person is to miss the point—*both* have an equal claim to that title. The relatively well-behaved, "normal" Jack is merely the socially acceptable façade of the uncompromising desire that is Tyler.

Žižek neatly details this duality using an example from Fritz Lang's 1945 film *The Woman in the Window*, about a man who murders someone, then wakes up and realizes it was all a dream. He notes that

> the message of the film is not consoling, not: "it was only a dream, in reality I am a normal man like others and not a murderer!" but rather: *in our unconscious, in the real of our desire, we are all murderers.* . . . We could say that the professor awakes *in order to continue his dream* (about being a normal person like his fellow men), that is, to escape the real (the "psychic reality") of his desire.[18]

Like the professor, who on waking from his dream must reassure himself that he is not a murderer, Jack *needs* to destroy Tyler to convince himself that *he is not really Tyler*. The very fact that Jack has to shoot *himself* to defeat Tyler, of course, demonstrates just how much Jack *is* Tyler—Jack's Symbolic-integrated public persona cannot be separated from the Real of his desire.

Even as Jack "kills" Tyler, seemingly reasserting the authority of the Symbolic order, the film's ending makes clear the impossibility of ever truly containing the Real. Narratively, Tyler's demolition plans— which involve destroying the financial records on which ordered society is based—succeed even after his "death." Formally, the image track concludes with a quick pornographic insert, recalling a scene from earlier in the movie where Tyler was splicing pornography into children's films. This shot reminds us that Tyler—the Real—is *always*

10.2. As *Fight Club* (1999) ends, Marla and Jack watch the skyscrapers outside explode. Though Jack appears to have destroyed Tyler, the film's final shots serve as a reminder that the Real is *always* present and ready to challenge the Symbolic order.

present "behind the scenes." Jack's victory will be short lived, for Tyler remains an integral part of him, waiting for the next opportunity to break through the barrier holding the Real in check.

CASE STUDY: *HAIRSPRAY* AND THE REAL OF THE MUSICAL

In all three of these films (*Disturbia*, *The Matrix*, and *Fight Club*), a plot involving the inability of the Symbolic to contain the Real is mirrored by DSS-driven formal elements in which the Real expands from the multi-channel soundtrack into the image track. And as these examples illustrate, this eruption of the Real into the Symbolic *can* occur in all sorts of films. One genre, though, is built entirely around this rupture: the musical. Unlike the classic operas of Mozart's era or the rock operas of more recent years, the film musical is rarely a story set entirely to music. Instead, it portrays an otherwise normal diegetic world with the one quirk that the characters spontaneously break into song (and often dance). The story freely switches back and forth between "regular" talking scenes and song-and-dance numbers, with no one commenting on their odd juxtaposition. It is hardly a stretch to suggest that the musical segments represent an intrusion of the Real into the otherwise ordered "reality" of the diegetic world.

Add to this the musical's inherent reliance on sound, and the genre suggests itself as a promising testing ground for the issues raised in this chapter. Chapter 2 offered one example of a musical's use of multi-channel to separate the real from reality: *Dancer in the Dark* (2000) distinguishes its fantasy-based musical sequences from other scenes showing the mundane reality of life through employing sur-round sound in the former scenes and a monophonic soundtrack in the latter. Close examination of *Moulin Rouge!* (2001), which sparked the recent revival of the live-action musical, reveals that its mix too varies as the film shifts between musical and non-musical segments.

Both these films deserve further examination in the context of multi-channel sound and/or psychoanalysis. For the final case study of this book, though, it seemed inappropriate to focus on the auteur-driven, urgently unique *Moulin Rouge!* or *Dancer in the Dark*; examin-ing a more classically styled Hollywood musical will better demonstrate digital surround sound's influence on this well-established cinematic form. Thus the object of inquiry here will be 2007's *Hairspray*, the film version of the popular stage musical (itself based on the 1988 film of the same name). Aside from the fact that the film's plot revolves around an *American Bandstand*–style teen dance show, which provides a real-world excuse for a few of the musical numbers, *Hairspray* sticks to the classical musical formula, where characters will suddenly burst out singing in the middle of diegetic "reality."

The film's plot deals with cultural norms (reality), the desires that threaten them (the Real), and the inability of the former to contain the latter. At one level of the story, this battle pits those who wish to main-tain the status quo of segregation between blacks and whites against those promoting integration. At another, this society-wide struggle is mirrored by the personal battles of the film's heroine, Tracy Turnblad (played by Nikki Blonsky), to become a dancer on *The Corny Collins Show* and win the heart of the show's star, Link (Zac Efron), despite be-ing overweight and thereby not conforming to societal norms of beauty.

That both Tracy's personal ambitions and the broader fight for integration represent the Real of desire attacking societal conventions is made clear by the lyrics of the film's songs. Indeed, *Hairspray*'s first words are Tracy's sung expression of an inner drive for something be-yond what society gives her: "Woke up today, feeling the way I always do—hungry for something that I can't eat—then I hear that beat." The battle over integration is couched in similar terms. Motormouth May-belle (Queen Latifah), host of the monthly "Negro Day" dance show, reveals that she keeps fighting because of something inside her: "It's a voice that comes from deep within. There's a cry asking why, I pray the answer's up ahead." Like Tracy, Maybelle hungers for something the law—in both the literal and Lacanian senses—says she cannot have and insists on pursuing that drive regardless of the consequences.

Affirming its status with *The Matrix, Disturbia*, and *Fight Club* as a "psychotic" film, *Hairspray*'s formal structure mirrors this narra-tive battle between the Real and reality. As explained above, musical sequences in general can be read as intrusions of the Real into the Symbolic. But categorizing *Hairspray*'s sequences into "musical" and "non-musical" oversimplifies the situation—the movie incorporates two distinct varieties of musical sequence. Some, such as the sing-ing and dancing numbers that are part of *The Corny Collins Show*, are at least partially integrated into the reality of the movie. Others, like Tracy's opening number "Good Morning Baltimore" or "I Can Hear the Bells," in which she imagines her future with Link, exist in a fantasy space.

These two types of musical scenes, moreover, employ the multi-channel environment quite differently from each other. Both utilize DSS's entire 5.1 surroundscape, but they do not do so in the same way.[19] For the reality-based musical sequences like those within *The Corny Collins Show*, the multi-channel soundscape is used to create a con-cert-style environment. Singing and instrumentation originate from the screen channels, with the rears used for reverberation and ambient sounds. The combined effect is that of hearing an on-stage musical performance from a seat in the audience at an enclosed venue—the music clearly originates in the front but reverberates around the entire space to envelop the audience.

In contrast, the fantasy-based musical scenes use the surround channels much more aggressively. Individual instruments are panned to different speakers around the theater, and while the primary singer always remains in the center channel, chorus effects and other voices originate in the rears. If the reality-based songs acoustically place film-

10.3. *Hairspray* (2007) varies its use of the multi-channel environment during musical sequences depending on how diegetically grounded they are. For numbers, such as this one performed on *The Corny Collins Show*, that occur in the "reality" of the film's world, *Hairspray* uses a "concert-style" multi-channel mix.

goers at a concert, these sequences place them in the middle of the orchestra, literally surrounded by instruments. A few of the musical numbers lie between these two extremes. "(You're) Timeless to Me" and "(The Legend of) Miss Baltimore Crabs," for example, include portions in the diegetic world and portions that are clearly fantasies. These scenes follow the same rules as their more homogeneous counterparts; their reality-based segments use a front-heavy mix, while their fantasy portions not only bring up the volume of the rear channels but also allow instrumentation to spread into the surrounds.

These variations in mixing exemplify the association between multi-channel sound and the Real: the more fantastical a musical sequence becomes—the more it diverges from *reality*—the more the rear channels are employed. Even in the surround-intensive "Good Morn-

10.4. *Hairspray*'s "fantasy"-based musical sequences use a more aggressive surround mix than its reality-based ones. "I Can Hear the Bells" is clearly a fantasy-driven number, as this shot makes clear: Tracy's singing goes unremarked upon by her driving instructor, who (in the diegetic reality) does not hear her singing. Accordingly, this song's soundtrack moves some instruments and voices into the surround channels rather than keeping them all onscreen. *Hairspray* (2007).

ing Baltimore," the single most immersive moment comes when Tracy herself gets so lost in the music that she disconnects from the world around her; too busy dancing to notice everyone around her getting on the bus, she misses it and must find an alternate transport to school. To be sure, *all* the movie's musical sequences represent an intrusion of the Real into reality. Even the front-centric, concert-style mixing of the diegetically motivated musical scenes departs from "reality," as it creates a listening environment not literally corresponding to that portrayed onscreen. For instance, when "Run and Tell That" moves from a classroom out into the streets, the reverb in the rear channels does not change significantly despite the onscreen move from an enclosed space to an open one—the sound remains that of an idealized performance space, not that of the literal diegetic space. Nevertheless, *Hairspray* distinguishes the *degree* to which the Real intrudes by tightly tying its surround usage to how "fantastical" a given musical sequence is.

Hairspray also confirms this chapter's assertion that in the digital surround era the Real, represented here by the musical sequences, cannot be permanently contained. Tracy acknowledges as much in the opening number, singing that "something inside of me makes me move when I hear that groove. My ma tells me no, but my feet tell me go!" Nor is Tracy's "ma," representative of the "law" to her teenaged daughter, alone in trying and failing to prohibit the real from erupting into her orderly world. Mrs. Pingleton—mother of Tracy's best friend Penny—scrupulously follows the laws set out in the Bible and by her government, even heeding the pricey Cold War–era recommendation to build her own nuclear bomb shelter. Yet neither her adherence to the dictates of society nor the strict rules Mrs. Pingleton lays down for her daughter can contain the Real of desire. She imprisons both Tracy and Penny to keep them from further participation in pro-integration activities, but they escape—which Mrs. Pingleton only learns when she sees Penny on television kissing her African American boyfriend. Velma, the television station's manager, similarly tries to maintain societal norms by vehemently opposing both Tracy's inclusion on and the integration of *The Corny Collins Show.* But her plans reveal the inadequacy of the Symbolic order in suppressing the Real. Policemen (the law) stationed outside the TV studio by Velma specifically to keep Tracy *out* of the studio unwittingly carry a concealed Tracy *into* it. Then, during the movie's climactic live broadcast, the white teenagers and their black peers ignore Velma's long-standing prohibitions against mixing onscreen by acting on their own desires and spontaneously integrating the show.

This final scene might seem to suggest an assimilation of the Real into the Symbolic order. After all, at the end Tracy and her friends succeed in integrating *The Corny Collins Show,* Tracy gets her man, and everyone seems happy with these outcomes. Yet the fact that everyone seems happy when the film cuts to credits does not mean societal norms have suddenly shifted. It merely diverts attention from the reality of how difficult changing societal norms actually is. Two races mingling for the length of one song hardly puts an end to racism; as

10.5. Though representatives of societal authority (the law) try to prevent integration, ultimately they cannot contain the Real. By the end of *Hairspray*, teenagers and adults of all races, ages, and sizes dance together on live television. Here Motormouth Maybelle leads a verse of "You Can't Stop the Beat," the film's concluding number, backed by teens both black and white. *Hairspray* (2007).

Maybelle wryly tells two students of different races who have fallen in love, "You two better brace yourselves for a whole lotta ugly coming at you from a never-ending parade of stupid." Even as the rest of the cast sings and dances in harmony on a newly integrated *Corny Collins Show*, Velma and Mrs. Pingleton—representatives of the Symbolic/societal order threatened by interaction—refrain from joining the dance, instead stubbornly continuing their already-failed struggle to repress the real. Velma tries to reassert control over the program, lamenting that the show is "turning to gumbo" despite growing cheering and clapping in the soundtrack suggesting the audience is quite pleased with how it is unfolding. Mrs. Pingleton, meanwhile, is last seen scrubbing her television screen, desperately trying to change the skin color of her daughter's new boyfriend in the live image.

    Hairspray's final scene ultimately represents not a merging of the Real *with* reality, but a temporary triumph of the Real *over* reality's efforts to keep it in check. The barrier between the two breaks down, and the Real quickly overtakes the entire field until no differentiations remain. Since its opening song, where Tracy vocalizes the real of her desire as "that beat," the film has intermittently given us eruptions of the real into reality through singing and dancing. For the final number, where the Symbolic order has been overcome by the Real, *everyone*— black, white, old, young, fat, slim—can join the dance. The title and chorus of this concluding song boisterously declare "You Can't Stop the Beat," a claim true not only for *Hairspray* but for the DSS-era musical in general. Since the Real cannot be repressed, music ("the beat") must eventually break into the reality of the diegetic world, just as *Fight Club*'s Jack can never permanently contain Tyler.

Before leaving the musical and this chapter, it is worth pointing out that *Hairspray* does not, outside its pre-title opening sequence, exhibit many of the traits of the digital surround style. Its image track relies heavily on wide shots and maintains spatial orientation through classical continuity editing and shooting practices. And its soundtrack employs a heavily screen-centric mix for all non-musical sounds rather than aggressively panning them around the soundscape. In short, aside from aggressive use of the surrounds in its musical segments, *Hairspray* looks and sounds much like a pre-DSS film.

This may have more to do with the musical genre than with *Hairspray*'s particular style. Their extensive use of non-diegetic music makes musicals inherently ill suited to DSS-based diegetic immersion. Almost every feature film employs non-diegetic music at some point, of course, but this music is understood by the audience as part of the *movie* rather than as something originating within the diegetic world of the film. Musicals, on the other hand, rely on an inherent paradox: characters interact with, and sing along to, music originating outside their diegetic world. In such a situation, the tight image/sound matching that the digital surround style requires is impossible. If voices were spatially matched to the location of the characters singing but the instrumental background was not, this would draw unwanted attention to the ontological difference between the vocals and the rest of the music in relation to the diegetic world. Yet moving the instrumental tracks around the soundscape with the vocal tracks would be equally problematic: these sounds do not originate within the onscreen environment and hence logically should not be spatially associated with a particular area of the onscreen world. With no good way to spatialize musical sequences, even DSS-equipped musicals tend to adhere to classical screen-centric mixing practices and minimize use of direct sounds panned outside the screen.

The musical genre therefore serves as a reminder that while di-egetic immersion is a valuable overall conception of DSS aesthetics, it does not accurately describe every contemporary film. Rather, the aural and visual characteristics of a particular film or genre must be carefully examined to ascertain the degree to which that film or genre deploys the traits of this digital surround–based aesthetic. For musicals and other films that utilize relatively few of these elements, it is reasonable to assert that diegetic immersion is probably not the primary aesthetic. This does not mean, however, that digital surround sound technology does not play a significant role in those films' styles or construction.

Hairspray, for example, exploits DSS's multi-channel capabilities to distinguish the relative mixture of fantasy (Real) and reality (Symbolic) within its scenes. And though the film does not rely on the specific "digital surround style" of diegetic immersion outlined earlier, its vary-ing use of surround sound nevertheless *does* promote immersion in the onscreen world. Specifically, it places the audience in the *psychologi-cal* world of the characters, using musical sequences to present truths hidden to society at large—the audience, like the characters, becomes immersed in this fantastic musical world that seems more engrossing and important than the everyday reality from which both audience and characters remain at a distance. *Hairspray* thus ultimately employs a "variation" on diegetic immersion, demonstrating the overall applica-bility of that model when considered in terms of *function* rather than of specific stylistic execution.

CONCLUSION: MEDIA AND MEDIA STUDIES IN THE DIGITAL SURROUND AGE

This book began with a simple question: how has 5.1 surround sound impacted the cinema? That seemingly straightforward starting point blossomed into a wide-ranging exploration. Examination of the formal traits—aural and visual—encouraged by cinema's adoption of digital surround sound led to recognition of a specific style centered on diegetic immersion. This, in turn, established the need to develop new textual analysis methodologies capable of explicating multi-channel soundtracks and the complex relationships between sound and image employed by the digital surround style. And these analytic strategies were then used to investigate the way DSS and diegetic immersion relate to conceptions of how the cinema fundamentally works.

In short, this project has covered a lot of ground, including audiovisual aesthetics, textual analysis practices, and film theory. Yet in the end it presents a necessarily incomplete perspective on DSS's implications. Its final section, for instance, established the importance of reconsidering film theory in the light of DSS. But it limited its scrutiny to three select theoretical concepts, even though semiotics, authorship, realism, ideology, and other concerns are equally deserving of examination through the lens of 5.1 digital surround. Additionally, the current work has forgone the massive task of covering *all* DSS's effects on *all* media in favor of demonstrating its importance to both media production and media scholarship through the particular example of Hollywood feature film.

Ultimately the in-depth—but not comprehensive—exploration of DSS's consequences for the film industry and film scholarship offered by this book was designed not only to open its readers' eyes and ears to digital surround's importance in contemporary cinema but also to provide a foundation for further work on digital surround and multichannel sound, both in the cinema and outside it. It is in the nature of scholarly projects to suggest avenues for exploration beyond those that they themselves pursue—in that spirit, these last few pages outline some of the paths opened up by the current work.

DSS AND SPECIFIC CINEMATIC FORMS

Mainstream narrative cinema has to date been the largest exploiter of 5.1-channel surround's unique capabilities, which is why this book has relied primarily on Hollywood feature films for its examples. As digital surround has grown more prevalent, though, it has increasingly come within reach of filmmakers at all levels working on all types of projects. A college student with a laptop and a few hundred dollars worth of software can now create a 5.1 soundtrack, marry it to video shot on a cheap camcorder, burn it to a DVD, and send the finished product to friends, relatives, and festivals. Today, a 5.1 surround mix is increasingly an expectation, not a luxury, for any film seeking distribution.

This does not mean that the aesthetic effects of DSS are necessarily the same across all types of movies. Independent filmmakers often do not have the time, money, or expertise to create theater-quality surround mixes, and they may not even hear their movies on anything other than their computer speakers before sending those films off to festivals. Sound designer Glenn Morgan offers first-hand experience with this scenario, recalling that after an indie feature was picked up for distribution, "the studio called and said, 'We just bought this project, we would like for you to take a look at it and see if you can expand upon it and make it bigger.'"[1] The point, Morgan notes, was not that they wanted to "Hollywoodize" the movie, but that the sound design was too "thin" to work in a large theatrical space, as the film's director and producer themselves acknowledged after hearing their movie played in an actual cinema. In a scenario like this, the final movie may employ a mix of DSS-based and more traditional characteristics, depending on what changes are made at this stage, how much time and money is spent reworking the soundtrack, and how surround-aware the original filmmakers were in terms of their visual compositions and editing.

Budget and expertise are not the only factors at play in determining how a film uses DSS. Experimental and documentary films often adopt styles different from narrative features, and their use of 5.1 surround may likewise diverge in some ways from the narrative feature–oriented model outlined in this book. Even within mainstream narrative cinema, some genres are more likely than others to make extensive use of the digital surround style. Action, science fiction, and fantasy films tend to exploit DSS and diegetic immersion extensively; comedies, dramas, and period pieces generally do not. Musicals (as discussed in chapter 10) often make use of DSS's multi-channel capabilities, but not necessarily in service of the type of diegetic immersion promoted by the digital surround style. And animation is a mixed bag: while Pixar has created some of the most aggressively immersive surroundscapes of recent years, animated films from Dreamworks and Fox have generally employed more screen-centric approaches (though 3-D has encouraged a movement toward greater surround use). All these variations illustrate that an examination of surround aesthetics in the context of genres would be of great value. To this point, the only major work in this arena has been a thoughtful chapter in William Whittington's *Sound Design & Science Fiction* on the relationship between surround sound and science fiction. This book will, I hope, encourage other scholars of genre to follow Whittington's lead.

IDENTITY POLITICS

This project has intentionally focused on texts and production practices, rather than on reception, a conscious strategy aimed at demonstrating the importance of digital surround sound. Certainly, as discussed in chapter 6, those studying contemporary cinema should make the necessary efforts to study films in their full multi-channel presentation. That said, in the real world not all audiences experience films in 5.1 surround all the time. Home theater ownership levels, for instance, vary with household income.[2] Though prices have come down in recent years, even low-end 5.1 home theater systems cost several hundred dollars, and 5.1 is ultimately a luxury item, not a necessity. Not even all those who can afford home theater systems choose to purchase them; research indicates that surround sound is not equally important across all demographic groups, with age, race/ethnicity, and family status affecting decisions to buy home theater systems.[3]

Surround sound usage is not much more consistent outside the home. Even aside from any question of whether different demographic groups may prefer different *movies*, class, race, location, and income levels have an impact on what *theaters* moviegoers attend. Upscale first-run houses will likely feature well-maintained (though not always correctly configured) 5.1 systems, while theaters further down the theatrical hierarchy may not have 5.1 surround or may have installed systems but then failed to repair or maintain them after installation. At the second-run dollar-a-show multiplex near me, for example, some screens have fully functional 5.1 sound systems, while others feature surround systems in various stages of decay or non-functionality. One of the most frustrating theatrical experiences I have ever had was watching *Adventureland* (2009) at this theater on a day where the center speaker was not producing mid to high frequencies. At best, this was merely distracting, such as when a bicycle traveled across the screen—its sound originated in the front right channel, disappeared as it reached the center, and reappeared as the bike reached the left side of the frame. More often, the missing frequencies made it difficult to decipher the dialogue and kept me from following parts of the movie.

Since not everyone has an equal opportunity (or desire) to experience movies in 5.1 surround either at the theater or at home, a study of digital surround sound in the context of identity and ideology would be a valuable supplement to this project. The very idea of a "digital surround style" suggests that some movies *must* be experienced in 5.1—the above-mentioned differences in where and how movies are actually screened might suggest that movies in this category are made specifically for a particular economic, ethnic, or geographic demographic. This leads to a larger question about cinema's role as an equal-opportunity art; not everyone can afford to attend operas or Broadway musicals, but movie tickets are relatively cheap and generally available to everyone—does the digital surround style make cinema less of a democratic form?

Questions in the opposite direction can also be asked: if certain genres or categories of films tend to employ the DSS-driven style while others do not, what does this say about the people to whom those films are meant to appeal? For example, romantic comedies rarely employ heavily surround-based soundtracks. Is this because the digital surround style is inherently poorly suited to the genre, or because the women and couples who form the primary market for those films prefer screen-centric movies? The latter possibility raises the particularly intriguing question of surround sound and gender. In general, women have better hearing than men,[4] yet the genres most associated with surround sound are those often considered male oriented. This book explored the digital surround style and its ramifications for film scholarship; work tackling identity-based questions such as those listed here would productively build on that work, helping to expose the societal ramifications of that style and its use.

BEYOND CINEMA: DSS IN OTHER AUDIO-VISUAL MEDIA

Although digital surround sound originated in the cinema, it did not take long to expand its reach beyond the cinema's walls. Laserdisc was the first non-theatrical format to experiment with digital surround, including 5.1 digital tracks on some releases starting in the mid-1990s. When DVD supplanted laserdisc a few years later, its massive success—and the fact that all DVDs were required to include at least one DSS-encoded soundtrack—spurred the explosive growth of home theater and the purchase of 5.1 systems for home use. Yet DSS's adoption by laserdisc and DVD is essentially an extension of its roots in film; most people use these home formats primarily to watch movies originally created for theatrical release. Thus the effects of DSS on DVD are largely the same as its effects in the cinema.

The same does not necessarily hold true, though, for the other media to which 5.1 has spread now that DVD has brought digital surround into a significant number of homes. High-definition television followed DVD in setting 5.1 digital surround as its audio standard, and television style may shift to accommodate its new sonic capabilities. But there is no guarantee that it will be affected in the same ways the cinema was, especially since the two media forms already employ notably different styles. Additionally, television is currently in the same situation as cinema during the first few years after DSS's introduction, with infrastructure limitations making mediamakers leery of exploiting its full capabilities—though much prime-time programming is now *broadcast* in 5.1, television producers and broadcasters realize that most people *hear* those mixes downconverted to two-channel stereo for playback over their television speakers, making it difficult to incorporate surround design as an integral part of their shows' aesthetics.

This combination of interest in adopting digital surround sound with hesitancy about assuming audiences will hear their television programs in 5.1 is apparent in the 2009 episode "Day 7: 9:00 PM–10:00 PM" of the television show 24. This episode uses an aggressive multi-channel mix—including dialogue panned to the surround channels—to enhance the real-time immediacy and authenticity of its world. Scenes in the Oval Office, for instance, often include the sound of a reporter's voice, which diegetically originates from a television opposite the president's desk. As the camera cuts to different angles around the office, this voice jumps around the multi-channel soundscape to maintain appropriate spatial matching between sound and source.[5] In short, the mix maintains the "reality" of a complete space existing all around the audience and matching the visual perspective, precisely the type of immersion that characterizes the digital surround style. At the same time, however, 24 does not fully spatialize the environment. Of the various voices heard on the soundtrack, it is only the reporter's voice— essentially serving as environmental ambience—that is allowed to leave the center channel; the voices of the main characters are consistently mixed front and center lest they go unheard by audiences watching TV without a 5.1 surround system. As home theater grows more prevalent, television producers will likely grow more comfortable with employing the aggressive surround mixing practices made possible by DSS, but until this happens, exactly how they will choose to deploy those capabilities—and in particular whether DSS's impact on television style will be the same as its effect on feature filmmaking practices—remains to be seen.

INTERACTIVE SURROUND

Surround sound in video games is in some ways an even more promising area of inquiry. In gaming, the "audience" (i.e., the player) can affect the media experience, rather than just taking in a pre-existing set of sound and images as in the cinema or television. This difference means that games can deploy multi-channel in ways significantly different from other media. First-person shooters such as *Dead Space* (2008), *Halo 3* (2007), and *Brothers-in-Arms: Hell's Highway* (2007), for instance, specifically place effects around the 5.1 soundscape to alert the player to other characters or events. Conceptually, this approach fits the diegetic immersion model, as it informs players that the world of the game extends a full 360 degrees around them and locates their perspective literally in the midst of the action. Practically, though, it pushes diegetic immersion beyond the limits of its cinematic incarnation. The surroundscape not only informs players about the world beyond the screen but also forces them to *react* to that information—they must quickly decide whether a sound in the surrounds merits investigation or whether it is wiser to continue looking in the current direction. Explains Akihiko Mukaiyama, director of the acclaimed game *Panzer Dragoon Orta* (2002), 5.1 sound can "give players information that cannot be visually described on-screen. . . . allowing them to anticipate key plot points or enemies approaching from different directions, which makes game play experience that much more immersive."[6] The intended result is precisely the "exit door effect" the cinema strives so hard to avoid—noises in the surrounds are designed to *attract* players' attention and suggest that they look away from "the screen."

The intriguing possibility this raises is that some games may be completely unplayable in a non-5.1-equipped environment. In the midst of a firefight, being able to identify the direction from which enemy gunfire is coming is a crucial advantage, meaning that games utilizing this manner of surround design become much more difficult when played in mono or traditional two-channel stereo. Why the video game industry has been so quick to embrace the possibilities of media that *requires* 5.1 surround is worthy of further exploration. One possible explanation is that the gaming world is simply more accustomed to adopting and exploiting new technologies than the cinema or television. Alternatively, perhaps the immersive nature of 5.1 is a natural fit for the interactivity of video games. And as yet another possibility, the industry may have assumed that those consumers who could afford—and chose to purchase—a pricey video game system were likely to already own, or at least have the means to purchase, a home theater system as well.

Aesthetically, 5.1 surround has been deployed in video games in a variety of ways, suggesting that DSS may have had more disparate effects on that media form than it has had on the cinema. At least three distinct approaches to 5.1 surround use have emerged. One is the immersive first-person approach already described, where the soundscape surrounds the player and shifts in accordance with the onscreen perspective. A second is a "third-person" approach, where the soundtrack suggests action beyond the frame, but the player occupies an outside perspective not identical to that of an onscreen character hearing. Here the location of offscreen sounds conveys information about their location relative to the game field, rather than to the actual player as in the first approach. In *Lego Batman* (2008), for instance, offscreen sounds in the surround channels (as well as the front left and right) let the player know where additional enemies lie, but the soundtrack's orientation does not change as Batman moves or turns since the player is not *literally* hearing Batman's aural perspective. Finally, a third approach uses surround to create a three-dimensional soundscape not oriented to specific onscreen action. *Rock Band 2* (2008) is an excellent example. During gameplay, the image track presents a barrage of shots from a variety of angles, cut together to mimic a concert video; the 5.1 soundtrack, meanwhile, remains consistent throughout, spreading the instruments across the front three channels and placing crowd cheers (or jeers) in the two rear speakers.

This variety of approaches to surround shows that the ultimate consequences of DSS for gaming are anything but a settled question. It *is* clear that surround sound will continue to be an integral part of video games into the foreseeable future. 5.1 made its first foray into gaming in the early 2000s, with the hugely successful *Halo* (2001) being one of several games exciting players and audiences about the possibilities of surround sound gaming. As *Halo*'s audio director noted, "having this technology . . . allows me to add a level of realism and dramatic effect to my games that is not possible otherwise."[7] Today virtually all games for Microsoft's Xbox 360 and Sony's PlayStation 3 are released in 5.1 (Nintendo's Wii does not support DSS), and a few recent games even surpass cinematic multi-channel capabilities by incorporating full 7.1-channel soundtracks.[8] Considering video games' varied and changing deployments of DSS and the unique immersive possibilities afforded by their intrinsically interactive nature, gaming certainly offers fertile ground for future work on surround sound and media.

5.1 MUSIC

Music recordings, unlike television, film, or video games, exist without any visual referent, and hence have engendered passionate debate about the "right" way to mix in surround sound without a screen as the focus of audiences' attention. Since this issue first arose in the 1970s with quad sound, the music industry has not arrived at any definitive answer. Some records, particularly those in the classical and jazz genres, use surround to reproduce a typical concert environment, placing the performance in the front channels and using the surrounds for ambient sounds, crowd noise, and reverb. Often this type of surround mix is not created from scratch in the studio but derives from a multi-channel microphone setup capturing the actual acoustics of the original performance space. Other mixes employ an "in the band" perspective, placing different instruments in different places around the multi-channel environment. And some even push this strategy a step further, using in-your-face surround effects with no corollary in real performance. The 5.1 release of "Bootylicious" by Destiny's Child, for example, cycles a guitar sample through all five main speakers, creating the effect of a guitar whizzing around the borders of the listening space.

Like the gaming world, then, the music industry has employed a variety of surround sound aesthetics. Where 5.1 surround sound has been highly successful in video games, though, 5.1 surround in music has never been embraced by consumers. Attempting to capitalize on DSS's success in cinema and the subsequent home theater boom, in the late 1990s and early 2000s the music industry introduced three different 5.1-channel music formats: Sony's super audio compact disc

(SACD), Philips's DVD-Audio (DVD-A), and DTS's DTS-CD or "5.1 Music Disc." Despite acclaim by audiophiles and demonstrable technological superiority over compact discs, none of these formats achieved mainstream success. Even at the peak of their popularity in 2002–2003, SACD and DVD-A sales combined equaled less than two million discs (DTS-CD sales were never tracked separately). By 2006, annual sales had dropped to less than a quarter of 2002–2003's already low levels,[9] and in 2008 the Recording Industry Association of America (RIAA) determined that sales in both formats were too low to continue tracking.[10]

The failure of these 5.1 music formats raises the provocative question of why DSS, such a success in theaters and home video, met with resounding indifference from purchasers of recorded music. One of several plausible explanations is that consumers were perfectly happy with the quality of CDs and did not see any reason to pay for the playback equipment needed to handle the new formats. DVD's massive success demonstrates that consumers are willing to pay for a new format if it represents a clear improvement over the current norm: compared to VHS, DVD offered better picture, better sound, more special features, and random access. But DVD-A and SACD, unlike DVD, offered few new features other than the ability to play music in 5.1. Their most touted improvement over CDs was their higher resolution audio signals, yet most people cannot even hear the difference between CDs and the high-resolution music formats.[11] One industry executive probably speaks for many in recalling his first 5.1 music experience as being notably underwhelming: "I remember putting it on and blasting on the new system and I really wanted to love it. I wanted to stand in the middle of it and go, 'This is so cool!' . . . but it didn't really translate into a superior experience for me."[12]

Another possibility is that pre-recorded music simply does not lend itself well to 5.1 presentation. For maximum effect, surround sound requires a stationary listener placed at the "sweet spot" in the middle of all the speakers. Most people, however, rarely listen to music in this way. As film music executive Mike Knobloch laments,

> When I was a kid you could just listen to music and that was enough, but today . . . the multitasking or hypertasking mode that everyone is in, maybe just listening to music—whether it's stereo or 5.1—is not as

satisfying an experience as it used to be. . . . It's not so much about how many speakers it comes out of as it is "do people just enjoy listening to high quality music, and not doing anything else at the same time."[13]

Tomlinson Holman concurs that "it's a lifestyle thing. People just don't sit down and listen to music as they once did."[14] Music listening today occurs over the radio or CD player in cars (where each seat hears a different mix of the various speakers), in the background as people go about their business at work or at home, or over headphones as people exercise or travel. None of these cases provide a good venue to really hear the difference between 5.1 and stereo, or even between stereo and mono. "If you were listening to two channels of music and you move around the room . . . it's going to sound different," as one sound editor puts it. "I'm not sure anyone necessarily needs 5.1 or more channels to listen to music."[15]

Perhaps the most intriguing possible factor in 5.1 music's failure is that surround sound is most effective in the context of an audio-*visual* experience. The digital surround style relies not just on DSS's aural capabilities but on the relationship between the soundscape and the onscreen images. 5.1 surround may thus impact audio-only media forms like music much less than audio-visual ones like cinema or video games. Chapter 6 cited an experimental study demonstrating that—in certain cases—viewers rate movie clips differently depending on whether they heard the clips in 5.1 surround or two-channel stereo. The same study found that for music excerpts, sound presentation mode had *no* significant effect on audience ratings.[16] This study, moreover, included a wide range of musical styles and approaches to surround mixing, indicating that even for the most aggressive surround mixes (the "Bootylicious" track mentioned above was one of the samples used), audiences responded no differently to the 5.1 mix than to the 2-channel stereo mix. Follow-up investigations are under way, but at the very least this research indicates that the effects of surround sound may depend as much on visual stimuli as on sound itself.

A LOOK TO THE FUTURE . . .

Nearly two decades after its first appearance in theaters, digital surround sound technology continues to push forward. Theaters and home systems now commonly go beyond 5.1, employing 6.1- and 7.1-channel systems. Digital cinema promises that in the near future theatrical soundtracks will offer higher-resolution audio and lossless compression, while some Blu-Ray discs already offer lossless audio to home viewers. And advanced configurations incorporating 10.2 (or more) channels are, though not yet commonplace, already a reality. Not necessarily coincidentally, for the first time in a century the cinema's visual technology is also changing as exhibitors gradually adopt digital projection. Even 3-D is making a comeback thanks to committed executives and filmmakers like Jeffrey Katzenberg, Robert Zemeckis, and James Cameron. Perhaps DSS can claim some share of the credit for this movement—as the soundtrack has expanded and grown, it may have spurred a desire to help the image "catch up" with the immersive capabilities of the soundtrack.

Clearly the cinema is currently in a period of significant change, and it is not yet clear when and whether digital projection, 3-D, and other new technologies will be universally adopted or fall by the wayside as 3-D has done before. At the same time, the nature of digital surround sound itself is changing, as expanded channel configurations are introduced and DSS expands into new media forms within and beyond the cinema, where it may or may not be used the same way it has been in mainstream narrative cinema. But if the future is uncertain today—twenty years into the digital surround age—at least one thing does seem clear: digital surround sound will only grow in its importance to the audio-visual arts for the foreseeable future.

This book's introduction noted the failure of cinema studies thus far to even notice surround sound, likening the practice of studying contemporary Hollywood films in mono or stereo to writing about color films after only seeing them in black and white. The ensuing exploration of digital surround sound's impact on filmmaking, film analysis, and film theory hopefully backed this assertion with ample evidence that adding consideration of surround sound to any type of work on the cinema pays significant dividends. But getting scholars to screen films in their intended soundtrack format is only one step toward the larger goal of moving the field beyond its visual origins; eventually, cinema studies must upgrade not just its sound systems but also its thinking about sound and image. Cinema may have started as an image-only medium, but it has been a fully audio-visual medium for nearly a century, and a surround-equipped one (albeit in a variety of different ways) for at least half that time. Only by learning to consistently consider its object of study for what it is now, rather than for what it was a hundred years ago, will cinema studies be fully equipped to explore and explain contemporary film.

APPENDIX A: TIMELINE OF COMMON SOUND EXHIBITION FORMATS

The Mono Era (1927 to late 1970s)

The first sync sound films were in mono, with a single channel of audio played back through a speaker located in the front of the auditorium at the horizontal center of the screen. Various multi-channel analog formats appeared over the years, starting with *Fantasia's* Fantasound in 1940. Some of these multi-channel formats, such as CinemaScope, Todd-AO, and Cinerama, enjoyed some success during the widescreen boom of the 1950s. None, however, supplanted monophonic sound as a widely adopted standard until the 1970s.

The Dolby Stereo Era (mid-1970s to mid-1990s)

In the mid-1970s, Dolby introduced a method for encoding four channels of audio—left, center, and right across the width of the screen (L, C, R) and a surround channel (S) in the space of the theater—into the same space on 35mm film prints that had been used for a mono soundtrack. This configuration was highly successful and remained the norm for theatrical exhibition until digital systems appeared in the early 1990s. Dolby Stereo first appeared as a three-channel format (L, C, R) in *Lizstomania* (1975); the four-channel matrix configuration (L, C, R, S) did not appear until 1976's *A Star is Born*. Its use in blockbuster films such as *Star Wars* (1977) and *Close Encounters of the Third Kind* (1978) encouraged adoption of Dolby's sound system across the industry.

In 1986, Dolby Laboratories introduced Dolby SR encoding. In its 35mm incarnation, Dolby SR uses the same four-channel-matrixed configuration as Dolby Stereo but offers a greater dynamic range (difference between the loudest and the softest sounds possible). The first theatrical releases with Dolby SR–encoded soundtracks were *Innerspace* (1987) and *Robocop* (1987). Dolby SR would remain the standard for film exhibition until it was supplanted by digital surround sound systems in the 1990s. Even today, though, 35mm prints continue to include Dolby SR soundtracks, both to ensure compatibility with non-digitally equipped theaters and to serve as a backup in case of technical problems with the digital soundtrack.

The Digital Surround Era
(early 1990s to present)

The specifications for theatrical digital surround sound systems were created by the Society of Motion Picture and Television Engineers (SMPTE) in 1987. Their specifications included at least three front channels across the width of the screen (left, center, right), at least two surround channels (left surround, right surround), and a separate low-frequencies-only channel (LFE, for low-frequency effects), all of which were to be discrete (rather than matrixed). This configuration would come to be known as 5.1-channel (pronounced "five point one") sound, with the ".1" being the frequency-limited LFE channel.

After some initial market shakeout, by the mid-1990s three digital surround sound formats remained. The first was Dolby Digital (initially dubbed Dolby SR-D), which officially debuted in 1992 with *Batman Returns*. The original Dolby Digital format utilized the 5.1-channel configuration specified by SMPTE. Dolby Digital Surround EX, or Dolby Surround EX, later expanded this system to 6.1 channels by adding a matrixed center surround channel; this system was first used for 1999's *Star Wars Episode I: The Phantom Menace*. The second was DTS, whose 5.1-channel base configuration first appeared in *Jurassic Park* (1993). The original DTS codec left room for expansion, a capability exploited by the discrete 6.1-channel DTS-ES format that debuted with *The Haunting* (1999). Like Dolby Surround EX, this configuration added a center surround channel to the normal 5.1 setup. The third format was Sony Dynamic Digital Sound (SDDS), which premiered in 1993's *Last Action Hero*. SDDS specifies an eight-channel configuration with five channels across the width of the screen (L, LC, C, RC, R) in addition to stereo surround channels and the LFE channel, though the format can also encode traditional 5.1-channel mixes. SDDS stopped selling decoding equipment in the early 2000s, though film prints continue to include SDDS to maintain compatibility with SDDS-equipped theaters. Since 2007, however, no films have been mixed with a full eight-channel SDDS soundtrack.

APPENDIX B:FILM SOUND PERSONNEL CITED

The sound designers, editors, mixers, engineers, and executives quoted in this work have hundreds of collective credits. This alphabetical listing includes a few selected credits and awards for each filmmaker to provide the reader some context for their comments.

The Cinema Audio Society (CAS) is a professional society of mixers and annually presents CAS Awards to recognize outstanding television and film sound mixing. Motion Picture Sound Editors (MPSE) is an honorary society for film sound editors; it annually presents Golden Reel Awards honoring the best film and television sound editing.

Erik Aadahl

Sound designer: *Transformers* (2007), *Superman Returns* (2006), *I, Robot* (2004)

Sound editor: *Transformers: Revenge of the Fallen* (2009), *Valkyrie* (2008), *Kung Fu Panda* (2008), *The New World* (2005)

Awards: 4 Emmy nominations, 9 Golden Reel nominations (2 wins)

Richard Anderson

Sound editor: *Shrek the Third* (2007), *Planet of the Apes* (2001), *Sleepy Hollow*

(1999), *Being John Malkovich* (1999), *The Lion King* (1994), *Batman Returns* (1992), *Edward Scissorhands* (1990), *The Goonies* (1985), *48 Hrs.* (1982), *Poltergeist* (1982), *Raiders of the Lost Ark* (1981)

Awards: 2 Oscar nominations plus Special Achievement Award for sound effects editing, 1 Emmy win, 12 Golden Reel nominations plus MPSE Career Achievement Award

Steve Bissinger

Sound editor: *I Love You, Beth Cooper* (2009), *3:10 to Yuma* (2007), *Marie Antoinette* (2006), *Daddy Day Care* (2003), *Behind Enemy Lines* (2001), *Tombstone* (1993)

Awards: 1 Emmy nomination, 4 Golden Reel nominations (1 win)

David Bondelevitch

President of Motion Picture Sound Editors 2003–2005

Sound editor: *Strangers with Candy* (2005), *Battlestar Galactica* (TV) (2004), *Jeepers Creepers 2* (2003), *Thinner* (1996)

Awards: 1 Emmy win, 20 Golden Reel nominations (2 wins)

Ben Burtt

Sound designer and sound editor: *Star Trek* (2009), *WALL-E* (2008) (also re-recording mixer), *Indiana Jones and the Kingdom of the Crystal Skull* (2008), *Munich* (2005), *Star Wars* Episodes I, II, III, V (1980/1999/2002/2005) (also picture editor on I, II, III),

Sound designer and re-recording mixer: *Indiana Jones and the Last Crusade* (1989), *Always* (1989), *Indiana Jones and the Temple of Doom* (1984), *Return of the Jedi* (1983)

Awards: 10 Oscar nominations (2 wins) plus 2 Special Achievement Awards for sound effects and sound effects editing, 1 CAS Award nomination, 6 Golden Reel nominations (1 win) plus MPSE Career Achievement Award

Midge Costin

Sound editor: *Armageddon* (1998), *Con Air* (1997), *The Rock* (1996), *Broken Arrow* (1996), *Crimson Tide* (1995), *Hocus Pocus* (1993), *Days of Thunder* (1990)

Currently the Kay Rose Professor in the Art of Dialogue & Sound Editing at the University of Southern California

Andy Daddario (a.k.a. Andy D'Addario)

Re-recording mixer: the *Rush Hour* series (1998/2001/2007), *Brothers and Sisters* (TV) (2006–2009), *Wedding Crashers* (2005), *Shanghai Knights* (2003), *Stir of Echoes* (1999)

Dane Davis

Sound designer and sound editor: *Speed Racer* (2008), *Ghost Rider* (2007), *Aeon Flux* (2005), *The Forgotten* (2004), the *Matrix* series (1999/2003/2003), *Treasure Planet* (2002), *Red Planet* (2000)

Awards: 1 Oscar win, 1 Emmy nomination, 9 Golden Reel nominations (4 wins)

Thom "Coach" Ehle

Sound consultant for Dolby: *Role Models* (2008), *Forgetting Sarah Marshall* (2008), *Red Dragon* (2002), *8 Mile* (2002), *Collateral Damage* (2002), *O Brother, Where Art Thou?* (2000), *The Straight Story* (1997), *L.A. Confidential* (1997), *From Dusk till Dawn* (1996), *Glengarry Glen Ross* (1992), *Days of Thunder* (1990)

Steve Flick (a.k.a. Stephen Hunter Flick)

Sound editor: *The Unborn* (2009), *Leatherheads* (2008), *Constantine* (2005), *Terminator 3: Rise of the Machines* (2003), *The Long Kiss Goodnight* (1996), *Apollo 13* (1995), *Speed* (1994), *Pulp Fiction* (1994), *Robocop* (1987)

Sound designer: *The Invisible* (2007), *Hostage* (2005), *Spider-Man* (2002), *My Dog Skip* (2000)

Awards: 4 Oscar nominations (1 win) plus Special Achievement Award for sound effects editing, 3 Emmy wins, 6 Golden Reel nominations (3 wins)

Tomlinson Holman

Sound engineer and member of the Society for Motion Picture and Television Engineers

Inventor of 10.2 audio system; member of committees that developed the standards for 5.1-channel digital surround sound and those for the Digital Cinema Initiative (DCI)

Technical Achievement Award from Academy of Motion Picture Arts and Sciences (for work on theater sound systems), CAS Career Achievement Award

Marti Humphrey

Re-recording mixer: *Drag Me to Hell* (2009), *The Strangers* (2008), *The Exorcism of Emily Rose* (2005), *The Grudge* (2004)

Awards: 3 Emmy nominations (2 wins), 1 CAS Award nomination, 1 Golden Reel nomination

Suhail Kafity

Sound editor: *Apocalypto* (2006), *Harold & Kumar Go to White Castle* (2004), *Timeline* (2003), *Bad Boys II* (2003), *Sweet Home Alabama* (2002), *Remember the Titans* (2000), *Gone in Sixty Seconds* (2000), *Red Corner* (1997), *Crimson Tide* (1995)

Awards: 5 Golden Reel nominations

Andy Kennedy

Sound editor: *Harry Potter* films 2–6 (2002/2004/2005/2007/2009), *Sherlock Holmes* (2009), *The Golden Compass* (2007), *Batman Begins* (2005), *The Hours* (2002), *The World Is Not Enough* (1999)

Awards: 2 Emmy wins, 6 Golden Reel nominations (1 win)

Richard King

Sound designer and sound editor: *The Dark Knight* (2008), *The Assassination of Jesse James by the Coward Robert Ford* (2007), *The Prestige* (2006), *War of the Worlds* (2005), *Signs* (2002), *Unbreakable* (2000), *Magnolia* (1999)

Sound editor: *Gattaca* (1997), *Twister* (1996), *Waterworld* (1995), *L.A. Story* (1991)

Awards: 3 Oscar nominations (2 wins), 8 Golden Reel nominations (3 wins)

Mike Knobloch

President of Film Music for Universal Pictures

Albert Lord III

Sound editor: *Fortress 2* (1999), *Eve's Bayou* (1997), *In Search of Dr. Seuss* (1994), *Blue Ice* (1992)

Awards: 10 Emmy nominations (1 win), 1 Golden Reel nomination

Paul Massey

Re-recording mixer: *It's Complicated* (2009), *This is It* (2009), the *Night at the Museum* films (2006/2009), *Pirates of the Caribbean: Dead Man's Chest* (2006), *Walk the Line* (2005), *The Weather Man* (2005), *Kingdom of Heaven* (2005), *Master and Commander: The Far Side of the World* (2003), *Old School* (2003), *Hannibal* (2001), *Air Force One* (1997)

Awards: 6 Oscar nominations, 5 CAS Award nominations (2 wins)

F. Hudson Miller

Sound editor: *Déjà Vu* (2006), *Hitch* (2005), *The Chronicles of Narnia: The Lion, The Witch, and the Wardrobe* (2005), *National Treasure* (2004), *Man on Fire* (2004), *Spy Game* (2001), *Pearl Harbor* (2001), *Enemy of the State* (1998), *The Rock* (1996), *Patriot Games* (1992)

Awards: 1 Oscar nomination, 8 Golden Reel nominations

Glenn Morgan

Sound editor: *Star Trek* (2009), *Bobby* (2006), *The Day After Tomorrow* (2004), *Open Water* (2003) (also sound designer), *Monster's Ball* (2001) (also sound designer), *The Boondock Saints* (1999)

Awards: 1 Emmy nomination, 5 Golden Reel nominations

Walter Murch

Re-recording mixer and picture editor: *Jarhead* (2005), *Cold Mountain* (2003), *The Talented Mr. Ripley* (1999), *The English Patient* (1996), *Apocalypse Now* (1979) (also sound designer), *The Conversation* (1974) (also sound editor)

Awards: 9 Oscar nominations (3 wins), 1 CAS Award won plus CAS Career Achievement Award

Richard Portman

Re-recording mixer: *The Pelican Brief* (1993), *The Hand That Rocks the Cradle* (1992), *Presumed Innocent* (1990), *Fletch* (1985), *The River* (1984), *On Golden Pond* (1981), *Heaven's Gate* (1980), *The Deer Hunter* (1978), *Star Wars* (1977), *Young Frankenstein* (1974)
    Awards: 11 Oscar nominations (1 win), 2 Emmy nominations

Christopher Reeves

Sound editor: *Flash Forward* (TV) (2009), *Alias* (TV) (2001–2006), *The Practice* (TV) (1997–1998), *The X-Files* (TV) (1993)
    Awards: 8 Emmy nominations (2 wins), 8 Golden Reel nominations (1 win)

Gary Rydstrom

Sound designer and re-recording mixer: *Finding Nemo* (2003), *Hulk* (2003), *Minority Report* (2002), *Monsters, Inc.* (2001), *The Haunting* (1999), *Saving Private Ryan* (1998), *Toy Story* (1995), *Jurassic Park* (1993), *Terminator 2: Judgment Day* (1991)
    Re-recording mixer: *Punch-Drunk Love* (2002), *Star Wars* Episodes I and II (1999/2002), *Titanic* (1997), *Mission: Impossible* (1996)

Awards: 14 Oscar nominations (7 wins), 4 CAS Award nominations (2 wins) plus CAS Career Achievement Award, 12 Golden Reel Award nominations (5 wins) plus MPSE Career Achievement Award

Randy Thom

Sound designer and re-recording mixer: *A Christmas Carol* (2009), *Ratatouille* (2007), *The Polar Express* (2004), *Avalon* (2001), *Cast Away* (2000), *Mars Attacks!* (1996)
    Sound designer: *The Simpsons Movie* (2007), *War of the Worlds* (2005), *The Iron Giant* (1999), *Starship Troopers* (1997)
    Awards: 14 Oscar nominations (2 wins), 1 Emmy nomination, 4 CAS Award nominations (1 win) plus CAS Career Achievement Award, 15 Golden Reel nominations (5 wins)

Frank Warner

Sound editor: *St. Elmo's Fire* (1985), *Raging Bull* (1980), *Close Encounters of the Third Kind* (1977), *Taxi Driver* (1976), *Shampoo* (1975), *Harold and Maude* (1971)
    Awards: Special Achievement Award for sound effects editing from Academy of Motion Picture Arts and Sciences, MPSE Lifetime Achievement Award

Introduction

The epigraph is from Sergi, *Dolby Era*, 3–4.

1. Grainge, "Selling Spectacular Sound," 266–267.
2. Sergi, *Dolby Era*, 31.
3. Beck and Grajeda, "Introduction," 2.
4. Lastra, *Sound Technology*, 181.
5. Sergi, *Dolby Era*, 3.
6. Sobchack, "When the Ear Dreams," 1.
7. Sergi, *Dolby Era*, 31–32.
8. Marti Humphrey, personal interview by author, 5 August 2006.
9. Richard King, personal interview by author, 28 July 2006; Tomlinson Holman, personal interview by author, 15 July 2004.
10. Though a number of DVDs and Blu-Rays are now available with 6.1- and 7.1-channel content available, for consistency all the films discussed in this book were analyzed on a standard 5.1-channel setup.

1. Cinema's Hidden Multi-channel History and the Origins of Digital Surround

The epigraph is from Holman, interview, 2004.

1. Readers desiring a more complete history of multi-channel sound technologies should see Beck, "Quiet Revolution," or Holman, 5.1.
2. Beck, "Quiet Revolution," 60.
3. Ibid., 64.
4. Ibid., 65.
5. Holman, 5.1, 12; Kellogg, "Final Installment," 212–213.
6. Holman, 5.1, 12.
7. Beck, "Quiet Revolution," 67.
8. Kellogg, "Final Installment," 212–213.
9. Beck, "Quiet Revolution," 68–69.
10. Altman, "Sound Space," 48.
11. Ibid., 49. This setup obviously only works when dialogue and music do not appear at the same time, but until 1933 this was essentially the case due to the difficulty of mixing together multiple tracks of audio that had been recorded separately. See Altman, "Introduction," 6.
12. Kellogg, "Final Installment," 212.
13. Carr and Hayes, *Wide Screen Movies*, 239.
14. Bernard, "All About Surround Sound," 52; Holman, 5.1, 12.
15. Handzo, "Appendix," 419. See also Holman, interview, 2004, and Kellogg, "Final Installment," 213.

16. Kellogg, "Final Installment," 213. Emphasis added.

17. Holman, *5.1*, 12.

18. Handzo, "Appendix," 419.

19. Ibid., 418–419; Kellogg, "Final Installment," 213.

20. Beck, "Quiet Revolution," 69–70.

21. Holman, *5.1*, 13.

22. Kellogg, "Final Installment," 215–216.

23. Hull, "Surround Sound."

24. Handzo, "Appendix," 419.

25. Carr and Hayes, *Wide Screen Movies*, 178–180.

26. Belton, "Magnetic Sound," 156; Beck, "Quite Revolution," 72. Beck also notes that this was not a cheap obligation to meet; the sound system upgrades required to outfit a monophonic theater for CinemaScope cost about $25,000.

27. Belton, "Magnetic Sound," 156.

28. Handzo, "Appendix," 420; Hull, "Surround Sound," 1; Holman, LoBrutto interview, *Sound-on-Film*, 206.

29. Bernard, "All About Surround Sound," 51. This led to the name "effects channel"—see Hull, "Surround Sound," 1.

30. Belton, "Magnetic Sound," 163.

31. Ibid., 165.

32. Handzo, "Appendix," 420.

33. Belton, "Magnetic Sound," 157.

34. Ibid.

35. While CinemaScope's attempts to standardize stereophonic audio was a qualified failure, the format's visual technology was much more successful—the anamorphic 35mm image process it introduced is still used today.

36. Handzo, "Appendix," 421.

37. Thompson and Bordwell, *Film History*, 374–376; Carr and Hayes, *Wide Screen Movies*, 165.

38. Belton, "Magnetic Sound," 157.

39. Ibid., 158.

40. Holman, *5.1*, 16; Hull, "Surround Sound," 1.

41. Hull, "Surround Sound," 1.

42. Mitchell, "Surround Sound," 48.

43. Bernard, "All About Surround Sound," 56.

44. Handzo, "Appendix," 421.

45. Sergi, "Sonic Playground," 5–6.

46. Beaupre, "Lang, Robson," 174.

47. Beck, "Quiet Revolution," 177.

48. Ibid., 128–129.

49. Ibid., 151.

50. Hull, "Surround Sound," 2–3; Homan, *5.1*, 15.

51. Ranada, "Inside Dolby Digital," 81; Holman, *Sound for Film*, 7; Beck, "Quiet Revolution," 131.

52. Beck, "Quiet Revolution," 132. Emphasis in original.

53. Mitchell, "Surround Sound," 48; Ranada, "Inside Dolby Digital," 81.

54. Bernard, "All About Surround Sound," 56.

55. Beck, "The Sounds of 'Silence,'" 70–75.

56. Holman, *5.1*, 15.

57. Mitchell, "Surround Sound," 47.

58. Beck, "Quiet Revolution," 171.

59. Holman, *5.1*, 16. This adaptation helped spell the demise of Sensurround, as 70mm Dolby Stereo could now offer the low-frequency rumbles that were Sensurround's primary selling point.

60. Beck, "Quiet Revolution," 135.

61. Holman, *5.1*, 16.

62. Except where the difference is relevant, hereafter "Dolby Stereo" will refer both to Dolby's original system and to the SR update.

63. Holman, *5.1*, 15.

64. Ibid., 18.

65. David Bondelevitch, personal interview by author, 28 July 2006.

66. King, interview, 2006.

67. Murch, LoBrutto interview, *Sound-on-Film*, 91.

68. Beck, "Quiet Revolution," 133.

69. Kramer, "DTS," 1.

70. Holman, 5.1, 19. By "CD-quality sound" SMPTE meant that the new system should use digital sampling parameters of at least 44.1 kHz, 16 bits—the sampling rate and bit depth used by CDs.

71. Hull, "Surround Sound," 4; Holman, 5.1, 16.

72. Holman, 5.1, 16; Hull, "Surround Sound," 4.

73. This sort of psychoacoustic research is typically summarized in "equal-loudness curves" (or "Fletcher-Munson curves," after the researchers who first published these results in the 1930s), which show how much physical energy different frequency sounds must carry to subjectively *sound* equally loud. Examples of equal-loudness curves can be found in Holman, 5.1, 65.

74. Holman, *Film and Television*, 34.

75. Holman, 5.1, 208.

76. The five full-range channels do carry their own low-frequency sounds. The LFE channel, though, provides a way to add extra volume and/or rumble in certain places where the full-range channels are inadequate for the desired effect. See chapter 2.

77. "Movies Featuring CDS."

78. Hodges, "Digital Cinema Arrives," 132.

79. Midge Costin, personal interview by author, 21 July 2004; F. Hudson Miller, personal interview by author, 20 July 2004; Thom Ehle, personal interview by author, 21 July 2004.

80. Ehle, interview, 2004.

81. "Movies Featuring CDS."

82. "Movies Featuring CDS." *Universal Soldier*, released on 10 July 1992, was the final CDS release; *Batman Returns* debuted Dolby's system on 19 June 1992.

83. Wright, "One Hand Clapping," 36.

84. Clark, "New Dolby Sound," C1.

85. Hodges, "Seizing the Day," 112.

86. Nunziata, "*Batman*," 11.

87. Homer, "*Batman* to Launch," Technology 11.

88. Nunziata, "*Batman*," 10.

89. Sheehan, "Montreal Theatres," D3; Van Bergen, "*Jurassic* on CD-ROM," 34.

90. Pendleton, "Soundtrack Firm," D3; Van Bergen, "*Jurassic* on CD-ROM," 34.

91. For example, see *Chicago Tribune*, 11 June 1993, Sect. 7G.

92. The film premiered on 18 June 1993.

93. Pasquariello, "Indiana Jones," 59; Hull, "Surround Sound," 2; "Questions and Answers about SDDS."

94. Kenny, "Digital Audio Today," 54.

95. Ehle, interview, 2004.

96. Nunziata, "Sony Enters," 55; Masters, ""Tamed Terminator," D1; Harmon, "Sound Wars," D1; Schaefer, "New Digital Sound Systems," S05.

97. Kramer, "DTS," 1.

98. Ehle, interview, 2004.

99. "NATO Statistics." Between the end of 1992 and the end of 1999, the number of non-drive-in screens in the United States increased from 24,344 to 36,448.

100. Whittington, *Sound Design*, 254.

101. "NATO Statistics."

102. Gary Johns, personal interview by author, 15 July 2004; Ehle, interview, 2004.

103. Klinger, *Beyond the Multiplex*, 4.

104. Hull, "Surround Sound," 4; Dolby Laboratories, "Dolby Surround."

105. Hull, "Surround Sound," 3–4; Mitchell, "Surround Sound," 48.

106. Dolby Stereo and Dolby Pro Logic use similar decoding schemes.

To differentiate its product lines, Dolby only uses "Dolby Pro Logic" and "Dolby Surround" for home systems, while reserving "Dolby Stereo" and "Dolby SR" for theatrical use.

107. Dolby, "Dolby Surround."

108. Kramer, "DTS," 1; Herranen and Doolen, "Laserdisc FAQ."

109. Hull, "Surround Sound," 5.

110. Johns, interview, 2004. Inside SDDS, the idea of a home version was periodically resurrected but never adopted.

111. Groves, "Pundits Ponder," 14. DVD-Video, commonly known simply as "DVD" was introduced in 1996 in Japan but did not appear in the United States until a year later.

112. Roberts, "Disc," 32; Groves, "Pundits Ponder," 14. For an explanation of why laserdisc failed while DVD succeeded, see Pohlmann, "Separated at Birth," 40.

113. Sherber, "DVD Leads," 1.

114. Hull, "Surround Sound," 4.

115. Consumer Electronics Association, "Digital America 2006."

116. Consumer Electronics Association, "Digital America 2008 Preview," 49. In early 2009, my parents (who are not early adopters) purchased a 5.1 sound system, indicating to me that home digital surround was indeed a mainstream technology.

117. Bondelevitch, interview, 2006.

118. Glenn Morgan, personal interview by author, 31 July 2006.

119. Suhail Kafity, personal interview by author, 20 July 2004.

120. See Holman, 5.1, 50: "50% of the public becomes annoyed" when image and sound are displaced more than 15 degrees.

121. Holman, interview, 2004. Thanks also to Mike Thomson of Malco Theatres for a demonstration of theater configuration techniques.

122. Klinger, "Beyond the Multiplex," 83.

123. See, for instance, the monthly DVD column in *American Cinematographer* or the reviews at http://www.dvdtalk.com, which gives star ratings to DVDs in areas such as "picture," "sound," and "extras," and tends to use the second category to penalize movies that do not have many effects placed in the rear channels.

124. Bondelevitch, interview, 2006.

125. "SDDS Movies."

126. Johns, interview, 2004. As of July 2004.

127. Dolby Laboratories, "Dolby TrueHD."

128. Holman, interview, 2004.

129. Ibid.

130. Hull, "Surround Sound," 4.

131. Buettner, "DTS-ES Discrete 6.1."

132. Ehle, interview, 2004.

133. Palenchar, "Onkyo Adds"; Palenchar, "Broad Integra Launch."

134. Christopher Reeves, personal interview by author, 31 July 2006.

135. Tomlinson Holman, personal interview by author, 9 August 2006.

136. Ibid.

137. Mike Thomson, personal interview by author, 21 August 2004.

2. The Sound of 5.1

The epigraph is from Warren, LoBrutto interview, *Sound-on-Film*, 132.

1. Holman, *Film and Television*, 119–120. A 35mm three-track magnetic soundtrack encoded with Dolby SR has a dynamic range of 98 dB. Dynamic range is frequency dependent; the numbers given here are averages across the mid-frequencies.

2. Warren, LoBrutto interview, *Sound-on-Film*, 132.

3. Murch, "Intro," 48.

4. Holman, *Film and Television*, 20.

5. Anonymous, personal interview by author. In some cases where they are criticizing the film industry in general and/or individual films, some interviewees asked not to have their names associated with those quotations lest it damage their professional careers.

6. Ehle, interview, 2004.

7. Allen, "Are Movies Too Loud?" 4.

8. Ehle, interview, 2004.

9. Anonymous sound editor, personal interview by author.

10. Morgan, interview, 2006.

11. Clarke, "The Future."

12. Bondelevitch, interview, 2006.

13. Morgan, interview, 2006.

14. Anonymous sound editor, personal interview by author.

15. Murch, LoBrutto interview, *Sound-on-Film*, 99.

16. Morgan, interview, 2006.

17. Thom, "Re: The Future."

18. Daddario, "Re: The Future."

19. Daddario, "Re: The Future."

20. Allen, "Are Movies Too Loud?" 4.

21. Thom, "Re: The Future."

22. Anonymous, personal interview by author.

23. Anonymous sound designer, personal interview by author.

24. Whittington, *Sound Design*, 201. *T2* came out in 1991, employing the now-defunct Cinema Digital Sound (CDS) format for its 5.1 digital soundtrack.

25. Figgis, "Silence," 2.

26. See Théberge, "Almost Silent," 51–67.

27. Chion, *Audio-Vision*, 57.

28. Théberge, "Almost Silent," 53.

29. Holman, LoBrutto interview, *Sound-on-Film*, 205.

30. Bissinger, "Re: The Future."

31. Erik Aadahl, personal interview by author, 20 July 2004.

32. Watters, Sonnenschein interview, *Sound Design*, 51.

33. Rydstrom, LoBrutto interview, *Sound-on-Film*, 233.

34. Bissinger, "Re: The Future."

35. King, interview, 2006.

36. Ibid.

37. Whittington, *Sound Design*, 201.

38. Murch, "Touch of Silence," 100–101.

39. Ibid., 100.

40. Arnott, "Re: The Future."

41. Ibid.

42. Bissinger, "Re: The Future."

43. King, interview, 2006.

44. Steve Flick, personal interview by author, 11 August 2006.

45. Costin, interview, 2004.

46. Flick, interview, 2006.

47. Whittington, *Sound Design*, 122.

48. Holman, interview, 2006.

49. Mike Knobloch, personal interview by author, 20 July 2004.

50. Dolby Laboratories, "Dolby—Cinema Sound FAQ."

51. Johns, interview, 2004.

52. Altman, "Introduction," 6.

53. Whittington, "Sonic Spectacle."

54. Murch, "Intro," 7. Emphasis in original.

55. Ibid.

56. Rydstrom, "Big Movie Sound Effects."

57. Sonnenschein, *Sound Design*, 31 and 80.

58. Murch, "Intro," 18.

59. Functions such as short-term memory can only consider five to nine separate "chunks" of information at one time. Murch's rules about how many "chunks" of sound can be productively played at once are lower, suggesting that sounds may not be processed in the same way as other information, or that one "layer" of sound correlates with more than one "chunk" of infor-

mation. See Miller, "Magical Number Seven," 81–97.

60. King, interview, 2006.
61. Aadahl, interview, 2004.
62. Altman, "The Sound of Sound," 71.
63. Théberge, 61–62.
64. Miller, interview, 2004.
65. Rydstrom, LoBrutto interview, *Sound-on-Film*, 238.
66. Flick, interview, 2006.
67. Paul Massey, personal interview by author, 8 August 2006.
68. Bondelevitch, interview, 2006.
69. Reeves, interview, 2006.
70. Whittington, *Sound Design*, 202.
71. Miller, interview, 2004.
72. Rydstrom, Sergi interview, *Dolby Era*, 170.
73. In many non-professional systems, such as those used in most home theaters, the low-frequency segments of this audio are shuttled to the subwoofer since inexpensive and/or small speakers generally cannot reproduce sounds all the way down to 20 Hz.
74. Beck, "Sounds of 'Silence,'" 71.
75. Costin, interview, 2004.
76. Several of the sound editors I interviewed cited *Crimson Tide* as one of their favorite all-around film soundtracks.
77. Reeves, interview, 2006.
78. Miller, interview, 2004.

3. The Look of 5.1

The epigraph is from Rydstrom, LoBrutto interview, *Sound-on-Film*, 245.

1. Salt, *Film Style & Technology*, 174.
2. Ibid., 214. Similar results are seen from films in the late 1910s and early 1920s. Films of the early 1910s had a slightly higher average and much more variation; this is not unexpected as the stylistic traits of the feature film

were still developing during this time. See also Ibid., 146–147.

3. Ibid., 239, 249, 266, 282, 296.
4. Chion, *Audio-Vision*, 151.
5. Ibid., 150.
6. Doane, "Voice in Cinema," 165.
7. Whittington, *Sound Design*, 126.
8. Claude Bailblé, quoted and translated in Doane, "Voice in Cinema," 165.
9. Chion, *Audio-Vision*, 151.
10. Žižek, *Looking Awry*, 40.
11. Whittington, *Sound Design*, 126.
12. Chion, *Audio-Vision*, 85.
13. Chion, "Quiet Revolution," 73.
14. Chion, *Audio-Vision*, 150.
15. Beck, "Sounds of 'Silence,'" 77. Emphasis added.
16. Žižek, *Looking Awry*, 40. The "sound aquarium" is a reference to Chion's claim that the multiple layers of sound in contemporary cinema may overwhelm the image. See Chion, "Quiet Revolution," 72.
17. Chion, *Audio-Vision*, 151.
18. The relationship between *Saving Private Ryan*'s unconventional approach to sound mixing and the film's thematic/narrative concerns is addressed in detail in Kerins, "The (Surround) Sounds."
19. Altman, "Sound Space," 62.
20. Doane, "Ideology," 57–58.
21. Chion, *Audio-Vision*, 150.
22. Morgan, interview, 2006.
23. Kafity, interview, 2004.
24. Holman, interview, 2006.
25. Midge Costin, personal interview by author, 1 July 2006.
26. Humphrey, interview, 2006. In the early part of the 1950s stereo boom, some films panned dialog across the wide screens of the day to correspond with actor locations onscreen, and Fox studio head Darryl Zanuck even encouraged his filmmakers to put actors on opposite sides of the screen in wide

shots to highlight these stereo effects. This effect was ultimately deemed distracting, and dialogue returned to the center of the screen. See Kellogg, "Final Installment," 212; Belton, *Widescreen Cinema*, 205–206.

27. Bondelevitch, interview, 2006.

28. Chion, *Audio-Vision*, 151.

29. Costin, interview, 2006.

30. Bondelevitch, interview, 2006.

31. Rydstrom, LoBrutto interview, *Sound-on-Film*, 234. Emphasis added.

32. Beck, "Sounds of 'Silence,'" 79.

33. Beck, "Sounds of 'Silence,'" 77. Emphasis added.

34. Neo's bullets, of course, sound different than the guards'.

35. Like *Saving Private Ryan* a year earlier, *The Matrix* finished the night second in Oscars won, behind only the Best Picture winner.

36. Humphrey, interview, 2006.

37. Chion, *Audio-Vision*, 151.

38. Steve Flick, telephone interview by author, 13 May 2004.

39. Burtt, Sonnenschein interview, *Sound Design*, 90.

40. Chion, *Audio-Vision*, 151.

41. Rydstrom, Sergi interview, *Dolby Era*, 171.

42. Chion, *Audio-Vision*, 151.

43. Not all films with digital soundtracks employ a digital surround–driven style. Though *The Thin Red Line* was released in 1998 with a DSS soundtrack, its soundtrack and visuals adhere to Dolby Stereo–based principles.

44. The *Terminator* franchise, with four films spanning twenty-five years, itself offers an interesting demonstration of the impact of DSS on cinematic aesthetics. The first film was released in mono (but well after the introduction of Dolby Stereo), the second straddled the line between the Dolby Stereo and DSS eras (it employed a digital 5.1 soundtrack in 1991, before 5.1 systems had been broadly introduced), and the third and fourth films were released well into the DSS era. And as one would expect, the extent to which the films employ the various DSS-linked aesthetic traits discussed in this and the previous chapter notably increases over the course of the four-film series.

45. Costin, interview, 2006; Bondelevitch, interview, 2006.

46. Holman, interview, 2006; Murch, *Blink*, 118–124.

47. Bondelevitch, interview, 2006.

48. Holman, interview, 2006.

49. Bondelevitch, interview, 2006.

4. Decoding the Digital Surround Style

The epigraph is from Thom, "Acceptance Speech."

1. Chion, "Silence in the Loudspeakers."

2. Vernallis, "New Cut-Up Cinema."

3. Ibid.

4. Lipscomb, "Perception of Audio-Visual Composites," 37–67.

5. Vernallis, "New Cut-Up Cinema."

6. Ibid. Emphasis in original.

7. Ibid.

8. Ibid.

9. Ibid.

10. Though Vernallis does mention some non-musical sounds in her analysis, she considers them only for their musical or rhythmic properties.

11. Vernallis, "New Cut-Up Cinema."

12. Robert Towne famously claimed that he had to write the story to *Mission: Impossible II* (2000) around a list of action scenes director John Woo wished to shoot. See "*Mission: Impossible II* (2000)—Trivia." Roger Ebert's

review of *Bad Boys II* (2003) imagines that one chase scene with no obvious relation to the storyline was similarly put in solely because someone thought it would be a "cool" scene. See Ebert, "*Bad Boys II.*"

13. Kafity, interview, 2004.

14. Bordwell, "Intensified Continuity," 16.

15. Ibid., 22.

16. Ibid., 16.

17. Ibid. Emphasis in original.

18. Ibid., 22.

19. Ibid., 23.

20. Ibid., 22–24.

21. Ibid., 20. "Indeed, the scene's most distant framing may well come at the very end, as a caesura."

22. Ibid., 17.

23. Ibid., 24.

24. Ibid. Possibly Bordwell means that the viewer is riveted to the *events* (including sound and image) happening "onscreen," rather than to the *screen* itself. Nevertheless, his language is revealing.

25. Vernallis, "New Cut-Up Cinema."

26. This should not be confused with the fleeting sound/image interactions of "The New Cut-Up Cinema," which are intermittent rather than continuous and dependent on audience perceptions of accent points rather than on spatial matches between image and sound.

27. Bordwell, "Intensified Continuity," 25.

28. Ibid.

29. Ibid.

30. Sobchack, "When the Ear Dreams," 3.

31. Ibid., 2.

32. Ibid., 8–9.

33. Ibid., 8.

34. Chion, *Audio-Vision*, 100. Chion does not specify whether he heard

these trailers in standard 35mm Dolby Stereo or in 70mm magnetic Dolby Stereo; as noted in chapter 1, the latter system employed a configuration almost identical to that of modern 5.1 digital surround systems. The fact that he is specifically discussing the sound of large, THX-certified theaters makes it possible, and even likely, that the trailers were actually played (perhaps without Chion knowing it) in 5.1-channel discrete surround rather than in the 4-channel-matrixed surround of standard Dolby Stereo.

35. Holman, LoBrutto interview, *Sound-on-Film*, 204. Emphasis added.

36. Holman, interview, 2006.

37. Ibid.

38. Chion, *Audio-Vision*, 100.

39. Holman, interview, 2006. For those not familiar with the terminology, in sound design parlance "wet" and "dry" refer to how much of a sonic element is the clean, "dry," original sound and how much is affected or altered ("wet"). In terms of theater design, a "dry" theater is one with a short reverberation time so you hear little echo, while a "wet" one is one where the sound bounces around the theater at a perceptible level longer.

40. Sobchack, "When the Ear Dreams," 6.

41. See ibid., 7, "with the exception of 'Stomp'"; 8, "Except again for 'Stomp'"; 11, "In all but 'Stomp'"; 13, "With the exception of 'Stomp.'"

42. Ibid., 13.

43. Farinella, "Battle of the Trailers."

44. Sobchack, "When the Ear Dreams," 3.

45. At the end of 2003, there were 35,361 indoor screens in the United States, at least 10,000 of which had been built since the introduction of digital surround. See "NATO Statistics."

46. For a discussion of Dolby's "branding" efforts to make its name a synonym for "quality sound," see Grainge, "Selling Spectacular Sound," 251–268.

47. "Dolby—Movie Sound FAQ."

48. Humphrey, interview, 2006.

49. Sobchack, "When the Ear Dreams," 7–8.

50. Ibid., 8.

51. Ibid., 7.

52. Ibid., 11.

53. Murch, "Intro," 4. See also Branigan, "Sound and Epistemology," 313.

54. See, among others, Doane, "Voice in Cinema," 169–171; Murch, "Intro," 4; Silverman, *Acoustic Mirror*. Additionally, chapter 9 of this book centers on apparatus theory, which is deeply concerned with the relationship between cinema and the "primitive stage" of being in the womb.

55. Branigan, "Sound and Epistemology," 313.

56. Schreger, "Altman, Dolby," 351.

57. Johns, interview, 2004.

58. Massey, interview, 2006.

59. Malsky, "Sounds of the City," 118.

60. Belton, "Magnetic Sound," 158; see also Belton, *Widescreen Cinema*, 202–204. Bruno Toussaint has proposed a "hybrid" model for surround sound use, combining diegetic immersion and a cinema of sonic attractions. In this model, surround sound simultaneously causes "sound immersion . . . the disappearance of the classical separation between the room and the screen" *and* "sideration . . . a medical state, defined as staggering, dumbfounded and amazed. Something you might call the 'Wow effect.'" Toussaint's ideas are provocative, but the "Wow effect"— which implies an awareness of the workings of the movie itself—seems to contradict the principle of immersion in the diegetic world, making it dif-

ficult to imagine how the two function as a single style. See Bruno Toussaint, "Sound Design."

61. Sergi, "Sonic Playground."

62. Sergi, *Dolby Era*, 20.

63. Parts of Sergi's argument here are drawn from his work on Dolby Stereo and others from his thoughts on contemporary multi-channel sound in general. But as Sergi himself asserts that digital surround sound and Dolby Stereo adhere to exactly the same aesthetic principles, this seems a legitimate pairing. See *Dolby Era*, 30–31.

64. Wright, "Making Films Sound Better," 64. Emphasis added.

65. Whittington, *Sound Design*, 122. Whittington finds that digital sound has the same effect in *home* theaters, writing that "home theater systems have taken up the idea of immersive sound (surround sound) and embedded audio technology into the design of the home. . . . The audio elements create a shroud of sound that masks the 'real' and immerses audiences in a film's extended diegesis."

66. Maltby, *Hollywood Cinema*, 259.

67. Miller, interview, 2004.

68. "Dolby—Cinema Sound FAQ."

69. Chion, "Quiet Revolution," 72–73.

70. Holman, 5.1, 221.

71. Holman, interview, 2004. The *ideal* 5-channel configuration for creating envelopment is somewhat different than that used by 5.1 systems, notably for its inclusion of a center back speaker rather than a center front. 6.1-channel systems add this missing piece and should therefore be more enveloping than standard 5.1 arrangements.

72. Ibid.

73. This also confirms that the surround channels are more important to the digital surround style than to the "one wall" aesthetic of Dolby Stereo:

in the latter the filmgoer watches the action at a distance, making what is behind him of relatively less importance, while in the former he is placed in the midst of the action, with important things occurring on all sides.

74. It is possible through camera moves and blocking to shift the 180-degree line within a scene, allowing filmmakers to "cross the (original) line" without violating continuity rules. In general, though, this admittedly simplified version of the 180-degree rule accurately reflects the limitation of continuity shooting and editing.

75. Bordwell, "Intensified Continuity," 25.

76. Costin, interview, 2006.

77. King, interview, 2006.

78. Thom, "Acoustics of the Soul," 1–2.

79. Aadahl, interview, 2004.

80. Kafity, interview, 2004. Emphasis added.

81. Costin, interview, 2006. Emphasis added.

82. Morgan, interview, 2006.

83. This statement was presented to them in written form, italics included, to ensure both that I explained it in the same way with each interview and that my interviewees had the opportunity to study it and think about it rather than just responding with the first thing that came to mind.

84. Thom, "Acoustics," 1.

85. Holman, interview, 2006.

86. King, interview, 2006.

87. Erik Aadahl, personal interview by author, 9 August 2006.

88. Bondelevitch, interview, 2006.

89. Flick, interview, 2006.

5. Using the Digital Surround Style

The first epigraph is from Humphrey, interview, 2006. The second epigraph is from King, interview, 2006.

1. Sergi, *Dolby Era,* 147.

2. Chion, "Quiet Revolution," 73.

3. Ehle, interview, 2004.

4. Massey, interview, 2006.

5. Murch, "Intro," 20–21.

6. Holman, interview, 2006.

7. Miller, interview, 2004.

8. Kafity, interview, 2004.

9. Costin, interview, 2006.

10. Murch, "Intro," 23.

11. Morgan, interview, 2006.

12. Anonymous sound designer, personal interview by author. As in chapter 2, some of the sound professionals interviewed asked that certain comments not be associated with their names to avoid offending any filmmakers with whom they may work in the future.

13. "Alan Parker." Emphasis added.

14. Ebert, *"Last Action Hero."*

15. Savlov, *"Last Action Hero."*

16. Howe, *"Last Action Hero."*

17. The Internet Movie Database (IMDB) puts the film's worldwide grosses at $137 million, a weak financial performance for a film budgeted at about $85 million.

18. Anonymous sound editor, personal interview by author.

19. King, interview, 2006.

20. Ehle, interview, 2004.

21. Bondelevitch, interview, 2006.

22. Burtt, LoBrutto interview, *Sound-on-Film,* 148.

23. Aadahl, interview, 2006.

24. Warner, LoBrutto interview, *Sound-on-Film,* 38.

25. Kafity, interview, 2004.

26. Ehle, interview, 2004.

27. Anonymous sound editor, personal interview by author.

28. Anonymous sound designer, personal interview by author.

29. Costin, interview, 2006; Flick, interview, 2006.

30. King, interview, 2006.

31. Flick, interview, 2006; Costin, interview, 2004.

32. Bondelevitch, interview, 2006.

33. Aadahl, interview, 2006.

34. Ibid.

35. Ehle, interview, 2004.

36. Kennedy, *Film Sound Daily* interview.

37. Anonymous sound editor, personal interview by author.

38. Anonymous re-recording mixer, personal interview by author.

39. Anonymous sound designer, personal interview by author.

40. Anonymous sound editor, personal interview by author.

41. Massey, interview, 2006.

42. Anonymous, personal interview by author.

43. Portman, LoBrutto interview, *Sound-on-Film*, 49.

44. Anonymous mixer, personal interview by author.

45. King, interview, 2006.

46. Anonymous sound designer, personal interview by author.

47. Just as with digital surround sound, 3-D has historically affected the aesthetics of the films in which it has been used. In particular, 3-D movies tend to have lots of objects coming directly "out into the audience," a device rarely seen in non-3-D films. This may not, however, be the case with future 3-D releases; discussing 3-D's current resurgence, Dreamworks Animation head Jeffrey Katzenberg points out that most 3-D films today avoid these "in your face" effects due to their association with the "cheesy" 3-D of years past. Like surround sound, 3-D seems to have the potential to function either as "spectacle" or as "immersion," depending on the specific way it is employed.

48. Holman, interview, 2004. This is quite possibly an apocryphal tale; its striking similarity to the legend of audiences running screaming from the first Lumière screening to avoid being hit by a train suggests roots in that story rather than in fact. But whether it is true or not is beside the point: its mere existence demonstrates that people in the film industry *believe* in the exit door effect.

49. Rydstrom, Sergi interview, *Dolby Era*, 172. What it means to "design the soundtrack properly" to protect against the exit door effect is considered later in this chapter.

50. Whittington, *Sound Design*, 115. Emphasis added.

51. Holman, interview, 2004.

52. Anonymous, personal interview by author.

53. Anonymous sound designer, personal interview by author.

54. King, interview, 2006. He also notes that this was early in the DSS era, and that this director has since come to appreciate the possibilities surround sound offers.

55. Flick, interview, 2006.

56. Anonymous sound designer, personal interview by author.

57. Anonymous, personal interview by author.

58. Anonymous, personal interview by author.

59. Anderson, LoBrutto interview, *Sound-on-Film*, 160.

60. Aadahl, interview, 2006.

61. Murch, "Intro," 51.

62. Aadahl, interview, 2006; Miller, interview, 2004, offers a similar perspective.

63. Thom, "Re: The Future."

64. "Alan Parker," 4.

65. Murch, "Intro," 51.

66. Julstrom, "High-Performance," 60.

67. Altman, "Sound of Sound," 70. Emphasis added.

68. King, interview, 2006.

69. Ibid.

70. Reeves, interview, 2006.

71. King, interview, 2006.

72. Holman, interview, 2004.

73. Costin, interview, 2004. This is not to say that Steven Spielberg and his ilk offer no creative input on the soundtrack, but rather that they are willing to trust in their crews to make some choices about how to implement their visions.

74. Ibid.

75. See, for instance, ibid.

76. Bondelevitch, interview, 2006.

77. Kafity, interview, 2004. With *Jurassic Park* set as the first DTS release, he may also have wanted to give the crew additional time to figure out the quirks of the new format.

78. Aadahl, interview, 2006.

79. Ibid.

80. Ehle, interview, 2004.

81. Holman, interview, 2004.

82. Humphrey, interview, 2006.

83. Portman, LoBrutto interview, *Sound-on-Film*, 47.

84. Flick, interview, 2004.

85. Knobloch, interview, 2004.

86. Bondelevitch, interview, 2006.

87. King, interview, 2006. Emphasis added.

88. Ibid.

89. Miller, interview, 2004.

90. Reeves, interview, 2006.

91. Kafity, interview, 2004.

92. Ibid.

93. King, interview, 2006.

94. Costin, interview, 2006.

95. Flick, interview, 2006. *Predator,* a 1987 release, predates digital surround systems but was mixed in the equivalent of 5.1 for its 70mm six-track magnetic release. Despite being released in the pre-DSS era, the film employs many of the stylistic traits—visual and aural—of the digital surround style, including heavy use of close-ups, shooting from within the dramatic space, aggressive movement of sounds around the soundscape, etc.

96. Flick, interview, 2006; Massey, interview, 2006. Ambient recordings do not include the ".1" LFE channel.

97. Reeves, interview, 2006. "Walla" is a term for usually indistinguishable background voices, such as the sound of diners in a crowded restaurant. Walla is made up of voices but is considered part of the ambient sound of a space rather than "dialogue" since it is not meant to be understood but merely to help create environment around the main action.

98. For a detailed dissection of the ambient sound in *Finding Nemo's* opening scene, see Kerins, "Narration," 44–46.

99. This was a conclusion that none of my interviewees volunteered on their own, but several of them agreed with this once I stated it as a possibility. See, for example, Bondelevitch, interview, 2006.

100. Flick, interview, 2006.

101. Rydstrom, Sergi interview, *Dolby Era*, 172.

102. Flick, interview, 2006.

103. Ibid.

104. Murch, "Intro," 43.

105. Aadahl, interview, 2004.

106. Morgan, interview, 2006.

107. Massey, interview, 2006.

108. Costin, interview, 2006.

109. David Tolchinsky was the first person to mention this example; raising this issue in discussion with others later, I found many people reported the same experience.

110. Recalling Steve Flick's comments about ambient sounds in the surrounds needing to be "readily identifiable," car drive-bys and cheering are easily recognizable, particularly in a movie about a race car.

111. Wright, "Making Films Sound Better," 53.

112. Altman, "Sound Space," 60.

113. David Tolchinsky, personal conversation, February 2003.

114. Costin, interview, 2006.

115. Portions of this example first published as Kerins, "Narration," 41–54. Copyright ©2006 by the University of Texas Press. All rights reserved.

116. Aadahl, interview, 2004. Aadahl credits the film's effects re-recording mixer, Doug Hemphill, for this unexpected use of the surround environment.

117. Whittington, *Sound Design*, 126.

118. Aadahl, interview, 2004. Given the earlier discussion of condensed schedules and lack of communication, it should be noted that this effective but initially unplanned design only materialized because the schedule allotted the post-audio crew enough time to try out different approaches.

119. Rydstrom, Sonnenschein interview, *Sound Design*, 178. David Tolchinsky notes that this specific instance is also particularly effective because it "inverts" the world: the semi-hearing loss audio sounds much like the underwater audio from earlier in this scene, symbolizing that for Miller the world has been flipped upside down.

120. Rydstrom, Sergi interview, *Dolby Era*, 178.

121. *Spider-Man 2* (2004) includes a similar scene where Norman's son Harry is confronted by the voice of his father. In this latter case, though, Norman's voice is accompanied by his image. As before, the audience sees and hears exactly what a character (Harry Osborn in this case) is seeing and hearing; since they know that his father is dead, though, it is immediately clear that Harry Osborn has gone insane.

122. Flick, interview, 2006.

123. Costin, interview, 2006.

124. Ibid.

125. Box office, budget, and Academy Award data is drawn from the Internet Movie Database (http://us.imdb.com). Annual box office rankings are drawn from Box Office Mojo (http://www.box-officemojo.com/yearly/).

126. These numbers change only slightly if outliers (such as *The Dark Knight*, which earned over $100 million more than any other nominated film, and *Letters from Iwo Jima*, which earned less than half of the next lowest grossing nominee) are excluded.

127. Replacing 35mm film with digital projection is another major shift, but one that on its own seems unlikely to have a major effect on aesthetics.

128. Quittner, "Next Dimension," 54.

129. Ibid., 58.

130. Ebert, "*Monsters vs. Aliens.*"

131. Sperling, "3-D Movie Preview," 34. Emphasis added.

132. Katzenberg, "*Monsters vs. Aliens.*"

133. Quittner, "Next Dimension," 62.

134. Katzenberg, "*Monsters vs. Aliens.*"

135. Other diegetic immersion–based exhibition technologies are in the works as well, though 3-D is the only one that has seen significant adoption. For instance, one company is marketing "enhanced movie theater seat technology" (a cross between Sensurround and an amusement park ride), claiming it "offers theatergoers an unparalleled realistic experience where they are immersed in the film, experiencing every jolt, wave, breeze and explosion." See Finke, "Is That a Quake."

136. Murch, LoBrutto interview, *Sound-on-Film*, 99. Emphasis in original.

137. Holman, LoBrutto interview, *Sound-on-Film*, 209.

138. Holman, interview, 2004.
139. Ibid. Emphasis in original.
140. "Hear What the Buzz."
141. Holman, interview, 2006.

6. Studying Multi-channel Soundtracks

The epigraph is from Sergi, *Dolby Era*, 136.

1. Beck, "Sounds of 'Silence,'" 79.
2. Ibid., 78. Emphasis added.
3. Ibid., 82. Emphasis added.
4. Whittington, *Sound Design*, 119.
5. Ibid., 120.
6. Of course, scholars who repeatedly "practice" close listening through soundtrack analyses will learn to pick up on more subtle sonic elements.
7. Sergi, *Dolby Era*, 77.
8. Newman, "Paderewski," 154.
9. Bordwell and Thompson, *Film Art*, 316–317.
10. Altman, "Film Fallacies," 39–40.
11. Rydstrom, Sergi interview, *Dolby Era*, 170; Rydstrom, LoBrutto interview, *Sound-on-Film*, 245.
12. Warner, LoBrutto interview, *Sound-on-Film*, 33.
13. Kerins and Lipscomb, "Presentation Mode."
14. Albert Lord, personal interview by author, 8 July 2006. This approach obviously works only for sections where all principal dialogue is in the center channel.
15. A chart of this breakdown can be found in Bellour, *Analysis of Film*, 32–49.
16. See Ibid., 107–174.
17. Honan, "Spielberg."

7. Studying Image/Sound Interactions

The epigraph is from Murch, "Intro," 46. Emphasis added.

1. Aadahl, interview, 2004.

2. Thanks to Christopher Reeves for suggesting this example.
3. See, for instance, Marshall and Cohen, "Effects," 95–112.
4. Boltz, "Musical Soundtracks," 427–454.
5. See Lipscomb and Kendall, "Perceptual Judgment," 60–98; also Lipscomb, "Perception of Audio-Visual Composites," 37–67.
6. Cook, *Analysing Musical Multimedia*, 98.
7. Ibid., 98.
8. Ibid., 103. Emphasis added.
9. The line between complementation and contest is inherently subjective, hence the use of "could."
10. See Cook, *Analysing Musical Multimedia*, 105–106.
11. Eisenstein, Pudovkin, and Alexandrov, "A Statement," 84.
12. Chion, *Audio-Vision*, 221.
13. Ibid., 187.
14. Ibid., 187–188.
15. Ibid., 192.
16. Ibid., 192.
17. Ibid., 21.
18. Cook, *Analysing Musical Multimedia*, 21.
19. See ibid., 151–152.
20. Ibid., 6.
21. Ibid.
22. Ibid.
23. Chion, *Audio-Vision*, 190–191.
24. Unusual visual techniques such as split-screen and superimpositions can make the image "multiple," but the "norm" in mainstream filmmaking is one that one shot is on the screen at a time.
25. Chion, *Audio-Vision*, 187.
26. Note that this mixing strategy requires the discrete configuration of DSS and could not work in Dolby Stereo.

NOTES TO PAGES 259–281 · 349

8. Body and Voice

The epigraph is from Chion, *Voice*, 166.

1. Chion, *Voice*, 5. Emphasis in original.
2. Humphrey, interview, 2006.
3. Ehle, interview, 2004.
4. Chion, "Wasted Words," 104. Emphasis added.
5. Thompson and Bordwell, *Film History*, 92.
6. Chion, *Audio-Vision*, 101.
7. Doane, "Voice in Cinema," 163.
8. Doane, "Ideology," 56.
9. Quoted in Chion, *Voice*, 131.
10. Johnson, "Sound and Image," 31. Emphasis added.
11. Chion, *Voice*, 127. Emphasis added.
12. Holman, LoBrutto interview, *Sound-on-Film*, 201. Emphasis added.
13. See Metz, "Aural Objects," 157–158.
14. In general, the terms "offscreen" and "onscreen" are of little use in describing non-diegetic sounds, though parodic films such as *Spaceballs* and *Blazing Saddles* play with this distinction by revealing sounds initially interpreted as non-diegetic to have been "offscreen."
15. Belton, "Magnetic Sound," 163.
16. Chion, *Audio-Vision*, 131.
17. Chion, *Audio-Vision*, 84.
18. Chion, *Voice*, 127.
19. This example comes from Whittington, *Sound Design*, 119.
20. Chion, *Voice*, 141.
21. Jordan, "Visible Acousmêtre," 65.
22. Chion, *Voice*, 141.
23. Chion, *Voice*, 150.
24. Edward Norton's character is listed in the credits only as "Narrator," even though his actual name in the film is "Tyler." For clarity in distin-guishing between the Norton and Brad Pitt versions of "Tyler," I have adopted the language of the film's marketing campaign, which calls Norton's character "Jack."
25. Quoted in Chion, *Voice*, 148.
26. Chion, *Voice*, 24.
27. In reality, the break in the soundtrack would not be heard at the same time the spliced image was onscreen; the filmmakers likely opted for synchrony between the two (even though technically "incorrect") to make the effect clear to the audience.

9. Apparatus Theory

The first epigraph is from Aadahl, interview, 2004. The second epigraph is from Knobloch, interview, 2004.

1. Beck and Grajeda, "Introduction," 18. Emphasis in original.
2. Johnson, "Sound and Image," 24.
3. Lastra, *Sound Technology*, 11.
4. Altman, "Sound on Sound," 69.
5. Lastra, *Sound Technology*, 11. See also Corrigan and White, *Film Experience*, 456.
6. Baudry, "Apparatus," 767.
7. Carroll, "Jean-Louis Baudry," 786.
8. This example highlights one of the problems with multi-channel sound in comparison to mono: its more limited "sweet spot." While most seats in a modern movie theater are deemed "good enough," only a small portion of the audience is correctly positioned to hear the *intended* surround mix.
9. Baudry, "Apparatus," 770.
10. Carroll, "Jean-Louis Baudry," 786. Carroll also claims that Baudry's theory hinges on the "seated" immobile spectator and argues that, since a movie is the same whether viewed standing or sitting, Baudry's claims are wrong. I

disagree with Carroll about his initial assumption, as Baudry later links the cinema with dreaming, which is usually done in a prone position. In either case, the important issue here is lack of "motoricity," not the seated position itself.

11. Carroll, "Jean-Louis Baudry," 786.
12. Baudry, "Apparatus," 765.
13. Ibid., 775.
14. Ibid., 772. Emphasis in original.
15. Ibid.
16. Carroll, "Jean-Louis Baudry," 790.
17. Ibid., 790. Emphasis added.
18. Ibid.
19. Ibid., 789.
20. Ibid., 781.
21. Doane, "Voice in Cinema," 170. For more on this argument, see Silverman, Acoustic Mirror.
22. Doane's "The Voice in Cinema," for example, was originally published in 1980.
23. Smith et al., "Intelligibility of Sentences," 347–353.
24. Baudry, "Apparatus," 773. Emphasis added.
25. Doane, "Voice in Cinema," 164. Emphasis added.
26. Baudry, "Apparatus," 773.
27. It is telling and unfortunate that neither Baudry nor Carroll explores the non-visual aspects of the cinema.
28. Lehrer, "Inside a Baby's Mind," 5P.
29. Ibid.
30. Corrigan and White, Film Experience, 456.
31. See, for instance, Partridge, "Plato's Cave," 239–257; Irwin, "Computers, Caves, and Oracles," 5–15; and Boettke, "Human Freedom," 145–158.
32. Whittington, Sound Design, 13. Emphasis in original.
33. Carroll, "Jean-Louis Baudry," 781.
34. Davis, Sonnenschien interview, Sound Design, 154.
35. Baudry, "Apparatus," 773. Emphasis added.

10. The Real and the Symbolic

The epigraph is from Casetti, Theories of Cinema, 167.

1. For a brief summary of the way in which Baudry and others deploy psychoanalysis in film theory, see Casetti, Theories of Cinema, 160–165.
2. For instance, Modleski, Women; Gordon, Dial "M" for Mother; and Samuels, Hitchcock's Bi-Textuality.
3. Casetti, Theories of Cinema, 162.
4. Ibid., 160.
5. Ibid.
6. Griffin, "Mamae Eu Quero."
7. Ibid.
8. Žižek, Looking Awry, viii.
9. Chion, "Quiet Revolution," 72.
10. Žižek, Looking Awry, 40.
11. Ibid., 41.
12. Chion, "Quiet Revolution," 73.
13. Žižek, Looking Awry, 15.
14. Ibid., 14.
15. Ibid., 20.
16. Ibid., 42–43. Emphasis added.
17. Ibid., 15.
18. Ibid., 16–17. Emphasis in original.
19. 5.1-channel music recordings similarly fall into two categories, matching the mixing styles described here. See this book's conclusion.

Conclusion

1. Morgan, interview, 2006.
2. Research and Markets, "Digital Home Theater."
3. Ibid.
4. "Study Reveals." For abstract of original presentation, see Murphy, Themann, and Franks, "Hearing Levels," 2395–2396.

5. See, for example, "Day 7: 9:00 PM–10:00 PM," first aired 16 March 2009.

6. "Dolby Digital 5.1."

7. "Dolby Surrounds the Xbox 360."

8. Blasucci, "DTS Delivers."

9. Recording Industry Association of America (RIAA), "2007."

10. RIAA, "2008."

11. Holman, interview, 2006.

12. Knobloch, interview, 2004.

13. Ibid.

14. Holman, interview, 2004.

15. Bondelevitch, interview, 2006.

16. Kerins and Lipscomb, "Presentation Mode."

BIBLIOGRAPHY

"Alan Parker Talks about Sound for Film." *Dolby News: Cinema Edition* (Fall 2004): 2–4. http://www.dolby.com/uploadedFiles/zz-_Shared_Assets/English_PDFs/About/Newsletters/mp_nw_0409_ShowEast2004_9664_100_percnt_pages.pdf (16 February 2009).

Allen, Ioan. "Are Movies Too Loud?" 22 March 1997. http://www.dolby.com/uploadedFiles/zz-_Shared_Assets/English_PDFs/Professional/54_Moviestooloud.pdf (9 April 2009).

Altman, Rick, ed. "Four and a Half Film Fallacies." In *Sound Theory/Sound Practice*, ed. Rick Altman, 35–45. New York: Routledge, 1992.

———. "Introduction." *Yale French Studies* no. 60 (1980): 3–15.

———. "The Sound of Sound." *Cineaste* 21, no. 1–2 (1995): 68–71.

———. "Sound Space." In *Sound Theory/Sound Practice*, ed. Rick Altman, 46–64. New York: Routledge, 1992.

———. *Sound Theory/Sound Practice*. New York: Routledge, 1992.

Anderson, Richard. Interview by Vincent LoBrutto. *Sound-on-Film*. London: Praeger, 1994.

Arnott, Robert. robertlarnott@gmail.com. "Re: The Future for Hollywood Sound. . . ." 9 March 2009. sound-article-list@yahoogroups.com (9 March 2009).

Baudry, Jean-Louis. "The Apparatus: Metapsychological Approaches to the Impression of Reality in Cinema." In *Film Theory and Criticism*, ed. Leo Baudry and Marshall Cohen, 760–777. New York: Oxford University Press, 1999.

Beaupre, Lee. "Lang, Robson Want Audiences to 'Feel' as Well as See *Earthquake*." *Daily Variety*, 18 March 1974. Quoted in Jay Beck, "A Quiet Revolution" (Ph.D. diss., University of Iowa, 2003), 174.

Beck, Jay. "A Quiet Revolution: Changes in American Film Sound Practices, 1967–1979." Ph.D. diss., University of Iowa, 2003.

———. "The Sounds of 'Silence': Dolby Stereo, Sound Design, and *The Silence of the Lambs*." In *Lowering the Boom*, ed. Jay Beck and Tony Grajeda, 68–83. Urbana: University of Illinois Press, 2008.

Beck, Jay, and Tony Grajeda. "Introduction: The Future of Film Sound

Studies." In *Lowering the Boom*, ed. Jay Beck and Tony Grajeda, 1–20. Urbana: University of Illinois Press, 2008.

——, eds. *Lowering the Boom: Critical Studies in Film Sound*. Urbana: University of Illinois Press, 2008.

Bellour, Raymond. *The Analysis of Film*, ed. Constance Penley. Bloomington: Indiana University Press, 2000.

Belton, John. "1950's Magnetic Sound: The Frozen Revolution." In *Sound Theory/Sound Practice*, ed. Rick Altman, 154–167. New York: Routledge, 1992.

——. *Widescreen Cinema*. Cambridge, Mass.: Harvard University Press, 1992.

Bernard, Josef. "All About Surround Sound." *Radio-electronics* 61, no. 6 (1990): 51–58.

Bissinger, Stephen. steve@sinelanguage.com. "Re: The Future for Hollywood Sound. . . ." 9 March 2009. sound-article-list@yahoogroups.com (9 March 2009).

Blasucci, Dave. "DTS Delivers Cutting Edge Audio to Video Games with DTS Neural Surround." 25 March 2009. http://www.reuters.com/article/pressRelease/idUS226569+25-Mar-2009+BW20090325 (15 June 2009).

Boettke, Peter J. "Human Freedom and the Red Pill." In *Taking the Red Pill: Science, Philosophy, and Religion in The Matrix*, ed. Glenn Yeffeth and David Gerrold, 145–158. Dallas: BenBella Books, 2003.

Boltz, Marilyn G. "Musical Soundtracks as a Schematic Influence on the Cognitive Processing of Filmed Events." *Music Perception* 18, no. 4 (2001): 427–454.

Bordwell, David. "Intensified Continuity: Visual Style in Contemporary American Film." *Film Quarterly* 55, no. 3 (2002): 16–28.

Bordwell, David, and Kristin Thompson. *Film Art: An Introduction*. 5th ed. New York: McGraw-Hill, 1997.

Branigan, Edward. "Sound and Epistemology in Film." *Journal of Aesthetics and Art Criticism* 47, no. 4 (1989): 311–324.

Buettner, Shane. "DTS-ES Discrete 6.1." http://www.dtsonline.com/consumer/dts-es.pdf (12 March 2002).

Burtt, Ben. Interview by David Sonnenschein. *Sound Design: The Expressive Power of Music, Voice, and Sound Effects in Cinema*. Studio City, Calif.: Michael Wiese Productions, 2001.

——. Interview by Vincent LoBrutto. *Sound-on-Film*. London: Praeger, 1994.

Carr, Robert E., and R. M. Hayes. *Wide Screen Movies*. London: McFarland and Co., 1988.

Carroll, Noël. "Jean-Louis Baudry and 'The Apparatus.'" In *Film Theory and Criticism*, ed. Leo Baudry and Marshall Cohen, 778–794. New York: Oxford University Press, 1999.

Casetti, Francesco. *Theories of Cinema, 1945–1995*, trans. Francesca Chiostri and Elizabeth Gard Bartolini-Salimbeni with Thomas Kelso. Austin: University of Texas Press, 1999.

Chicago Tribune, 11 June 1993, Sect. 7G.

Chion, Michel. *Audio-Vision*, trans. Claudia Gorbman. New York: Columbia University Press, 1994.

——. "Quiet Revolution . . . and Rigid Stagnation," trans. Ben Brewster. *October* 58 (1991): 69–80.

——. "Silence in the Loudspeakers," trans. Stephen Muecke with Noel King. http://www.sarai.net/mediacity/filmcity/essays/loudspeakers.htm (18 January 2005).

———. *The Voice in Cinema*, trans. Claudia Gorbman. New York: Columbia University Press, 1999.

———. "Wasted Words." In *Sound Theory/Sound Practice*, ed. Rick Altman, 104–110. New York: Routledge, 1992.

Clark, Don. "New Dolby Sound Headed for Homes." *San Francisco Chronicle*, 12 August 1992, C1.

Clarke, Stephen. sclarke1@uclan.ac.uk. "The Future for Hollywood Sound. . . ." 3 March 2009. sound-article-list@yahoogroups.com (3 March 2009).

Consumer Electronics Association. "Digital America 2006—Home Theater." http://www.ce.org/Press/CEA_Pubs/1994.asp (6 April 2009).

———. "Digital America 2008 Preview." http://www.ce.org/PDF/2k8_DA_Preview.pdf (6 April 2009).

Cook, Nicholas. *Analysing Musical Multimedia*. Oxford: Oxford University Press, 2000.

Corrigan, Timothy, and Patricia White. *The Film Experience*. Boston: Bedford/St. Martin's, 2004.

Daddario, Andy. andydadd@earthlink.net. "Re: The Future for Hollywood Sound. . . ." 8 March 2009. sound-article-list@yahoogroups.com (8 March 2009).

Davis, Dane. Interview by David Sonnenschein. *Sound Design: The Expressive Power of Music, Voice, and Sound Effects in Cinema*. Studio City, Calif.: Michael Wiese Productions, 2001.

Doane, Mary Ann. "Ideology and the Practice of Sound Editing and Mixing." In *Film Sound: Theory and Practice*, ed. Elisabeth Weis and John Belton, 54–62. New York: Columbia University Press, 1985.

———. "The Voice in Cinema: The Articulation of Body and Space." In *Film Sound: Theory and Practice*,

ed. Elisabeth Weis and John Belton, 162–176. New York: Columbia University Press, 1985.

"Dolby Digital 5.1 Turns Up the Volume for SEGA's Holiday Xbox Line-Up." 20 August 2002. http://www.thefreelibrary.com/Dolby+Digital+5.1+Turns+Up+the+Volume+for+SEGA%27s+Holiday+Xbox+Line-Up-a090541313 (15 June 2009).

Dolby Laboratories. "Dolby—Cinema Sound FAQ." http://www.dolby.com/consumer/motion_picture/dolby_in_pictures_tb03.html#q9 (6 April 2009).

———. "Dolby—Movie Sound FAQ—Cinema Questions Answered." http://www.dolby.com/consumer/motion_picture/dolby_in_pictures4.html#q4 (17 February 2009).

———. "Dolby Surround in the Age of Dolby Digital." 1998. http://www.dolby.com/ht/surr-age.pdf (19 March 2002).

———. "Dolby TrueHD." http://www.dolby.com/consumer/technology/trueHD.html (6 April 2009).

"Dolby Surrounds the Xbox 360." 17 November 2005. http://findarticles.com/p/articles/mi_m0EIN/is_2005_Nov_17/ai_n15857713/ (15 June 2009).

DTS, Inc. "DTS-HD Master Audio." http://www.dts.com/Technology/DTS-HD_Master_Audio.aspx (6 April 2009).

Ebert, Roger. "*Bad Boys II*." 18 July 2003. http://rogerebert.suntimes.com/apps/pbcs.dll/article?AID=/20030718/REVIEWS/307180301/1023 (15 June 2009).

———. "*Last Action Hero*." 18 June 1993. http://rogerebert.suntimes.com/apps/pbcs.dll/article?AID=/19930618/REVIEWS/306180301/1023 (9 November 2009).

———. "*Monsters vs. Aliens*." 25 March 2009. http://rogerebert

.suntimes.com/apps/pbcs.dll/ article?AID=/20090325/REVIEWS/ 903259989 (27 March 2009).

Eisenstein, Sergei, Vsevolod Pudovkin, and Grigori Alexandrov. "A Statement." In *Film Sound: Theory and Practice*, ed. Elisabeth Weis and John Belton, 83–85. New York: Columbia University Press, 1985.

Farinella, David John. "Battle of the Trailers." 1 July 1999. http:// mixonline.com/mag/audio_battle_ trailers/ (16 February 2009).

Fielding, Raymond, ed. A Technological History of Motion Pictures and Television: An Anthology from the pages of the Journal of the Society of Motion Picture and Television Engineers. Berkeley: University of California Press, 1967.

Figgis, Mike. "Silence: The Absence of Sound." In *Soundscape: The School of Sound Lectures 1998–2001*, ed. Larry Sider, Diane Freeman, and Jerry Sider, 1–14. London: Wallflower Press, 2003.

Finke, Nikki. "Is That a Quake . . . Or Your Theater Seat?" *Deadline Hollywood Daily*. 16 March 2009. http:// www.deadlinehollywooddaily.com/ is-that-an-earthquake-or-my-theater-seat/ (16 March 2009).

Forlenza, Jeff, and Terri Stone, eds. *Sound for Picture*. Winona, Minn.: MixBooks, 1993.

Gordon, Paul. *Dial "M" for Mother: A Freudian Hitchcock*. Cranbury, N.J.: Farleigh Dickinson University Press, 2008.

Grainge, Paul. "Selling Spectacular Sound: Dolby and the Unheard History of Technical Trademarks." In *Lowering the Boom*, ed. Jay Beck and Tony Grajeda, 251–268. Urbana: University of Illinois Press, 2008.

Griffin, Sean. "Mamae Eu Quero: Carmen Miranda Performing Maternal

Abundance." Paper presented at the annual conference of the Society for Cinema and Media Studies, Chicago, March 8–11, 2007.

Groves, Don. "Pundits Ponder How to Goose DVD Market." *Variety*, 5 November 2001, 14.

Handzo, Stephen. "Appendix: A Narrative Glossary of Film Sound Technology." In *Film Sound: Theory and Practice*, ed. Elisabeth Weis and John Belton, 383–426. New York: Columbia University Press, 1985.

Harmon, Amy. "Sound Wars Coming to a Theater Near You." *Los Angeles Times*, 25 May 1993, D1.

Harper, Graeme, Ruth Doughty, and Jochen Eisentraut, eds. *Sound and Music in Film and Visual Media: A Critical Overview*. London: Continuum, 2009.

"Hear What the Buzz Is about. . . ." http://www.tmhlabs.com/products/ 10_2.html (21 July 2009).

Herranen, Henrik, and Timm Doolen. "Laserdisc FAQ." 1 November 1998. http://www.oz.net/blam/LaserDisc/ FAQ (18 March 2002).

Hodges, Ralph. "Digital Cinema Arrives." *Stereo Review* 56, no. 1 (1991): 132.

———. "Seizing the Day." *Stereo Review* 57, no. 6 (1992): 112.

Holman, Tomlinson. Interview by Vincent LoBrutto. *Sound-on-Film*. London: Praeger, 1994.

———. *5.1 Surround Sound: Up and Running*. Boston: Focal Press, 2000.

———. *Sound for Film and Television*. Boston: Focal Press, 2002.

Homer, Steve. "*Batman* to Launch New Film Sound from Dolby." *Financial Times (London)*, 7 July 1992, Technology 11.

Honan, Edith. "Spielberg Ripped Off Hitchcock Classic: Lawsuit." 9 September 2008. http://www

.reuters.com/articlePrint?articleId=USN0844655020080909 (9 September 2008).

Howe, Desson. "*Last Action Hero.*" 18 June 1993. http://www.washingtonpost.com/wp-srv/style/longterm/movies/videos/lastactionheropg13howe_a0afd4.htm (9 November 2009).

Hull, Joseph. "Surround Sound Past, Present, and Future." 1999. http://www.dolby.com/ht/430.1.br.9904.surhist.pdf (19 March 2002).

Irwin, William. "Computers, Caves, and Oracles: Neo and Socrates." In *"The Matrix" and Philosophy: Welcome to the Desert of the Real*, ed. William Irwin, 5–15. Peru, Ill.: Open Court, 2002.

Johnson, William. "Sound and Image: A Further Hearing." *Film Quarterly* 43, no. 1 (1989): 24–35.

Jordan, Randolph. "The Visible Acousmêtre: Voice, Body, and Space across the Two Versions of *Donnie Darko.*" *Music, Sound, and the Moving Image* 3, no. 1 (2009): 49–72.

Julstrom, Stephen. "A High-Performance Surround Sound Process for Home Video." *Journal of the Audio Engineering Society* 35, nos. 7–8 (1987): 538. Quoted in Benjamin Wright, "Making Films Sound Better: The Transition to Dolby Sound in Hollywood Cinema" (M.A. thesis, Carleton University, 2005), 60.

Katzenberg, Jeffrey. "*Monsters vs. Aliens* and 3-D." Presentation to regional theatrical exhibitors at Webb Chapel Cinemark 17, Dallas, 10 December 2008.

Kellogg, Edward W. "Final Installment: History of Sound Motion Pictures." In *A Technological History of Motion Pictures and Television*, ed. Raymond Fielding, 205–220. Berkeley: University of California Press, 1967.

Kennedy, Andy. Interview by *Film Sound Daily.* 13 July 2007. http://filmsounddaily.blogspot.com/2007/07/harry-potter-and-order-of-phoenix-pt2.html (14 August 2007).

Kenny, Glen. "Digital Audio Today." *Stereo Review* 57, no. 10 (1992): 54–57.

Kerins, Mark. "Narration in the Cinema of Digital Sound." *Velvet Light Trap* 58 (Fall 2006): 41–54.

———. "The (Surround) Sounds of War in *Saving Private Ryan* and *The Thin Red Line.*" Paper presented at the annual conference of the Society for Cinema and Media Studies, London, 31 March–3 April 2005.

Kerins, Mark, and Scott D. Lipscomb. "Presentation Mode in the Cinematic and Music Listening Experiences: An Experimental Investigation." Paper presented at the biannual meeting of the Society for Music Perception and Cognition, Montreal, Canada, 30 July–3 August 2007.

Klinger, Barbara. *Beyond the Multiplex: Cinema, New Technologies, and the Home.* Berkeley: University of California Press, 2006.

Kramer, Lorr. "DTS: Brief History and Technical Overview." http://www.DTSonline.com/history8.pdf (12 March 2002).

Lastra, James. Sound Technology and the American Cinema: Perception, Representation, Modernity. New York: Columbia University Press, 2000.

Lehrer, Jonah. "Inside a Baby's Mind." *Dallas Morning News*, 24 May 2009, early edition, Sect. P.

Lipscomb, Scott D. "The Perception of Audio-Visual Composites: Accent Structure Alignment of Simple Stimuli." *Selected Reports in Ethnomusicology* 12 (2005): 37–67.

Lipscomb, Scott D., and R. A. Kendall. "Perceptual Judgment of the Relationship between Musical and Visual Components in Film." *Psychomusicology* 13, no. 1 (1994): 60–98.

LoBrutto, Vincent. *Sound-on-Film.* London: Praeger, 1994.

Malsky, Matthew. "Sounds of the City: Alfred Newman's 'Street Scene' and Urban Modernity." In *Lowering the Boom*, ed. Jay Beck and Tony Grajeda, 105–122. Urbana: University of Illinois Press, 2008.

Maltby, Richard. *Hollywood Cinema.* Oxford: Blackwell, 2003.

Marshall, S. K., and A. J. Cohen. "Effects of Musical Soundtracks on Attitudes toward Animated Geometric Figures." *Music Perception* 6, no. 1 (1988): 95–112.

Masters, Kim. "Can a Tamed Terminator Save Sony's *Last Action Hero?*" *Washington Post*, 29 May 1993, D1.

Metz, Christian. "Aural Objects." In *Film Sound: Theory and Practice*, ed. Elisabeth Weis and John Belton, 154–161. New York: Columbia University Press, 1985.

———. *The Imaginary Signifier: Psychoanalysis and the Cinema*, trans. Celia Britton, Annwyl Williams, Ben Brewster, and Alfred Guzzetti. Bloomington: Indiana University Press, 1982.

Miller, George. "The Magical Number Seven, Plus or Minus Two: Some Limits on Our Capacity for Processing Information." *Psychological Review* 63 (1956): 81–97.

"Mission: Impossible II (2000)—Trivia." http://us.imdb.com/title/tt0120755/ trivia (9 February 2009).

Mitchell, Peter W. "Surround Sound." *Stereo Review* 57, no. 4 (1992): 44–49.

Modleski, Tania. *The Women Who Knew Too Much.* New York: Routledge, 1988.

"Movies Featuring CDS." http:// us.imdb.com/List?tv=on&&soundmix=CDS (11 April 2005).

Murch, Walter. *In the Blink of an Eye.* Los Angeles: Silman-James Press, 2001.

———. Interview by Vincent LoBrutto. *Sound-on-Film.* London: Praeger, 1994.

———. "Intro/Womb Tone/Dense Clarity—Clear Density." *Transom Review* 5, no. 1 (2005). http://www.transom .org/guests/review/200504.review .murch.pdf (7 July 2009).

———. "Touch of Silence." In *Soundscape: The School of Sound Lectures 1998–2001*, ed. Larry Sider, Diane Freeman, and Jerry Sider, 83–102. London: Wallflower Press, 2003.

Murphy, William, Christa L. Themann, and John R. Franks. "Hearing Levels in US Adults Aged 20–69 Years: National Health and Nutrition Examination Survey 1999–2002." *Journal of the Acoustical Society of America* 117 (2005): 2395–2396.

"NATO Statistics: Number of U.S. Movie Screens." http://www .natoonline.org/statisticsscreens.htm (17 February 2009).

Newman, Nancy. "'We'll Make a Paderewski of You Yet!': Acoustic Reflections in *The 5,000 Fingers of Dr. T.*" In *Lowering the Boom*, ed. Jay Beck and Tony Grajeda, 152–170. Urbana: University of Illinois Press, 2008.

Nunziata, Susan. "*Batman* First Feature to Fly with Dolby Digital Sound." *Billboard*, 6 June 1992, 10–11.

———. "Sony Enters Digital-Sound Film Arena, Joins 2 Competing Formats in Field." *Billboard*, 7 March 1992, 55.

Palenchar, Joseph. "Broad Integra Launch Adds 9.2 AVRs." 21 September 2009. http://www.twice.com/article/354795-Broad_Integra_Launch_Adds_9_2_AVRs.php (2 November 2009).

———. "Onkyo Adds First 9.2-Channel AVRs." 24 August 2009. http://www.twice.com/article/328710-Onkyo_Adds_First_9_2_Channel_AVRs.php (2 November 2009).

Partridge, John. "Plato's Cave and The Matrix." In Philosophers Explore "The Matrix," ed. Christopher Grau, 239–257. Oxford: Oxford University Press, 2005.

Pasquariello, Nicholas. "Indiana Jones and the Last Crusade." In Sound for Picture, ed. Jeff Forlenza and Terri Stone, 57–61. Winona, Minn.: Mix-Books, 1993.

Pendleton, Jennifer. "Soundtrack Firm Gets Big Break in the Movies." Los Angeles Times, 28 December 1993, D3.

Pohlmann, Ken. "Separated at Birth." Stereo Review's Sound and Vision 65, no. 3 (2000): 40.

Portman, Richard. Interview by Vincent LoBrutto. Sound-on-Film. London: Praeger, 1994.

"Questions and Answers about SDDS." http://www.sdds.com/whatis/q_a.html (12 March 2002).

Quittner, Josh. "The Next Dimension." Time, 30 March 2009, 54–62.

Ranada, David. "Inside Dolby Digital." Stereo Review 61, no. 10 (1998): 81.

Recording Industry Association of America (RIAA). "2007 U.S. Manufacturers' Unit Shipments and Value Chart." http://76.74.24.142/81128FFD-028F-282E-1CE5-FDBF16A46388.pdf (18 May 2009).

———. "2008 U.S. Manufacturers' Unit Shipments and Value Chart." http://76.74.24.142/1D212C0E-408B-F730-65A0-C0F5871C369D.pdf (18 May 2009).

Research and Markets, "Digital Home Theater Playback Hardware in the United States 2006." http://www.researchandmarkets.com/reports/464942/digital_home_theater_playback_hardware_in.pdf (13 June 2009).

Roberts, J. L. "The Disc that Saved Hollywood." Newsweek, 20 August 2001, 30–32.

Rydstrom, Gary. "Big Movie Sound Effects." Presentation at meeting of the Motion Picture Sound Engineers, Los Angeles, 14 July 2004.

———. Interview by Gianluca Sergi. The Dolby Era. New York: Manchester University Press, 2004.

———. Interview by Vincent LoBrutto. Sound-on-Film. London: Praeger, 1994.

Salt, Barry. Film Style & Technology: History & Analysis. London: Starword, 1992.

Samuels, Robert. Hitchcock's Bi-Textuality: Lacan, Feminisms, and Queer Theory. New York: State University of New York Press, 1998.

Savlov, Marc. "Last Action Hero." 25 June 1993. http://www.austinchronicle.com/gyrobase/Calendar/Film?Film=oid%3A139388 (9 November 2009).

Schaefer, Stephen. "New Digital Sound Systems Are a Blast." Boston Herald, 24 June 1994, S05.

Schreger, Charles. "Altman, Dolby, and the Second Sound Revolution." In Film Sound: Theory and Practice, ed. Elisabeth Weis and John Belton, 348–355. New York: Columbia University Press, 1985.

"SDDS Movies." 2009. http://www.sdds.com/news_movies.cfm (2 November 2009).

Sergi, Gianluca. The Dolby Era. New York: Manchester University Press, 2004.

——. "The Sonic Playground: Hollywood Cinema and Its Listeners." 1999. http://www.filmsound.org/articles/sergi/index.htm (8 November 2005).

Sheehan, Henry. "Montreal Theatres Showing *Jurassic* Have New Sound System." *Gazette* (Montreal, Quebec), 11 June 1993, D3.

Sherber, Anne. "DVD Leads a Hardware Revolution." *Video Store*, 14 October 2001, 1+.

Sider, Larry, Diane Freeman, and Jerry Sider, eds. *Soundscape: The School of Sound Lectures 1998–2001*. London: Wallflower Press, 2003.

Silverman, Kaja. *The Acoustic Mirror*. Bloomington: Indiana University Press, 1988.

Smith, S. L., et al. "Intelligibility of Sentences Recorded from the Uterus of a Pregnant Ewe and from the Fetal Inner Ear." *Audiology & Neuro-Otology* 8, no. 6 (2003): 347–353.

Sobchack, Vivian. "When the Ear Dreams: Dolby Digital and the Imagination of Sound." *Film Quarterly* 58, no. 4 (2005): 2–15.

Sonnenschein, David. *Sound Design: The Expressive Power of Music, Voice, and Sound Effects in Cinema*. Studio City, Calif.: Michael Wiese Productions, 2001.

Sperling, Nicole. "3-D Movie Preview." *Entertainment Weekly*, 27 March 2009, 24–34.

"Study Reveals Who Hears Best." 13 June 2006. http://www.livescience.com/health/060613_best_hearing.html (13 June 2009).

Théberge, Paul. "Almost Silent: The Interplay of Sound and Silence in Contemporary Cinema and Television." In *Lowering the Boom*, ed. Jay Beck and Tony Grajeda, 51–67. Urbana: University of Illinois Press, 2008.

Thom, Randy. "Acceptance Speech for Sound Editing Academy Award." 2005. http://www.oscar.com/oscarnight/winners/win_34478.html (5 April 2005).

——. "Acoustics of the Soul." *Offscreen* 11, nos. 8–9 (2007): 1–2. http://www.offscreen.com/Sound_Issue/thom_diegesis.pdf (15 July 2009).

——. davidrandallthom@hotmail.com. "Re: The Future for Hollywood Sound. . . ." 8 March 2009. sound-article-list@yahoogroups.com (8 March 2009).

Thompson, Kristin, and David Bordwell. *Film History: An Introduction*. New York: McGraw-Hill, 1994.

Toussaint, Bruno. "Sound Design and *mise en scène*: Immersion, Sideration and Sonic Transcendence." Paper presented at annual *Screen* Studies Conference, Glasgow, Scotland, 4–6 July 2008.

Van Bergen, J. "*Jurassic* on CD-ROM." *TCI* 27, no. 34 (1993): 34.

Vernallis, Carol. "The New Cut-Up Cinema: Music, Speed, and Memory." Paper presented at annual *Screen* Studies Conference, Glasgow, Scotland, 4–6 July 2008.

Warner, Frank. Interview by Vincent LoBrutto. *Sound-on-Film*. London: Praeger, 1994.

Warren, Robert. Interview by Vincent LoBrutto. *Sound-on-Film*. London: Praeger, 1994.

Watters II, George. Interview by David Sonnenschein. *Sound Design: The Expressive Power of Music, Voice, and Sound Effects in Cinema*. Studio City, Calif.: Michael Wiese Productions, 2001.

Weis, Elisabeth. "Sync Tanks: The Art and Technique of Postproduction Sound." *Cineaste* 21, no. 1–2 (1995): 56–61.

Weis, Elisabeth, and John Belton, eds. *Film Sound: Theory and Practice.* New York: Columbia University Press, 1985.

Whittington, William. "Sonic Spectacle: Emergence of Spectacle in the Contemporary Film Soundtrack." Paper presented at the annual conference of the Society for Cinema and Media Studies, Minneapolis, 6–9 March 2003.

———. *Sound Design & Science Fiction.* Austin: University of Texas Press, 2007.

Wright, Benjamin. "Making Films Sound Better: The Transition to Dolby Sound in Hollywood Cinema." M.A. thesis, Carleton University, 2005.

Wright, Karen. "One Hand Clapping." *Scientific American* 260, no. 6 (1989): 35–37.

Žižek, Slavoj. *Looking Awry: An Introduction to Jacques Lacan through Popular Culture.* Cambridge, Mass.: MIT Press, 1998.

FILMOGRAPHY

Where appropriate, listings include the specific version of the soundtrack referenced.

12 Monkeys (1995)
24 (TV) season 7 (2009), Dolby Digital 5.1 broadcast mix
The 5,000 Fingers of Dr. T (1953)

Adventureland (2009), theatrical mix
The Alamo (1960)
Aliens (1986), Dolby Surround mix on DVD, ASIN: B000G6BM00
American Beauty (1999), DTS 5.1 mix on DVD, ASIN: B00003CWL6
American Graffiti (1973)
Apocalypse Now (1979)
Armageddon (1998), theatrical mix
Around the World in 80 Days (1956)
Avatar (2009)

Backdraft (1991)
Bad Boys II (2003)
Batman Returns (1992)
Battleship Potemkin (1925)
Being John Malkovich (1999), Dolby Digital 5.1 mix on DVD, ASIN: 6305807086
Ben-Hur (1959)
The Birds (1963)

The Bourne Ultimatum (2007)
Braveheart (1995), Dolby Digital 5.1 mix on DVD, ASIN: B00003CX95
Brother Bear (2003)

Cars (2006), Dolby Digital 5.1 mix on Blu-Ray, ASIN: B000V1Y43W
Cast Away (2000), DTS-ES mix on DVD, ASIN: B00003CXRP
Citizen Kane (1941)
Close Encounters of the Third Kind (1977)
The Color of Money (1986)
Contact (1997), Dolby Digital 5.1 mix on DVD, ASIN: 0790733226
The Conversation (1974)
Crimson Tide (1995), Dolby Digital 5.1 mix on DVD, ASIN: 6304765258

Dancer in the Dark (2000)
Daredevil (2003)
The Dark Knight (2008), Dolby Digital 5.1 mix on Blu-Ray, ASIN: B001GZ6QEC
Days of Thunder (1990), theatrical mix
Dick Tracy (1990)
Die Hard (1988)
Disturbia (2007), Dolby Digital Surround EX mix on DVD, ASIN: B000RO6K9E

Donnie Darko (2001), Dolby Digital 5.1 mix on director's cut DVD, ASIN: B0006GAOBI

Earthquake (1974)
The Empire Strikes Back (1980)
The End of the Spear (2005)
The Exorcist (1973) (re-release with new soundtrack, 2000)

Fahrenheit 9/11 (2004)
The Fall (2006)
Fantasia (1940)
Fight Club (1999), Dolby Digital 5.1 mix on DVD, ASIN: B00003W8NM
Finding Nemo (2003)
For Love of the Game (1999)
Frost/Nixon (2008), theatrical mix

Girl, Interrupted (1999)
Gladiator (2000), DTS-ES mix on DVD, ASIN: B00003CXE7
The Godfather Part II (1974)
The Green Mile (1999)

Hairspray (2007), Dolby Digital 5.1 mix on DVD, ASIN: B000W4KT6E
Harry Potter and the Chamber of Secrets (2002), Dolby Digital Surround EX mix on DVD, ASIN: B00008DDXC
Harry Potter and the Half-Blood Prince (2009), theatrical mix
Harry Potter and the Order of the Phoenix (2007), theatrical mix
Harry Potter and the Prisoner of Azkaban (2004), Dolby Digital 5.1 broadcast mix
Hill Street Blues (TV) (1981–1987)

I, Robot (2004), DTS-HD Master Audio 5.1 mix on Blu-Ray, ASIN: B0012GVKVY
Innerspace (1987)

The Jazz Singer (1927)
Joy Ride (2001), Dolby Digital 5.1 mix on DVD, ASIN: B0002WT4OE

Juno (2007), Dolby Digital 5.1 broadcast mix
Jurassic Park (1993)

Kinsey (2004), theatrical mix

Last Action Hero (1993), Dolby Digital 5.1 mix on DVD, ASIN: 0800127862
The Last of the Mohicans (1992)
Lawrence of Arabia (1962)
Leaving Las Vegas (1995)
Letter from Siberia (1957)
Lifted (2006), Dolby Digital 5.1 mix on *Ratatouille* Blu-Ray, ASIN: B000VBJEFK
The Lord of the Rings: The Fellowship of the Ring (2001), DTS-ES mix on DVD, ASIN: B000067DNF
The Lord of the Rings: The Return of the King (2003), DTS-ES mix on DVD, ASIN: B000634DCW
The Lord of the Rings: The Two Towers (2002), DTS-ES mix on DVD, ASIN: B00009TB5G

Master and Commander: The Far Side of the World (2003)
The Matrix (1999), Dolby Digital 5.1 mix on DVD, ASIN: B000P0J0AQ
Million Dollar Baby (2004), theatrical mix
Mission: Impossible II (2000)
The Mosquito Coast (1986)
Moulin Rouge! (2001), Dolby Digital 5.1 mix on DVD, ASIN: B00005QZ7U
The Mummy (1999)
Music and Lyrics (2007)

The New World (2005)
North by Northwest (1959)

Oklahoma! (1955)

The Patriot (2000)
Pearl Harbor (2001)
Platoon (1986), Dolby Digital 5.1 mix on DVD, ASIN: 079284646X
Pola X (1999), theatrical mix

Predator (1987)
Psycho (1960), mono mix on DVD,
 ASIN: 0783225849
Psycho (1998), Dolby Digital 5.1 mix on
 DVD, ASIN: BoooooIQVC

Ratatouille (2007), Dolby Digi-
 tal 5.1 mix on Blu-Ray, ASIN:
 BoooVBJEFK
Rear Window (1954)
Rear Window (1998), Dolby Surround
 mix on DVD, ASIN: Booo6HBL6E
Return of the Jedi (1983)
The Ring (2003), DTS 5.1 mix on DVD,
 ASIN: Boooo5JLTK
Robocop (1987)
The Rock (1996), Dolby Digital 5.1 mix
 on DVD, ASIN: Boooo59TPN
The Rules of the Game (1939)

Saving Private Ryan (1998), Dolby
 Digital 5.1 mix on DVD, ASIN:
 Boooo1ZWUS
Se7en (1995), DTS-ES mix on DVD,
 ASIN: Boooo5oFEN
Seven Swans (2005)
Signs (2002), Dolby Digital 5.1 mix on
 DVD, ASIN: Boooo5JL3T
The Silence of the Lambs (1991)
Singin' in the Rain (1952)
Speed (1994), DTS-HD Master Au-
 dio 5.1 mix on Blu-Ray, ASIN:
 BoooICLRHK
Spider-Man (2002), Dolby Digital 5.1
 mix on DVD, ASIN: Boooo5JKCH
Spider-Man 2 (2004)
Spy Game (2001)
Star Wars (1977)
*Star Wars Episode I: The Phantom
 Menace* (1999), Dolby Digital Sur-
 round EX mix on DVD, ASIN:
 Boooo3CX5P
*Star Wars Episode II: Attack of the
 Clones* (2002), Dolby Digital Sur-
 round EX mix on DVD, ASIN:
 Boooo6HBUJ
Strange Days (1995)

Superbad (2007), Dolby TrueHD
 5.1 mix on Blu-Ray, ASIN:
 BoooWZEZHC
Superman (1978)
Superman Returns (2006), theatrical
 mix
Surf's Up (2007)

The Terminator (1984)
Terminator 2: Judgment Day (1991),
 DTS-ES mix to Special Edition on
 DVD, ASIN: Boooo4TRD8
Terminator 3: Rise of the Machines
 (2003), Dolby Digital 5.1 mix on Blu-
 Ray, ASIN: Boo13ND36G
Terminator Salvation (2009), theatrical
 mix
The Texas Chainsaw Massacre (trailer)
 (2003), theatrical mix
The Thin Red Line (1998)
This is Cinerama (1952)
Timecode (2000), Dolby Digital 5.1 mix
 on DVD, ASIN: BooooAQVIA
Tommy (1975)
Touch of Evil (1958)
Traffic (2000)
Transformers (2007), Dolby Digi-
 tal 5.1 mix on Blu-Ray, ASIN:
 BoooNTPDT6
Transformers: Revenge of the Fallen
 (2009), theatrical mix
Twilight (2008)

Uncle Josh at the Moving Picture Show
 (1902)
Underworld (2003)
Universal Soldier (1992)

WALL-E (2008), DTS-HD Master
 Audio 5.1 mix on Blu-Ray, ASIN:
 Boo1EOQWF8
West Side Story (1961)
What Lies Beneath (2000), DTS 5.1 mix
 on DVD, ASIN: Boooo3CXI7
The Wizard of Oz (1939)
The Woman in the Window (1945)
Woodstock (1970)

INDEX

Page numbers in italics indicate pictures and their captions; *n* or *nn* indicates material contained in an endnote. If endnotes for multiple chapters appear on the same page, the chapter number is included, when necessary, to distinguish notes with the same number but from different chapters. For example, 335n1:11 refers to note 11 from chapter 1, found on page 335.

MARK KERINS is Assistant Professor of Cinema-Television in the Meadows School of the Arts at Southern Methodist University, where he works in both filmmaking and film studies.